UPON THIS ROCK

MODERN APOLOGETICS LIBRARY

UPON THIS ROCK

St. Peter and the Primacy of Rome
in Scripture
and the Early Church

BY

STEPHEN K. RAY

IGNATIUS PRESS   SAN FRANCISCO

Nihil Obstat: Reverend Robert Lunsford
                   Censor Librorum

Imprimatur: + Carl F. Mengeling
                   Bishop of Lansing

Cover art: Icon written by Brother Claude Lane, O.S.B.
Mount Angel Abbey, Oregon

Cover design by Riz Boncan Marsella

ISBN 0–89870–723–4
Library of Congress catalogue card number 98–74065
Printed in the United States of America ∞

DEDICATION

To Thomas Howard, who courageously journeyed beyond the boundaries of his Fundamentalist Protestant roots to discover the glory of the Catholic Church and, in so doing, broke through a hidden barrier, opening the door for thousands of orphaned souls to glimpse the light. But even more than that, he wrote *Evangelical Is Not Enough* and, in so doing, made it possible for me, my family, and countless friends and fellow Evangelicals to find the Catholic Church, which, from our birth, had been darkly shrouded by grotesque caricatures and misinformation. His life and pages have enabled us to embark on a great love affair with the ancient Church, which we have found to be forever young. For this great treasure, we owe an eternal debt of gratitude.

To Fr. Ed Fride, the first Catholic priest our family ever knew and the one who baptized our children, confirmed all six of us, and received us with tears of joy into the Roman Catholic Church. In the subsequent years he has been a stalwart model of godliness, strength, faithfulness, and orthodoxy. He has become a great friend, and we have "adopted" him into our family (with a special ceremony and certificate). We admire his dedication to holiness, the Lord Jesus, the Catholic Church, and the See of Rome. We are honored to follow such a shepherd, who daily lays down his life for the sheep and serves in the sure line of the apostolic succession.

To Dave Palm, another Evangelical Protestant who came into the Catholic Church about the same time as our family and who has been a friend *extraordinaire*. He has a degree in New Testament studies and is thoroughly acquainted with the issues surrounding the Papacy, as well as with all other matters Catholic. But most of all, he has a contagious love for Jesus and the Church. He graciously critiqued my manuscript. Blessed be God forever for such brothers in our Lord Jesus Christ.

And finally, to Bishop Carl Mengeling, bishop of Lansing, Michigan, who read the entire manuscript and offered many helpful suggestions, as well as his Imprimatur. I am honored to have such a faithful shepherd.

Most of the biographical information on the Fathers used in the footnotes was gleaned from two excellent sources: *The Oxford Dictionary of the Christian Church*, edited by F. L. Cross and E. A. Livingstone, 2d rev. ed. (New York: Oxford Univ. Press, 1983), and *The Faith of the Early Fathers*, in three volumes, by William A. Jurgens (Collegeville, Minn.: Liturgical Press, 1970). Christendom Press was kind enough to grant permission for use of the chronology of St. Peter's life from their book *The Founding of Christendom*, by Warren H. Carroll. Our Sunday Visitor, Inc., graciously granted permission to use the chronological list of Popes that is reprinted in Appendix A.

"[Andrew] brought [Simon] to Jesus. Jesus looked at him, and said, 'So you are Simon the son of John? You shall be called Cephas' (which means Peter)."

—John 1:42

When Christ at a symbolic moment was establishing His great society, He chose for its cornerstone neither the brilliant Paul nor the mystic John, but a shuffler, a snob, a coward—in a word, a man. And upon this rock He has built His Church, and the gates of Hell have not prevailed against it. All the empires and the kingdoms have failed, because of this inherent and continual weakness, that they were founded by strong men and upon strong men. But this one thing, the historic Christian Church, was founded on a weak man, and for that reason it is indestructible. For no chain is stronger than its weakest link.

G. K. Chesterton, in *Heretics*

My grace is sufficient for you, for my power is made perfect in weakness.

2 Corinthians 12:9

CONTENTS

INTRODUCTION

St. Peter and the Primacy of Rome

There is little in the history of the Church that has been more heatedly contested than the primacy of Peter and the See of Rome. History is replete with examples of authority spurned, and the history of the Church is no different. As we proceed with this overview of history, we will allow the Scriptures, the voice of the apostles, and the testimony of the early centuries of the Christian community to speak for themselves. In many quarters, over the last few centuries, the din of opposition and uninformed dissent has drowned out the voices of these ancient witnesses. Novel ideas, like a voracious flood, have tried to erode the foundations and the clear historical precedents provided by the Holy Spirit's work in the primitive Church.

History has a clear and distinct voice, but it does not force itself upon us uninvited. History is prudent and waits quietly to be discovered. Conversely, the ingenious inventions of recent theologians and innovators are loud and demanding, bursting upon our ears and minds, our lives and hearts, demanding our immediate attention and loyalties. The riches of history fall quietly aside as the prattling innovators blast their trumpets and loudly parade their followers through new streets, trampling the knowledge of the ages under their cumulative feet.

Here we will allow the voices of the past to speak again—for themselves. And what the reader will find is that the utterances of the past still resound with one voice, with clarity and force. To study those who have gone before us, following in the footsteps of the Lord Jesus, his apostles, and our Fathers in the faith is to lose interest in much of the clamor of modern notions. We find these theological innovations and ecclesiastical groups poorly devised, if not disingenuous. This is what John Henry Newman, a Protestant clergyman at the time, found as he studied the primitive Church. He concluded: "To be deep in history is to cease being a

Protestant."[1] As the Protestant churches continue to fragment and lose the fervor and orthodoxy of their past reform efforts, many Evangelicals and Fundamentalists are looking to the past to hear what the early Fathers have to say today. They are beginning to listen to the unobtrusive voice of the early Church, and they are finding it is quite different from what they have been taught. Reading the writings of the early Church allows us to tap into the very heartbeat of the apostolic teaching and tradition of the primitive Church—the very Church bequeathed to us by the apostles.

Sometimes silence is more eloquent than words. This is especially true in Church history. We hear so much about what the Fathers *say* and so little about what they *do not say*. This is revealing and should play a significant role in our research. William Webster has written a book that we will refer to several times in our study. Webster is an ex-Catholic who decided to abandon the Church and cast his lot with the Fundamentalist Protestants. His book is entitled *Peter and the Rock* and asserts that, as the blurb on the back of the book says, "The contemporary Roman Catholic interpretation [of Peter and the rock] had no place in the biblical understanding of the early church doctors." To ascertain whether or not such an assertion is true is one of the main goals of this book. But along with what the Fathers *say*, we need to hear their silence as well.

While reading Webster's book, I noticed, along with his selective use of the Fathers in attempting to discredit the Catholic Church's teaching on the Papacy, that there are no citations "revealed" in his book in which a Christian, especially a Church Father, explicitly denies the Petrine primacy or the Petrine succession. Webster collects a large number of passages that are supposed to prove that the Fathers oppose Catholic teaching, yet never is there a flat-out denial of the Petrine primacy or the primacy of Rome. *This is a silence that speaks volumes!* We may find differing interpretations of Peter's primacy, which is what we should expect, according to John Henry Newman, yet we find no denial of that primacy.

I wrote to William Webster and asked him if he knew of any Church Father who denied the primacy of Peter or of his successors. Mr. Webster's response was very telling, and I wish he had

---

[1] John Henry Cardinal Newman, *An Essay on the Development of Christian Doctrine*, in *Conscience, Consensus, and the Development of Doctrine* (New York: Doubleday, 1992), 50.

been forthright about this matter in his book. His return E-mail stated, "No father denies that Peter had a primacy or that there is a Petrine succession. The issue is how the fathers interpreted those concepts. They simply did not hold to the Roman Catholic view of later centuries that primacy and succession were 'exclusively' related to the bishops of Rome."[2] What an extraordinary admission; what an extraordinary truth. Many of the Fathers were in theological or disciplinary disagreement with Rome (for example, Cyprian and Irenaeus), yet they never denied Rome's primacy. They may have debated what that primacy meant, or how it was to work out in the universal Church, but they *never denied the primacy*. The quickest way to achieve jurisdictional or doctrinal victory is to subvert or disarm the opponent. In this case it would have been as simple as proving from the Bible or from tradition that Peter, and subsequently his successors in Rome, had no primacy, no authority to rule in the Church. Yet, as even Webster freely admits, this refutation never occurred. Irenaeus may challenge the appropriateness of a decision made by Victor, but he never challenges Victor's authority to make the binding decision. Cyprian may at times disagree with a decree of Stephen's on baptism, but he never rejects the special place of the Roman See, which would have been the easiest means of winning the debate. The bishop of Rome was unique in assuming the authority and obligation to oversee the Churches. Clement and Ignatius make this clear from the first century and the beginning of the second. If the authority exercised had been illegitimate, or wrongly arrogated, it would have been an act of overzealousness at one end of the spectrum, of tyranny at the other. Yet no one ever stood up and said, "No, you have no authority. Who are you to order us, to teach us, to require obedience from us, to excommunicate us?" If the jurisdictional primacy of Rome had been a matter of self-aggrandizement, someone would have opposed it as they opposed other innovations and heresies in the Church. The silence is profound.

As doctrines develop, as authority develops, as even a family or society develops, there is discussion relating to authority and its exercise. Amazingly enough, this is also true for the canon of the New Testament, which was not finally collected and codified for almost four hundred years after the death of Christ. Does the fact

---

[2] E-mail from William Webster dated August 16, 1997.

that there were various interpretations of what the New Testament was, or which books it contained—a discussion, by the way, that raised its head again in the teaching of Martin Luther—in any way prove that somehow the New Testament held by the Protestant is uncertain or in doubt because there were various applications or perceptions of that canon in the early years? The faithful Christian may have believed various things about the canon, but he never denied that the Scriptures held a special place. He may have clung to a different collection of books, yet he always understood that there were "apostolic" books. In the same way, early Fathers, especially Eastern Fathers, may have defined the primacy of Peter and the supremacy of his successors in nuanced ways, yet they never denied that the primacy or authority was attached to Peter and his See in Rome.

Authority has always been an object of distrust and, very often, defiance. The nation of Israel refused to hear authority: they rejected the authority of the prophets[3] and rejected their Messiah sent by the Father.[4] The apostles themselves were abused and rejected.[5] Should it surprise us that many in our present day reject and demean the unifying authority God has ordained in his Church? In the primitive Church, as we learn from St. Irenaeus, the greatest theologian of the second century, many groups splintered off from the apostolic Church and "assembled in unauthorized meetings".[6] Rejecting the Church and spurning her shepherd is nothing new to our day.

---

[3] Mt 23:37: "O Jerusalem, Jerusalem, killing the prophets and stoning those who are sent to you! How often would I have gathered your children together as a hen gathers her brood under her wings, and you would not!"

[4] Jn 1:10–11: "He was in the world, and the world was made through him, yet the world knew him not. He came to his own home, and his own people received him not."

[5] Paul says in 2 Timothy 1:15, "You are aware that all who are in Asia turned away from me, and among them Phygelus and Hermogenes." The Apostle John writes in 1 John 2:19, "They went out from us, but they were not really of us; for if they had been of us, they would have remained with us; but they went out, in order that it might be shown that they all are not of us."

[6] "Since, however, it would be very tedious, in such a volume as this, to reckon up the successions of all the Churches, we do put to confusion all those who, in whatever manner, whether by an evil self-pleasing, by vainglory, or by blindness and perverse opinion, assemble in unauthorized meetings; [we do this, I say,] by indicating that tradition derived from the apostles, of the very great, the very

Christians of many traditions are currently espousing recent Protestant traditions and modern schisms; yet they all claim the early Church as their own—asserting that they are the rightful heirs to the teachings of our Lord, the apostles, and the Fathers of the apostolic Church. Are they? Do they have a legitimate claim to the theology of the early Church? Was the early Church essentially "Protestant" in her theology and polity, or was she Catholic?

Much of the distinctive character of the Church through the centuries has been based on the teaching concerning Peter and his place within the apostolic company and in the Church. Was he chosen for a special position? Did Jesus separate Peter out from the Twelve? Did Peter have authority over the body of Christ, the one sheepfold? Was the position of bishop carried on by his successors? How did the first generations of Christians relate to Peter? These are questions we will try to answer as we proceed with this study.

Holy Scripture must be interpreted, since it is not laid out simply in the form of a Church manual or textbook. One principle of proper interpretation involves studying a topic or passage within its context, both the immediate context and the context of the whole Bible. If this is neglected or done poorly, a plethora of problems arises. Historical context must also be taken into account.

In studying Peter and the subject of primacy, it is especially important to consider who or what makes up the foundation of the Church. The many facets of the Church are like the multiple surfaces of a diamond glistening in the sunlight. These facets are written about from different angles, and the metaphors used— foundations, builders, stones, and so on—are as varied as the gem's surfaces. In grammar school we learn not to mix metaphors. Mixing metaphors makes clear communication difficult and can lead to misunderstandings. This confusion of context is especially pronounced in much of the Fundamentalist and Evangelical Protestant understanding of the foundation of the

---

ancient, and universally known Church founded and organized at Rome by the two most glorious apostles, Peter and Paul; as also [by pointing out] the faith preached to men, which comes down to our time by means of the successions of the bishops" (Irenaeus, *Against Heresies* 3, 3, 2, in *The Ante-Nicene Fathers*, ed. Alexander Roberts and James Donaldson, rev. A. Cleveland Coxe [Grand Rapids, Mich.: Eerdmans, 1985], 1:415 [hereafter ANF]).

Church. However, even George Salmon, no friend to Catholic teaching (in fact he has proven himself a hero to many opposed to the Catholic Church and wrote *The Infallibility of the Church* to undermine the teachings of the Catholic Church), understood the need to understand properly the metaphors used in Scripture. I provide an extended quotation from Salmon's book to lay the foundation (pun intended) for understanding the biblical and patristic references to Peter and the foundation of the Church.

> It is undoubtedly the doctrine of Scripture that Christ is the only foundation [of the Church]: "other foundation can no man lay than that is laid, which is Jesus Christ" (1 Cor 3:11). Yet we must remember that the same metaphor may be used to illustrate different truths, and so, according to circumstances, may have different significations. The same Paul who has called Christ the only foundation, tells his Ephesian converts (2:20):—"Ye are built upon the foundation of the Apostles and Prophets, Jesus Christ himself being the chief corner-stone." And in like manner we read (Rev 21:14):—"The wall of the city had twelve foundations, and on them the names of the twelve Apostles of the Lamb." How is it that there can be no other foundation but Christ, and yet that the Apostles are spoken of as foundations? Plainly because the metaphor is used with different applications. Christ alone is that foundation, from being joined to which the whole building of the Church derives its unity and stability, and gains strength to defy all the assaults of hell. But, in the same manner as any human institution is said to be founded by those men to whom it owes its origin, so we may call those men the foundation of the Church whom God honoured by using them as His instruments in the establishment of it; who were themselves laid as the first living stones in that holy temple, and on whom the other stones of that temple were laid; for it was on their testimony that others received the truth, so that our faith rests on theirs; and (humanly speaking) it is because they believed that we believe. So, again, in like manner, we are forbidden to call anyone on earth our Father, "for one is our Father which is in heaven." And yet, in another sense, Paul did not scruple to call himself the spiritual father of those whom he had begotten in the Gospel. You see, then, that the fact that Christ is called the rock, and that on Him the Church is built, is no hindrance to Peter's also being, in a different sense, called rock, and being said to be the foundation of the Church; so that I consider there is no ground for the fear entertained by some, in ancient and in modern

times, that, by applying the words personally to Peter, we should infringe on the honour due to Christ alone.[7]

Our current study comprises four interrelated topics. The first two sections examine the life and ministry of the Apostle Peter from biblical and historical sources. The last two sections examine the continuing authority of Peter through the centuries, carried on through apostolic succession and the primacy of Rome. We divide the study in this way:

1. The Life and Ministry of Peter
    A. Biblical study: Peter the man, the apostle, the rock: What is his place in the teachings of Jesus and in the New Testament?
    B. Historical study: Did Peter travel to Rome, oversee the Church as bishop, and die a martyr's death in the city of Rome?

2. The Primacy of Peter in the Early Church
    A. Earliest document study: The primacy of Rome in the earliest non-canonical writings of the Church, authored by Clement of Rome and Ignatius of Antioch.
    B. Early Church study: Peter and the primacy of Rome taught and practiced throughout the first five centuries.

Certainly, it is not possible to compile *every* passage from the Fathers that pertains to the study of Peter and the primacy. This is true, first of all, because such passages are too abundant and, secondly, because many times the primacy is not demonstrated by written teachings per se, but by the *actions* of the Fathers in particular historical situations. Some Fathers write of the Petrine primacy and later change their stance as they move away from orthodoxy or from a literal understanding of Scripture or when they enter into a personal conflict with the bishop of Rome. Lately, several books have come out that are hostile to the Catholic Church's teaching on papal primacy (we will discuss these books in the course of our study). A perusal of these books shows that their inability to deal fairly with the issue stems from their ten-

---

[7] George Salmon, *The Infallibility of the Church* (London: John Murray, 1914), 338–39.

dency to "proof-text", by which they point out things that seem to support their contentions and ignore everything that does not.

Another reason these opponents find it difficult to comprehend the Papacy is a perspective, inherited from the Protestant Reformation, that is essentially anti-sacramental, anti-mediational, and anti-incarnational. God's economy, however, always involves mediation. The people of God, for example, stepped back and demanded that God not speak to them directly, for they were afraid and stood at a distance. Then they said to Moses, "You speak to us, and we will hear; but let not God speak to us, lest we die" (Ex 20:19). Take another example—Paul. God could very well have "saved" him directly, but instead the great Paul was sent to the lowly Ananias for baptism and instructions. Paul later went to Peter for approval and to make sure he "was not running in vain", even though he had received revelations and had even been taken up to the "third heaven" (2 Cor 12:2). No Christian baptizes himself; this is done though the mediating agency of another person. Without an understanding of how God works through mediation, it is difficult to understand the fullness of the faith.[8]

It would take volumes to deal thoroughly with every biblical passage, every Father's writings, and every argument against the Papacy. However, we will provide ample material to establish the firm foundation of Catholic teaching and to refute the opposition. In the process we will attempt to be fair with the material, analyzing not only the Catholic position but the interpretation espoused by the opposition.

Much can be said about each of these topics and detailed accounts can be read from other sources listed in the bibliography.

---

[8] The objection will arise, "But we have only 'one mediator between God and men, the man Christ Jesus' " (1 Tim 2:5). To this the Catholic offers a hearty *Amen!* Yet we see, not four verses earlier, Paul commanding Timothy to pray for all men—to intercede (from the Latin *intercedere*, to intervene or go between, to mediate). Yes, Jesus is the mediator of the New Covenant, for such a unique covenant takes a unique mediator (Heb 8:6). But do we assume that, because Christ is the mediator of a better covenant, there is no longer any mediation in the Church? Prayer is mediation. *We* are mediating God's message to a sinful world when we preach the gospel. No finite human being can mediate an eternal covenant between God and man, but a pastor can certainly mediate God's word, and a simple soul can certainly intercede for the mighty. Mediation is alive and well as we enter into the New Covenant and participate in the mediating work of Christ.

In our journey through the Scriptures and the primitive Church, we will consult our first brethren in Christ. We will conclude by looking at the current teaching of the Catholic Church as well as the widespread opposition.

Now let us journey back in time to the New Testament period and the generations that followed in the footsteps and the teachings of Jesus and the apostles.

PART ONE

THE APOSTLE PETER

Biblical Study
Peter the Man, the Apostle, and the Rock

Why should we consider someone so impulsive, outspoken, and unstable as Peter to be capable of leading the band of apostles in founding and governing the Church, the Household of God? Because he is respected and loved by Jesus, being the first among the closest associates of Jesus. Jesus often separated out Peter, James, and John for intimate times of prayer and special instruction. Jesus also specifically chose Peter to be the leader and spokesman for the apostles and the primitive Christian community.

Every list of the twelve apostles in the New Testament has Peter prominently placed at the top of the list, and Judas is listed last.[1] Peter was the first of three special disciples whom Jesus included in his inner circle.[2] Peter is repeatedly mentioned by name when the others are referred to simply as "disciples" or "the eleven".[3] He always stands out as the leader, the spokesman, and the chosen "first" among equals. The names Peter, Simon, or Cephas are used 191 times in the New Testament. Except for Christ himself, no other person receives nearly as much attention as Simon Peter does through biblical references.[4] Before Jesus called this fisherman and renamed him Peter, his name was Simon, son of Jonas.

---

[1] Mt 10:2; Lk 6:13–16; Acts 1:13.

[2] Mt 17:1; Mk 5:37; 9:2; 14:33; Lk 8:51; 9:28.

[3] Mk 16:7; Acts 1:15; 2:14; 2:37; 8:14; 10:45; 1 Cor 9:5; 15:5.

[4] This is especially significant when we recall that the Gospels were written many years after the historical events. The Gospel of John, for example, was probably not written until the end of the first century, sixty or seventy years after the Resurrection of Christ; yet even decades after the original events, Peter is mentioned as being most significant among the apostles. "John, often regarded as equal in eminence with Peter (or nearly so), is next in frequency with only forty-eight appearances, and James considerably less than that. . . . Archbishop Fulton Sheen reckoned that all the other disciples combined were mentioned one hundred and thirty times. Assuming this is correct Peter is named a remarkable 60% of the time any disciple is referred to. . . . Surely, such consistent predominance is beyond coincidence" (Dave Armstrong, "Forty-five New Testament Proofs", in *Hands On Apologetics*, September/October 1995, 12).

Jesus gave Simon a new, descriptive name, Peter, which means "rock" in Greek, and from that time forward he was known as Simon Peter. Jesus in Caesarea Philippi also called him Cephas (Aramaic for "rock").[5] As we see from the naming of the twelve sons of Jacob, names were very significant in Jewish society. In the Torah and in Jewish tradition, a name change meant a change in status. Abraham, the father of the Jews who received the covenant sign of circumcision, had his name changed by God from Abram, meaning "father", to Abraham, meaning the "father of nations" (Gen 17:1–5). Now, at the inception of the new covenant, we see Simon's name changed by Jesus from Simon to *Kepha*, Peter, signifying a new designation, a new commission, and a new status.

Peter was the son of Jonas[6] and the brother of Andrew.[7] It appears from the Gospel record, and from Paul's writings, that Peter was married and owned his own house just south of the synagogue in Capernaum, on the northern shore of the Sea of Galilee. Peter may have lived with his mother-in-law and possibly his wife (Lk 4:38). The first-century stone pavement and the dark rocks of the original synagogue foundation, where Jesus taught "as one having authority" (Mk 1:21), can still be seen today. Archeologists have discovered that the site of Peter's home was venerated as early as the first century, and several churches were later built over the site in honor of St. Peter.[8] We get bits of information from

---

[5] Mt 16:18; Jn 1:42. Cephas (*Kepha*) and Peter are not different names. They are merely the same name, *Rock*, in two different languages, Aramaic and Greek, respectively. Cephas is the Greek transliteration of the Aramaic *Kepha*. This name was appropriately given to Peter near Caesarea Philippi. The water that flowed from the massive rock there was the source of the Jordan River.

[6] Jn 1:42; Mt 16:17.

[7] Mt 10:2; Jn 6:8.

[8] Tradition and modern archeology have uncovered the house of Peter in the ancient city of Capernaum, north of the Sea of Galilee. Next to the archeological remains, archeologists discovered the synagogue in which Jesus "taught. And they were amazed at his teaching" (Mk 1:21–22). "The traditional house of St. Peter was used for community gatherings as early as the third quarter of the first century A.D. . . . We have shown that the Christian community of Capharnaum paid a special attention to the house of Simon Peter. That house became very soon 'the house' of the followers of Jesus, i.e. a domus-ecclesia [house church]. As a matter of fact, the rediscovered house of Peter is the first example of a domus-ecclesia in the Christian world" (Stanislao Loffreda, *Recovering Capharnaum* [Jerusalem: Franciscan Printing Press, 1993], 57). "About 400 the pilgrim Egeria wrote: 'At Capharnaum the house of the Prince of the Apostles has

Clement of Alexandria (c. A.D. 150–215) that provide possible enlightenment about Peter's family. Clement writes, "They say, accordingly, that the blessed Peter, on seeing his wife led to death, rejoiced on account of her call and conveyance home, and called very encouragingly and comfortingly, addressing her by name, 'Remember thou the Lord.' Such was the marriage of the blessed, and their perfect disposition toward those dearest to them."[9] Clement also mentions that the apostles Peter and Philip both had children.[10] The Apostle Paul informs us that Peter, along with the other married apostles, perhaps took his wife with him on his apostolic journeys (1 Cor 9:5).

Peter and John were not highly educated; in fact, the rulers of the people and elders watched "Peter and John, and perceived that they were uneducated, common men."[11] Peter's brother Andrew, who was a disciple of John the Baptist at the time, introduced Peter to Jesus.[12] Peter owned fishing boats and a family fishing business in partnership with James and John, the sons of Zebedee.[13] It was from Peter's boat that Jesus chose to speak to the multitudes (Lk 5:3). Peter and his brother Andrew, along with James and John, left their everyday life and businesses to follow

---

become a Church: the walls of the house are still preserved. There our Lord healed the paralytic. There is the Synagogue where our Lord healed the demoniac, to which access is given through numerous stairs; this synagogue is made of cut stones' " (Eugene Hoade, *Guide to the Holy Land* [Jerusalem: Franciscan Printing Press, 1976], 759).

[9] *Stromata* 7, 11, ANF 2:541.

[10] *Stromata* 3, 6, ANF 2:390.

[11] Acts 4:13; cf. 1 Cor 1:26–27. "The court was *astonished by the courage of Peter and John*, particularly because they were *unschooled* [*agrammatoi*, meaning not that they were illiterate, but that they had received no proper training in Rabbinic theology) and *ordinary men* (*idiōtai*, meaning 'laymen' or 'non-professional', from which we get our English word 'idiot'). But then *they took note that these men had been with Jesus*, who also lacked both a formal theological education (Jn 7:15) and professional status as a Rabbi" (John Stott, *The Spirit, the Church and the World* [Downers Grove, Ill.: InterVarsity Press, 1990], 98).

[12] Jn 1:35–42. It appears that Jesus met them here, but the actual time they left their nets to follow Jesus may have been at a later date (see Mt 4:18–20).

[13] Mt 4:18; Lk 5:2, 3, 10. St. Maximus of Turin (d. c. A.D. 408) wisely observed, "Of how great merit before his God was Peter, that, after rowing his little boat, there should be consigned to him the helms of the whole Church" (*Homily* 3 *De Eod. Fest.*, in Joseph Berington and John Kirk, comps., *The Faith of Catholics*, ed. T. J. Capel [New York: F. Pustet & Co., 1885], 2:43).

Jesus as his disciples. What happened to their boats and nets? What happened to their fishing business? We do not know. Maybe the business was carried on by family members, possibly by Zebedee and his hired servants (Mk 1:20). After the Resurrection, Peter and the other disciples were again fishing from a boat in the Sea of Galilee (Jn 21:3), so it is probable that Peter still owned the fishing vessels.

The New Testament is peppered with biographical details about the personality and life of Peter. For three years Peter and the disciples followed Jesus as he crisscrossed the rocky terrain of Israel. Peter walked on the water (Mt 14:28–31) and pulled a coin from a fish's mouth to pay a tax for himself and Jesus (Mt 17:24–27). Peter was the one who received a revelation from God that enabled him to confess the true identity of Jesus (Mt 16:16), and he saw Jesus transfigured, along with Moses and Elijah, on the mountain, which he mentions later in his second epistle.[14] Peter, along with John, was selected to prepare the Passover meal, which would be transformed into the Eucharist (Lk 22:8). Peter was bold and spoke his mind—sometimes too quickly, not thinking before he did so. He was rebuked by Jesus for his wrong-headed conclusions (Mt 16:23), though Jesus loved his devotion and courage. After pledging loyalty and even martyrdom for Jesus' sake, Peter reneged and vehemently denied the Lord three times—and then (unlike Judas) repented and wept bitterly because of his betrayal.[15] Another time, he impulsively drew his sword and slashed off Malchus' ear (Jn 18:10). Even though he was brash and impulsive, however, he had a gentle heart and was extremely sensitive to his sin and shortcomings.[16]

There may be too much made of Peter's impulsiveness. As a successful businessman with a prominent house in the community, Peter must also have had organizational and leadership abilities—to which the event of Pentecost added charisms of faith and leadership, grace building upon nature. He could not have succeeded in business if he had allowed impulse alone to rule him. But he may very well have overestimated his own abilities. He took it on himself to lead wherever he was, speaking often for the other disciples, and even once for Jesus.

---

[14] Mk 9:2–9; 2 Pet 1:18.
[15] Mt 26:35; Lk 22:57–62.
[16] Lk 5:8; 22:61–62.

Peter was the first man to see Jesus after the Resurrection.[17] Peter was given the special commission to pray for his brethren and strengthen them and was appointed by Jesus to feed and tend his sheep.[18] After Pentecost, Peter took the leading role in the fledgling Church.[19] He preached the first gospel message (Acts 2:14–40), and, with the assistance of the other apostles, he baptized over three thousand people that day.

After exposing their deception, Peter condemned Ananias and Sapphira, who lied to the Holy Spirit and fell dead at the feet of Peter (Acts 5:1–11). Peter changed the course of the young Church by baptizing Cornelius and his household, the first Gentiles to become Christians. Paul came to visit Cephas (Peter) and "remained with him fifteen days" (Gal 1:18). Later, Paul again came to Jerusalem to submit his gospel to Peter and the leading apostles to make sure he was not running in vain (Gal 2:2). When confusion arose over how the law of circumcision applied to the Gentile converts, Peter made the authoritative doctrinal decision at the first Church council in Jerusalem (Acts 15), to which all those in attendance acquiesced. Peter traveled extensively, preaching the gospel and establishing churches all over the Roman Empire.[20] There are many more biographical passages focusing on Peter in the Scriptures, more than we can detail in this short introduction.

---

[17] Lk 24:34; 1 Cor 15:5.

[18] Lk 22:32; Jn 21:15–17.

[19] "We can see that St. Peter, immediately after our Lord's Ascension, entered on his office of visible head of the Church. He declared in the presence of a hundred and twenty of the faithful that another apostle must be chosen in the place of Judas, and they did exactly as he told them, without seeing any pretension or arrogance in his thus putting himself forward; for they, one and all, knew that our Blessed Lord had appointed him to be the chief pastor of His Church" (Frederick Justus Knecht, *A Practical Commentary on Holy Scripture* [St. Louis, Mo.: B. Herder Book Co., 1930], 736–37).

[20] Acts 11:12–13; 1 Cor 1:12; 9:5; 1 Pet 1:1. This topic will be covered in some detail as we progress in the book. However, we know from Bishop Dionysius of Corinth in his letter to Pope Soter in Rome, written about A.D. 166/174, that Peter had labored and planted in Corinth as well as in Rome. Eusebius records Dionysius' words: " 'You have thus by such an admonition bound together the planting of Peter and of Paul at Rome and Corinth. For both of them planted and likewise taught us in our Corinth. And they taught together in like manner in Italy, and suffered martyrdom at the same time.' I have quoted these things in order that the truth of the history might be still more confirmed" (Eusebius, *The*

How does Peter fit into the whole scheme of things? Did Jesus really treat Peter differently from the others? Did Jesus favor Peter or set him apart? What about the other disciples? Did they recognize Peter as first, in a place of preeminence? John was the disciple "Jesus loved", the one who rested his head on Jesus' breast while at the Passover dinner,[21] but it was Peter who was given a special place of leadership, the shepherd of the sheep and the one who "strengthens" his fellow apostles.[22] But the single event that most clearly shows Peter's prominence in the New Testament is recorded in the Gospel of St. Matthew. Jesus commissions Peter, and his words have probably caused more spilled ink over the last five centuries than any other biblical passage.[23]

The Gospels, Acts, and the letter to the Galatians give us the most information about the ministry of Peter after the Resurrection. The Acts of the Apostles begins with Peter at the center of activity in Jerusalem; and then, after the Council of Jerusalem, Paul takes center stage in the drama. According to Michael Winter,

> After this decision [in Jerusalem regarding the Gentiles] has been reached, the book of the Acts leaves the Jerusalem community and relates in detail the mission to the gentiles. It is natural that atten-

---

Church History 2, 25, 8, in Philip Schaff, ed., *Nicene and Post-Nicene Fathers*, 2d series [Grand Rapids, Mich.: Eerdmans, 1983], 1:130 [hereafter NPNF2]).

[21] Jn 13:23–25; Eusebius, *Church History*, 3:31, NPNF2, 1:163.

[22] Jn 21:15–17; Lk 22:31–32.

[23] It will be helpful to eliminate early on in our study one attempted dismissal advanced against this important Matthean passage. Because of the import of this passage, especially with regard to the existence of a "Church" in Jesus' theology and the Church's claim to a Petrine primacy, many have suggested that this passage is a later interpolation, added by someone promoting an ecclesiastical agenda. However, this suggestion has been discredited and summarily dismissed. Anglican John Lowe writes, "The dominant critical view until recently among non-Roman Catholic scholars, and it is still strongly maintained by some, is that we have here a community production arising out of local rivalries over leadership in the early Church. I leave on one side the suggestion that the passage is a late intrusion into the text of Matthew, designed to bolster up incipient Roman claims, a suggestion unsupported by any textual evidence and abandoned by responsible scholars. One obvious and certain fact is the marked Semitic colouring of the language. Even Bultmann, a strong opponent of genuineness, admits that the passage must have taken shape in Aramaic-speaking Palestinian circles. Whether spoken by Jesus or not, the saying is an integral part of the First Gospel, and ante-dates any argument about the claims of Rome" (John Lowe, *Saint Peter* [New York: Oxford Univ. Press, 1956], 48).

tion should henceforth center on St. Paul, but the lesson of the first half of the book is not thereby invalidated. The picture of St. Peter is just the same as that of the gospels. Without any attempt to force the meaning of the text, he is seen in a position of particular authority, and although the precise amplitude of his powers cannot be decided without reference to the gospels he is rightly seen to be the director of the infant church. There is no suggestion here that St. Peter is about to be demoted, and although little more is said about him, no evidence can be found to show that it was the intention of Christ or the infant church that he should relinquish his position of authority.[24]

Quite the contrary. As we enter the fascinating period of the apostolic Church, we see that the place of Peter, and his martyrdom in Rome, had a universal acceptance among the writings and beliefs of the earliest Christians.

Now we will plunge into the Scriptures to discover passages related to Peter and his primacy in the early Church, a primacy that was passed on in the Church through the office of the bishop of Rome.

The Gospel of John
   —event c. A.D. 30
   —written by St. John about A.D. 90–100

"One of the two who heard John speak, and followed him, was Andrew, Simon Peter's brother. He first found his brother Simon, and said to him, 'We have found the Messiah' (which means Christ). He brought him to Jesus. Jesus looked at him, and said, 'So you are Simon the son of John? You shall be called Cephas' (which means Peter)."[25]

---

[24] Michael M. Winter, *Saint Peter and the Popes* (Baltimore, Md.: Helicon Press, 1960), 29.

[25] Jn 1:40–42. When Jesus met Simon he said, "You shall be called Rock." Peter (Πέτρος) and Cephas (Κηφᾶς) are not different names, but the same name in different languages, Greek and Aramaic, respectively. "*You will be called Cephas*: doubtless in Aramaic the expression was *kêpā'*, a word meaning 'rock' " (Evangelical scholar D. A. Carson, *The Gospel according to John* [Grand Rapids, Mich.: Eerdmans, 1991], 156). John, writing his Gospel about sixty years after

The Gospel of Matthew
  —event c. A.D. 30
  —written in the last half of the first century

"The names of the twelve apostles are these: first, Simon, who is called Peter, and Andrew his brother; James the son of Zebedee, and John his brother; Philip and Bartholomew; Thomas and Matthew the tax collector; James the son of Alphaeus, and Thaddaeus; Simon the Cananaean, and Judas Iscariot, who betrayed him." [26]

The Gospel of Luke
  —written in the last half of the first century

"Now about eight days after these sayings he took with him Peter and John and James, and went up on the mountain to pray. . . . Now Peter and those who were with him were heavy with sleep." [27]

---

the death and Resurrection of the Lord and about thirty years after the death of Peter, recalls the time when Jesus appointed Peter as the "Rock". The Old Testament provides the precedents for the changing of names at the onset of an appointment or calling (Gen 17:5; 32:28; 41:45).

[26] Mt 10:2–4. Matthew not only lists Peter first but even calls him *first*. In Greek the word is πρῶτος, *first* or *chief*. According to William F. Arndt and F. Wilbur Gingrich, *A Greek–English Lexicon of the New Testament and Other Early Christian Literature* (Chicago: Univ. of Chicago Press, 1957), 733, "[In Matthew 10:2 this] is not meant to indicate the position of Simon in the list, since no other numbers follow, but to single him out as the *most prominent* one of the twelve" (emphasis added). It is not insignificant, in this regard, that Judas Iscariot is listed last.

R. V. G. Tasker says, "There is little doubt that *The first* (*prōtos*) means 'first and foremost'. It is not surprising that this designation of Peter is not found in Mark, for the leading apostle was humble enough not to harp upon the position assigned him by Jesus [in the Gospel written by Mark]" (*The Gospel according to Matthew*, Tyndale New Testament Commentaries [Grand Rapids, Mich.: Eerdmans, 1978], 106).

[27] Lk 8:45; 9:28, 32. Because the four Gospels were written much later than the actual time of the events they describe, it is significant how many times Peter is distinguished from the other disciples. Peter, though a leader and spokesman during the lifetime of Jesus, was recognized all the more as the appointed shepherd after the Ascension of Christ. Those who wrote the Gospels later, in view of the first decades of the Church, mention Peter as leader, faithful to the tradition passed on orally by the apostles.

An Angel
 —recorded in the Gospel of Mark
 —event about A.D. 30
 —written in the last half of the first century

"And entering the tomb, they saw a young man sitting on the right side, dressed in a white robe; and they were amazed. And he said to them, 'Do not be amazed; you seek Jesus of Nazareth, who was crucified. He has risen, he is not here; see the place where they laid him. But go, tell his disciples and Peter that he is going before you to Galilee; there you will see him, as he told you.' " [28]

The Gospel of Luke

"And they rose that same hour and returned to Jerusalem; and they found the eleven gathered together and those who were with them, who said, 'The Lord has risen indeed, and has appeared to Simon!' " [29]

Paul in his *First Letter to the Corinthians*
 —written about A.D. 57

"For I delivered to you as of first importance what I also received, that Christ died for our sins in accordance with the scriptures, that he was buried, that he was raised on the third day in accordance with the scriptures, and that he appeared to Cephas, then to the twelve. Then he appeared to more than five hundred brethren at one time." [30]

---

[28] Mk 16:5–7. Jesus wants Peter to know that he is not rejected after having denied his Lord. However, there is more to the reason he is mentioned in particular. The Orthodox archbishop Blessed Theophylact wrote from Constantinople in the eleventh century, "He names Peter separately from the other disciples, as Peter was the foremost of the apostles" (*The Explanation by Blessed Theophylact of the Holy Gospel according to St. Mark* [House Springs, Mo.: Chrysostom Press, 1993], 141).

[29] Lk 24:33–34. The King, Jesus, has made a special point of appearing to the apostle who is "first and foremost", in order to secure for all time the reality and historicity of his physical Resurrection. Peter, as the leader of the apostles, is again set apart for an exclusive privilege.

[30] 1 Cor 15:3–6.

Jesus Christ in *The Gospel of Matthew*[31]

"Now when Jesus came into the district of Caesarea Philippi,[32] he asked his disciples, 'Who do men say that the Son of man is?'

---

[31] Papias (c. A.D. 60–130) wrote, "Matthew put together the oracles [of the Lord] in the Hebrew language, and each one interpreted [translated] them as best he could" (*Fragments of Papias* 6, ANF 1:155). Irenaeus, writing about A.D. 180, informs us, "Matthew also issued a written Gospel among the Hebrews in their own dialect" (*Against Heresies* 3, 1, 1, ANF 1:414). Origen (c. A.D. 185–254), consistent with the early witnesses, wrote, "Among the four Gospels, which are the only indisputable ones in the Church of God under heaven, I have learned by tradition that the first was written by Matthew, who was once a publican, but afterwards an apostle of Jesus Christ, and it was prepared for the converts from Judaism, and published in the Hebrew language" (*Commentary on Matthew*, quoted in Eusebius, *Church History* 6, 25, NPNF2, 1:273). Aramaic, the language of Jesus, was closely related to Hebrew.

[32] The significance of Caesarea Philippi as the site for his appointment of Peter did not escape Jesus. "The situation of the ancient Caesarea Philippi (1,147 feet above the sea) is, indeed, magnificent.... The western side of a steep mountain, crowned by the ruins of an ancient castle, forms an abrupt rock-wall. Here, from an immense cavern, bursts a river. These are 'the upper sources' of the Jordan. This cave, an ancient heathen sanctuary of Pan, gave its earliest name of Paneas to the town.... The views, sheer down the precipitous sides of the mountain, into the valleys and far away, are magnificent" (Alfred Edersheim, *The Life and Times of Jesus the Messiah* [Grand Rapids, Mich.: Eerdmans, 1972], 2:74). The city was originally named Paneas, "the city of Pan, the god of springs and shepherds of ancient Greece, who was worshiped here in the first centuries A.D. The cult of Pan seems to have flourished on the rock escarpment above the town.... [It was] the northernmost point visited by Jesus and his disciples" (Rivka Gonen, *Biblical Holy Places* [Herzlia, Israel: Palphot, 1994], 46). So Jesus took the disciples out of the Jewish populated areas around Jerusalem and Judea, into the Gentile districts, to the site of Pan, the pagan god of shepherds and flocks (see Pierre Grimal, *The Dictionary of Classical Mythology* [New York: Basil Blackwell, 1985], 340), to appoint Peter as the rock. Jesus, the true God of shepherds, appointed Peter as the steward of his kingdom and shepherd of his flock. By choosing this location for the appointment, Jesus clearly shows that he is setting up his divine kingdom in opposition to the worldly kingdom of the Roman Caesars, who claimed divinity for themselves.

During the time of Christ, a temple to Caesar Augustus sat at the pinnacle of the rock wall overlooking Caesarea Philippi. In about A.D. 95, Josephus wrote, "So when he [Herod] had conducted Caesar to the sea, and was returned home, he built him a most beautiful temple, of the whitest stone of Zenodorus's country, near the place called Panium. This is a very fine cave in a mountain, under which there is a great cavity in the earth, and the cavern is abrupt, and prodigiously deep, and full of a still water; over it hangs a vast mountain; and under the caverns arise the springs of the river Jordan. Herod adorned this

And they said, 'Some say John the Baptist, others say Elijah, and others Jeremiah or one of the prophets.' He said to them, 'But who do you say that I am?' Simon Peter replied, 'You are the Christ, the Son of the living God.'[33] And Jesus answered him, 'Blessed are you, Simon Bar-Jona![34] For flesh and blood has not revealed this to you, but my Father who is in heaven.[35] And I

---

place, which was already a very remarkable one, still further by the erection of this temple, which he dedicated to Caesar" (Josephus, *Jewish Antiquities* 15, 10, 3, in *Josephus, Complete Works*, trans. William Whiston [Grand Rapids, Mich.: Kregel Pub., 1980], 333).

"The epithet ['thou art Peter'] is explained and it is all so much clearer as they stand there before that actual rock which supports the temple dedicated to the lord of the Palatine [Caesar Augustus]. The foundation rock of the spiritual temple which Jesus will build to the Lord of heaven, namely, his Church, is to be the disciple who first declared him the Messias and truly the Son of God" (Giuseppe Ricciotti, *The Life of Christ*, trans. Alba Zizzamia [Milwaukee, Wis.: Bruce Pub. Co., 1947], 404). And, as the water flowed from the rock at Caesarea Philippi to feed the Jordan River, Peter was to be the rock and leader of the Church, and from that Church would flow the water of truth and life to the whole world, offering life, the salvation of Israel, both to the Jew and to the Gentile (see Ezek 47:1, 9). For a detailed history of the site and its relationship to Matthew 16, see Stanley L. Jaki's *And on This Rock* (Front Royal, Va.: Christendom Press, 1997).

[33] Many of the Church Fathers, as we will see as we proceed, used this passage in their apologetics to prove the deity of Jesus Christ. By divine revelation Peter declares that Jesus is the Messiah and that he is divine, being the Son of the Living God.

[34] The name "Bar-Jona" is a confirmation that Jesus himself was speaking in Aramaic, not in Greek, during his discourse with Peter. Before the Christian era, Aramaic had become the language of the Jews in Palestine. Jesus preached in Aramaic, and parts of the Old Testament and much of the rabbinical literature were written in Aramaic. This passage in Matthew is loaded with Hebrew parallelisms and Aramaic phrases that confirm that Jesus actually spoke to Peter in Aramaic, a fact that is further confirmed by the name "Bar-Jona". "The word 'bar' is Aramaic for 'son' " (Daniel J. Harrington, *The Gospel of Matthew* [Collegeville, Minn.: Liturgical Press, 1991], 247). Watchman Nee speculates, " 'Bar' means son. 'Jonah' means 'dove'. Combined, the surname of Simon means having the revelation of the Holy Spirit. . . . 'Bar-Jonah' means son of the Holy Spirit" (*The King and the Kingdom of Heaven* [New York: Christian Fellowship Pub., 1978], 192–93).

[35] A divine privilege was granted to Peter by way of a divine revelation. In a sense, God the Father, in choosing to make the revelation to Peter alone, chose Peter as the rock. Through the revelation, and Simon's statement of faith, Jesus, working in cooperation with the Father, recognized or "agreed with" the Father's choice and appointed Peter as the *Kepha*, the rock and the steward who would carry the keys of the kingdom.

tell you, you are Peter,[36] and on this rock[37] I will build my church,[38] and the powers of death shall not prevail against it. I

---

[36] W. F. Albright, eminent Protestant scholar and internationally regarded as the "dean of biblical studies", writes, "This is not a name, but an appellation and a play on words. There is no evidence of Peter or Kephas as a name before Christian times. . . . *Peter* as *Rock* will be the foundation of the future community. Jesus, not quoting the Old Testament, here uses Aramaic, not Hebrew, and so uses the only Aramaic word that would serve his purpose. In view of the background of verse 19, . . . one must dismiss as confessional interpretation any attempt to see *this rock* as meaning the faith, or the messianic confession, of Peter. To deny the pre-eminent position of Peter among the disciples or in the early Christian community is a denial of the evidence. . . . The interest in Peter's failures and vacillations does not detract from this pre-eminence; rather, it emphasizes it. Had Peter been a lesser figure his behavior would have been of far less consequence (cf. Gal 2:11ff.)" (W. F. Albright and C. S. Mann, *The Anchor Bible: Matthew* [Garden City, N.Y.: Doubleday & Co., 1971], 195).

David Hill, Presbyterian minister and senior lecturer of biblical studies, University of Sheffield, writes, "It is on Peter himself, the confessor of his Messiahship, that Jesus will build the Church. . . . Attempts to interpret the 'rock' as something other than Peter in person (e.g., his faith, the truth revealed to him) are due to Protestant bias, and introduce to the statement a degree of subtlety which is highly unlikely" (*The Gospel of Matthew*, New Century Bible Commentary [Grand Rapids, Mich.: Eerdmans, 1972], 261). For more information on this point, see James T. Shotwell and Louise Ropes Loomis, *The See of Peter* [1927; reprint, New York: Columbia Univ. Press, 1991], especially 23–24).

Name changes held great weight in Eastern cultures. Abraham's name change from Abram (father) to Abraham (father of nations) is a prime example. It signified a change of status or mission. Jesus changed Peter's name from Simon to Rock. Jesus is making it obvious that something important is taking place; Peter's status has changed for all time, and, as with Abraham, this change would have a continuing impact on the new covenant community. The fisherman was now the steward of a kingdom. Fundamentalists may object, "Only Christ can be the rock." However, the same figures of speech can be applied to more than one person in Scripture. In one illustration, Jesus is called the cornerstone, not the foundation, while the apostles *are* called the foundation (see Rev 21:14). God is called rock in Deuteronomy 32:4, and the name is now given to Peter, who shares in God's rock-ness. Jesus is the one with the keys (Rev 3:7), but the keys are delegated to Peter. Jesus is the Good Shepherd, but Peter is also given the responsibility of shepherd (Jn 21:15–17). The apostles were to share in the authority and work of Christ. We should remember George Salmon's words quoted earlier: "Yet we must remember that the same metaphor may be used to illustrate different truths, and so, according to circumstances, may have different significations" (*The Infallibility of the Church* [London: John Murray, 1914], 338).

[37] We know that Jesus spoke Aramaic, not Greek. The Greek words "Peter" (Πέτρος) and "rock" (πέτρα) would have been the same Aramaic word *Kepha* (from which we get *Cephas*). There was no distinction between the two words as

Jesus spoke them. James G. McCarthy, seeming to ignore all recent scholarship on this Matthean passage, writes, in *The Gospel according to Rome* (Eugene, Ore.: Harvest House Pub., 1995), 242: "Why did not the Holy Spirit just repeat the word *petros*, as Catholic defenders speculate He did in the Aramaic? Then Matthew 16:18 would read, 'You are Peter (*Petros*), and upon this rock (*petros*) I will build My church.'" The simplest reply, which should be understood by anyone with the most rudimentary knowledge of biblical Greek, is that in the Greek language nouns have grammatical gender—something we do not have in English. In Greek, *petra* is feminine, and *Petros* is masculine. "Rock" is feminine in Greek, and when the Aramaic *Kepha* was translated into Greek, *Petros* (masculine) was used for Peter's name. Why? For the same reason my mother named me Stephen instead of Stephanie, and James McCarthy's mother named him James instead of Jacqueline (both from *Jacob*)—Simon could not be given a feminine name. Remember, "Peter" was not just a description but a new name. Jesus said, "You are Rock [*Kepha*] and upon this rock [*kepha*] I will build my Church." Thus, the Holy Spirit, through the author of Matthew, used the word *Petros* to provide a masculine form for the feminine *petra*.

Fundamentalists have also tried to disassociate Peter from the "rock" by making a distinction between Peter (*Petros*) and rock (*petra*) in the Greek text. But, in the *Theological Dictionary of the New Testament* (ed. Gerhard Kittel and Gerhard Friedrich [Grand Rapids, Mich.: Eerdmans, 1968], 6:98), we read, "The obvious pun which has made its way into the Greek text as well suggests a material identity between πέτρα and Πέτρος, the more so as it is impossible to differentiate strictly between the meanings of the two words. On the other hand, only the fairly assured Aramaic original of the saying enables us to assert with confidence the formal and material identity between πέτρα [*petra*] and Πέτρος [*Petros*, or Peter]: Πέτρος = ['rock' in Aramaic] = πέτρα. Elsewhere in the NT the individual Christian is never called πέτρα. . . . Rightly understood, Christ alone is πέτρα. If, then, Mt. 16:18 forces us to assume a formal and material identity between πέτρα and Πέτρος, this shows how fully the apostolate, and in it to a special degree the position of Peter, belongs to and is essentially enclosed within, the revelation of Christ. Πέτρος himself is this πέτρα, not just his faith or his confession. He is this, of course, only as the Simon whom Christ has taken in hand. But in this way, like the one who walked on the sea, he truly is this Πέτρος. If Christ is to build a spiritual house, the [Church] on this πέτρα, Πέτρος is the foundation of this [Church] on the basis of the saying of Christ: 'Thou art Peter'."

Protestant scholar Oscar Cullmann, the author of the article, goes on to say, "But what does Jesus mean when He says: 'On this rock I will build my church'? The idea of the Reformers that He is referring to the faith of Peter is quite inconceivable in view of the probably different setting of the story. For there is no reference here to the faith of Peter. Rather, the parallelism of 'thou art Rock' and 'on this rock I will build' shows that the second rock can only be the same as the first. It is thus evident that Jesus is referring to Peter, to whom he has given the name Rock. He appoints Peter, the impulsive, enthusiastic, but not persevering man in the circle, to be the foundation of His *ecclesia* [church]. To this extent Roman Catholic exegesis is right and all Protestant attempts to evade this interpretation are to be rejected" (6:108).

Craig Keener helps solidify this point. "In Aramaic, 'Peter' and 'rock' are the same word; in Greek (here), they are cognate terms that were used interchangeably by this period" (*The IVP Bible Background Commentary: New Testament* [Downers Grove, Ill.: InterVarsity Press, 1993], 90).

A different attempt is made by James White to equate πέτρα [rock] with Peter's confession of faith rather than with Peter himself. White writes, "The rock of which the Lord speaks is that common confession made by all who are part of the Church: Jesus is the Christ, the Son of the living God. This is seen, I believe, in the fact that while the Lord is addressing Peter directly, He changes from the direct address to the third person, 'this rock', when speaking of Peter's confession" (James White, *The Roman Catholic Controversy* [Minneapolis: Bethany House Pub., 1996], 118.). He believes that the third person designates something other than Peter himself, namely, his confession. Though this may seem feasible on the surface, especially for one wanting desperately to shed the Catholic interpretation, a much better explanation of the third-person use of πέτρα, and one that fits the text more adequately, is that the third person not only refers to Peter, as Cullmann has already told us it must, but also includes something even more extensive: the stewardship of Peter, the primacy, the *office* of the universal shepherd. It includes Peter, yes, but projects out through time; *and time is an important element in this passage*, extending beyond the individual man to the perpetual *office* being established. James White's "third person" observation only strengthens the Catholic understanding of the passage. One must also realize that Jesus is standing in front of a massive rock (see Stanley L. Jaki's *And upon This Rock* for an excellent treatment of Matthew 16). This fact is too often ignored. Jesus, standing in front of the massive rock in Caesarea Philippi upon which stands the "false church", the temple to the "divine" Caesar Augustus, says to Peter ,"You are Rock", making a correlation. Then, after the correlation has been made, he looks at Peter *and* the massive rock and says, "And upon this Rock I will build my Church." The fact that Jesus uses the third person only emphasizes the Catholic position and strengthens the understanding of the Petrine office in the Catholic Church.

[38] In this metaphorical description, Jesus himself could not be the *foundation*, because in this illustration he presents himself as the *builder*. The following is very important. In Scripture Jesus is variously depicted as the foundation (1 Cor 3:11), the builder (Mt 16:18), the cornerstone (Acts 4:11), and the temple itself (Rev 21:22). We also see the apostles and/or believers as the foundation (Eph 2:20; Rev 21:14), the builders (1 Cor 3:10), the stones, λίθος, not πέτρα (1 Pet 2:5), the building (1 Cor 3:9), and the temple (Eph 2:21). Many illustrative metaphors are used to explain various aspects of the Church. One cannot simply substitute one descriptive figure of speech for another in any one illustration, thereby mixing metaphors. It does great violence to the textual illustration itself and is a good example of roughshod "proof-texting", wrongly "dividing the word of truth" (2 Tim 2:15). The Bible does not set up a dichotomy—*either* Jesus *or* Peter; rather, it presents us with *both* Jesus *and* Peter as foundation stones. Jesus is establishing the man who will be the focal point of unity within the Church, the foundation. He who builds on sand has a structure that crumbles (Mt 7:24–27). Jesus built his Church upon the rock of his choice, and, by his protection, the Church has stood the test of time. The powers of hell have failed to destroy or corrupt her.

will give you the keys of the kingdom of heaven,[39] and whatever you bind on earth shall be bound in heaven, and whatever you loose on earth shall be loosed in heaven.'[40] Then he strictly charged the disciples to tell no one that he was the Christ."[41]

---

[39] Too many people struggle to resist the Catholic understanding of this passage. They invariably fail to listen carefully or understand the words of our Lord. The keys entrusted to a man have always represented the delegation of authority. In Isaiah 22, the king's steward carried the keys of authority as a vice regent of the king and exercised the king's own authority—for example, Joseph for Pharaoh. Jesus knows he is leaving this earth soon, and he is assigning a vice regent, or steward, to be over his "house". Peter is given keys and the authority to administer affairs for the King in his absence. This gives Peter, and the office he fills, tremendous responsibility and influence. (For a more detailed discussion, see appendix B.)

[40] Attempts are often made to soften Jesus' words, to make them appear to give Peter no real authority, by stating that what the apostles bind and loose on earth ratifies a prior decision in heaven or that Peter (and subsequently all who believe) is only given the right to tell others that their sins are forgiven if they believe in Jesus. However, this is not what the passage says. Peter is given the prerogative to make binding decisions upon the Church that God will ratify from heaven; thus, God binds himself to Peter's decisions. Therefore, God watches over each pronouncement made by Peter and his successors, since God himself has promised to ratify what the Church determines. "The judgment of Peter, and by implication that of the church, reflects what is in accord with what is settled in heaven as the fully determined will of God. Whether this is already decreed in the will of God or subsequently ratified as the will of God is not the issue here. Peter's authority, in short, is such that he speaks on behalf of heaven (i.e., God)" (Donald A. Hagner, *Matthew 14–28*, Word Biblical Commentary [Waco, Tex.: Word Books, 1995], 33b:474). John C. Fenton writes, "Peter has authority in the Church to make pronouncements (whether legislative or disciplinary) which will be ratified at the last judgment" (*The Gospel of Saint Matthew* [Baltimore, Md.: Penguin Books, 1963], 270). Peter, as the steward and shepherd of the Church, speaks on God's behalf, and what he proclaims and determines on earth and in the Church is ratified by God in heaven and will be executed on the final Day of Judgment. (See also Alfred Edersheim, *The Life and Times of Jesus the Messiah* [Grand Rapids, Mich.: Eerdmans, 1972], 2:85).

[41] "Binding" and "loosing" are often reduced simply to Peter's "preaching the gospel to open the gates of heaven", especially to the Gentiles. However, this reduction ignores the meaning and usage of these technical terms ("binding" and "loosing") during the lifetime of Jesus. These terms have been defined as follows: "Rabbinic terms used in Mt. 16:19 of Peter's doctrinal authority to declare things forbidden or permitted; and in Mt. 18:18 of the disciples' disciplinary authority to condemn and absolve" (*The Illustrated Bible Dictionary*, ed. J. D. Douglas [Wheaton, Ill.: InterVarsity Press and Tyndale House Pub., 1980], 1:199). Protestant writer and Aramaic scholar George Lamsa writes of binding

The Prophet Isaiah[42]

"Thus says the Lord God of hosts, 'Come, go to this steward, to Shebna, who is over the household,[43] and say to him: What have you to do here and whom have you here, that you have hewn here a tomb for yourself, you who hew a tomb on the height, and carve a habitation for yourself in the rock? . . . I will thrust you from your office,[44] and you will be cast down from your station. In that day I

---

and loosing, " 'He has the key,' means he can declare certain things to be lawful and others unlawful; that is, to bind or to loose, or to prohibit or to permit, or to forgive" (*Old Testament Light* [San Francisco: Harper & Row, 1964], 657). This prerogative, delegated to Peter and the other apostles in conjunction with him, can be seen in the Council of Jerusalem in Acts 15 and in all subsequent ecumenical councils of the Catholic Church.

"No other terms were in more constant use in Rabbinic canon-law than those of *binding* and *loosing*. They represented the *legislative* and *judicial* powers of the Rabbinic office. These powers Christ now transferred . . . in their reality, to his apostles; the first, here to Peter" (Marvin R. Vincent, *Word Studies in the New Testament* [1887; reprint, Grand Rapids, Mich.: Eerdmans, 1980], 1:96). For further study of this passage, refer to *Jesus, Peter and the Keys*, by Scott Butler, Norman Dahlgren, and David Hess (Santa Barbara, Calif.: Queenship Pub., 1996).

[42] The Gospel of Matthew was written primarily for Jews. Every educated Jew who read Matthew 16 would immediately associate the appointment of Peter with this passage in Isaiah 22. Jesus most obviously referred to Isaiah 22 by the very words he employed; and the context places Peter as the royal steward of Jesus' New Kingdom, Jesus being the son of David and heir to the eternal throne. Isaiah, the great prophet of Israel, is pronouncing judgment, displacing Shebna, the royal steward of the king, and appointing Eliakim to succeed him as the steward. The office of royal steward was a permanent office within the Eastern kingdoms. For a detailed discussion, see appendix B.

[43] The "steward" or one "over the house" or "master of the palace" was second to the king. The steward ruled in his place and in his absence. "One is reminded of our Lord's words to Peter, the Vizier of the Kingdom of Heaven (Mt 16:19). Like the Egyptian vizier, the master of the palace was the highest official in the state" (Roland de Vaux, *Ancient Israel* [New York: McGraw-Hill, 1961], 130). In this case, Eliakim replaced Shebna as the royal steward for Hezekiah, king of Judah (2 Kings 18:18). Jotham was "over the house" as regent or vicar of the kingdom in the absence of the king, as was the vizier in the absence of the Pharaoh, as was Peter in the physical absence of Christ.

[44] Concerning this passage in the prophet Isaiah, John D. W. Watts writes, "What follows is the fullest description of this position of honor and authority that exists in Scripture" (*Word Biblical Commentary*, s.v. Is. 1–33 [Waco, Tex.: Word Books, 1985], 24:289). That the position of steward was an office is not disputed. The office was dynastic in that it was a continuing position and was

will call my servant Eliakim the son of Hilkiah, and I will clothe him with your robe, and will bind your girdle on him,[45] and will commit your authority to his hand;[46] and he shall be a father to the inhabitants of Jerusalem and to the house of Judah.[47] *And I will*

---

filled whenever vacated. Peter was appointed by Christ as the steward of his kingdom, and the office would, like that of royal steward, demand a successor. Notice the incredible parallel that Jesus draws by alluding to Isaiah 22. The King (Jesus) is appointing Peter as the steward of his kingdom in his absence, until he comes again. He is giving Peter his own authority to rule his new kingdom, the Church. Peter stands in the King's place, exercising authority in his name.

[45] According to *Matthew Henry's Commentary* (McLean, Va.: MacDonald Pub., n.d.), 4:121, the robe is "the badge of honour", and the girdle is "the badge of power". This could be seen to reflect the primacy of honor and jurisdiction held by the bishop of Rome, as the successor of Peter, the "steward" of the visible Church. Matthew Henry also suggests that "clothe him" be followed by "strengthen him", which implies that God gives strength and protection to the one to whom he gives authority.

[46] "Shebna is officially described as 'over the house.' This was the name given to an office of state of great importance in both kingdoms (1 Kings 4:6, 18:3), in fact the highest office of all, and one so vastly superior to all others (Is 36:3, 37:2), that it was sometimes filled by the heir to the throne (2 Chron 26:21). . . . The person 'who was over the house' had the whole of the domestic affairs of the sovereign under his superintendence, and was therefore also called the socēn or administrator . . . as standing nearest to the king" (C. F. Keil and F. Delitzsch, *Isaiah*, vol. 7 of *Commentary on the Old Testament* [Grand Rapids, Mich.: Eerdmans, 1978], 398). As Evangelical Edward J. Young comments, "A man in such an exalted position would wield an influence of great power over the king" (*The Book of Isaiah* [Grand Rapids, Mich.: Eerdmans, 1969), 2:114).

[47] The king's steward in Isaiah 22 is clearly the backdrop against which the Lord Jesus proclaims Peter the keeper of the keys. He builds upon this prophetic passage, as any Jew would immediately recognize. The royal steward in Judah is called a "father", as is the "successor" to the Petrine chair in the reestablished Davidic kingdom. Protestant commentator Geoffrey W. Grogan writes, "The word 'father' suggests both his authority over the people of Jerusalem and also the provision he would make for them in virtue of his office. Verse 22 is not intended figuratively but literally, for the steward would have the large master key of the palace fastened to the shoulder of his tunic." He later comments in endnote 15: "The official in charge of the royal buildings and supplies would certainly have considerable and probably increasing power" (*The Expositor's Bible Commentary*, ed. Frank Gaebelein [Grand Rapids, Mich.: Zondervan, 1986], 6:143, 144). Being part of the Jewish culture, and knowing the social and religious context of Jesus' words, the disciples would have had no doubt that Jesus was appointing Peter to a very singular and prominent office in his Church. Just as the Pope is called *Father*, so the steward was called a *father* to the inhabitants of Jerusalem, which is a figure of the Church. As the steward and

place on his shoulder the key of the house of David,[48] *he shall open, and none shall shut; and he shall shut, and none shall open.*[49] And I will

his successors were the "fathers" of the Jewish nation, the visible representative of the king, so the Church has Peter and his successors as the visible representative of Christ over the Church. Matthew Henry explains, "Rulers should be fathers to those that are under their government, to teach them with wisdom, rule them with love, and correct what is amiss with tenderness, to protect them and provide for them, and be solicitous about them as a man is for his own children and family" (*Matthew Henry's Commentary*, 4:122). Jesus fully utilizes the symbolism of Isaiah's prophecy to express his future plans for Peter and the visible leadership of his Church.

[48] This mention of the key(s) is found three times in Scripture (Is 22:22; Mt 16:19; Rev 3:7). In Revelation 3:7 we find: "The words of the holy one, the true one, who has the key of David, who opens and no one shall shut, who shuts and no one opens." Jesus possesses the keys. In using the terminology of Isaiah, Jesus is telling the Church that Peter has been given *his* key, *his* authority, as one delegates authority to a vicar or deputy. Whereas Christ is the invisible head of the Church, Peter is to be the visible head of the Church. "The key was properly handled by the king (Rev 3:7), and therefore by the 'house-mayor' only in his stead. The power of the keys consisted not only in the supervision of the royal chambers, but also in the decision who was and who was not to be received into the king's service. There was a resemblance, therefore, to the giving of the keys of the kingdom of heaven to Peter under the New Testament" (Keil and Delitzsch, *Isaiah*, 398). With the royal steward as the historical backdrop, Peter and his successors hold the authority of the keys during Jesus' visible absence. And what kind of authority? "The keys of the kingdom would be committed to the chief steward in the royal household and with them goes plenary authority" (*The Interpreter's Bible*, ed. George Buttrick et al. [Nashville, Tenn.: Abingdon, 1980], 7:453). So, as the royal steward of the new Davidic kingdom, Peter has been given full and complete authority to rule over the new kingdom with the powers of binding and loosing.

[49] Isaiah declares that Eliakim is given the authority of the keys to open and close in the name of, and in the place of, the king. But Peter's authority extends farther than just opening and closing, because Jesus changes the parallel words to "binding" and "loosing", indicating that Peter has power to exercise administrative and legislative authority with a mandate from heaven. In Jewish rabbinical teaching (Jesus was called *Rabbi*), "binding" and "loosing" were technical terms for excluding from or granting readmission to the community or for declaring what is forbidden or permitted according to the law. "In the vast majority of cases, binding and loosing occur in a *doctrinal* sense, i.e. to 'prohibit' or 'permit' by means of legal rules as interpreted by a teacher of the law (scribe); less frequently the terms are used in a disciplinary sense, i.e. to 'expel from' or 'receive back into' the congregation" (*The Zondervan Pictorial Encyclopedia of the Bible*, ed. Merrill Tenney [Grand Rapids, Mich.: Zondervan, 1978], 1:611–12).

According to Watts (*Isaiah 1–33*), "He [the steward with the keys] also served as the chief of ministers in the royal government. He made decisions which fasten him like a peg in a sure place, and he will become a throne of honor to his father's house. And they will hang on him the whole weight of his father's house, the offspring and issue, every small vessel, from the cups to all the flagons."[50]

The Prophet Isaiah

"Hearken to me, you who pursue deliverance, you that seek the Lord; look to the rock from which you were hewn,[51] and to the quarry from which you were digged. Look to Abraham your father, and to Sarah who bore you; for when he was but one I called him, and I blessed him, and made him many."[52]

---

carried royal authority and could not be appealed" (292). Peter, in the image of the steward, has administrative power in the Church to make binding decisions and exercise authority in the name of Christ.

[50] Is 22:15–16, 19–24 (emphasis added).

[51] In attempting to make his point, that only God, never a man, is referred to as a "rock" in the Bible, James G. McCarthy writes, "Matthew wrote his Gospel for a Jewish audience. He expected his readers to be familiar with Old Testament imagery. How would a Jewish reader interpret 'upon this rock'? G. Campbell Morgan answers, 'If we trace the figurative use of the word rock through Hebrew Scriptures, we find that it is never used symbolically of man, but always of God' " (*The Gospel according to Rome* [Eugene, Ore.: Harvest House, 1995], 240–41). So, as challenged by McCarthy, we ask ourselves: How would a Jew understand the Aramaic phrase "upon this rock"? New Testament scholar William Barclay gives us a hint: "Whatever else this is [Simon's new name "Rock"], it is a word of tremendous praise. It is a metaphor which is by no means strange or unusual to Jewish thought. The Rabbis applied the word *rock* to Abraham. They had a saying: 'When the Holy One saw Abraham who was going to arise, he said, "Lo, I have discovered a rock (*petra*) to found the world upon." Therefore he called Abraham *rock* (*sur*), as it is said: "Look unto the rock whence ye are hewn." ' Abraham was the rock on which the nation and the purpose of God were founded" (*The Gospel of Matthew* [Philadelphia: Westminster Press, 1975], 2:140). Abraham was the patriarchal head of the first covenant, and his name was changed from Abram to Abraham to signify his change of status. Would we be amazed, especially if we were Jewish, to find that Abraham is referred to as a rock in Isaiah 51:1–2? Abraham was the pinnacle or fountainhead of the covenant people. Peter is given the office of shepherd and designation of "rock" as a "patriarch" of the New Covenant. As Abram's name was changed, so was Simon's, to show a change in status and to point to him as the starting point and foundation of the Church. McCarthy, in his hurried attempt to refute the Catholic Church, stumbles in his biblical research and thus fails to prove his point.

[52] Is 51:12: At the beginning of the great Abrahamic covenant, God says he set up a rock from which the nation of Israel was hewn. Along with the designation

Flavius Josephus[53]
—C. A.D. 37–c. 100

"And now the Pharisees joined themselves to her to assist her in the government. . . . But these Pharisees artfully insinuated themselves into her [Alexandra's] favour by little and little, and became themselves the real administrators of the public affairs: they banished and reduced whom they pleased; they bound and loosed [men] at their pleasure; and, to say all at once, they had the enjoyment of the royal authority."[54]

---

as *rock*, Abram's name was changed from Abram (father) to Abraham (father of a multitude). Again in Matthew 16, God changes a name, this time giving Simon the name of Rock, upon which the Church will be established. In referring to Matthew 16, and to Peter as the Rock, Presbyterian professor David Hill writes, "In favour of interpreting the word-play as a personal reference is the rabbinic saying about Abraham: 'when the Holy one wanted to create the world, he passed over the generations of Enoch and of the Flood; but when he saw Abraham who was to arise, he said: 'Behold, I have found a rock on which I can build and found the world': therefore he called Abraham rock, as it is said [Is 51:1] 'Look to the rock from which you were hewn' [Yalkut 766 on Numbers 23:9, quoting an earlier source, Tanchuma B, Yelamdenu]" (David Hill, *The Gospel of Matthew*, The New Century Bible Commentary [Grand Rapids, Mich.: Eerdmans, 1972], 261). The Jewish listeners would immediately understand the import of Jesus' words, richly couched in their Jewish heritage. The parallels were drawn between Abraham and Peter: in both cases there were name changes to indicate a new status, a designation as "rock", and a position at the fountainhead of the two major covenants of God with his people. In each case, God began with one person to achieve a much larger goal.

[53] Josephus was non-Christian, a Jewish historian, and a native of Palestine. He was educated in the Jewish law and of priestly descent. In A.D. 77–78, he published his *Wars of the Jews*. Later in life he wrote a history of the Jewish nation entitled *Antiquities of the Jews*.

[54] *Wars of the Jews* 1, 5, 2, in *Josephus: Complete Works*, trans. William Whiston (Grand Rapids, Mich.: Kregel Pub., 1980), 434. Josephus gives us a glimpse back in time to help us understand the common terms and usage of "binding" and "loosing" in first-century Jewish culture. The Pharisees, under Hasmonean Queen Alexandra (reigned 76–67 B.C.), were in possession of the royal authority and were therefore able to bind and to loose men from obligations, to punish and absolve, to make actions lawful or unlawful, and so on. These were not obscure terms in the first century but were widely used to describe religious, legislative, and judicial authority. This was the cultural context of Jesus' delegation of authority to Peter in the kingdom of God. "[D]isputes among [the Rabbis] were so numerous in Jesus' time as to let the expression 'to loose and to bind' become a standard reference to the endless disagreements that raged a

Jesus Christ to His Twelve Apostles

"If your brother sins against you, go and tell him his fault, between you and him alone. If he listens to you, you have gained your brother. But if he does not listen, take one or two others along with you. . . . If he refuses to listen to them, tell it to the church; and if he refuses to listen even to the church,[55] let him be to you as a Gentile and a tax collector.[56] Truly, I say to you, whatever you bind on earth shall be bound in heaven, and whatever you loose on earth shall be loosed in Heaven." [57]

---

little earlier between the two main rabbinical authorities, Shamma and Hillel. What the one loosed, the saying went, the other bound, and vice versa. Josephus Flavius did not hint at anything novel in referring to the power of binding and loosing" (Stanley L. Jaki, *The Keys of the Kingdom* [Chicago: Franciscan Herald Press, 1986], 43). Jesus put an end to the raging disputes over who has the real authority to bind and loose. He gave it to Peter, the steward and vizier of his New Kingdom—promising to ratify in heaven what Peter bound or loosed on earth.

[55] The adverb *even* implies a sense of disbelief that anyone would dare to defy the authority of the Church any more than one would dare to defy Moses. The Jews understood authority and had the example of Korah, who "rose up before Moses together with some of the sons of Israel, two hundred and fifty leaders of the congregation" (Num 16:2), in which judgment fell and the earth swallowed the 250 men who despised Moses' unique position among God's people. Korah's death, at the "feet" of Moses, could be a foreshadowing of Peter's authority displayed in the case of Ananias and Sapphira (Acts 5:1–11).

[56] To the Jew, a Gentile was a dog and outside the covenant of God; a tax collector was ostracized and separated from religious life, considered ceremonially unclean on account of his continual contact with Gentiles and his need to work on the Sabbath. The Jew would be forbidden to eat with such a one; and thus in the Church, one who is excommunicated is to be considered an outsider and one who is unclean. No one would dare fellowship or share the eucharistic meal with such an excommunicated person—at least, in principle.

[57] Mt 18:15–18. For Jesus' instructions to be feasible, the Church must be a visible, unified, and recognizable entity with universal jurisdiction and binding authority. The Christian must "listen to the Church". The Church (ἐκκλεσία) is singular, with the definite Greek article signifying and pointing to a particular entity. It is not plural, churches divided up into competing factions. Matthew is referring to the Catholic Church as understood by the Fathers, in many locations though still unified as one house. This Church Jesus founded can be appealed to for judiciary purposes, and her rulings are binding upon the hearts and souls of the believers universally. In today's denominational climate, where is the Church? What church can a Baptist brother take his Methodist brother to for reproof and judgment? The words of our Lord are reduced to nonsense in our age of ever-dividing factions and independent sects and groups.

Jesus Christ as recorded in the *Gospel of John*

"And I have other sheep, that are not of this fold; I must bring them also, and they will heed my voice. So there shall be one flock, one shepherd."[58]

"I do not pray for these only, but also for those who believe in me through their word, that they may all be one; even as thou, Father, art in me, and I in thee, that they also may be in us, so that

---

Notice that Matthew 16 is referring to the universal Church, but the promises are given to Peter alone. In Matthew 18 the same power of "binding and loosing" is given to the whole apostolic college, whose members have the same authority in the local churches, the obvious jurisdiction discussed in Matthew 18, where a localized situation is at issue. Christ has given his authority to Peter and the apostles to rule his Church, both universal and local. Jesus informs his apostles that he is going to establish a hierarchy within his Church and that what Peter and the apostles (and their successors, since an office has been established: see Acts 1:20) determine in the Church *will be ratified by Christ in heaven.* Moses had authority to establish and adjudicate the law in the Old Covenant; Peter and the apostles are granted the authority to interpret the law of Christ and rule the Church.

[58] Jn 10:16. The primary thrust of these words is that Jesus is expanding his covenant to include Gentile believers; but they also emphasize Jesus' desire for the visible unity of the Christian community. It is clear from Jesus' words that the Church should never be divided into many separate folds—competing flocks with disunited shepherds. In 1519, Martin Luther wrote to Pope Leo X. We have a record of this in the work of Protestant historian d'Aubigné: "Yet [Luther] still felt esteem for the ancient Church of Rome, and had no thought of separating from it. 'That the Roman Church . . . is honoured by God above all others is what we cannot doubt. Saint Peter, Saint Paul, forty-six popes, many hundreds of thousands of martyrs, have shed their blood in its bosom, and have overcome hell and the world, so that God's eye regards [the Roman Church] with especial favour. Although every thing is now in a very wretched state there, this is not a sufficient reason for separating from it. On the contrary, the worse things are going on within it, the more should we cling to it; for it is not by separation that we shall make it better. We must not desert God on account of the devil; or abandon the children of God who are still in the Roman communion, because of the multitude of the ungodly. There is no sin, there is no evil that should destroy charity or break the bond of union. For charity can do all things, and to unity nothing is difficult" (J. H. Merle d'Aubigné, *History of the Reformation of the Sixteenth Century*, one-vol. ed., trans. H. White [1846; reprint, Grand Rapids, Mich.: Baker Book House, 1987], 159–60). "It may be well to recall that Luther, before he formally separated himself from obedience to Rome, and when he seemed to abhor such a course, declared, 'I never approved of a schism, nor will I approve of it for all eternity' " (Patrick F. O'Hare, *The Facts about Luther* [Rockford, Ill.: TAN Books, 1987], 356).

the world may believe that thou hast sent me. The glory which thou hast given me I have given to them, that they may be one even as we are one, I in them and thou in me, that they may become perfectly one [perfected in unity], so that the world may know that thou hast sent me and hast loved them even as thou hast loved me." [59]

---

[59] Jn 17:20–23. A sheepfold provides a distinct enclosure whereby the sheep are protected, kept together, and fed. The Church is, as the Nicene Creed declares, "*one, holy, catholic (universal) and apostolic*". Jesus never meant the Church to be rent by divisions, torn asunder into competing denominations and sects. He prayed that the Church, his flock, would be one and perfected in unity. This cannot be relegated to an "invisible" unity, for only a visible and organic unity can be seen and observed by the world. Even the small Evangelical or Fundamentalist congregation understands the essential need of a pastor, a visible leader and teacher, to maintain doctrine, faith, and unity. The shepherd is essential to the unity and coherence of the flock. Christ appointed Peter as the shepherd of his sheep (Jn 21:15–17). The shepherd is essential to maintain the unity of the flock. Can we do without a visible shepherd and claim Christ as the only head of the Church? What Protestant group would make such an assertion in its own congregation? Did not Jesus appoint Peter shepherd? Did not Paul acknowledge shepherds in the Church (Eph 4:11)? From ancient times, as we shall see in the current study, the bishop of Rome, occupying the See of Peter, has been the shepherd of the universal Church, maintaining the true faith and the essential unity, that the Church may be perfected in one, visible, universal flock. When the unifying office of the Pope is abandoned, the various groups go off in thirty thousand different and competing directions. The only unifying factor among them is the denial of papal primacy. Hans Urs von Balthasar writes, "The negation created a purely formal unity, but this unity, deriving from negation—within every non-Catholic church as well as between them—remains *abstract* in content, because the most concrete factor of unity has been eliminated. . . . Wherein then lies the unity of the Church, the unity of the different churches, if this focal point is removed? Döllinger, in his early writings, cites a Protestant theologian: 'It is untrue and confusing to speak of unity when this is merely sought after, existing only as a concept, and when nothing can be presented that shows the alleged unity numerically.' Mohler says in his *Die Einheit in der Kirche*: 'To call the external manifestation of internal unity the "empirical concept" of the Church, which must be replaced by the "ideal", means to put an abstraction, an empty concept, death, in the place of *life*.' In what, we may further ask, could such an ideal consist if it were not at the same time the concretely manifested reality of unity? That is why the Anglican Newman complained that the (then) existing unity of the English church was *abstract*; in truth one should speak about 'churches' " (Hans Urs von Balthasar, *The Office of Peter and the Structure of the Church* [San Francisco: Ignatius Press, 1986], 82, 83). The latter point could just as easily be applied to Evangelical Protestantism.

Jesus Christ in the *Gospel of Matthew*
    —written in the latter half of the first century

"These twelve Jesus sent out. . . . He who receives you receives me, and he who receives me receives him who sent me."[60]

"Then said Jesus to the crowds and to his disciples, 'The scribes and the Pharisees sit on Moses' seat;[61] so practice and observe

---

[60] Mt 10:5, 40. Jesus does an amazing thing by actually investing his apostles with his own authority. Those who reject them reject him and in turn reject God the Father. The apostles have a special office in the kingdom of God. In Luke 10:16, Jesus says to his seventy, "He who hears you hears me, and he who rejects you rejects me, and he who rejects me rejects him who sent me." This caveat substantiates the authority invested in the apostles. As Robert Gundry writes, "Great emphasis falls on the authority of the disciples as representatives of Jesus and the Father who sent him" (Robert H. Gundry, *Matthew: A Commentary on His Literary and Theological Art* [Grand Rapids, Mich.: Eerdmans, 1982], 201). One should think carefully before despising and rejecting the authority of Christ invested in his apostles and the bishops within his Church.

[61] Within the Jewish synagogues a stone chair was reserved for the authoritative teacher and expositor of the law of Moses. Alfred Edersheim tells us, "In the middle of the synagogue (so generally) is the *Bima*, or elevation, on which there is the *Luach*, or desk, from which the Law is read. This is also called the *Kurseya*, chair, or throne, or *Kissé*, and *Pergulah*. Those who are to read the Law will stand, while he who is to preach or deliver an address will sit" (Edersheim, *The Life and Times of Jesus the Messiah*, 1:436). I studied one such chair in the Israel Museum in Jerusalem—an authentic stone chair from the first or second century. The placard describes the synagogue in Chorazin and comments on the chair: "Remarkable example of 'Galilean' type of synagogue. This important wall had two raised daises. One was for the placement of the Holy Ark, the second with its imposing chair, 'the seat of Moses', from where the Bible was read." Interestingly, the "seat of Moses" is not formally decreed in the Old Testament, but Jesus nevertheless recognizes it as an authentic development of the Jewish oral tradition. James White tries to dismiss the importance of such a chair with the comment: "Synagogue worship, of course, came into being long after Moses' day, so those who attempt to make this an oral tradition going back to Moses are engaging in wishful thinking" (*The Roman Catholic Controversy*, 100). Frankly, I do not recall any "Roman apologists" who claim that synagogue worship or the actual stone chair goes back to Moses. Rather, Moses' authority as the teacher of Israel was understood to be successive and was represented in the time of Jesus by the "seat of Moses" in the synagogue. The tradition of Moses' teaching authority—embodied in the "seat of Moses"—is based on Exodus 18:13, 15–16: "On the morrow Moses sat to judge the people [NIV: "Moses took his seat"], and the people stood about Moses from morning till evening. . . . And Moses said to his father-in-law, 'Because the people come to me to inquire of God; when they have a dispute, they come to me and I decide between a man and his neighbor,

whatever they tell you, but not what they do; for they preach, but do not practice.' " [62]

---

and I make them know the statutes of God and his decisions.' " Does Jesus deride the tradition and the teaching authority of Moses and his successors? No; in fact, he commands the listeners to obey those who teach and judge from the seat of Moses—Do what they say, not what they do. The Greek word Matthew used for seat is *kathedra* (καθέδρα), from which comes the Latin phrase *ex cathedra* (from the chair) and the word *cathedral*, which means the "church containing the throne of the bishop".

Eusebius writes, "The chair of James, who first received the episcopate of the church at Jerusalem from the Saviour himself, . . . has been preserved until now, the brethren who have followed him in succession there exhibiting clearly to all the reverence which both those of old times and those of our own day maintained and do maintain for holy men on account of their piety" (Eusebius, *Church History*, 7, 19, finished in A.D. 325, in NPNF2, 1:305).

[62] Mt 23:1–3. The Church was born from Jewish roots and culture. The "seat of Moses" in the synagogue became the "seat of the bishops" in the early churches. "Sitting on 'Moses' seat' referred to a place of dignity and the right to interpret the Mosaic law. The scribes were the successors and the heirs of Moses' authority and were rightfully looked to for pronouncements upon his teaching. . . . Jesus does not appear to challenge this right" (*Encyclopedia of the Bible*, ed. Walter A. Elwell [Grand Rapids, Mich.: Baker Book House, 1988], 2:1498). Notice the mention of "successors", "right to interpret", and "heirs of authority". Evangelical commentator D. A. Carson writes, "Moreover, 'to sit on X's seat' often means 'to succeed X' (Exod 11:5; 12:29; 1 Kings 1:35, 46; 2:12; 16:11; 2 Kings 15:12; Ps 132:12; cf. Jos. Antiq. VII, 353 [xiv.5]; XVIII, 2 [i.1]. This would imply that the 'teachers of the law' are Moses' legal successors, possessing all his authority—a view the scribes themselves held. . . . *Panta hosa* ('everything') is a strong expression and cannot be limited to 'that teaching of the law that is in Jesus' view a faithful interpretation of it'; they cover *everything* the leaders teach, including the oral tradition as well" (Gaebelein, *Expositor's Bible Commentary*, 8:472). Carson later dismisses the whole passage by relegating it to irony, which even James White rejects (*Roman Catholic Controversy*, 100). The Jewish people understood the authority of the "seat of Moses". And the first Christians, being Jewish, clearly understood that the bishops succeeded the apostles in the Church, carrying on their authority, just as the teachers of Israel succeeded Moses and carried on *his* authority (see St. Marcarius later in this study). Jesus had earlier transferred the rabbinic authority from the Jewish leaders to the apostles (Mt 16:19; 18:18). The Church through her apostles and bishops became the new voice of God, and they ruled and shepherded the flock, defined doctrine, interpreted Scripture, and preserved the apostolic teaching and tradition. This fact is very helpful in ascertaining the early Christians' understanding of the authority and succession of bishops and the primacy of Rome. For an interesting study of the Jewish roots of this passage, see John Lightfoot, *Commentary on the New Testament from the Talmud and Hebraica* (Peabody, Mass.: Hendrickson, 1995), 2:289–90.

Jesus Christ in the *Gospel of Luke*
  —written in the latter half of the first century

"Simon, Simon, behold, Satan demanded to have you [plural],
that he may sift you [plural] like wheat, but I have prayed for you
[singular] that your faith may not fail; and when you [singular]
have turned again, strengthen your brethren." [63]

Jesus Christ in the *Gospel of John*
  —speaking to Peter after the Resurrection[64]

"'Simon, son of John, do you love me more than these?' He said to
him, 'Yes, Lord; you know that I love you.' He said to him, 'Feed

---

[63] Lk 22:31–32. Why does Jesus pray for Peter and not for the other eleven?
The singular and plural pronouns in this passage are very telling. Jesus speaks
directly to Simon, uttering his name twice for emphasis. Jesus tells Peter that
Satan has demanded to sift them all as wheat, a passage reminiscent of Job 1:8–
12. Jesus then tells Peter that he has prayed for him (singular, not the other
eleven), that his faith will prevail, and that when he has gone through the trial,
Peter should strengthen the other apostles. "Strengthen" means to confirm, fix,
establish, make stable, place firmly, and set fast. This is confirmation of the fact
that Christ had made Peter the leader, the rock, and had invested him with the
keys; Luke was not ignorant of the authority invested in Peter by our Lord. The
whole apostolic band would be strengthened by the one for whom the Lord
prayed—the one whom the Lord appointed as shepherd of his flock.
  Saint John Chrysostom (c. A.D. 347–407) wrote, "[Peter] always is the first to
begin the discourse. Lo, there were a hundred and twenty [Acts 1:15]; and he
asks for one out of the whole multitude. Justly: he has the first authority in the
matter, as having had all entrusted to him. For to him Christ said, and 'thou
being converted, confirm thy brethren' " (*Acts of the Apostles, Homily 3*, in Berington and Kirk, *Faith of Catholics*, 2:34).
  [64] Peter is always listed first in the Gospel narratives. Jesus and all the writers of
the New Testament documents gave him a place of preeminence. About seventy
years after the Resurrection, John recalls that Peter was unique, singled out by
the risen Lord. John, the last living apostle, probably wrote this Gospel at the
end of the first century and speaks more of Peter than any previous author
(more than thirty times). "[John] sets the claims of Peter who at the time John
wrote had already been dead more than thirty years: he, Peter, was to be shepherd of the entire flock. But Peter was long dead! Why, then, this tremendous
insistence on his [Peter's] position? Simply because Peter was living on in his
successors who even during John's own lifetime—as we see in the case of Pope
Clement's letter to the Corinthian Church—were exercising Peter's prerogative
of shepherding the entire flock. Whatever John's position, . . . he was still inferior not only to Peter but to Peter's successors, for to John was not given the

my lambs.' A second time he said to him, 'Simon, son of John, do you love me?' He said to him, 'Yes, Lord; you know that I love you.' He said to him, 'Tend my sheep.' He said to him a third time, 'Simon, son of John, do you love me?' Peter was grieved because he said to him the third time, 'Do you love me?' And he said to him, 'Lord, you know everything; you know that I love you.' Jesus said to him, 'Feed my sheep.' " [65]

---

supreme commission to feed the entire flock of Christ" (Hugh Pope, "The Papacy in the New Testament", in *The Papacy*, ed. C. Lattey [London: Burns, Oates & Washbourne, 1923], 17).

John records Peter's divine commission. "[This passage] assumes what in ancient times was regarded as a traditional shape: it can be described, that is to say, as a 'divine Commission'. In no fewer than twenty-seven passages of the Old Testament, a literary form has been found in which there is this sort of delegation of power and a commissioning by God. The formula consists of a regular series of elements. . . . This form of utterance appears very frequently not only in the Old Testament, but also in various other parts of the New Testament as well. Indeed, the latter contains no fewer than thirty-three examples of a comparable sort of commission. Jesus' command, as it has come down to us, is clearly intended to formulate the establishment of a new Church community. . . . Peter needed all the authority he could get. Much came from his prime role in the aftermath of Jesus's death, and much more could be derived from the assertion that Jesus had explicitly commissioned him. In any case, Peter was now establishing his unquestioned leadership. . . . Paul in *Galatians* admits Peter's supremacy, of which apparently even the distant converts he was addressing in that letter were aware. . . . The general evidence will admit no rivalry to the leadership of Peter after Jesus's death" (Michael Grant, *Saint Peter* [New York: Scribner's, 1995], 106–7).

[65] Jn 21:15–17. After rising from the dead, Jesus spends forty days with his apostles, teaching them about the kingdom of God and his Church (Acts 1:3; Mt 28:18–20). He invests Peter with a singular and special commission. Peter is to be the shepherd over Jesus' sheep—a visible, recognizable leader. Jesus earlier said he has other sheep, but he will now bring them into one fold with one shepherd (Jn 10:16). Jesus commands Peter to *feed* and *tend* his sheep and lambs. The word *feed* is βόσκω and means literally "to feed" and figuratively to teach and promote in every way the spiritual welfare of the members of the Church. The second word, *tend*, is ποιμαίνω and means literally to tend or shepherd the sheep and figuratively to govern or rule. Jesus appoints Peter the universal shepherd of his whole flock. Protestant scholar Joachim Jeremias writes, "Only in Jn. 21:15–17, which describes the appointment of Peter as a shepherd by the risen Lord, does the whole Church seem to have been in view as the sphere of activity" (*Theological Dictionary of the New Testament*, 6:498). The Good Shepherd appoints Peter to participate in his own authority as shepherd, to exercise delegated authority and leadership over the flock. What is this but a veritable primacy of jurisdiction? There are two sides to every coin: *When Jesus commands Peter to govern his sheep,*

The Acts of the Apostles
   —written in the latter half of the first century
   —event c. A.D. 30

"Then [the apostles] returned to Jerusalem from the mount
called Olivet, which is near Jerusalem, a sabbath day's journey
away; and when they had entered, they went up to the upper
room, where they were staying. . . . All these with one accord devoted themselves to prayer, together with the women and Mary the
mother of Jesus, and with his brethren. In those days Peter stood
up among the brethren (the company of persons was in all about
a hundred and twenty), and said, 'Brethren, the scripture had to
be fulfilled, which the Holy Spirit spoke beforehand by the mouth
of David, concerning Judas who was guide to those who arrested
Jesus. . . . For it is written in the book of Psalms, 'Let his habitation
become desolate, and let there be no one to live in it'; and 'His
office let another take.' [66] So one of the men who have accompa-

---

he implicitly commands the sheep to submit to and obey the universal shepherd—Peter. St.
Augustine writes, "There are many other things which most justly keep me in her
[the Catholic Church's] bosom. . . . The succession of priests keeps me, beginning
from the very seat of the Apostle Peter, to whom the Lord, after His resurrection,
gave it in charge to feed His sheep, down to the present episcopate [bishop]"
(*Against the Epistle of Manichaeus,* in *Nicene and Post-Nicene Fathers,* 1st series, ed.
Philip Schaff [Grand Rapids, Mich.: Eerdmans, 1983], 4:130 [hereafter NPNF1]).

[66] Peter quotes the Old Testament scriptures to explain the need for a man to
fill the "office" vacated by Judas Iscariot. The position is exactly that, an office—
an office that needs to be filled. He quotes David in Psalm 109, in which David
is grieving over an enemy who has unjustly accused him—an ungrateful enemy
who has unjustly charged him with a capital offense. David laments, "They beset
me with words of hate, and attack me without cause. In return for my love they
accuse me, even as I make prayer for them. So they reward me evil for good, and
hatred for my love" (Ps 109:3–5). The context is parallel to the unjust accusation against Jesus and his betrayal by Judas. David prays that his enemies' "days
will be few", or that they will come to a premature death, as did Judas.
   The word for "office" used in the Greek Septuagint, obviously the text cited
by Peter, is *episkopē* (ἐπισκοπὴ), from which we get our English word "episcopal",
meaning of, suited to, or belonging to a bishop. The King James version of the
Bible renders this phrase: "and his bishoprick let another take". It is defined by
William Arndt and F. Wilbur Gingrich as a "position or office as an overseer
(Num 4:16) of Judas' position as an apostle. . . . esp. the office of a bishop" (*A
Greek-English Lexicon,* 299). Here we see the office of apostle being referred to by
Peter as the office of overseer or bishop. Also important, we see that the office is
one of succession—another man succeeds to the office on the death of Judas.

nied us during all the time that the Lord Jesus went in and out among us, beginning from the baptism of John until the day when he was taken up from us—one of these men must become with us a witness to his resurrection.' And they put forward two, Joseph called Barsabbas, who was surnamed Justus, and Matthias. And they prayed and said, 'Lord, who knowest the hearts of all men, show which one of these two thou hast chosen to take the place in this ministry and apostleship from which Judas turned aside, to go to his own place.' And they cast lots for them, and the lot fell on Matthias; and he was enrolled with the eleven apostles." [67]

The Acts of the Apostles

"But Peter, standing with the eleven, lifted up his voice and addressed them, 'Men of Judea and all who dwell in Jerusalem, let this be known to you, and give ear to my words.' "[68]

The word *episkopē* is the same word used in 1 Timothy 3:1, "The saying is sure: If any one aspires to the *office of bishop*, he desires a noble task" (emphasis added), and in Acts 20:28, "Take heed to yourselves and to all the flock, in which the Holy Spirit has made you *guardians*, to feed the church of the Lord which he obtained with his own blood" (emphasis added). This was a dynastic position, an office of authority, and an office that continued through succession after the current occupant ceased to hold the position.

[67] Acts 1:12–16, 20–26. Again, it is Peter who stands up among the other apostles and is their spokesman. He also applies the Scripture to a contemporary situation, and no one questions his judgment. Why did not Jesus assign an "alternate" apostle, knowing of Judas' betrayal and demise, as is done in modern jury systems or in the theater. After his Resurrection, Jesus himself could very well have chosen a replacement to fill Judas' office, but he left that decision up to his apostles, namely, Peter.

[68] Acts 2:14. At this early event in the history of the Church, the preaching of Peter on the day of Pentecost, Peter is already set apart as the leader of the Church, and the other apostles have acquired a title of "the eleven", which many translations capitalize: "the Eleven". Simon Kistemaker, Reformed theologian and member of the Evangelical Theological Society, writes, "Immediately after Jesus' ascension, Peter assumes the leadership role within the company of the 120 believers. . . . Peter shows the crowd that he is the leader of the twelve apostles. In earlier days, the multitudes came to listen to Jesus. Now they come to the apostles and Peter realizes that the task of giving leadership belongs to him. . . . The presence of the other apostles next to him conveys to the crowd that Peter speaks on their behalf" (*Acts*, New Testament Commentary [Grand Rapids, Mich.: Baker Book House, 1990], 87–88). This pattern continues to develop in the early Church's structure of leadership.

St. Paul to the Galatians
    —written in the middle of the first century

"I did not confer with flesh and blood, nor did I go up to Jerusalem to those who were apostles before me, but I went away into Arabia; and again I returned to Damascus. Then after three years I went up to Jerusalem to visit Cephas, and remained with him fifteen days. But I saw none of the other apostles except James the Lord's brother." [69]

Luke the Physician in the *Acts of the Apostles*
    —chronicling the Council of Jerusalem c. A.D. 49–50

"But some men came down from Judea and were teaching the brethren, 'Unless you are circumcised according to the custom of Moses, you cannot be saved.' . . . The apostles and the elders were

---

[69] Gal 1:16–19. When Paul finally "made contact" with the Church, it was Peter he went to visit. As is his regular designation for Peter in his epistles, Paul refers to him as "Rock" (Cephas), the Greek transliteration of the Aramaic *Kepha*, which Jesus named Peter at Caesarea Philippi. By referring to Simon Peter as Cephas, Paul acknowledges the special position of Peter signified by that name. Why did Paul visit Peter only, a point emphasized by Paul; and what did they discuss for fifteen days? Commenting on this passage, and on the Greek word translated by "visit", St. John Chrysostom (c. 347–407) says of St. Paul: "What can be more lowly than such a soul? After such successes, wanting nothing of Peter, not even his assent, but being of equal dignity with him, (for at present I will say no more,) he comes to him as his [Paul's] elder and superior. And the only object of this journey was to visit Peter; thus he pays due respect to the Apostles, and esteems himself not only not their better but not their equal. . . . He says, 'to visit Peter'; he does not say to see (ἰδεῖν,) but to visit and survey (ἱστορῆσαι,), a word which those who seek to become acquainted with great and splendid cities apply to themselves. Worthy of such trouble did he consider the very sight of Peter; and this appears from the Acts of the Apostles also" (*Commentary on Galatians* 1, 18, NPNF1, 13:12–13). F. F. Bruce, in his book *Paul: Apostle of the Heart Set Free* (Grand Rapids, Mich.: Eerdmans, 1977), 84, informs us, "The purpose of Paul's going to Jerusalem on this occasion was to make the acquaintance of the leading apostle—and not merely to make his acquaintance but to inquire of him (for that is the force of the verb *historēsai* which he uses). For Peter was a primary informant on matters which it was now important that Paul should know—the details of Jesus' ministry and the 'tradition' of teaching which derived from him. There is in some quarter considerable resistance to the idea that Paul was interested in acquiring information of this kind, but even if Paul had no such interest (which is incredible), what would Peter talk about in those fifteen days?"

gathered together to consider this matter. And after there had been much debate, Peter rose and said to them, 'Brethren, you know that in the early days God made choice among you, that by my mouth the Gentiles should hear the word of the gospel and believe.' . . .[70] And all the assembly kept silence; and they listened to Barnabas and Paul as they related what signs and wonders God had done through them among the Gentiles. After they finished speaking, James replied, 'Brethren, listen to me.[71] Symeon has related how God first visited the Gentiles, to take out of them a

---

[70] Peter exercises his authority at this first Church council along with the apostles and elders—legislating in the Church. The council is marked by much disputing as everyone waits for Peter to speak. Peter "rose" up and proclaimed the Church's teaching, binding on all believers—and "all the assembly kept silence." After giving due deference to Peter, Paul and Barnabas recount their experiences. James makes practical implementations based on Peter's teaching and the words of the prophets. The authoritative teaching of the Church silences the opposition. A letter is composed that can be considered the first decree of an ecumenical council, considered infallible by the Church and the recipients—the Holy Spirit speaking through the Magisterium of the Church. Peter is a decisive factor in doctrinal and political unity and speaks for the whole Church.

"This meeting is seen as the first general council of the Church, that is, the prototype of the series of councils of which the Second Vatican Council is the most recent. Thus, the Council of Jerusalem displays the same features as the later ecumenical councils in the history of the Church: a) it is a meeting of the rulers of the entire Church, not of ministers of one particular place; b) it promulgates rules which have binding force for all Christians; c) the content of its decrees deals with faith and morals; d) its decisions are recorded in a written document—a formal proclamation to the whole Church; e) Peter presides over the assembly" (The Acts of the Apostles in the *Navarre Bible* [Dublin: Four Courts Press, 1992], 160–61).

[71] James White makes the assertion that "At this point James speaks up and, using the imperative mode (v. 13), commands the assembly to listen to his words" (*Roman Catholic Controversy*, 112, n. 246; also see 246, n. 6), implying that the imperative indicates that St. James possessed the ultimate authority at the council, in that he *commands* everyone to listen to him. However, Robert A. Sungenis informs us that "The Greek word translated as 'hear me' in Acts 15:14 is *akouoo*, which is used hundreds of times in the New Testament. For example, the same word is used in two verses prior in Acts 15:12 in the Greek indicative mood and translated as 'and heard [*akouoo*] Barnabas and Paul.' It is a word that, in itself, does not connote authority. Placing *akouoo* in the Greek imperative mood in Acts 15:14 can simply be understood as a request for those gathered to give their undivided attention to what will subsequently be spoken. The use of the imperative mood can be made strong or weak depending upon the

people for his name. And with this the words of the prophets agree.' ... [Peter, the apostles, and the elders wrote to the Gentiles, saying], 'For it has seemed good to the Holy Spirit and to us to lay upon you no greater burden than these necessary things.' "[72]

---

context in which it is placed, but the use of the imperative does not necessarily denote any official authority of the one using the mood. The imperative mood of *akouoo* can be used for ANY desire of one person seeking the attention of another. It can be used, for example, in a simple request such as, 'Listen, did you hear that noise?' ... These different senses of the imperative mood are used throughout the New Testament (e.g., Acts 22:1 ['fathers, listen to my defense'], James 2:5 ['hear me, my beloved brothers']...). Again, these uses do not necessarily mean that the speaker is vested with authority over the person or group he is addressing; rather, it can be as simple as requesting their attention to the things he wishes to tell them" (Scott Butler, Norman Dahlgren, and David Hess, *Jesus, Peter and the Keys* [Santa Barbara, Calif.: Queenship Pub., 1996], 96–97). Fundamentalist commentator G. Campbell Morgan agrees with Sungenis: "An emphatic pronoun depends after all upon the tone and emphasis. The emphatic *I* must be interpreted in harmony with the rest of the New Testament and the Bible. It is absurd to believe that James at this moment gave his personal opinion as the final word, from which there could be no appeal.... The very emphasis on the I shows that he was only expressing a personal conviction" (*The Acts of the Apostles* [Westwood, N.J.: Fleming H. Revell, 1924], 362–63).

[72] Acts 15:1, 6–7, 12–15, 28. Many have used this passage in an attempt to invalidate Peter's primacy by drawing attention to James as having the "final word", but this interpretation is sadly misguided. Hugh Pope writes, "Now what is there in this episode which runs counter to Peter's primacy of jurisdiction? Is it not rather in fullest conformity with it? St. James is the bishop of the city, yet not only does Peter speak first—he settles the question; St. James endorses what he says, and simply provides a practical way of meeting the difficulty which has arisen" ("The Papacy in the New Testament", in Lattey, *Papacy*, 23). "You're right in saying that [James] went beyond Peter's decision, but he was not decreeing or deciding as Peter had done. He states, to begin with, that it is his judgement. Peter didn't speak for himself; he spoke for the whole Church. What James added had nothing to do with the doctrinal decision which had [already] been settled [by Peter]" (Daniel W. Martin, *The Church of the Scriptures* [St. Louis, Mo.: Confraternity Home Study Service, 1959], 83). Peter's theological pronouncement was the watershed of the council; Paul gave testimony; and James concludes with pastoral, practical implementation. St. John Chrysostom writes, "See how Paul speaks after Peter, and no one restrains: James waits and starts not up, for he (Peter) it was to whom had been entrusted the government (primacy)" (*Acts of the Apostles*, Homily 33 in Berington and Kirk, *Faith of Catholics*, 2:34). Though papal opponents often cite this passage as a proof text for *sola Scriptura*,

Paul to the Galatians
    —written in the middle of the first century

"Then after fourteen years I went up again to Jerusalem with Barnabas, taking Titus along with me. I went up by revelation; and I laid before them (but privately before those who were of repute) the gospel which I preach among the Gentiles,[73] lest somehow I should be running or had run in vain. . . . [A]nd when they perceived the grace that was given to me, James and Cephas and John,[74] who were reputed to be pillars, gave to me and Barnabas

---

asserting that James goes to the Bible alone for his summary, it is interesting to note that James quotes *two* authorities as he summarizes the proceedings: Peter and the Old Testament—"Symeon has related" and "with this the words of the prophets agree" (Acts 15:14–15).

[73] The phrase "laid before them" means to declare, communicate, refer, with the added idea that the person to whom a thing is referred is asked for his opinion or judgment; to lay something before someone for consideration, as in, "I laid my gospel before them" (see Arndt and Gingrich, *A Greek–English Lexicon*, 61). This verb is used also in Acts 25:14.

[74] Why do we find James listed first? Does it imply a primacy for James, over and against Peter? Although several ancient Greek manuscripts do list Peter's name first, it is quite sure that the correct rendering has James' name leading the list. The list seemed so unnatural that the following ancient writers produced this list with Peter's name first: Marcion, Irenaeus, Tertullian, Origen, Gregory of Nyssa, Jerome, Ambrose, Ephraim, and Augustine (see Winter, *Saint Peter,* 37). Thomas Aquinas says that "James is mentioned first, as being the Bishop of Jerusalem where these events took place" (St. Thomas Aquinas, *Commentary on Saint Paul's Epistle to the Galatians*, trans. F. R. Larcher [Albany, N.Y.: Magi Books, 1966], 44). Protestant commentator Charles John Ellicott fleshes this out further: "In some few [manuscripts] and patristic quotations the reading is *Peter and James and John.* This doubtless arose from the tendency to exalt St. Peter [in the first centuries], though the reading (which is found in Tertullian and Origen, and therefore must run up into the second century) is too early to be directly connected with the pretensions of the Papacy. The way in which St. Paul speaks respectively of St. Peter and St. James is in strict accordance with the historical situation. When he is speaking of the general work of the Church (as in the last two verses) St. Peter is mentioned prominently; when the reference is to a public act of the Church of Jerusalem the precedence is given to St. James [who was the Bishop of Jerusalem]" (*The Epistles to Galatians, Ephesians, and Philippians* [London: Cassel & Co., n.d.], 32).

[75] Paul reports that after his meeting with the "pillars of the Church" (see 1 Tim 3:15), they confirmed his gospel, and he was given the "right hand of fellowship." Being able to announce to the Judaizers that he had received the right hand of fellowship from Peter, James, and John gave Paul great credibility,

the right hand of fellowship;[75] that we should go to the Gentiles, and they to the circumcised."[76]

Paul to the Galatians

"But when Cephas came to Antioch I opposed him to his face,[77] because he stood condemned. For before certain men came from

---

verification, and authority in his argument. Paul is arguing with the Judaizers, who believed that the Gentiles had to be circumcised before becoming Christians. His opponents dismissed him as less influential. "Paul, said the Judaizers, does not rank with Peter, John, James the Less, and the rest of the Twelve; he did not get his knowledge of Christ at first hand, he only picked it up from others. And so he is unreliable. . . . [But Paul was vindicated and the apostles] gave their approval to his policy of receiving Gentiles without obligating them to observe the Jewish law" (Ronald Knox, *It Is Paul Who Writes: Based on the Translation of the Epistles of Saint Paul and of the Acts of the Apostles by Ronald Knox*, arr. Ronald Cox [New York: Sheed and Ward, 1944], 77, 79).

[76] Gal 2:1–2, 9. Opposition to the Catholic Church has caused many to belittle Peter's office of primacy in the Church by quoting Paul's words that the apostles in Jerusalem "seemed to be pillars" or were "reputed to be pillars", as though Paul were mocking the authority of Peter and the apostles. According to Kittel, it refers to "those who are of particular repute in the Jerusalem community. . . . In the light of these passages there is no reason to suspect irony ('those who want to be something'). On the other hand, the abbreviation in verse 2:6b, and the fourfold repetition, indicate the use of a slogan coined by Paul's opponents" (*Theological Dictionary of the New Testament*, 2:233). In the same vein, Evangelical Richard N. Longnecker observes, "Contrary to many who deny irony in Paul's usage, it seems hard to ignore at least a certain 'dismissive' tone in Galatians 2—a dismissal, however, not of [Peter or] the Jerusalem apostles themselves, but of the Judaizers' claims for them" (*Galatians*, Word Biblical Commentary [Waco, Tex.: Word Books, 1990], 41:48). Martin Luther comments, "This is not idle talk; for they really were reputed to be pillars. The apostles were revered and honored throughout the Church. They had the authority to approve and declare the true doctrine and to condemn the opposite" (*Lectures on Galatians*, in *Luther's Works*, ed. Jaroslav Pelikan [St. Louis, Mo.: Concordia Pub., 1963], 26:100).

[77] Does this passage in Galatians prove beyond doubt that the Petrine primacy is a myth? Here is what Loraine Boettner tells his audience: "In other words, Paul gave the 'Holy Father' a 'dressing down' before them all, accusing him of not walking uprightly in the truth of the Gospel. Surely that was no way to talk to a pope! Imagine anyone today, even a cardinal, taking it upon himself to rebuke and instruct a real pope with such language! Just who was Paul that he should rebuke the Vicar of Christ for unchristian conduct? If Peter was the chief it was Paul's duty and the duty of the other apostles to recognize him as such and to teach only what he approved. Obviously Paul did not regard Peter as infallible

James, he ate with the Gentiles; but when they came, he drew back and separated himself, fearing the circumcision party. And with him the rest of the Jews acted insincerely, so that even Barnabas was carried away by their insincerity. But when I saw that they were not straightforward about the truth of the gospel, I said to Cephas before them all, 'If you, though a Jew, live like a Gentile and not like a Jew, how can you compel the Gentiles to live like Jews?' "[78]

in faith and morals, or recognize any supremacy on his part" (*Roman Catholicism* [Phillipsburg, N.J.: Presbyterian and Reformed Pub. Co., 1962], 115). Why, one may ask, would Paul's action in any way prove he "did not regard Peter as infallible in faith and morals"? Why would Paul be out of line in correcting some wrong practice of Peter? Does Peter claim perfection? Does the Catholic Church ever claim that the *successor* to Peter is any more perfect in his conduct than Peter was himself? Does the Catholic Church teach that either Peter or the current Pope is impeccable, sinless, always perfect in his conduct, always practicing perfectly what he preaches, never in need of confession? The Catholic Church's teaching on papal infallibility applies only to the official teaching office of the Pope, certainly not to his personal moral conduct or consistency. Papal opponents really ought to be more careful in ascertaining what the Catholic Church actually teaches. The Pope goes to confession regularly, because he knows he is less than perfect—less than irreproachable in his everyday life. If Popes are guilty of imprudent or immoral conduct, they can be, should be, and often have been reproved. A classic example of this occurred when Catherine of Siena (c. 1347–1380) severely reproved Pope Gregory XI and ultimately persuaded him to return the Papacy from Avignon to Rome. "Catherine arrived at Avignon on June 18, 1376, and soon had a conference with Pope Gregory, to whom she had already written six times, 'in an intolerably dictatorial tone, a little sweetened with expressions of her perfect Christian deference' " (Alban Butler, *Butler's Lives of the Saints*, rev. Herbert Thurston and Donald Attwater [Allen, Tex.: Christian Classics, 1995], 2:195–96). Can anyone imagine a fourteenth-century woman reproving the Pope, especially with an "intolerably dictatorial tone"? And imagine, she was not only canonized a saint, but she was declared a Doctor of the Church! So much for the Pope's insulation from reproof and criticism.

[78] Gal 2:11–14. The Protestant Reformer John Calvin comments on this passage, "And here the Roman Papacy is struck down by another thunderbolt. . . . [Paul] reproves Peter in the presence of the whole Church, and Peter obediently submits to correction. The whole debate on those two points was nothing less than the overthrow of the tyrannical primacy which the Romanists prate was founded on divine right" (*Calvin's New Testament Commentaries*, trans. T. H. L. Parker [Grand Rapids, Mich.: Eerdmans, 1965], 11:34). Does this passage overthrow the primacy of Peter? Paul says he withstood Cephas ("Rock") and, by using his new name, emphasizes the significance of Peter and the gravity of his action. There is nothing whatever in this passage that undermines papal primacy or infallibility if one understands these terms correctly. Paul's rebuke did not deny Peter's supremacy, quite the opposite. Peter's example compelled

First Epistle of Peter
   —written from Rome c. A.D. 65

"So I exhort the elders among you, as a fellow elder and a witness of the sufferings of Christ as well as a partaker in the glory that is to be revealed.[79] Tend the flock of God that is your charge, not by

---

Christians—even Paul's missionary partner, Barnabas—to imitate him because of his authority. Paul's example did not have the same compelling power. In other words, in the same room everyone followed Peter's example and not Paul's. Peter had acted to preserve peace. Paul had done the same in a similar incident when he had Timothy circumcised for the sake of peace (Acts 16:3). Peter Kreeft writes, "Papal infallibility certainly seems to be a specifically Catholic dogma that Protestants cannot accept. But they often misunderstand it. First, they often think of the Pope as an autocrat rather than the head of a body. . . . Second, they often think of the Church along political lines and want it to be a democracy. But Scripture thinks of the Church along organic lines, and no organic body is a democracy. Third, they often misunderstand infallibility as attaching to the Pope personally. In fact, it attaches to the office, not the person, and only when defining a doctrine of faith or morals" (*Fundamentals of the Faith* [San Francisco: Ignatius Press, 1988], 270). Leslie Rumble comments, "St. Peter was supreme head of the Church and infallible in his doctrinal teaching, but it does not follow that he would not be indiscreet in some act of administration. Now no doctrinal error was involved in this particular case. . . . To cease from doing a lawful thing for fear lest others be scandalized is not a matter of doctrine. It is a question of prudence or imprudence. . . . St. Cyprian, who lived in the third century, knew of this passage and certainly understood Christianity. Yet he did not perceive any objections against St. Peter's supremacy in this case. He writes, 'Peter, whom the Lord chose to be first and upon whom He built His Church, did not proudly assert the primacy he possessed, nor despise Paul who had once been a persecutor of the Church; but he accepted meekly, giving us an example of patience.' St. Hilary, in the fifth century, says, 'Both Paul and Peter are to be admired; Paul because he did not fear to point out the right practice to his superior; Peter because, knowing that all acknowledged his primacy, he had too much humility to resent any reproach offered to himself" (*Radio Replies*, ed. Charles Carty [1938; reprint, Rockford, Ill.: TAN Books, 1979], 1:82–83). Finally, Tertullian comments, "Moreover, if Peter was reproached [by Paul] because, after having lived with the gentiles, he later separated himself from their company out of respect for persons, the fault certainly was one of procedure and not of doctrine" (*The Demurrer against the Heretics* 23, 10, in William A. Jurgens, *The Faith of the Early Fathers* [Collegeville, Minn.: Liturgical Press, 1970], 1:121). Does an imprudent action on Peter's account prove it is impossible for a fallible man, protected by God, to provide an infallible interpretation of truth? If so, must we also deny, then, the infallible writings of Scripture, inasmuch as they also are provided through fallible men?

[79] In the Greek, the word "elder" is *presbuteros* (πρεσβύτερος), and simply means *elder*. Many have claimed that Peter's humility with the title of "fellow elder"

constraint but willingly, not for shameful gain but eagerly, not as domineering over those in your charge but being examples to the flock. And when the chief Shepherd is manifested you will obtain the unfading crown of glory. Likewise you that are younger be subject to the elders. Clothe yourselves, all of you, with humility toward one another." [80]

---

implies that he considered himself on an equal plane with all other elders, denying any primacy and disproving Catholic teaching. An example of this unfortunate reasoning is given by Norman Geisler, who writes, "By Peter's own admission he was not *the* pastor of the church but only a '*fellow* presbyter'", and again, "Peter referred to himself in much more humble terms as 'an apostle' (1 Pet 1:1) not the apostle and 'fellow-presbyter' (1 Pet 5:1), not the supreme Bishop, the Pope, or the Holy Father" (Norman L. Geisler and Ralph E. Mac-Kenzie, *Roman Catholics and Evangelicals: Agreements and Differences* [Grand Rapids, Mich.: Baker Books, 1995], 209, 212). Of course, if we accept Geisler's assumption, it would seem that Peter no longer considered himself an authoritative apostle either, for in this verse (taken on its own) he only claims to be a "fellow-elder". But clearly, Peter is only practicing the very humility he is exhorting his readers to practice (see 1 Pet 3:8; 5:5–6). Peter certainly does not deny the primacy the Lord Jesus had bestowed on him. When the president of the United States addresses the nation, he does not start out by saying, "I am your superior, the highest authority in the land, the most powerful man in the world"; rather, he humbly addresses the American citizens with the words: "My fellow Americans". Is this a denial of presidential authority? Of course not. The president is *both* a fellow citizen *and* the most powerful political figure in the world. In his 1993 encyclical *The Splendor of Truth* (Boston, Mass.: St. Paul Books & Media, 1993), 9, John Paul II addresses his readers in this way: "Venerable Brothers in the Episcopate, Health and the Apostolic Blessing!" Do the Pope's words of equality and fraternity contradict the primacy of his office? Again, of course not. Peter's humility only enhances his position. Eastern Orthodox theologian and professor of New Testament studies Nicholas Koulomzine says of 1 Peter 5:1, "These are words of shining humility when the great Apostle speaks them; but surely they prove just the opposite—that his real title as Christ's Apostle placed him in a much higher position than that of a mere elder in a local church" (*The Primacy of Peter*, ed. John Meyendorff et al. [Crestwood, N.Y.: St. Vladimir's Seminary Press, 1992], 23). J. B. Lightfoot adds further support: "St. Peter, giving directions to the elders, claims a place among them. The title 'fellow-presbyter,' which he applies to himself, would doubtless recall to the memory of his readers the occasions when he himself had presided with the elders *and guided their deliberations*" (J. B. Lightfoot, *St. Paul's Epistle to the Philippians* [Lynn, Mass.: Hendrickson Pub., 1982], 198 [emphasis added]).

[80] 1 Pet 5:1-5. Peter informs us that Jesus Christ is the "Shepherd and Guardian" of their souls (1 Pet 2:25). The King James version renders this "Shepherd and Bishop". Peter exhorts his fellow elders to "feed [shepherd] the flock" and care for "your charge" [exercising oversight]. (The word for "your charge" is

St. Paul to Timothy
   —written c. A.D. 67

"I hope to come to you soon, but I am writing these instructions to you so that, if I am delayed, you may know how one ought to behave in the household of God, which is the church of the living God, the pillar and bulwark [foundation] of the truth."[81]

---

episkopeo, which is related to the Greek word for *bishop.*) If Christ is the "Shepherd and Guardian" of our souls, is it not intruding on his prerogatives and authority for Peter and the elders to arrogate to themselves the titles of shepherd and bishop? Bishops share in Christ's "shepherd-ness" and his "bishop-ness". They do not detract from him; rather, they are drawn deeper into his apostolate, and so he is glorified, much as a father is glorified in the success of his sons. Peter draws strong allusions to Gospel passages, especially John 21:15–17, Luke 22:31–32, and Matthew 16:18–19, using his special calling and primacy to encourage others who are tending the local Churches.

[81] 1 Tim 3:14–15. For the Fundamentalist or Evangelical, the Bible is the pillar and foundation of the truth, even though the Bible gives this place of honor to the Church and, therefore, to the hierarchy that gives her visible form. In *The Expositor's Bible Commentary* (ed. Frank Gaebelein), Ralph Earle comments, "Taken together these two terms [pillar and foundation] emphasize the certainty and firmness of 'the truth' that is revealed in God's Word [the Bible]" (11:370). One might reasonably ask: Where does Paul mention the Bible in this passage? This classic Protestant assertion is made because the Evangelical and Fundamentalist cannot comprehend the concept of a universal and visible Church used by God to preserve his truth infallibly. But what *does* Paul say? Does he say the Bible is the pillar and foundation of the truth? No, he says the Church is. Protestant scholar Donald Guthrie has a problem with this verse: "The phrase *the pillar and ground of the truth* has caused difficulties, mainly because it appears to give greater eminence to the Church than to the truth" (*The Pastoral Epistles,* Tyndale New Testament Commentaries [Grand Rapids, Mich.: Eerdmans, 1980], 88). Guthrie then goes on at length to fit this passage into the Protestant mold. If this passage did indeed refer to the Bible, it would become the strongest—no, the only—biblical passage to imply *sola Scriptura,* and it would become the blazing banner carried aloft by those espousing it. However, as Paul says it is the *Church* that is the "pillar and foundation of the truth", there is an unmistakable silence and general partisan dismissal of the true meaning of the text. However, the Fathers understood that the Church is the bank into which Christ and the apostles deposited the fullness of the faith and that the Church was to be the guardian and defender of that truth. Protestants see the deposit of faith as lodging exclusively in the Bible. But Jude says we should "earnestly contend for the faith which was once delivered unto the saints". Where was the faith deposited? Into the Bible? There was no collected New Testament canon for several hundred years. The truth had been delivered unto the saints; deposited into the Church! It is not *either* the Church *or* the Bible; it is rather *both* the Church *and* the Bible.

So we come to the conclusion of the first section of our study, searching the scriptural passages relating to Peter's commission as steward and shepherd. We have looked at the biblical passages relating to Peter and the Church. We have briefly touched upon the biographical information contained in the New Testament and the passages that affirm Peter's special standing, his primacy in the Church. Since the Protestant Reformation, many have ignored, even attacked the ancient teachings of the Church and have tried to empty the biblical passages of any hierarchical significance.[82] The winds of freedom and democracy that have

---

The early Christians had a perspective much different from that proposed by today's Protestant traditions. Irenaeus (c. 130–c. 200), the disciple of Polycarp, who was a disciple of the Apostle John, writes, "The Church, having received this preaching and this faith, although scattered throughout the whole world, yet, as if occupying but one house, carefully preserves it. She also believes these points [of doctrine] just as if she had but one soul, and one and the same heart, and she proclaims them, and teaches them, and hands them down [tradition], with perfect harmony, as if she possessed only one mouth" (*Against Heresies* 1, 10, 2, ANF 1:331). "Since therefore we have such proofs, it is not necessary to seek the truth among others which it is easy to obtain from the Church; since the apostles, like a rich man [depositing his money] in a bank, lodged in her hands most copiously all things pertaining to the truth: so that every man, whosoever will, can draw from her the water of life. For she is the entrance to life; all others are thieves and robbers. On this account are we bound to avoid them, but to make choice of the thing pertaining to the Church with the utmost diligence, and to lay hold of the tradition of the truth.... For how should it be if the apostles themselves had not left us writings? Would it not be necessary, [in that case,] to follow the course of the tradition that they handed down to those to whom they did commit the Churches? To which course many nations of those barbarians who believe in Christ do assent, having salvation written in their hearts by the Spirit, without paper or ink, and, carefully preserving the ancient tradition" (*Against Heresies* 3, 4, 1–2, ANF 1:416–17).

[82] Fundamentalist Protestants have argued that the rock upon which the Church would be built was not Peter but Christ, the confession of faith, or Peter's faith, but not Peter and his successors. "Modernists" have tried to dismiss the relevance of the passage by asserting that it is a later addition inserted into Matthew by redactors. "These are the arguments from two separate standpoints against the office of Simon. But in both cases the real reason for denying it, a reason never explicitly or frankly stated, is the premise that it was 'impossible' that Jesus should confer that office. This 'impossibility' is absolute, indisputable, transcendent, and much more valid indeed than the clarity and the authenticity of the text" (Ricciotti, *Life of Christ*, 406). In other words, preconceived biases or anti-Catholic sentiments, and not an objective study of the passage itself, compel the objector to resist the clear meaning of the biblical passage.

swept Europe in the past few centuries have not failed to have an impact on biblical study and perceptions of Church government. Too often the Church is perceived as a democracy instead of as a kingdom. Jesus Christ reestablished the eternal throne of David and also reestablished the office of royal steward "over the house" when he chose Peter, investing him with the keys of the kingdom of heaven. Peter may have died, but his office continues, and his successors, as we shall discover shortly, continue to fill his office of royal steward and continue to preserve the sacred deposit of truth entrusted to the Church by the apostles.

As we continue working from the base we have established here, we shall see how the earliest Christians, our first brothers and sisters in Christ, understood these biblical passages and the authority of the Church.

We will now delve into the later life of Peter, after he escaped Herod's persecution in Jerusalem, after "he departed, and went into another place" (Acts 12:17). Get ready to step back into history, to become better acquainted with the great Prince of the Apostles, and to witness the rise of the persecuted Church of the first century.

HISTORICAL STUDY
Was Peter in Rome, Was He the First Bishop of Rome, and Was He Martyred in Rome?

The details of Peter's life, especially his later life, are sketchy, for no detailed record has been passed down through the centuries.[1] Luke, on the other hand, one of Paul's traveling companions, wrote an account of Jesus' life and also chronicled select portions

---

[1] The New Testament documents afford little historical information about the apostles and the early years of the Church. What do we know of Thomas, Matthew, Andrew, and the others beyond the biblical record? Very little indeed. And consider that the first twelve chapters of Acts cover a whole decade! The apostles were too busy *making* history to write about it! They were too concerned with spreading the gospel to keep chronological travel logs. Most of the New Testament documents were written, not to give us a detailed account of the early Church or a manual for Church polity, but to defend the fledgling gospel, to correct a faulty practice, or to commend or rebuke local Churches. Early Christians did not write history as we know history in the modern world. Luke informs Theophilus that he compiled his Gospel "so that you [Theophilus] might know the exact truth about the things you have been taught" (Lk 1:4). The Book of Acts carries on where Luke's Gospel leaves off. Luke's main intent is *not* to give a comprehensive historical account of the early Church but to affirm certain aspects of the gospel that he considers crucial. Commenting on the historical aspects of the book of Acts, Fundamentalist G. Campbell Morgan writes, "The title of the book is an unfortunate one. To one taking up the book for the first time, that title, 'The Acts of the Apostles', would seem to suggest that in the book we should find a chronicle of all the doings of all the apostles. We know this is not so. . . . Some of the apostles are never named beyond their inclusion in the list given before the account of the Pentecostal effusion. Further, not all the acts of any one apostle are recorded. The book as history is merely a fragment, and in some senses a disappointing fragment" (*The Acts of the Apostles* [Westwood, N.J.: Fleming H. Revell, 1924], 8).

Early documents were destroyed during persecutions, disintegrated due to age, or were just neglected. We know of two epistles written by Paul that did not survive the first century. Secular historians tell us very little; they largely ignored the "Jewish sect" that attracted the lower levels of society, considering it unworthy of attention. For these and many other reasons, detailed knowledge of the birth of Christianity is scarce, and we can be thankful to God that we have as much available as we do.

of Paul's ministry so that Theophilus "might know the exact truth about the things [he] had been taught" (Lk 1:4). Even with Paul's life, there are long periods of activity about which we are told nothing. Take, for example, the fourteen-year period before his return to Jerusalem after his conversion (Gal 2:1), or his two years of house arrest in Rome, or his trip to Spain, or his second journey to Rome, or, of course, his martyrdom. We have precious little information about the other apostles after the day of Pentecost. To illustrate the point further, what do we know with certainty from the Scriptures about the life and ministry of Thomas, who preached in India, Matthew, who traveled widely, or John, who cared for the Blessed Virgin Mary and oversaw the Churches of Asia? And what of Bartholomew, Philip, Andrew, Matthias, James the son of Alphaeus, Judas son of James, and the others? What happened to Lazarus, Jesus' friend? Those who accept the doctrine of *sola Scriptura* and have the attitude that nothing can be known, and nothing matters, outside the text of the New Testament are deprived of much understanding and knowledge about the continuing work of the Holy Spirit among Christ's flock. Later in this book, we will look at some of the views opposing the presence and bishopric of Peter in Rome. But first, we will look at all the evidence available, which will demonstrate without a doubt Peter's residence and accomplishments in Rome.

We cannot assume that the silence of the New Testament is an indication that the seldom-mentioned apostles ceased their apostolic ministries after the Ascension of Christ, or that they were not important in the first century and beyond. Quite the contrary. We know from history that they were bustling with missionary and ecclesiastical activity. The New Testament was never intended as a complete history of, or manual for, the primitive Church. The Church herself has kept the tradition of the apostles alive and intact, and she has pondered and celebrated it through the centuries.

Even though we have in the New Testament only fragmentary documentation of Peter's travels and ministry, in this section of our study we will gather together what historical information is available on this subject. We will use New Testament sources as well as the historical documents, along with the tradition carefully preserved by the Church Fathers.

Peter opened the doors of the Church to the various ethnic groups. After Pentecost (c. A.D. 30), when Peter preached the gospel to the Jews, the Acts of the Apostles tells us that Peter stayed in Jerusalem for several years, traveling to Samaria to open the door of salvation to the Samaritans (Acts 8:4–25) and later to Joppa (Acts 9:32–43), where he stayed until called by God to visit Caesarea. There he admitted the first Gentile convert into the Church—Cornelius, the Roman centurion. This took place about ten years after the Resurrection of Christ. Peter then returned to Jerusalem to report that the Gentiles had accepted the gospel and received the Holy Spirit just as the Jews had ten years earlier on Pentecost (Acts 10:40; 11:18). During this time, Peter led the Church in Jerusalem, where, at least in the early years, the early Christians worshiped in the Jewish temple, in Solomon's porch (Acts 3:11; 5:12).

Persecution arose in Jerusalem, and the Apostle James was beheaded in c. A.D. 42–44 by Herod Agrippa I (Acts 12:2). After the martyrdom of James, Peter was imprisoned by Herod and miraculously released through the intervention of an angel (Acts 12:7). Peter then fled Jerusalem, around A.D. 44; the Acts of the Apostles tells us that Peter "departed and went to another place" (Acts 12:17). We know from references in Scripture and the writings of the primitive Church that Peter traveled extensively, preaching in the East, spending a good amount of time in Antioch (Gal 2:11–21), perhaps using this city as a home base for apostolic journeys. During these years he traveled to Rome and established the Church there, as we shall clearly see. He also journeyed through the provinces of Asia Minor and later wrote to these Churches in the provinces of "Pontus, Galatia, Cappadocia, Asia, and Bithynia" (1 Pet 1:1).[2] He also visited Corinth, where Dionysius says he "planted" along with Paul. That he traveled widely and spread the gospel is well attested in the writings of the early Christians.[3]

---

[2] Eusebius writes, "And in how many provinces Peter preached Christ and taught the doctrine of the new covenant to those of the circumcision is clear from his own words in his epistle already mentioned as undisputed, in which he writes to the Hebrews of the dispersion in Pontus, Galatia, Cappadocia, Asia, and Bithynia" (*Church History* 3, 4, 2, NPNF2, 1:136).

[3] Paul alludes to the traveling missionary work of Cephas and the other apostles in 1 Corinthians 9:5: "Do we not have the right to be accompanied by [take along] a wife, as the other apostles and the brothers of the Lord and Cephas?" The

Early records mention Peter as the head of the Church in
Antioch.[4] Luke informs us that Peter returned to Jerusalem for the
first Church council in Jerusalem between A.D. 49 and 51.[5] The
Council was held about eight years after Peter had fled Jerusalem,
following the death of the Apostle James. The Council defined
theological issues, promulgated disciplinary obligations, and removed certain ceremonial restrictions. These decrees were binding upon the visible, universal Church and were implemented in
order to assist in the absorption of the new Gentile converts.

After the Jerusalem Council, in which Peter, John, James the
Righteous, Paul, and Barnabas, among others, all came together
in Jerusalem, we have very little in Scripture to give us information
about Peter, other than his first epistle, where he mentions that he
is writing from Rome, under the pseudonym of Babylon. However,
the early history recorded in the writings of the Fathers provides
us adequate information on the apostolic ministry of Peter. This
will be the main focus of this section of our study.

A very workable time line for the life and ministry of Peter, from
the death and Resurrection of Christ up to his own martyrdom,
consistent with both scriptural and historical evidence, has been
provided by Warren Carroll. The following table is based on his
time line:[6]

Corinthians would have been familiar with the fact that Peter traveled through
Asia Minor, possibly with other apostles, accompanied by their wives.

[4] See Eusebius, *Church History* 3, 36, NPNF2, 1:166, and Origen's *In Lucam,
Homily 6*, 938A. We are told that Peter appointed Evodius as the first in the line
of Antiochian bishops to succeed him as bishop of Antioch. Evodius was succeeded by Ignatius of Antioch, who was later martyred by wild beasts in Rome
about the year 106. We will discuss the life and apostolate of St. Ignatius in more
detail later in our study.

[5] The Jerusalem Council is described in some detail in Acts 15. Peter was
present along with other important Church leaders. Paul and Barnabas arrived
together. Simon J. Kistemaker writes, "Together with Barnabas, Paul visited
Jerusalem a third time when the Council convened (49 A.D.) prior to the beginning of Paul's second missionary journey in Acts 15:4" (*Acts*, New Testament
Commentary [Grand Rapids, Mich.: Baker Book House, 1990], 533). Others
consider the date of the Council to be between A.D. 50 and 51. There is reason
to believe that all the apostles returned to Jerusalem for this Council and that
Mary, the Mother of our Lord, was also present and died during this time frame
(see Warren Carroll, *The Founding of Christendom*, A History of Christendom, vol.
1 [Front Royal, Va.: Christendom College Press, 1993], 413–14).

[6] Carroll, *Founding of Christendom*, 422.

The Apostolic Ministry of St. Peter
A.D. 30–67

c. 30   The death, Resurrection, and Ascension of Jesus; Pentecost

30–37   Peter head of the Church in Jerusalem

38–39   Peter's missionary journeys in Samaria and on the coast of Palestine

40–41   Peter in Antioch

42   Imprisonment in Jerusalem, escape, and departure to "another place"

42–49   First sojourn in Rome

49   Expulsion from Rome by the edict of Claudius against its Jews

49–50   In Jerusalem for the Apostolic Council

50–54   In Antioch, Bithynia, Pontus, Asia, and Cappadocia (or some of them)

54–57   Second sojourn in Rome; Gospel of Mark written under Peter's direction

57–62   In Bithynia, Pontus, and Cappadocia (or some of them); Mark in Alexandria, Egypt

62–67   Third sojourn in Rome; canonical Epistles of Peter; Mark with Peter in Rome

67   Martyrdom in Rome and burial near the Necropolis at the Vatican

We will now go back in time, beyond the clamor of the present age, to walk among the apostles and Church Fathers. We will allow their quiet voices from ancient times to be heard again with clarity. As we listen to their wisdom, preserved for almost two thousand years, we will humbly learn what our first Christian brethren believed and practiced, especially regarding Peter and the Church. We will learn from their written pages, which have been graciously preserved through the many intervening centuries. We will see the life of Peter emerge as he carries out the apostolic mandate given him by Jesus Christ. We will get glimpses of Peter, the Rock, as he exercises the authority of the keys and stands at the helm, maneuvering the ship toward the eternal shores. The Fathers will explain the "passing on of authority" as the apostles are succeeded by others in the office of bishop and in the office of Peter in the See of Rome.

Jesus Christ to Peter as recorded by the Apostle John
    —written c. A.D. 90–100 [7]

" 'Truly, truly, I say to you, when you were young, you girded
yourself and walked where you would; but when you are old, you
will stretch out your hands, and another will gird you and carry
you where you do not wish to go.' (This he said to show by what
death [Peter] was to glorify God.) And after this he said to him,
'Follow me.' " [8]

---

[7] The Apostle John probably wrote his Gospel about sixty to seventy years
after Christ's Resurrection and twenty-five to thirty years *after* the martyrdom of
Peter. Jesus' words have the mysterious obscurity of prophecy, but after the
prophecy was fulfilled in the Roman Circus, during the persecution of Nero,
John realized what Jesus had meant. He added a parenthetical comment explaining Jesus' prophecy of Peter's death, which by A.D. 90 was well known
throughout Christendom. Tradition reports that Peter was crucified in Rome.
Peter also recalls Jesus' prophecy when he refers to his imminent death: "I know
that the putting off of my body will be soon, as our Lord Jesus Christ showed me"
(2 Pet 1:14).

[8] Jn 21:18–19. The crucifixion of Christ was still clearly etched in the apostles'
minds when Jesus spoke these words several days after his Resurrection on the
shores of the Sea of Galilee. As he wrote his Gospel, the Apostle John had no
doubt what Jesus meant, since he was writing well after the martyrdom of Peter.
    Jesus' prophecy foretelling Peter's death significantly reinforces the unchal-
lenged early accounts that Peter was crucified in Rome about A.D. 64–67 under
Emperor Nero. Jesus knew Peter would be in Rome and die a martyr's death.
The common practice of crucifixion in the Roman Empire was to spread the
condemned man's arms out on the crossbeam of a cross, attaching him with
ropes or nails, and then forcing him to drag his cross to the site of execution,
where the cross would then be hoisted vertically into place. This crucifixion
procedure graphically fulfills the prophecy given by Jesus. (See D. A. Carson,
The Gospel according to John [Grand Rapids, Mich.: Eerdmans, 1991], 679.)
    With the exhortation "Follow me", Jesus commands Peter to imitate his Lord,
not only in life but in death, even to death on a cross. Peter therefore did in fact
fulfill his impetuous promise to his Lord when he said, "I will lay down my life
for you" (Jn 13:37). Jesus was the Chief Shepherd and was crucified for the
sheep; Peter, commissioned by the Chief Shepherd to tend the flock, was also
crucified for faithfully tending the sheep. Peter and Jesus had discussed this
matter earlier, just before Jesus was taken away by the Roman soldiers: "Simon
Peter said to him, 'Lord, where are you going?' Jesus answered, 'Where I am
going you cannot follow me now; but you shall follow afterward.' Peter said to
him, 'Lord, why cannot I follow you now? I will lay down my life for you' " (Jn
13:36–37). "Since being a shepherd involves laying down one's life for the
sheep (Jn 10:11), the command to Simon to feed Jesus' sheep leads into the
next section of the scene (21:18–23) where Peter's death is predicted in terms

Peter (martyred in Rome c. A.D. 67) in his *First Epistle*

"Peter, an apostle of Jesus Christ. To the exiles of the Dispersion.
. . . By Silvanus, a faithful brother as I regard him, I have written
briefly to you. . . . She [the Church] who is at Babylon [Rome],
who is likewise chosen, sends you greetings; and so does my son
Mark."[9]

---

suggestive of martyrdom. . . . Simon's martyrdom is a witness consonant with his
shepherd's duty of laying down his life" (*Peter in the New Testament*, a collabora-
tive assessment by Protestant and Roman Catholic scholars, ed. Raymond E.
Brown, Karl P. Donfried, and John Reumann [Minneapolis: Augsburg Pub.,
1973], 145–46).
Several sources, including Eusebius (*Church History* 3, 1), refer to Peter's
head-down crucifixion. We are told that Peter requested this inverted crucifixion since he did not consider himself worthy to die in the same manner as his
Lord. The Roman moralist Seneca is an independent witness to the Roman
practice of inverted crucifixion (*Consolation to Marcia* 20).
    [9] 1 Pet 1:1; 5:12–13. Only as a result of the sixteenth-century Reformation did
anyone attempt to deny that Peter was in Rome or that he died there. "Babylon",
as used here by Peter himself, refers figuratively to the city of Rome. As Babylon
had persecuted God's people (2 Kings 24), so Rome now persecuted the Church.
The contemporary Jews living in Rome also referred to Rome as Babylon (*Orac.
Sybil.* 5, 159f.; *4 Esdras* 3:1; *Apoc. Baruch*, vis. 2, 1; Rev 14:8; 16:19; 17:5; 18:2, 10, 21).
    Protestant scholar J. N. D. Anderson writes, "The key to the problem, in the
view of most critics, lies in the fact that in the 1st cent. 'Babylon' was becoming
in Jewish and Christian circles a symbolic title for Rome. For the prophets (e.g.,
Is 13; 43:14; Jer 50:29; 51:1–58) the name had denoted the proud, immoral,
godless city which dominated their world, and it was natural for later Jews to see
this as the type of the Rome they knew and which embodied these very characteristics. So we find Rome referred to as 'Babylon' in the rabbinical literature. . . .
'She who is in Babylon' simply means 'the church at Rome'. . . . So the church in
Rome is in Babylon because Rome is its place of exile" (*A Commentary on the
Epistles of Peter and Jude* [Grand Rapids, Mich.: Baker Book House, 1969], 218–
19). Protestant Alan Stibbs states in his commentary, "The name 'Babylon' is
used in Rev. 17, 18 to refer to Rome, and it can be so understood here. *Only at and
since the Reformation have some preferred to treat the word literally* as a reference either
to Babylon in Mesopotamia or to a military station called Babylon in Egypt. Since
in the opening salutations Peter described his intended readers in Asia Minor as
'elect . . . sojourners of the Dispensation' (1:1, RV), it seems appropriate here
that he should describe the Christian congregation in Rome as sharing the same
election . . . and sojourning in Babylon itself, the world-centre of organized
godlessness" (*The First Epistle General of Peter*, Tyndale New Testament Commentaries [Grand Rapids, Mich.: Eerdmans, 1981], 176, emphasis added).
    Eusebius, who wrote in A.D. 325, refers to Clement and Papias (c. A.D. 60–
130, who was acquainted with the Apostle John), "Clement in the eighth book

Clement of Rome in his *First Epistle to the Corinthians*
  —written from Rome c. A.D. 96
  —mentioned in Philippians 4:3
  —contemporary of Peter and Paul[10]

"But, to leave the examples of antiquity, let us come to the athletes who are closest to our own time. Consider the noble examples of our own generation.[11] Through jealousy and envy the greatest and most righteous pillars [of our Church in Rome] were persecuted, and they persevered even to death. Let us set before our eyes the good Apostles: Peter, who through unwarranted jealousy suffered not one or two but many toils, and having thus given testimony went to the place of glory that was his due. Through jealousy and strife

---

of his Hypotyposes gives this account, and with him agrees the bishop of Hierapolis named Papias. And Peter makes mention of Mark in his first epistle which they say that he wrote in Rome itself, as is indicated by him, when he calls the city, by a figure, Babylon, as he does in the following words: 'The church that is at Babylon, elected together with you, saluteth you; and so doth Marcus my son'" (*Church History* 2, 15, NPNF2, 1:116).

By way of summary, "The tradition connecting St. Peter with Rome is early and unrivalled. Against it can be placed only the silence of the New Testament. . . . The identification of 'Babylon' in 1 Pet 5:13 with Rome seems highly probable" (*Oxford Dictionary of the Christian Church*, ed. F. L. Cross and E. A. Livingstone [New York: Oxford Univ. Press, 1989], 1068).

[10] According to the Fathers, Clement of Rome (fl. c. A.D. 96) was the third bishop of Rome after Peter (Peter was bishop until his martyrdom about A.D. 67; Linus, c. 67–c. 79 [mentioned in 2 Tim 4:21]; Anacletus, c. 79–c. 85; and Clement of Rome, c. 85–c. 96). Eusebius wrote in 325, "Clement also, who was appointed third bishop of Rome, was, as Paul testifies, his co-worker and fellow-soldier [Phil 4:3]" (*Church History* 3, 4, NPNF2, 1:137). Irenaeus, in the second century, says this of Clement, "The blessed apostles, then, having founded and built up the Church, committed into the hands of Linus the office of the episcopate. Of this Linus, Paul makes mention in the Epistles to Timothy. To him succeeded Anacletus; and after him, in the third place from the apostles, Clement was allotted the bishopric. This man, as he had seen the blessed apostles, and had been conversant with them, might be said to have the preaching of the apostles still echoing [in his ears], and their traditions before his eyes. Nor was he alone [in this], for there were many still remaining who had received instructions from the apostles" (*Against Heresies* 3, 3, 3, ANF 1:416).

[11] The words "our own generation" place Clement, his fellow Roman Christians, and his readers in the midst of the apostolic age. Clement is appealing to the martyrdom of Peter and Paul as examples, examples that were still fresh in the minds of the eyewitnesses of his own generation and whose teaching and courage were known firsthand.

Paul showed the way to the prize for endurance. . . . He passed from the world and was taken up to the holy place. . . . To these men who lived such holy lives there must be added a multitude of the elect, who suffered terrible indignities and tortures on account of jealousy, and who became shining examples in our midst."[12]

The Testament of Hezekiah
—written c. A.D. 75–100[13]

"And now, Hezekiah and Josab my son, these are the days of the consummation of the world; and after it is consummated, Beliar [the Antichrist], a great angel, the king of this world, will descend. He has ruled it since it began and he will descend from his firmament in the form of a man, a king without law, the murderer of his mother [Nero]. He himself, even this king, shall persecute the plant [Church] which the twelve apostles of the Beloved shall plant and one of the twelve shall be delivered into his hands."[14]

---

[12] *1 Clement* 5:1–6, in William A. Jurgens, *The Faith of the Early Fathers* [Collegeville, Minn: Liturgical Press, 1970], 1:7–8). Clement, a disciple of Peter and personally ordained by him, tells of Peter's presence, position, and martyrdom in Rome. He refers to pillars in their midst, that is, Rome. He refers to "our generation", meaning during his own lifetime. Clement is acknowledging intimate knowledge and close association with the two great apostles. No details are given, which implies that the Corinthians understood all the circumstances and that a brief reminder was all it would take to bring the events alive again. Referring to Peter and Paul as "pillars", Clement may be alluding to the words of Paul in Galatians 2:9 and 1 Timothy 3:15. Johannes Quasten, in *Patrology* (Westminster, Md.: Christian Classics, 1993), 1:44, says, "[Clement] bears reliable testimony to St. Peter's sojourn to Rome, St. Paul's journey to Spain and the martyrdom of the two Princes of the Apostles."

[13] "*The Ascension of Isaiah* is a curious, composite work, thrown together by an unknown editor of the second or third century. . . . The elements of which it is composed are three, each originally a distinct document. The first, the *Martyrdom of Isaiah* . . . is a Jewish legendary history of the sawing asunder of the prophet and was written, probably, sometime during the first century of our era. The second, the *Testament of Hezekiah*, is an apocalyptic tract of Christian authorship, cast in the guise of a vision seen by King Hezekiah during an illness and related to him afterwards by Isaiah and Josab, Isaiah's sons. Its date can be more definitely determined than that of the *Martyrdom*, as somewhere between the years 75 and 100" (James T. Shotwell and Louise Ropes Loomis, *The See of Peter* [New York: Columbia Univ. Press, 1991], 69).

[14] *Ascension of Isaiah* 4, quoted in ibid., 71. The prophecy foretells the coming of the Antichrist, who is described unmistakably as Nero, who will persecute the

Ignatius of Antioch (c. A.D. 35–c. 107)[15]

"Ignatius, also called Theophorus, to the Church that has found mercy in the transcendent Majesty . . . which also presides in the chief place of the Roman territory.[16] . . . Not like Peter and Paul do I issue any order to you. They were Apostles, I am a convict; they were free, I am until this moment a slave."[17]

Church and kill "one of the twelve". The writer cannot be referring to Paul, since he was not included among the twelve foundation stones of the Church. "Only within the last few years have scholars realized its value as the most ancient of surviving testimonies as to the manner of Peter's death" (ibid., 70).

[15] Ignatius of Antioch, a saint, bishop of Antioch, friend of the apostles, and a martyr, is categorized as one of the apostolic Fathers of the Church. He referred to himself as Theophorus (Greek for "God-bearer") and is believed to have been a disciple of the Apostle John and probably of Peter as well, due to his presence in Antioch. Ignatius was condemned and devoured by wild beasts during the reign of the Roman emperor Trajan. On his way from Antioch to Rome in chains (over 1,300 miles), where the execution took place, he wrote seven letters. Of these, five were addressed to the Christian communities of Ephesus, Magnesia, Tralles, Philadelphia, and Smyrna—cities in Asia Minor that had sent representatives to greet him as he passed through. The other letters were addressed to Polycarp, the bishop of Smyrna, and to the Christian community residing at his destination—Rome. His letters are an important source of information about the beliefs and organization of the early Christian Church. Ignatius wrote them as warnings against heretical doctrines, thus providing his readers with detailed summaries of Christian doctrine. He also gave a vivid picture of Church organization as a community of love gathered around a presiding bishop assisted by a council of presbyters (elders) and deacons. In his writings he stressed the virgin birth of Christ, the threefold hierarchy of the Church (bishops, priests, and deacons), the Eucharist as a sacrifice, and the Real Presence of Christ; and he was the first person known to have used the term *catholic* to describe the universal Church.

[16] This phrase used by Ignatius regarding the Church of Rome has great significance as an early witness to the primacy of Rome. It will be discussed in detail in the third section of our study.

[17] *Epistle of St. Ignatius to the Romans* 1, 4, in *The Epistles of St. Clement of Rome and St. Ignatius of Antioch*, trans. James A. Kleist, Ancient Christian Writers (New York: Newman Press, 1946), 1:82. It is clear from Ignatius, a contemporary and associate of Peter and Paul, that both of these great apostles preached and presided over the Church of Rome. "Significant also is the fact that although Ignatius admonishes to unity and harmony in all his Epistles he does not do so in the one addressed to the Romans. He does not presume to issue commands to the Roman community, for it has its authority from the Princes of the Apostles. . . . This testimony also makes Ignatius an important witness to Peter and Paul's sojourn in Rome" (Quasten, *Patrology*, 1:70). Ignatius was the second bishop of Antioch after Peter and would have been well acquainted with Peter's travels.

Phlegon, quoted by Origen[18]
— during the reign of Hadrian (A.D. 117–138)

"Now Phlegon, in the thirteenth or fourteenth book, I think, of his Chronicles, not only ascribed to Jesus a knowledge of future events (although falling into confusion about some things which refer to Peter, as if they referred to Jesus), but also testified that the result corresponded to His predictions."[19]

Papias, Bishop of Hieropolis (c. A.D. 60–130)[20]
—See quotation from Eusebius in n. 9, pp. 69–70.

---

[18] "The following excerpt, derived from the writings of Origen, is trivial enough at first sight but grows in interest as one begins to grasp its implications. Phlegon was a favorite freedman of the emperor Hadrian and the reputed author of historical and other works, most of which have long been lost. Spartianus . . . says that Hadrian himself actually wrote many of the books which passed as Phlegon's and that he preferred to publish under his freedman's name rather than under his own. It is therefore possible that the *Chronicles* mentioned in our quotation were composed by the emperor. In any case, the author, a member of the Roman imperial court, knew some facts or reports about Peter as well as about Christ and found it easy to confuse Peter with the founder of Christianity" (Shotwell and Loomis, *See of Peter*, 73).

[19] Origen, *Against Celsus* 2, 14, ANF 4:437. "Phlegon (supposed to be the Emperor Hadrian writing under the name of a favorite slave) is said by Origen (*Contra Celsum*, II. 14) to have confused Jesus and Peter in his *Chronicles*. This is very significant as implying that Peter must have been well known in Rome" (NPNF2, 1:129, n. 7). The early date and the confusion of the Roman emperor between Jesus and Peter implies a very firm knowledge of the presence of Peter in the city of Rome, enough to make even the emperor confuse him with the Founder of the faith.

[20] Protestant A. Cleveland Coxe, D.D., writes, "Papias has the credit of association with Polycarp, in the friendship of St. John himself, and of 'others who had seen the Lord'. . . . Later writers affirm that he suffered martyrdom about 163 A.D.; some saying that Rome, others that Pergamus, was the scene of his death" (ANF 1:151). Concerning Papias, Irenaeus says, "These things are borne witness to in writing by Papias, the hearer of John, and a companion of Polycarp, in his fourth book; for there were five books compiled . . . by him" (*Against Heresies* 5, 33, 4, ANF 1:563). Papias wrote of himself, "But I shall not be unwilling to put down, along with my interpretations, whatsoever instructions I received with care at any time from the elders, and stored up with care in my memory, assuring you at the same time of their truth. For I did not, like the multitude, take pleasure in those who spoke much, but in those who taught the truth; nor in those who related strange commandments, but in those who rehearsed the commandments given by the Lord to faith, and proceeding from truth itself. If,

Dionysius (bishop of Corinth; fl. c. A.D. 166/174)
  —writing to Pope Soter in Rome[21]

"*That both [Peter and Paul] suffered martyrdom at the same time is affirmed as follows, by Dionysius, Bishop of Corinth, when writing to the Romans:* 'You have also, by your very admonition, brought together the planting that was made by Peter and Paul at Rome and at Corinth; for both of them alike planted in our Corinth and taught us; and both alike, teaching similarly in Italy, suffered martyrdom at the same time.' "[22]

---

then, any one who had attended on the elders [apostles] came, I asked minutely after their sayings,—what Andrew or Peter said, or what was said by Philip, or by Thomas, or by James, or by John, or by Matthew, or by any other of the Lord's disciples: which things Aristion and the presbyter John, the disciples of the Lord, say. For I imagined that what was to be got from books was not so profitable to me as what came from the living and abiding voice [tradition]" (*From the Exposition of the Oracles of the Lord*, ANF 1:153). Notice in passing the great interest in the living oral tradition over and above writings.

[21] Dionysius was bishop of Corinth during the bishopric of St. Soter in Rome (A.D. 166–175). He wrote several letters that are briefly described by Eusebius. In one of his letters he thanks the Roman Church for assisting the Corinthian Church and mentions that Clement's letter (written in A.D. 96) was habitually read in their Church, presumably in the same manner as "canonical" documents.

[22] *The Letter of Dionysius of Corinth to Soter of Rome*, quoted in Eusebius, *History of the Church* 2, 25, 8, in Jurgens, *Faith of the Early Fathers*, 1:45. Notice the claim that Peter had been to Corinth as well as to Rome, which is corroborated by Paul's epistles. This claim gives us further insight into the travels and ministry of Peter after he left Jerusalem. Dionysius would have had access to documents in Corinth, along with reliable oral tradition and testimony, to substantiate his statements. Why would anyone challenge this historical evidence, denying that Peter had been to Corinth and Rome, if it were not that a strong tradition forced them to oppose anything that might substantiate the claims of the historical Catholic Church? Some Fundamentalists even refer to this historical evidence of the Fathers as "legends" (see Loraine Boettner, *Roman Catholicism* [Philadelphia: Presbyterian and Reformed Pub. Co., 1962], 117). If any early Christian knew Peter was *not* in Rome and Corinth, why was there no rebuttal to this kind of ubiquitous historical evidence? The early Church was *very* conservative and very careful not to add to or take away from the life and teachings [tradition] of the apostles. If Peter did not preside as bishop of Rome and eventually die there, why did no one refute the claims of Dionysius, Ignatius, Clement, Gaius, and the others? If Peter died somewhere else, why did no other city claim his bones or exalt itself as the place of his martyrdom? We know the Church in Rome from the very beginning claimed the bones of Peter and Paul.

Gaius [or *Caius*], a Roman presbyter (fl. c. A.D. 198/217)[23]

"Thus publicly announcing himself as the first among God's chief enemies, he [Nero] was led on to the slaughter of the apostles.[24] It is, therefore, recorded that Paul was beheaded in Rome itself, and that Peter likewise was crucified under Nero. This account of Peter and Paul is substantiated by the fact that their names are preserved in the cemeteries of that place even to the present day. It is confirmed likewise by Caius, a member of the [Roman] Church, who arose under Zephyrinus, bishop of Rome [A.D. 198–217]. He, in a published disputation with Proclus, the leader of the Phrygian heresy, speaks as follows concerning the places where the sacred corpses of the aforesaid apostles are laid: 'But I can show the trophies [tombs][25] of the apostles. For if you will go

---

[23] Little is known of Gaius other than the remaining fragments of his *Disputation with Proclus*, most of which have been preserved by Eusebius. Proclus was a Montanist heretic; Gaius, an orthodox presbyter in Rome, debated him in writing.

[24] Tacitus (c. A.D. 52–c. 117), the non-Christian Roman historian, gives us a vivid account of the Neronian persecution in his *Annales* 15, 44, where he writes, "Therefore, to overcome this rumor [that Nero had caused the fire that had destroyed a large part of the city of Rome], Nero put in his own place as culprits, and punished with most ingenious cruelty, men whom the common people hated for their shameful crimes and called Christians. Christ, from whom the name was derived, had been put to death in the reign of Tiberius by the procurator Pontius Pilate. The deadly superstition, having been checked for a while, began to break out again, not only throughout Judea, where this mischief first arose, but also at Rome, where from all sides all things scandalous and shameful meet and become fashionable. Therefore, at the beginning, some were seized who made confessions; then, on their information, a vast multitude was convicted, not so much of arson as of hatred of the human race. And they were not only put to death, but subjected to insults, in that they were either dressed up in the skins of wild beasts and perished by the cruel mangling of dogs, or else put on crosses to be set on fire, and, as day declined, to be burned, being used as lights by night. Nero had thrown open his gardens for that spectacle, and gave a circus play, mingling with the people dressed in a charioteer's costume or driving in a chariot. From this arose, however, toward men who were, indeed, criminals and deserving extreme penalties, sympathy, on the ground that they were destroyed not for the public good, but to satisfy the cruelty of an individual" (Joseph Cullen Ayer, *A Source Book for Ancient Church History* [New York: Charles Scribner's Sons, 1948], 6–7).

[25] For a discussion of the word "*tomb*", we turn to Philip Hughes in *A History of the Church* (New York: Sheed & Ward, 1948), 1:61–62. "[It has been] suggested that it designates not the tombs of the Apostles but simple commemorative

to the Vatican or to the Ostian way, you will find the trophies of those who laid the foundations of this church.' " [26]

Irenaeus (c. A.D. 130–c. 200)
—disciple of Polycarp
—bishop of Gaul
—defender of the faith against the Gnostics[27]

"For, after our Lord rose from the dead, [the apostles] were invested with power from on high when the Holy Spirit came down

---

monuments. Even so it remains true that Rome, at the end of the second century, was still mindful of the memory 'of the founders of the church.' But there is nothing to disprove that the term in question means 'tomb'; we find it used with this meaning, and Eusebius, who had before him the complete text of Caius, so uses it. It is, in point of fact, the only possible meaning in this context. Caius is answering the boast of Proclus that Asia retains the bodies of the four prophetess-daughters of Philip and their father, too, and must in turn be claiming that Rome, more gloriously still, possesses, not merely a memorial, but the very tombs of the Apostles."

[26] Fragment of *Disputation with Proclus* preserved in Eusebius, *Church History* 2, 25, 5, NPNF2, 1:129–30. Gaius authored a written disputation with Proclus, a Montanist. Living in Rome, very close in time to the historical events, Gaius had access to documents and records long since destroyed in the fires and pillaging of many persecutions. He testifies that during his lifetime the grave sites and monuments of Peter and Paul were well known in Rome. He used this historical and empirical evidence against the heretics of his day with absolute confidence in its verifiability. The burial sites of the two apostles were well known to everyone and widely venerated. He could *never* have spoken so boldly had the facts been otherwise or open to refutation. His whole argument rests on the credibility of verifiable historical facts. Eusebius, about a century later, continued to assert the same fact and knew of no one who would dare rise to refute it.

[27] Irenaeus is one of the most important witnesses to the Christianity of the second century. He was a disciple of Polycarp (c. A.D. 69–c. 155), who, in turn, was a disciple of John the Apostle and thus an important link between the apostolic age and the great writers of the second century. Irenaeus of Lyons says this about himself, "For, when I was still a boy, I knew you (Florinus) in lower Asia, in Polycarp's house, when you were a man of rank in the royal hall, and endeavoring to stand well with him. I remember the events of those days more clearly than those which happened recently, for what we learn as children grows up with the soul and is united to it, so that I can speak even of the place in which the blessed Polycarp sat and disputed, how he came in and went out, the character of his life, the appearance of his body, the discourses which he made to the people, how he reported his intercourse

[upon them], were filled from all [His gifts], and had perfect knowledge: they departed to the ends of the earth, preaching the glad tidings of the good things [sent] from God to us, and proclaiming the peace of heaven to men, who indeed do all equally and individually possess the Gospel of God. Matthew also issued a written Gospel among the Hebrews in their own dialect, while Peter and Paul were preaching at Rome, and laying the foundations of the Church. After their departure, Mark, the disciple and interpreter of Peter, did also hand down to us in writing what had been preached by Peter." [28]

"We do put to confusion all those who . . . assemble in unauthorized meetings; [we do this, I say,] by indicating that tradition derived from the apostles, of the very great, the very ancient, and universally known Church founded and organized at Rome by the two most glorious apostles, Peter and Paul. . . . The blessed apostles, then, having founded and built up the Church, committed into the hands of Linus the office of the episcopate. Of this Linus Paul makes mention in the Epistles to Timothy." [29]

---

with John and with the others who had seen the Lord, how he remembered their words, and what were the things concerning the Lord which he had heard from them, and about their miracles, and about their teachings, and how Polycarp had received them from the eye-witnesses of the Word of Life, and reported all things in agreement with the Scriptures. I listened eagerly even then to these things through the mercy of God which was given me, and made notes of them, not on paper, but in my heart, and ever by the grace of God do I truly ruminate on them" (Eusebius, *History of the Church* 5, 20, 5–7, in Quasten, *Patrology*, 1:287).

[28] *Against Heresies* 3, 1, 1, in ANF 1:414. Irenaeus lived in Gaul, which is in modern-day France. His writings again confirm the universal knowledge of the primitive Church affirming Peter's presence in Rome and his founding of the Church there. This was unchallenged, and no tradition contradicted it; it was common knowledge from one end of the Roman Empire to the other. There was no hint of dissent, not even from heretics, who would have loved to challenge the authority of Rome. It is curious that many today would dare to defy the clear historical evidence of the first centuries, when no one in those centuries in any way questioned the fact that Peter founded the Church in Rome.

[29] Ibid., 3, 3, 2–3, in ANF 1:415–16. This passage from Irenaeus, where he ably disputes the heretics, is significant in that it again clearly demonstrates that the earliest Christians enjoyed unchallenged knowledge of Peter's presence in Rome—not presence only, but his role as the founder and organizer of the Church in Rome. Irenaeus is not simply stating a historical fact for the sake of doing so; he is battling for the faith; and he employs the fact that Peter and Paul founded the Church of Rome and were subsequently martyred in that city as the

Tertullian (C. A.D. 160–c. 225)[30]

"And accordingly it makes no difference whether a man be washed in a sea or a pool, a stream or a fount, a lake or a trough; nor is there any distinction between those whom John baptized in the Jordan and those whom Peter baptized in the Tiber."[31]

"For this is the way in which the apostolic Churches transmit their lists: like the Church of the Smyrnaeans, which records that Polycarp was placed there by John; like the Church of the Romans where Clement was ordained by Peter."[32]

"[R]un through the apostolic Churches in which the very thrones [*cathedrae*, in Latin] of the Apostles remain still in place; in which their own authentic writings are read. . . . If you are near to Italy, you have Rome, whence also our authority derives. How happy is that Church, on which Apostles poured out their whole doctrine along with their blood, where Peter endured a passion like that of the Lord [crucifixion], and where Paul was crowned in a death like John's [beheading]."[33]

---

key point in his argument. Could he be so bold with this defense of the faith if anyone questioned the truth of his assertion? If he had been proved wrong on this one point, his whole defense would have been devastated.

[30] Tertullian was born and raised in Carthage, Africa, of pagan parents. He was educated in literature and rhetoric, and he practiced as a lawyer. He became a Christian before A.D. 197. He was a distinguished apologist, writing many rigorous and strong defenses of the faith and doctrinal treatises. He later joined a fringe group called the Montanists. Even so, he was given the title of Father of Latin Theology. A zealous champion of Christianity, Tertullian wrote many theological treatises, of which thirty-one have survived. In his various works he strove either to defend Christianity, to refute heresy, or to argue some practical point of morality or Church discipline. He is an authentic witness to the early apostolic tradition. In this study we will distinguish between writings before and during his Montanist period.

[31] *On Baptism* 4, ANF 3:670–71. This treatise was written between 200 and 206. John the Baptist baptized in the Jordan River, which flowed through Israel, and Peter baptized converts in the Tiber River coursing through Rome. This is a remarkable witness to the apostolate of Peter in the city of Rome.

[32] *The Demurrer against the Heretics* 32, 1, in Jurgens, *Faith of the Early Fathers*, 1:122. There is no doubt in Tertullian's mind—and he was widely traveled and well-read, living less than one hundred years after the death of the Apostle John—that Peter had served in Rome and appointed successors to succeed him. We will discuss Clement further in the third section of our study.

[33] Ibid., 36, 1, in Jurgens, *Faith of the Early Fathers*, 1:122. Besides confirming Peter's presence and authority in Rome, Tertullian brings several interesting

"And if a heretic wants a faith backed by public record, let the archives of the empire speak, as would the stones of Jerusalem. We read the lives of the Caesars. In Rome Nero was the first to stain with blood the rising faith. Peter was girded about by another (Jn 21:18), when he was made fast to the cross. Paul obtained a birth suited to Roman citizenship, when in that city he was given re-birth by an ennobling martyrdom."[34]

---

things to light. First, that the apostolic Churches had "chairs" of the apostles (cf. Mt 23:2). Second, Tertullian says "our authority" is derived from Rome and, third, that the bishops were "from the apostolic seed", products of succession, and that they were ordained by the apostles. It is interesting to recall in this context that Eusebius writes, "The chair [throne] of James, who first received the episcopate of the church at Jerusalem from the Saviour himself . . . has been preserved until now, the brethren who have followed him in succession there exhibiting clearly to all the reverence which both those of old times and those of our own day maintained and do maintain for holy men on account of their piety" (Eusebius, *Church History* 7, 19, NPNF2, 1:305). From earliest times there were two chairs venerated in Rome upon which Peter was alleged to have sat: one at the Vatican and the other near the tomb of St. Peter. "Near the tomb of St. Peter, as De Rossi has proved, stood a second Pontifical seat, distinct from the one which the Abbot John saw on the other side of the stream. Not far from the Via Salaria, the savants of our time have discovered the most ancient catacomb in Rome, the Ostrian Cemetery, 'where Peter baptized'. Here, then, as it would certainly seem, the pilgrim from Lombardy venerated the first Chair of which he speaks, more ancient than that at the Vatican; for on the Papyrus of Monza, as well as in the Martyrologies and Calendars of the period, it is called 'the first whereon Peter was seated' " (Constant Fouard, *Simon Peter and the First Years of Christianity* [New York and London: Longmans, Green, and Co., 1893], 409). Again, Peter's founding of the Church in Rome, and the ancient attestation to his episcopal chair, was common knowledge and went unchallenged in all of Christendom, until the Reformers attempted to overthrow the early tradition in order to extricate themselves from the authority of Rome and the successor of Peter.

[34] *Antidote against the Scorpion* 15, 3, written c. A.D. 211/212, in Jurgens, *Faith of the Early Fathers*, 1:152. Tertullian was defending martyrdom against the Gnostics, who treated it with contempt. Tertullian defends the noble call of martyrdom by recalling the hero's death experienced by the Apostles Peter and Paul, whose leadership and martyrdom in Rome were a matter of "public record", filed in the "archives of the empire". There were undoubtedly hundreds of documents available to these early writers that have been lost over the centu-ries. Notice Tertullian's citation of Jesus' cryptic prophesy in John 21:18–19.

This is a good place to comment on the deaths of Peter (by crucifixion) and Paul (by beheading with the sword). As we know from Acts 22:25–29, not only was Paul a Roman citizen but Roman citizens were treated with greater legal consideration than non-citizens. In the same way, Roman citizens were exempted

"Let us see what milk the Corinthians drank from Paul; to what rule of faith the Galatians were brought for correction; what the Philippians, the Thessalonians, the Ephesians read by it; what utterance also the Romans give, so very near (to the apostles), to whom Peter and Paul conjointly bequeathed the gospel even sealed with their own blood. We have also St. John's foster churches."[35]

Clement of Alexandria (c. A.D. 150–c. 215)
—text preserved by Eusebius[36]

"Again, in the same books, Clement gives the tradition of the earliest presbyters, as to the order of the Gospels, in the following manner: The Gospels containing the genealogies, he says, were

---

from the severe cruelty reserved for others. David Stern writes, "[The cross was] used by the Romans to execute criminals who were not Roman citizens (Roman citizens sentenced to death were given a less painful way to die)" (*Jewish New Testament Commentary* [Clarksville, Md.: Jewish New Testament Publications, 1994], 41). The *Illustrated Bible Dictionary* comments further, "Only slaves, provincials and the lowest types of criminals were crucified, but rarely Roman citizens. Thus tradition, which says that Peter, like Jesus, was crucified, but Paul was beheaded, is in line with ancient practice" (ed. J. D. Douglas [Wheaton, Ill.: Tyndale House, 1980], 1:342–43).

[35] *Tertullian against Marcion* 4, 5, ANF 3:350.

[36] Clement of Alexandria was born of pagan parents, probably in Athens. After he became a Christian, he traveled extensively in Italy, Syria, and Palestine. His purpose was to seek instruction from the most famous Christian teachers. He explains that he "was privileged to hear" discourses of "blessed and truly remarkable men" (*Stromata* 1, 1, 11, ANF 2:301). He became head of the School of Catechumens in Alexandria. He wrote about later historical events in the life of the Apostle John. He claims a close association with the apostolic tradition in *The Stromata* (1, 1), writing, "Well, they preserving the tradition of the blessed doctrine derived directly from the holy apostles, Peter, James, John, and Paul, the sons receiving it from the father (but few were like the fathers), came by God's will to us also to deposit those ancestral and apostolic seeds. And well I know that they will exult; I do not mean delighted with this tribute, but solely on account of the preservation of the truth, according as they delivered it. For such a sketch as this, will, I think, be agreeable to a soul desirous of preserving from escape the blessed tradition" (ANF 2:301). Eusebius recalls, "In Book I he [Clement] shows that he himself was almost an immediate successor of the apostles. . . . In his work *The Easter Festival* he declares that his friends insisted on his transmitting to later generations in writing the oral traditions that had come down to him from the earliest authorities of the Church" (Eusebius, *The History of the Church* 6, 13, trans. G. A. Williamson

written first. The Gospel according to Mark had this occasion. As Peter had preached the Word publicly at Rome, and declared the Gospel by the Spirit, many who were present requested that Mark, who had followed him for a long time and remembered his sayings, should write them out. And having composed the Gospel he gave it to those who had requested it. When Peter learned of this, he neither directly forbade nor encouraged it. But, last of all, John, perceiving that the external facts had been made plain in the Gospel, being urged by his friends, and inspired by the Spirit, composed a spiritual Gospel. This is the account of Clement."[37]

" 'Marcus, my son, saluteth you' [1 Pet 5:13]. Mark, the follower of Peter, while Peter publicly preached the Gospel at Rome before some of Caesar's equites, and adduced many testimonies to Christ, in order that thereby they might be able to commit to memory what was spoken by Peter, wrote entirely what is called the Gospel according to Mark."[38]

"They say, accordingly, that the blessed Peter, on seeing his wife led to death, rejoiced on account of her call and conveyance home, and called very encouragingly and comfortingly, addressing her by name, 'Remember thou the Lord.' Such was the marriage of the blessed, and their perfect disposition towards those dearest to them."[39]

[Harmondsworth, Middlesex, England: Penguin Books, 1965], 191). The early Church was very conservative and not given to innovations. She was extremely concerned with passing on the apostolic tradition intact, with nothing added and nothing subtracted.

[37] Eusebius, *Church History* 6, 14, NPNF2, 1:261. Clement, writing from Alexandria, Egypt, relays the undisputed truth—that Peter preached the gospel in Rome. The writings of Clement of Alexandria are preserved by Eusebius, who quotes from a work (written c. A.D. 198–202) that has since been lost but was still readily available at the end of the third century.

[38] *Comments on the First Epistle of Peter*, by Clement of Alexandria, ANF 2:573. Here again is the unquestioned teaching of the primitive Church that Peter preached in Rome. Clement of Alexandria is a very early witness, having traveled the Roman Empire searching for the apostolic truth from the heirs to the apostles. He gleaned the orthodox teachings, and nowhere is there the slightest hint that Peter had not founded the Church in Rome; rather, it is assumed as an incontrovertible historical fact.

[39] *Stromata* 7, 11, ANF 2:541. This is an interesting anecdote about the death of Peter's wife, probably in Rome under the persecution of Nero. It might be assumed that Peter's wife was a vocal and active part of the Church since she

Origen of Alexandria (c. A.D. 185–c. 254)[40]

"Meanwhile the holy apostles and disciples of our Saviour were dispersed throughout the world. Parthia, according to tradition, was allotted to Thomas as his field of labor, Scythia to Andrew, and Asia to John, who, after he had lived some time there, died at Ephesus. Peter appears to have preached in Pontus, Galatia, Bithynia, Cappadocia, and Asia to the Jews of the dispersion. And at last, having come to Rome, he was crucified head-downwards; for he had requested that he might suffer in this way. What do we need to say concerning Paul, who preached the Gospel of Christ from Jerusalem to Illyricum, and afterwards suffered martyrdom in Rome under Nero? These facts are related by Origen in the third volume of his Commentary on Genesis."[41]

Porphyry of Tyre (c. A.D. 230–300)[42]

"So one wonders why Jesus gave the keys of heaven to such a man as Peter and why in such a time of disorder and tumult, beset with

---

evidently gained sufficient attention to warrant martyrdom. Other stories, probably legends, mention a daughter named Petronilla and a son (see Michael Grant, *Saint Peter* [New York: Scribner's, 1994], 56–57, and William Steuart McBirnie, *The Search for the Twelve Apostles* [Wheaton, Ill.: Tyndale House, Living Books, 1973], 68–69).

[40] Origen was probably the brightest scholar and most powerful intellect of all the Fathers living at the end of the second century. With unlimited access to historical and ecclesiastical documents, both in the library of Alexandria, which was second to none, and also the libraries of the Empire and the documents and traditions of the local Churches, Origen was in an unparalleled position to speak on the events of the first century, especially since he himself was born within eighty-five years of the death of the Apostle John.

[41] *Commentary on Genesis*, as relayed in Eusebius, *Church History* 3, 1, NPNF2, 1:132–33. Clement and Gaius from Rome, Dionysius from Corinth, Tertullian from Africa, Irenaeus from Lyons, Clement from Alexandria, and Ignatius and Origen from Syria: From every corner of the Empire, all echo the same truth— Peter was in Rome. Early confirmation of Peter's ministry, which corroborates the New Testament allusions, repeatedly confirms Peter's travels to and ministry in Rome.

[42] "The author of this [letter] was one Macarius Magnes . . . who was a member of the church party hostile to Chrysostom. He wrote in five books an imaginary dialogue between himself and a pagan philosopher, in the course of which the philosopher criticised or ridiculed various passages in the New Testament and he himself defended them. The speeches of the philosopher seem to have

such grave dangers, he said: 'Feed my lambs'. . . . Furthermore, it is recorded that Peter fed the lambs for several months only before he was crucified,[43] although Jesus had said that the gates of hell should not prevail against him. . . . Now let us notice what he says about Paul. 'Then spake the Lord to Paul in the night by a vision, "Be not afraid but speak. . . . For I am with thee and no man shall set on thee to hurt thee." ' Notwithstanding, this fine fellow was overpowered at Rome and beheaded, he who had said that we should judge angels, even as Peter, who had received the right to feed the lambs, was fastened to the cross and crucified."[44]

Eusebius (c. A.D. 260–340)[45]
—bishop of Caesarea and father of Church history

"Second year of the two hundred and fifth olympiad: the Apostle Peter, after he has established the Church in Antioch, is sent to

---

been culled mainly from the treatise of the Neoplatonist Porphyry, *Against the Christians*, composed about the year 280 and now lost. Macarius does not expressly say, as he does in other instances, that our quotations are from Porphyry, but they are both like Porphyry in style and scathing sarcasm. Porphyry himself spent much time at Rome about the middle of the third century and came into relations with the Christians there. It is clear that he investigated their writings and traditions with unusual care" (Shotwell and Loomis, *See of Peter*, 91).

[43] "The writer, who knew the New Testament so well, cannot mean that Peter's death occurred only a few months after his master's. It is more reasonable to suppose that he is alluding to the length of Peter's activities in Rome before his martyrdom" (ibid., 92, n. 81). It is also possible that he was exaggerating in his normal style, to deprecate the work and successes of Peter.

[44] Marcarius Magnes, presumably citing Porphyry in *Unigenitus* 3, 33; 4, 4, in ibid., 92–93. This is the only known existing pagan source to shed light on the presence and martyrdom of Peter in Rome. Sarcasm drips from his words as he belittles Christians for following such men as succumbed to ignominious deaths at the hand of the Romans, after claiming such "grandiose" schemes of redemption and freedom. The presence and suffering of Peter and Paul in Rome were assumed to be common knowledge and provide a significant basis for Porphyry's ridicule.

[45] Eusebius of Caesarea was a theologian, Church historian, and scholar, probably born in Palestine. Eusebius left Caesarea for Tyre, from which he subsequently fled during the persecutions of Christians at the beginning of the fourth century. It appears he was immediately imprisoned on his arrival in Egypt. After A.D. 310 the persecutions ceased, and he was released. About 314 he became bishop of Caesarea. At the Council of Nicaea in 325 Eusebius delivered the opening address and was made the leader of the Semi-Arians, the

Rome, where he remains as bishop of that city, preaching the gospel for twenty-five years. . . . Third year of the two hundred and fifth olympiad: the Evangelist Mark, interpreter of Peter, announces Christ in Egypt and Alexandria. . . . Fourth year of the two hundred and eleventh olympiad: Nero is the first, in addition to all his other crimes, to make a persecution against the Christians, in which Peter and Paul died gloriously at Rome."[46]

"In the same reign of Claudius [emperor of Rome, A.D. 41–54], the all-gracious and kindly providence of the universe brought to Rome to deal with this terrible threat to the world, the strong and great apostle, chosen for his merits [virtue] to be spokesman for all the others, Peter himself.[47]

"It is also recorded that under Claudius [10 B.C.–A.D. 54], Philo [c. 20 B.C.–c. A.D. 50] came to Rome to have conversations with Peter, then preaching to the people there. This would not be improbable, as the short work to which I am referring, and which he produced at a considerably later date, clearly contains the rules of the Church still observed in our own day."[48]

"So brightly shone the light of true religion on the minds of Peter's hearers [in Rome] that, not satisfied with a single hearing or with the oral teaching of the divine message, they resorted to appeals of every kind to induce Mark (whose Gospel we have), as he was a follower of Peter, to leave them in writing a summary of the instruction they had received by word of mouth, nor did they

---

moderate party, who were averse to discussing the nature of the Trinity and preferred the simple language of the Scriptures to the subtleties of metaphysical distinctions. At Nicaea he accepted the Athanasian position of the Nicene Creed. Eusebius stood in high favor with Constantine I, emperor of Rome, and was one of the most learned men of his time. His *History of the Church* is an invaluable resource for understanding the mind of the apostles, the bishops who succeeded them, and the daily life of the early Christians and the Church.

[46] *The Chronicle* 42, 43, and 68, in Jurgens, *Faith of the Early Fathers*, 1:291. Written c. A.D. 303, *The Chronicle* was a complete history of the Greeks as well as of the barbarians. Only fragments remain.

[47] Eusebius, *History of the Church* 2, 14, 6, Williamson trans., 49.

[48] Eusebius, *History of the Church* 2, 17, 1, ibid., 50. Philo was a Jewish thinker and writer who belonged to a prosperous priestly family of Alexandria, Egypt. Little is known of his life other than the fact that he did visit Rome. According to *Chambers Biographical Dictionary* (Edinburgh: W & R Chambers, 1984), "When over fifty [years old,] he went to Rome to plead for certain Alexandrians who had refused to worship the insane Caligula, described in his *De Legatione*" (1052).

let him go till they had persuaded him, and thus became responsible for the writing of what is known as the Gospel according to Mark. It is said that, on learning by revelation of the spirit what had happened, the apostle was delighted at their enthusiasm and authorized the reading of the book in the churches. Clement quotes the story in *Outlines* Book VI, and his statement is confirmed by Bishop Papias of Hierapolis, who also points out that Mark is mentioned by Peter in his first epistle, which he is said to have composed in Rome itself, as he himself indicates when he speaks of the city figuratively as Babylon." [49]

"As to the rest of his followers, Paul testifies that Crescens was sent to Gaul; but Linus, whom he mentions in the Second Epistle to Timothy as his companion at Rome, was Peter's successor in the episcopate of the church there, as has already been shown." [50]

Peter of Alexandria (d. c. A.D. 311)[51]

"Peter, the first chosen of the Apostles, having been apprehended often and thrown into prison and treated with ignominy,[52] at last

---

[49] Eusebius, *History of the Church* 2, 15, Williamson trans., 49.

[50] Eusebius, *Church History* 3, 4, 9, NPNF2, 1:137.

[51] St. Peter of Alexandria died a martyr's death about 311 after being the head of catechetics at Alexandria and later the bishop of Alexandria. Only fragments remain of what were fourteen canons, part of the law collection of the Eastern Church.

[52] The inhuman cruelty perpetrated by the Romans upon prisoners, especially non-citizens, is described in graphic terms by George F. Jowett, "Historians write of it [Mamertine or Tullian Keep] as being the most fearsome on the brutal agenda of mankind. Over three thousand years old, it is probably the oldest torture chamber extant, the oldest remaining monument of bestiality of ancient Rome, a bleak testimony to its barbaric inhumanity, steeped in Christian tragedy and the agony of thousands of its murdered victims. It can be seen to this day. . . . The only entrance [into the underground pit] is through the aperture in the ceiling . . . light never entered and it was never cleaned. The awful stench and filth generated a poison fatal to the inmates of the dungeon, the most awful ever known. . . . It is said that the number of Christians that perished within this diabolic cell is beyond computation" (*The Drama of the Lost Disciples* [London: Covenant Pub., 1970], 176). C. Bernard Ruffin adds, "Tradition holds that Peter was kept nine months in a noisome and fetid dungeon called the Tullian Keep, chained to a column. The Roman authorities had to change guards constantly, because Peter was converting them almost as soon as they were assigned to him" (*The Twelve* [Huntington, Ind.: Our Sunday Visitor, 1984], 54).

was crucified in Rome. And the renowned Paul, oftentimes having been delivered up and put in peril of death, having endured many evils, and boasting of his numerous persecutions and afflictions, was even himself put to the sword and beheaded in the same city."[53]

Lactantius of Africa (c. A.D. 240–c. 320)[54]

"When Nero was already reigning Peter came to Rome, where, in virtue of the performance of certain miracles which he worked by that power of God which had been given to him, he converted many to righteousness and established a firm and steadfast temple to God. When this fact was reported to Nero, he noticed that not only at Rome but everywhere great multitudes were daily abandoning the worship of idols, and, condemning their old ways, were going over to the new religion. Being that he was a detestable and pernicious tyrant, he sprang to the task of tearing down the heavenly temple and of destroying righteousness. It was he that first persecuted the servants of God. Peter, he fixed to a cross; and Paul, he slew."[55]

"But the disciples, being dispersed through the provinces, everywhere laid the foundations of the Church, themselves also in the name of their divine Master doing many and almost incredible miracles; for at His departure He had endowed them with power and strength, by which the system of their new announcement might be founded and confirmed. But He also opened to them all things which were about to happen, which Peter and Paul preached at Rome; and this preaching being written for the sake of remembrance."[56]

---

[53] *Penance,* canon 9, in Jurgens, *Faith of the Early Fathers,* 1:259. This excerpt from Peter's tract *Penance* was written about A.D. 306. Again, this reflects the unquestioned and reliable historical understanding of those in the Christian community, from one end of the known world to the other.

[54] Lactantius was a Christian apologist. Before his conversion, Emperor Diocletian appointed him as the rhetorician at Nicomedia in Bithynia. When he became a Christian, about the year 300, he was deprived of his appointed post. As a Christian he was appointed tutor of Emperor Constantine's son Crispus. Lactantius must have had ready access to all the Roman historical archives as well as the records and written histories of the Church.

[55] *The Deaths of the Persecutors* 2, 5, written between A.D. 316 and 320, when Lactantius was in Rome, in Jurgens, *Faith of the Early Fathers,* 1:272.

[56] *The Divine Institutes* 21, in ANF 7:123.

Cyril of Jerusalem (c. A.D. 315–386)[57]

"[Simon Magus] after he had been cast out by the Apostles, came to Rome. . . . And he so deceived the City of Rome that Claudius set up his statue, and wrote beneath it, in the language of the Romans, 'Simoni Deo Sancto,' which being interpreted signifies, 'To Simon the Holy God'. As the delusion was extending, Peter and Paul, a noble pair, chief rulers of the Church, arrived and set the error right. . . . And marvellous though it was, yet no marvel. For Peter was there, who carrieth the keys of heaven."[58]

Pope St. Damasus I (A.D. 304–384)[59]

"The most blessed Apostle Paul, who contended and was crowned with a glorious death along with Peter in the City of Rome in the time of the Caesar Nero—not at a different time, as the heretics prattle, but at one and the same time and on one and the same day: and they equally consecrated the above-mentioned holy Roman Church to Christ the Lord; and by their own presence and by their venerable triumph they set it at the forefront over the others of all the cities of the whole world. The first see, therefore, is that

---

[57] Cyril of Jerusalem is recognized as a saint and a Father and Doctor of the Church. He was born in Jerusalem and later became the bishop of Jerusalem. During his episcopal reign, he was banished from Jerusalem because of his strong stand against the heresy of Arianism, which claimed that Jesus was a creature. Arius accused him of selling the treasures of his church to feed the poor in a time of famine; for this the assembly deposed him. He was deposed and restored several times during his life by heretics and Roman emperors alike. His writings are invaluable as a source of information on the early Church. They consist of twenty-three treatises, eighteen of which are addressed to catechumens and five to the newly baptized.

[58] *Catechetical Lectures* 6, 14–15, NPNF2, 7:37–38. The history and tradition of Peter's presence, authority, and crucifixion in Rome are too deep and too consistent to be set aside, and there is absolutely no sign of any contradictory tradition. If Peter had not been to Rome, where were the orthodox believers denying this? Notice the acknowledgment of Peter's authority in reference to the keys he possessed.

[59] St. Damasus is known for having commissioned Jerome's translation of the Scriptures and for changing Church liturgy from Greek to Latin, which was then becoming the universal language. St. Damasus was very active in suppressing heresy (Arianism, Donatism, Macedonianism, and Luciferianism). At a council, probably held in Rome in 382, he promulgated a canon of scriptural books, since the New Testament had not yet been collected or canonized.

of Peter the Apostle, that of the Roman Church, which has neither
stain nor blemish nor anything like it." [60]

> "This place, you should know, was once the abode
>   of saints;
> Their names, you may learn, were Peter and likewise Paul.
> The East sent hither these disciples, as gladly we confess.
> For Christ's sake and the merit of his blood
>   they followed him among the stars
> And sought the realms of heaven and the kingdoms
>   of the righteous.
> Rome was deemed worthy to retain them as her citizens.
> May Damasus offer them these verses, new stars,
>   in their praise!" [61]

Doctrine of Addai (Syriac document dated c. A.D. 400)

"[Many years after his death, Aggai, who ordained holy priests for
the country, was martyred as he taught in the church by a rebellious son of Abgar. His successor, Palut, was obliged to go to
Antioch in order to get episcopal consecration, which he received from Serapion, Bishop of Antioch], who himself also
received the hand from Zephyrinus, Bishop of the city of Rome,
from the succession of the hand of the priesthood of Simon

---

[60] *The Decree of Damasus* 3, written A.D. 382, in Jurgens, *Faith of the Early Fathers,*
1:406. The first section of his decree addresses the Holy Spirit and the gifts; the
second part deals with the canon of Scripture; and the third part with the
primacy of Rome.

[61] *Inscription in the Platonia,* in Shotwell and Loomis, *See of Peter,* 109. The words
were inscribed on a placard written by Pope Damasus of Rome. It was erected
above the chamber presumably once sanctified by the holy relics of the apostles.
"Damasus and his secretary Philocalus were the first in the long line of Roman
church antiquarians . . . and they set themselves the serious task of identifying
and rescuing from oblivion the countless sacred graves and sites in and about
the city. . . . The observant visitor to the catacombs or the primitive basilicas can
still mark the discolored fragments of their memorial inscriptions on the
walls. . . . [These lines] are a translation of the inscription which Damasus set up
in the so-called Platonia or tomb chamber of the apostles. . . . The chamber,
now renovated almost beyond recognition, is a part of the crypt beneath the
church of San Sebastiano on the Via Appia" (ibid., 108–9). During a time of
extreme persecution, the remains of Peter and Paul were hidden in the catacombs.

Cephas,[62] which he received from Our Lord, who was there Bishop of Rome twenty-five years, in the days of the Caesar [Nero], who reigned there thirteen years."[63]

"But the Law and the Prophets and the Gospel, which ye read every day before the people, and the Epistles of Paul, which Simon Peter sent us from the city of Rome, and the Acts of the twelve Apostles, which John, the son of Zebedee, sent us from Ephesus, these books read ye in the Churches of Christ." [64]

Liber Pontificalis
—fourth-century sources[65]

"At the same time, Constantine Augustus built, by request of Silvester the bishop, the basilica of blessed Peter, the apostle, in

---

[62] "Doctrine of Addai", in *Catholic Encyclopedia* (New York: Robert Appleton Co., 1909), 5:88. "The anxiety of the writer to connect the Edessene succession with Rome is interesting; its derivation from the Petrine See of Antioch does not suffice for him" (ibid.). In other words, even at this early date, it is important to this distant Syrian Church to be in the apostolic succession, which can trace its "lineage" back to the Lord Jesus, through the Apostle Peter.

[63] Ibid.

[64] Ibid. We see further confirmation, from Syrian sources outside the Roman Empire, even outside the Greek-speaking world of the early Church, that Peter was in Rome and was believed to have sent the Syrians the epistles of Paul. The Syrian document also affirms the bishopric of Peter in Rome, the primacy of the bishop of Rome, the need for episcopal consecration, and apostolic succession.

[65] "The *Liber Pontificalis*, the oldest history of the Papacy, was put together [from earlier sources] by an unknown member of the Roman curia during the sixth or the seventh century. . . . It comprised a series of lives of individual popes from Peter to the writer's own day and incorporated and blended materials from many earlier sources. . . . It is no longer possible to doubt that Constantine actually built a basilica in honor of Peter over what he supposed to be the apostle's tomb. The form of ancient St. Peter's [Cathedral] was that of a 'tomb church,' constructed around and adapted to the requirements of a site already fixed by an older grave. During the fifteenth and sixteenth centuries, this basilica was torn down to make way for the present basilica, but the bricks taken from it show the Constantinian stamp. In 1594, when the masons were digging to lay the foundations for the modern high altar, they opened up a narrow shaft at the bottom of which they saw by the light of a torch a golden cross lying on the dark floor. Pope Clement VIII, who was summoned to witness the sight, ordered the shaft filled up at once and the spot has never since been disturbed. . . . All that can positively be asserted is that the fourth century did enshrine and venerate upon the traditional site of martyrdom what it believed to be Peter's very bones" (Shotwell and Loomis, *See of Peter*, 102–3).

the shrine of Apollo and laid there the coffin with the body of the holy Peter; the coffin itself he enclosed on all sides with bronze, which is unchangeable; at the head 5 feet, at the feet 5 feet, at the right side 5 feet, at the left side 5 feet, underneath 5 feet, and overhead 5 feet: thus he enclosed the body of blessed Peter, the apostle, and laid it away. And above he set porphyry columns for adornment and other spiral columns, which he brought from Greece. He made also a vaulted roof in the basilica, gleaming with polished gold, and over the body of the blessed Peter, above the bronze which enclosed it, he set a cross of purest gold, weighing 50 lbs., in place of a measure." [66]

Catalogus Liberianus
   —written c. A.D. 354 [67]

"In the reign of Tiberius Caesar our Lord Jesus Christ suffered under the constellation of the Gemini, March 25, and after his ascension blessed Peter instituted the episcopate. From his time we name in due order of succession every one who has been bishop, how many years he was in office and under what emperor. Peter, 25 years, 1 month, 9 days, was bishop in the time of Tiberius Caesar and of Gaius and of Tiberius Claudius and of Nero, from the consulship of Minucius and Longinus (A.D. 30) to that of Nero and Verus (A.D. 55). He suffered together with Paul, June 29, under the aforesaid consuls in the reign of Nero." [68]

"December 25 Birth of Christ in Bethlehem of Judaea. . . . January 20 Fabianus in the cemetery of Callistus and Sebastian . . . in the Catacombs. January 21 Agnes on the Nomentana. February 22 Anniversary of the chair of Peter. March 7 Perpetua and Felicitas . . . in Africa. . . . May 19 Parthenus and Calocerus . . . in the

---

[66] *Liber Pontificalis*, in ibid., 104.

[67] A manual or tour guide of Rome was compiled for the many Christian visitors and citizens of Rome in the fourth century. Included was a collection of miscellaneous information, historical facts, and lists.

[68] *Catalogus Liberianus*, in Shotwell and Loomis, *See of Peter*, 107. Christians visiting the city of Rome were given the information passed down along with the claim that Peter was in Rome as bishop for twenty-five years, which is quite within the time frame we looked at in Warren Carroll's *Founding of Christendom*.

cemetery of Callistus, in the 9th consulship of Diocletian and the 8th of Maximian (304). . . . June 29 Peter in the Catacombs and Paul on the Ostian Way, in the consulship of Tuscus and Bassus (258)."[69]

Optatus of Milevis (c. A.D. 370)[70]

"We must note who first established a see and where. If you do not know, admit it. If you do know, feel your shame. I cannot charge you with ignorance, for you plainly know. It is a sin to err knowingly, although an ignorant person may be blind to error. But you cannot deny that you know that the episcopal seat was established first in the city of Rome by Peter and that in it sat Peter, the head of all the apostles, wherefore he is called Cephas."[71]

Epiphanius of Salamis (c. A.D. 315–403)[72]

"At Rome the first Apostles and bishops were Peter and Paul; then Linus, then Cletus, then Clement, the contemporary of Peter and Paul, whom Paul remembers in his Epistle to the Romans. . . . The succession of the bishops in Rome is as follows: Peter and Paul, Linus and Cletus, Clement, Evaristus, Alexander,

---

[69] *Feriale Ecclesiae Romanae*, in the *Catalogus Liberianus* quoted in ibid., 107–8. These dates are taken from the calendar of Roman feasts, remembering important dates in the early Church and included in the above manual for Christian visitors to Rome. "The excerpt from the calendar of feasts is of considerable archeological interest but raises some troublesome questions" (ibid., 106). Among these questions is the significance of the date of 258. Many scholars have concluded that the date marks the peak of the Valerian persecution and "the bodies of both Peter and Paul were removed for safety from their original tombs on the Vatican and on the Ostian Way, and secreted temporarily in this obscure hiding place, thence to be produced in triumph under the peace of Constantine" (ibid.).

[70] Except for the fact that he was the bishop of Milevis in Africa, little is known of Optatus aside from an existing treatise he wrote entitled *Against Parmenian the Donatist*. This treatise refuted the Donatist heresy and was the starting point for St. Augustine's work refuting the same heresy.

[71] *De Schismate Donatistarum* 2, 2–3, in Shotwell and Loomis, *See of Peter*, 111–12.

[72] St. Epiphanius was a native of Palestine and the bishop of Salamis. He was an ardent upholder of the faith of Nicaea and was intolerant of any suspicion of heresy. He wrote a book refuting every heresy known to the Church from the beginning until his day.

Sixtus, Telesphorus, Hyginus, Pius, Anicetus, whom I have already mentioned above in my enumerating of the bishops."[73]

Prudentius (A.D. 348–c. 410)[74]

"More than their wont men gather and rejoice. Say, friend, why? All over Rome they hasten and exult in triumph. To us is returned the day of the victorious feast of the apostles, marked with the blood of noble Peter and Paul. The same day, tho' separated by the space of one full year, saw them both crowned with the lofty wreath of death. The marsh on the Tiber, laved by the bordering river, holds earth consecrated by two trophies and saw both the cross and the sword. . . . The sentence fell first to Peter, doomed by the laws of Nero to hang suspended from the tall beam."[75]

Augustine of Hippo
  —written c. A.D. 400[76]

"If the very order of episcopal succession is to be considered, how much more surely, truly, and safely do we number them from Peter himself, to whom, as to one representing the whole Church, the

---

[73] The *Panacea against All Heresies* 27, 6, in Jurgens, *Faith of the Early Fathers*, 2:72. The *Panacea* was written by St. Epiphanius between 374–377. It listed eighty heresies that he combated and gives us another confirmation of the unrefuted historical fact that Peter functioned as bishop of Rome. Epiphanius, too, had resources at his disposal long since unavailable to modern researchers. Had there been any reason to believe Peter had not been in Rome, Epiphanius would have challenged this fact as a false teaching and inaccurate history. He not only affirms the historical fact, however, he uses it in his refutation of the heretics. Epiphanius' arguments would have fallen flat if there had been any shadow of doubt or the least shred of evidence to the contrary.

[74] Prudentius Aurelius Clemens, a Spaniard, was a Latin poet and hymnwriter. He was a civil administrator and practiced law. His hymns are often apologetical, defending the faith against heresy in an artistic format. His writings give us a clear view of the Roman Church around the year 400.

[75] *Peristephanon* hymn 12, "On the Passion of Peter and Paul", in Shotwell and Loomis, *See of Peter*, 118.

[76] St. Augustine was the greatest of the Latin Fathers and one of the most eminent Doctors of the Western Church. Augustine was born on November 13, 354, in Tagaste, Numidia (Algeria). His father, Patricius, was a pagan (later converted to Christianity), but his mother, Monica, was a devout Christian who labored and prayed untiringly for her son's conversion. Augustine became an earnest seeker after truth. He considered becoming a Christian but experi-

Lord said: 'Upon this rock I will build My Church, and the gates of hell shall not conquer it.' Peter was succeeded by Linus, Linus by Clement, Clement by Anacletus, Anacletus by Evaristus, Evaristus by Sixtus, Sixtus by Telesphorus, Telesphorus by Hyginus, Hyginus by Anicetus, Anicetus by Pius, Pius by Soter, Soter by Alexander, Alexander by Victor, Victor by Zephyrinus, Zephyrinus by Callistus, Callistus by Urban, Urban by Pontianus, Pontianus by Anterus, Anterus by Fabian, Fabian by Cornelius, Cornelius by Lucius, Lucius by Stephen, Stephen by Sixtus, Sixtus by Dionysius, Dionysius by Felix, Felix by Eutychian, Eutychian by Caius, Caius by Marcellus, Marcellus by Eusebius, Eusebius by Melchiades, Melchiades by Sylvester, Sylvester by Mark, Mark by Julius, Julius by Liberius, Liberius by Damasus, Damasus by Siricius, Siricius by Anastasius. In this order of succession not a Donatist bishop is to be found."[77]

Jerome (c. A.D. 342–420)[78]

"Simon Peter, son of John, of the province of Galilee, of the village of Bethsaida, brother of Andrew the apostle, and himself chief of the apostles, after his bishopric at Antioch and his preaching to

---

mented with several philosophical systems before finally entering the Church. About 383 Augustine left Carthage for Rome, but a year later he went on to Milan as a teacher of rhetoric. In Milan he met St. Ambrose, then the most distinguished ecclesiastic in Italy. Augustine was attracted again to Christianity. At last one day, according to his own account, he seemed to hear a voice, like that of a child, repeating, "Take up and read." He interpreted this as a divine exhortation to open the Scriptures and read the first passage he happened to see, which was Romans 13:13–14. He immediately resolved to embrace Christianity. Ambrose baptized him, along with his natural son, on Easter Eve in 387. His mother, who had rejoined him in Italy, rejoiced at this answer to her prayers and hopes. She died soon afterward in Ostia. Augustine became bishop of Hippo in 395, an office he held until his death. John Calvin and Martin Luther, leaders of the Reformation, were both close students of Augustine's works. Augustine died at Hippo, August 28, 430.

[77] *To Generosus*, letter 53, 2, in Jurgens, *Faith of the Early Fathers*, 3:2. Written about the year 400, Augustine wrote to Generosus in the continuing debate with the sectarians called the Donatists. The fact that Peter was in Rome and presided as bishop over the Roman Church is never questioned by St. Augustine; in fact, he utilizes the fact, along with the line of bishops succeeding Peter in Rome, as the means of proving his point. Notice that he emphasizes his certainty with the words *surely, truly,* and *safely.*

[78] St. Jerome has been proclaimed a Father and Doctor of the Church and is acknowledged as the best biblical scholar in the early Church. His most

the dispersed of the circumcision who believed, in Pontus, Galatia, Cappadocia, Asia and Bithynia, in the second year of the emperor Claudius, went to Rome to expel Simon Magus and occupied there the sacerdotal seat for twenty-five years until the last year of Nero, that is, the fourteenth. By Nero he was fastened to a cross and crowned with martyrdom, his head downward toward the earth and his feet raised on high, for he maintained that he was unworthy to be crucified in the same manner as his Lord. . . . He was buried at Rome in the Vatican, near the Via Triumphalis, and is celebrated by the veneration of the whole world." [79]

From this point on, as the history of the Church flows from century to century, there is still no question raised about the historical

important work was a translation of the Bible into Latin known as the *Vulgate*. Jerome was born in Strido, on the border of the Roman provinces of Dalmatia and Pannonia, about A.D. 345. After studying in Rome, he journeyed to the desert, where he lived as an ascetic and pursued the study of Scripture. In 379 he was ordained a priest. He then spent three years in Constantinople with the Eastern Father St. Gregory Nazianzen. In 382 he returned to Rome, where he became secretary to Pope Damasus I and gained much influence. Many persons placed themselves under his spiritual direction. He fixed his residence at Bethlehem in 386, where he pursued his literary labors and engaged in controversy with the heretics Jovinian and Vigilantius and the adherents of Pelagianism. Because of his conflict with the Pelagians, Jerome went into hiding for about two years. He died soon after his return to Bethlehem in 419 or 420.

[79] *De Viris Illustribus* 1 and 5, in Shotwell and Loomis, *See of Peter*, 115–16 (see also Fouard, *St. Peter and the First Years of Christianity*, 407). Again, no one challenges or dissents from St. Jerome's historical statement, for no one in the East or West would set himself up for ridicule by denying universally held historical facts. Jerome was a scholar par excellence who studied in Rome and traveled the Christian world. He had access to historical documents and information no longer extant. As the *Oxford Dictionary of the Christian Church* (ed. Cross and Livingstone) so aptly says (731): "Jerome's writings issued from a scholarship unsurpassed in the early Church." Concerning the twenty-five year reign of Peter in Rome, we read, "If we desire to establish with precision the date at which St. Peter came to Rome and the length of his stay we are not any longer in a position to prove anything *demonstratively*. There are sources which all of them speak of a period of twenty-five years in connection with St. Peter's Roman apostolate, but they disagree as to the date where this period begins and also as to the events with which it is connected" (Hughes, *History of the Church*, 1:64). It is likely that Peter was in Rome sporadically between A.D. 42 and 67 and that he ruled the Church even though traveling, preaching the gospel, and fulfilling his charge as steward of the kingdom. Even today, the Pope is still the bishop of Rome even when he takes extended missionary journeys.

fact of Peter's sojourn and bishopric in Rome. Not, that is, until the Reformation in the sixteenth century. Even though the apocryphal writings of the Gnostics and Ebionites made up hundreds of fables about St. Peter, even they never placed his martyrdom or episcopal see anywhere but in Rome. How could they have done so in the face of the overwhelming historical proofs in support of those facts? Why is it that some in the last few centuries would deny the historical evidence and claim instead that Peter had never been to Rome? The answer is simple and has to do with authority.

The fact that Peter presided over the Church of Rome has been challenged only in modern times, and only because of the unfounded "doctrine" of *sola Scriptura*, instigated in an attempt to refute the primacy of Rome. *Sola Scriptura* is a doctrine of late origin, dating only from the Protestant Reformation of the sixteenth century, though the idea was beginning to develop somewhat earlier with John Wycliffe (c. 1329–1384) and Jan Hus (1373–1415). *Sola Scriptura* is the assertion that the Bible alone is the final and only infallible authority for faith and practice. It says that, if a doctrine cannot be proved explicitly by Scripture, it cannot be binding on all Christians. Some go even farther. Some who hold to *sola Scriptura* would have us believe that, since the New Testament does not specifically state that Peter was in Rome,[80] he must never have been there, or, at best, we cannot be certain.[81] They ignore all historical evidence outside the New Testament itself. But the Bible itself never claims to give a full accounting of all early Christian history. Those who espouse such a closed-minded and unscholarly methodology are disingenuous. The Bible never tells us that Nero persecuted Christians in Rome either, yet no one would dismiss the historical data outside the confines of the New Testament and claim the horrendous persecution never happened.

---

[80] Although it is understood by scholars that Peter's greetings from "Babylon" in 1 Peter 5:13 is a clear indication that Peter was in Rome. "Babylon" was the common, derisive name given to Rome by first-century Jews and Christians.

[81] Loraine Boettner, in his anti-Catholic tome, writes, "The remarkable thing, however, about Peter's alleged bishopric in Rome, is that the New Testament has not one word to say about it. . . . There is in fact no New Testament evidence, nor any historical proof of any kind, that Peter ever was in Rome. All rests on legend" (*Roman Catholicism*, 117). These are amazing allegations in the face of the universally consistent and unanimous testimony of the primitive Church.

Very few documents survived the first few centuries of the Church. Paper and pens were not what they are today. We know that two of Paul's epistles have not survived.[82] It is not surprising there is not more about the last days of Peter and Paul, not to mention the other apostles laboring in the Lord's vineyard. But the documents that did survive through the centuries clearly attest to the historical reality of Peter's long-standing and authoritative presence in the city of Rome.

Peter's presence in Rome is also denied in order to support an uninformed attack on the teachings and authority of the Catholic Church. Denying Peter's presence in Rome supposedly allows one to deny the Church's teaching on the primacy of Peter in the See of Rome. In other words, a certain preconception forces many to deny historical evidence—good and sufficient evidence—in order to uphold novel traditions. But in the ancient Church even those in dissent never had the temerity to deny Peter's sojourn in Rome. "We do not have even the slightest trace that points to any *other* place which could be considered as the scene of his death. . . . It is a further important point that in the second and third centuries, when certain churches were in rivalry with the one in Rome, it never occurred to a single one of them to contest the claim of Rome that it was the scene of the martyrdom of Peter."[83]

We have presented evidence from antiquity to establish firmly Peter's presence in Rome, his position as bishop, and his ultimate death by crucifixion at the hands of Nero. We will look at the implications of our findings for the Church as she spreads over the whole world in the first centuries, projecting herself on a steady course toward the twenty-first century. But first we will look briefly at a few who have ignored the historical evidence and have attempted to repudiate the clear and consistent historical records of Peter's presence in Rome in order to promote their anti-Catholic agenda.

---

[82] 1 Cor 5:9; Col 4:16.

[83] Oscar Cullmann, *Peter: Disciple, Apostle, Martyr,* trans. Floyd V. Filson (Philadelphia: Westminster Press, 1953), 114–15.

THE OPPOSITION

It is amazing the extent to which many will go to deny Peter's presence and influence in Rome. Their staunch opposition to the Catholic Church prods them to conclusions that others, non-partisan in their assessment, would never dare hold. Protestant commentator Alan Stibbs, as quoted earlier, recognizes that only the immediate precursors of the Reformation and those who followed tried to "remove" Peter from Rome: "Only at and since the Reformation have some preferred to treat the word [Babylon in 1 Pet 5:13] literally as a reference either to Babylon in Mesopotamia or to a military station called Babylon in Egypt."[1] Oscar Cullmann notes that the Waldensians, a small sect that had its origins in Peter Valdes of Lyons (d. between 1205 and 1218), were the first to raise the question. He writes, "The question [of Peter's stay in Rome] was first raised in the Middle Ages by Christians for whom the Bible was the only norm, the Waldensians. . . . For the Waldensians, the silence of the Bible was quite decisive. . . . For the next two hundred years we hear nothing of a real attack upon the tradition. Not until 1519–1520 does an anonymous author write an essay contending 'that the apostle Peter was never in Rome'. For him, too, as for the Waldensians, the chief argument is the silence of the sacred Scripture."[2] Now, beginning with the Reformation, we will take a quick look at a few of those opponents who denied that Peter ever resided in Rome.

---

[1] *The First Epistle General to Peter*, Tyndale New Testament Commentaries (Grand Rapids, Mich.: Eerdmans, 1959), 176.

[2] Oscar Cullmann, *Peter: Disciple, Apostle, Martyr*, trans. Floyd V. Filson (Philadelphia: Westminster Press, 1953), 71–72.

John Calvin (1509–1564)[3]

In commenting on the passage in 1 Peter 5:13 ("She who is at Babylon . . . sends you greetings"), John Calvin, the French reformer, says, "Many of the old commentators thought that Rome is here symbolically denoted. The Papists gladly lay hold on this comment, so that Peter seems to have been head of the Church of Rome. The infamy of the name does not deter them, provided they can pretend to the title, nor do they care greatly about Christ, provided Peter is left to them. Provided they can retain only the name of Peter's chair, they will not refuse to locate Rome in the infernal regions. But this old comment has no color of truth, nor do I see why it was approved by Eusebius and others, except that they were already led astray by the error that Peter had been at Rome. Add the fact that they are inconsistent with themselves. . . .[4] Since Peter had Mark as his companion when he wrote this Epistle, it is very probable that he was at Babylon; and this was in accordance with his vocation, for we know that he was appointed an apostle especially to the Jews.[5] He therefore visited chiefly

---

[3] John Calvin was French by birth but lived in Geneva, Switzerland, most of his life. He was a Protestant reformer and, second to Luther, was a key figure in the Protestant Reformation. He is the father of Reformed theology.

[4] Calvin seems to be unaware of the overwhelming consistency of the historical witness in regard to Peter's presence in Rome. Admittedly, Calvin was deprived of many of the early writings that have only recently been brought to light. But still, there is no inconsistency in the early witness—in fact, the very opposite is true, as we have seen. Had the early writers been led astray by false teaching about Peter being in Rome? If so, where is *any* documentation refuting the declarations of history? Why did not the heretics, at least, stand up with opposition to the Roman Church? Why did they not challenge the ubiquitous assertion of Peter's bishopric in Rome? Why does no other city claim the presence and bones of Peter? Why is there utter silence from all quarters in refuting Peter's presence in Rome? All testify that he was there—none would dare assert otherwise.

It is interesting to note here that Calvin produces no evidence to support his objection other than speculation and anti-Catholic rhetoric. In other words, he asserts it on the basis of his own authority. In logic, there is a saying: *Quod gratis asseritur, gratis negatur* (What is asserted without proof, is denied without proof).

[5] Calvin asserts that because Peter was called to preach to the circumcised (the Jews) he would not have been in Rome; but it is well known that there was a large Jewish population residing in Rome. Historian Paul Johnson writes, "The diaspora [Jewish dispersion], through which Paul and others eagerly traveled, was vast. The Roman geographer Strabo [c. 60 B.C.–c. A.D. 21] said that the Jews

those parts of the world where there was the greatest number of that nation [Jews]."[6] There is a certain arrogance displayed here; for Calvin seems to be saying, "Everyone in the first fifteen centuries has been deceived, not one has understood, not even those who knew Peter and followed in his footsteps. I alone have known the truth about Peter." This disdain for history and precedent is typical of many of the Reformers and their progeny.[7] We will look at only four representative examples, though others could be multiplied.

Loraine Boettner

Karl Keating, a prominent Catholic apologist, writes, "Loraine Boettner's *Roman Catholicism* might be called the 'Bible' of the

---

were a power throughout the inhabited world. . . . They had been in Rome for 200 years and now formed a substantial colony there; and from Rome they had spread all over urban Italy, and then into Gaul and Spain and across the sea into north-west Africa" (*A History of the Jews* [New York: Harper & Row, 1987], 132). In fact, their presence became so dominant that Suetonius (fl. A.D. 117–138) tells us: "Since the Jews constantly made disturbances at the instigation of Chrestus, Claudius [reigned A.D. 41–57] expelled them from Rome" (*Eerdmans' Handbook to the History of Christianity*, ed. Tim Dowley [Grand Rapids, Mich.: Eerdmans, 1977], 53). Finally, Peter Davids corrects Calvin by informing us, "Naturally it is possible that 'Babylon' might mean the city by that name in Mesopotamia. Had Peter been traveling earlier in the century, that would have been possible, but during the reign of Claudius the Jewish community left Babylon for Seleucia (Josephus, *Ant.* 18.9.8–9), and that was about the same time that Peter had to leave Jerusalem due to the persecution of Herod Agrippa I. Furthermore, Babylon was in decline generally during the first century so that by 115 Trajan would find it a ghost town (Dio Cassius, *Hist.* 68.30). Finally, there is no Syrian tradition of Peter's having traveled in the Mesopotamian area. Thus it is highly unlikely that Peter would ever have been in Babylon at the same time as Silvanus (who, we know, traveled in Asia Minor and Greece with Paul). That leaves Rome as the only viable option. That Rome was referred to as Babylon in both Jewish and Christian sources is known" (Peter Davids, *The First Epistle of Peter*, The New International Commentary on the New Testament [Grand Rapids, Mich.: Eerdmans, 1990], 202).

[6] *Calvin's New Testament Commentaries* (Grand Rapids, Mich.: Eerdmans, 1963), 12:322–23.

[7] Martin Luther actually concludes that "Babylon" in 1 Peter 5:13 refers to the city of Rome; however he goes on, "But I am willing to give everyone freedom here to interpret this verse as he chooses, for it is not vital" (*The Catholic Epistles*, in *Luther's Works*, ed. Jaroslav Pelikan [St. Louis, Mo.: Concordia Pub., 1967], 30:144).

anti-Catholic movement within fundamentalism. It is in this book that the anti-Catholic position is most extensively expressed. *Roman Catholicism* is worth examining, because what credibility the anti-Catholic movement has depends largely on the credibility of this one volume."[8]

Taking Keating's advice, we will see what Loraine Boettner has to say about Peter's presence and martyrdom in Rome. "According to Roman Catholic tradition Peter was the first bishop of Rome, his pontificate lasted twenty-five years, from 42 to 67 A.D., and he was martyred in Rome in 67 A.D. The Douay and Confraternity versions say that he was in Rome before the Jerusalem council of Acts 15, and that he returned to Jerusalem for that council, after which he went to Antioch, and then returned to Rome.[9] . . . The remarkable thing, however, about Peter's alleged bishopric in Rome, is that the New Testament has not one word to say about it.[10] The word Rome occurs only nine times in the Bible and never is Peter mentioned in connection with it. There is no allusion to Rome in either of his epistles. . . . There is in fact no

---

[8] Karl Keating, *Catholicism and Fundamentalism* (San Francisco: Ignatius Press, 1988), 28.

[9] The exact chronology as recited by Boettner is not part of official Catholic teaching as Boettner implies. Boettner's source is the introduction to *1 Peter* in the *Confraternity Bible*, which never claims that its introduction and explanatory comments are the final, authoritative, and infallible word on the details of Peter's life, any more than Ryrie's or Scofield's notes are considered to be the final, inspired word of God when they comment on select biblical background. They are meant to be guidelines and interpretations of historical research.

[10] One may think it strange that the Bible has little to say about Peter's apostolic ministry after he fled Herod's persecution in Jerusalem. We know very little about the first decade of the early Church, considering that the first twelve chapters of the Acts of the Apostles cover an astounding *ten years*. Actually, we know very little about many things that happened in the decades after the Ascension of Christ. The brief history contained in Acts covers over three decades and gives us precious few details. The first generations of Christians understood truth to be deposited in the Church, not solely in a book. Why is it surprising that we do not find a full account of Peter's later years? Is it not also surprising that the Scriptures give us so little information on the ministries of the other apostles? The burden of proof is not on the Catholic to prove Peter was in Rome; that has been accomplished overwhelmingly. The burden of proof lies with those who dismiss history, documents, and the early witness in an attempt to resist a dogma they dislike. Boettner has no argument, no evidence, but must defend on silence alone, and without evidence he can make no substantive case.

New Testament evidence, nor any historical proof of any kind, that Peter was in Rome. All rests on legend. . . . But there is no good reason for saying that 'Babylon' means 'Rome'."[11] One must ask why Boettner ignores the overwhelming testimony of the early Christians. Does he consider all the written documents of the first centuries to be "legends", even the documents that came out of the theological councils of the Church that defined the doctrines of the Blessed Trinity and the deity of Christ and those in which the canon of the New Testament was determined? Does he also consider all the other matters of history and fact from the same decades and centuries to be legends, or only those things that conflict with his tradition? Does he have proof of Peter being elsewhere? Absolutely not. Can he quote other sources or traditions that would support an opposing view? No. He has simply turned a blind eye in his loyalty to novel Fundamentalist notions.[12]

Harry A. Ironside (d. 1951)
—former Pastor of Moody Memorial Church in Chicago

The well-known Fundamentalist writer and preacher Harry A. Ironside peppers his commentaries and books with "anti-Romist" rhetoric. It is obvious in places that his conclusions are drawn not from scholarship as much as from a deeply embedded anti-Catholic bias. A simple example is found in his commentary entitled *James and Peter*, where he states, "This Letter is written at

---

[11] Loraine Boettner, *Roman Catholicism* (Philadelphia: Presbyterian and Reformed Pub., 1962), 117, 120. This is such an absurd statement in light of the scholarly work done on this matter that it deserves no comment. There are no reputable scholars today who deny that Peter went to Rome and that "Babylon", a term used by Jews and Christians alike in the first century, does indeed refer to the pagan and corrupt city of Rome.

[12] For anyone who has surveyed some of the historical and archeological evidence of the presence of Peter in Rome, it is almost humorous, if not sad, to read Boettner's summary paragraph: "The doctrine of the primacy of Peter is just one more of the many errors that the Church of Rome has added to the Christian religion. With the exposure of that fallacy the foundation of the Roman Church is swept away. The whole papal system stands or falls depending on whether or not Peter was a pope in Rome, and neither the New Testament nor reliable historical records give any reason to believe that he ever held that position or that he ever was in Rome" (ibid., 124). One wonders just how much evidence Boettner requires.

Babylon, which Romanists claim was pagan Rome."[13] Since the "Romanists" believe Rome is the See of Peter, the Fundamentalists must try to prove that Peter never traveled there, in an attempt to undermine the continuity of Catholic teaching, yet here again we see not a shred of evidence to substantiate their claim. Ironside makes the assertion based on his own authority.

Jimmy Swaggart
   —author and television evangelist

One of the main arguments used by Fundamentalists against the presence of Peter in Rome is based on silence. They observe that Paul, when he wrote his epistle to the Romans in about A.D. 58, does not mention Peter by name, which "proves" that Peter was never in Rome. Jimmy Swaggart, in his popular book *Catholicism & Christianity*, comes to this dogmatic conclusion: "Peter *may* have passed through or visited Rome at some time, but there is not a hint of scriptural evidence to confirm this. (Furthermore, outside of much-quoted, Catholic 'traditions,' neither is there any *historical* evidence of Peter's presence in Rome.) . . . [Turning to Paul's epistle to the Romans:] Since Peter was not mentioned here by Paul, it can be concluded with some certainty that he *was not there at that time!* This, of course, undermines the very *foundation* of the claimed apostolic succession of the Roman bishops. If Peter had been in Rome as bishop (as the Roman Catholic church claims), he would have been the first one to whom Paul would have referred! It is therefore a waste of time to consider such a groundless theory. To be frank, it is unlikely that Peter ever even *saw* the city of Rome in his lifetime!"[14]

Based on silence alone, a silence that can be easily explained, Swaggart totally dismisses Peter's presence in Rome as a "waste of time" and a "groundless theory". Not once does he mention the overwhelming historical witness of the first centuries, nor does he mention the fact that Peter's presence in Rome was considered a historical fact through all the early years of the Church. He offers not one piece of evidence to support his theory other than the

---

[13] Harry A. Ironside, *James and Peter* (Neptune, N.J.: Loizeaux Bros., 1947), 61.

[14] Jimmy Swaggart, *Catholicism & Christianity* (Baton Rouge, La.: Jimmy Swaggart Ministries, 1986), 23–24; emphasis his.

silence in Romans. He dismisses two thousand years of Christian history without one shred of supporting evidence.

Why Was Peter Not Mentioned in Paul's Epistle to the Romans?

Arguments from silence alone, without substantive evidence, are very unconvincing and are usually the only supports available for unhistorical and untenable theories. The fact that Paul does not mention Peter in Romans does not prove that Peter had never been in Rome.[15] There are many plausible reasons why Paul does not mention Peter. *First,* there is the possibility that Peter was traveling extensively at the time, preaching the gospel in other provinces, using Rome as a home base; or he may have been assisting a Church in another locale. Since he had been commissioned the "apostle to the circumcised", he would have felt obliged to travel the known world preaching to the Jews of the diaspora. Rome was probably his home base, at the center of the Empire and the center of the Church. We know, even from Paul's epistles, that Peter traveled widely, accompanied by his wife (1 Cor 9:5).

Second, it would be very probable, and certainly within the correct time frame (A.D. 49), that Peter had been expelled from Rome, along with all other Jews, by the decree of Emperor Claudius, possibly leaving behind only a small remnant of Gentile Christians. As already mentioned, we know that Claudius evicted all Jews from Rome because of disturbances caused by "Chrestus", which probably refers to Christ, in which case Peter, the leader of the "Jewish Chrestus sect", would have certainly been the first to be evicted.[16] Romans was written, according to most estimates,

---

[15] Paul is silent about the means, persons involved in, and time of the founding of the Roman Church other than to acknowledge that the foundation in Rome had already been laid, presumably by an apostle. This silence does not mean that Peter was not in Rome, nor does it deny that Peter was the founder of the Church in Rome. We know each Church had prominent leaders, Rome being no exception, and yet Paul does not address anyone in particular in his epistle. We certainly cannot conclude from this that the Church in Rome *had* no leadership. But if it did, why did Paul not address it as such? For a discussion of various arguments against Peter's being in Rome based on the silence of Romans and the rebuttals, refer to Michael Grant's biography *Saint Peter* (New York: Scribner's, 1995), 147–51.

[16] Suetonius, *Life of Claudius,* "The Twelve Caesars", chap. 25, sect. 4. We also have the expulsion of Jews confirmed by Luke in Acts 18:12: "After this he [Paul]

sometime in the mid-first century, which might easily have coincided with the period when the Jews were expelled.

Third, persecutions were a horrible reality in the first century, and it was a certain death sentence to be appointed bishop of Rome.[17] No Christian would have voluntarily exposed Peter or other leaders to harm, making them vulnerable to Roman retribution. Thus, risk of exposure provides another plausible reason for the silence in Paul's epistle. "The most ordinary prudence would make St. Paul avoid mentioning St. Peter as Bishop of Rome in written documents which might fall into the hands of the enemies of the Church. . . . Any hint that the head of the Church had taken up his abode in Rome, or was founding the See in the very heart of the Roman Empire would be disastrous if it came into the hands of the enemies of the Church. The Christians were most careful not to allow the movements and official acts of their Bishops to become known to the authorities of pagan society. St. Paul's remark that he was not going to build on 'another man's foundation' was sufficient reference for those to whom he was writing."[18]

Fourth, Paul may not have mentioned Peter because he may have been writing to a specific group within the larger Christian community in Rome. He does not address the community with the word "*church*" as he does his other epistles but instead addresses "all in Rome" in a general sort of way, as one who is unfamiliar with the landscape of the community there. He closes the last chapter by acknowledging what appear to be Christians of his personal

---

left Athens and went to Corinth. And he found a Jew named Aquila, a native of Pontus, lately come from Italy with his wife Priscilla, because Claudius had commanded all the Jews to leave Rome."

[17] Most, if not all, of the first thirty Roman bishops died as martyrs for their faith because they were leaders of the Church—they were lightning rods. To become the bishop of Rome was to accept martyrdom and to sign one's death warrant. Even Luther acknowledged, "That the Roman Church is more honored by God than all others is not to be doubted. St. Peter and St. Paul, forty-six Popes, some hundreds of thousands of martyrs, have laid down their lives in its communion, having overcome Hell and the world; so that the eyes of God rest on the Roman Church with special favor" (Letter of Martin Luther to Pope Leo X, January 6, 1519, in Patrick F. O'Hare's *The Facts about Luther* [Rockford, Ill.: TAN Books, 1987], 356).

[18] Leslie Rumble, *Radio Replies*, ed. with Charles M. Carty (1938; reprint, Rockford, Ill.: TAN Books, 1979), 2:92.

acquaintance. The Christian community in Rome was under-
standably large by A.D. 54, for we know the population of Rome
itself at the time far exceeded one million people.[19] Paul may have
been writing to a group of acquaintances to encourage them
during persecution and to bolster them in the faith, expecting the
epistles to be passed around to all the Christians in the vicinity.
Also, F. F. Bruce shows that Romans has come down to us with a
variety of endings, indicating the possibility that as the epistle
arrived in Rome, or as it was passed around, various endings were
attached or deleted depending upon the recipients. Bruce writes,
"There are a number of indications in the textual history of Romans that it circulated not only in the form in which we know it
but in one or even two shorter editions. These indications appear
mainly towards the end of the Epistle, but there are two pieces of
possibly significant evidence at the beginning."[20] He goes on to
show that several versions did not contain the phrase "in Rome"
and that there is "evidence for two shorter editions of the
Epistle—one ending at 15:33 and the other ending at 14:23."[21]
This could confirm the hypothesis that Paul was writing to several
small or local groups.

Fifth, it is quite possible that Paul *does* mention Peter in an
oblique manner both in his epistle and by revealing his travel
plans. Paul explains that he has not come to Rome because another man had already laid the foundation in that city. He writes,
"I have fully preached the gospel of Christ, thus making it my
ambition to preach the gospel, not where Christ has already been
named, lest I build on another man's foundation. . . . This is the
reason why I have so often been hindered from coming to you. But
now, since I no longer have any room for work in these regions,

---

[19] Protestant biblical scholar James Dunn writes, "Paul knew very few of the
purely local Christians in Rome, and . . . the Christians he actually does greet
were only a relatively small proportion of the overall Christian community. The
same chapter of Romans [16] confirms that the Christians must have met in a
number of house churches. . . . If the above deductions are correct, there must
have been at least several other house churches unknown personally to Paul"
(*Romans 1–8*, Word Biblical Commentary [Waco, Tex: Word Books, 1988],
38a:lii).

[20] F. F. Bruce, *The Epistle of Paul to the Romans*, Tyndale New Testament Commentaries (Grand Rapids, Mich.: Eerdmans, 1975), 25.

[21] Ibid., 28.

and since I have longed for many years to come to you, I hope to see you in passing as I go to Spain, and to be sped on my journey there by you, once I have enjoyed your company for a little" (Rom 15:19–20, 22–24). This passage makes it clear that someone had already founded the Church in Rome prior to the time of Paul's writing, some time near A.D. 54–58.[22] Paul had been hindered from coming to Rome because he was called to preach where the gospel had not yet been proclaimed. Paul says that someone, "another man", presumably an apostle (Eph 2:20), had already laid the foundation of the Church in Rome.[23] Paul therefore had reason to believe that the Roman Church had already been well founded (Rom 15:20); and even when he did plan on visiting Rome, he only intended to "pass through" and go by "way of you to Spain" (Rom 15:24, 28). Had the Roman Church been founded simply by stragglers from Jerusalem and other regions, and the Christian community planted by non-apostolic travelers, Paul would have felt obliged to become the establishing apostle. Obviously that was not the case.

John Calvin, as we have already seen, denies that Peter ever ventured to Rome, the "infernal regions", and thinks that anyone who disagrees with him is "led astray", even those of antiquity. Yet in his commentary on the Epistle of Paul to the Romans, Calvin writes, "It is not to be regarded as a fault that a successor was

---

[22] The Greek phrase "another man's foundation" is singular in number, implying a single apostle had already preached the gospel in Rome and had established the Church. Non-Catholics James T. Shotwell and Louise Ropes Loomis write, "The one most telling text in favor of regarding Peter as the founder of the Roman church is the reference of Paul in the fifteenth chapter of Romans (v. 20), when he says that he would not 'build upon another man's foundation,' which in view of the relations between Peter and Paul has been taken to refer to Peter. From the second century on, there was no doubt of the matter" (*The See of Peter* [1927; reprint, New York: Columbia Univ. Press, 1991], 59).

[23] Dunn, in his two-volume commentary on Romans, contends, "Klein has argued on the basis of Romans 15:20 that Paul thought the Christian community in Rome lacked an apostolic foundation and therefore intended to evangelize Rome itself. This is farfetched. . . . [Paul's] careful language of 15:24 ('passing through') and 15:28 ('by way of you to Spain') is just what we would expect from Paul writing to a church in whose founding he had played no part. . . . In accordance with Paul's theology of apostleship the existence of Christian groups in Rome was itself evidence of an 'apostolic foundation' " (*Romans 1–8*, 38a:lv, lvi).

appointed to fill the place of the apostle who established the Church [in Rome]. We may, therefore, regard the apostles as the founders of the Church, while the pastors who succeed them have the duty of protecting and also increasing the structure that they have erected. Paul refers to any foundation which has been laid by some other apostle as 'another man's foundation'." [24] The question then arises, especially for Calvin: If the foundation had already been laid in Rome, and laying foundations is the particular work of apostles, then which apostle laid the foundation in Rome? Which apostle does the early Church claim founded the Church in Rome? The "mystery" was no mystery at all until anti-Catholic prejudices compelled their adherents to create mysteries where none existed. The first Christians, and subsequent heirs of the faith through the centuries, would simply have said, "There is no mystery; we know from the Scriptures and the Fathers that Peter laid the apostolic foundations in Rome!"

Sixth, there is the distinct possibility that Paul and Peter were not the best of friends and that Paul would not go out of his way to see or write to Peter at this point in his ministry. Although this is a purely speculative explanation, there is evidence enough in Scripture that Paul had a strong and independent personality and had conflicts with more than one person. There is no reason to believe that these men, though great apostles and servants of God, did not have character flaws and interpersonal conflicts. [25] For one example, we can look at Acts 15:37–40: "And Barnabas was desirous of taking John, called Mark, along with them also. But Paul kept insisting that they should not take him along who had deserted them in Pamphylia and had not gone with them to the work. And there arose such a sharp disagreement that they separated from one another, and Barnabas took Mark with him and sailed away to Cyprus. But Paul chose Silas and departed." Barnabas and Paul

---

[24] *Calvin's New Testament Commentaries,* trans. T. H. L. Parker (Grand Rapids, Mich.: Eerdmans, 1965), 8:313.

[25] The record is sparse. There are passages that may imply respect and honor between the parties. In the second epistle of Peter, the writer refers to "our beloved brother Paul" (2 Pet 3:15). Even though Paul had the courage to oppose Peter to his face (Gal 2:11), there is no reason to assume personal animosity or hostility. The fact that he felt free enough to confront Peter in such a way implies a solid working relationship based on mutual goals and theological understandings.

had been "set apart" by the Holy Spirit to work together (Acts 13:2) and now are separated by sharp contention. What God had joined together, acute disagreement now split apart. John Mark later became Peter's "right hand" and interpreter in Rome and put Peter's gospel in writing. Peter affectionately refers to him as "my son Mark" (1 Pet 5:13). It is not inconceivable that Paul avoided Peter and Mark in Rome and for this reason failed to mention them in his epistle.

The possible explanations for Paul's silence concerning Peter in Rome abound. It must be remembered that the Scriptures are relatively silent on the later years of Peter's and Paul's lives, and it is here that the history and tradition of the early Church give us the information we need to fill in the gaps. This very tradition passed down though the writings of the Church was virtually unchallenged for sixteen centuries. Serious attempts to discredit the presence and primacy of Peter in the See of Rome only began through the impetus of the Protestant revolt.

To conclude this section we will provide three last quotations. The first is from the *Encyclopedia Britannica*, commenting on recent excavations in Rome, which confirm the early Christians' conviction that Peter was martyred and buried in Rome beneath the site of the basilica.[26] "In the early 4th century, the emperor Constantine (died A.D. 337) with considerable difficulty erected a basilica on the Vatican Hill. The difficulty of the task, combined with the comparative ease with which this great church might have been built on level ground only a slight distance to the south, may support the contention that the Emperor was convinced that the relics of Peter rested beneath the small Aedicula (shrine for a small statue) over which he had erected the ba-

---

[26] In the autumn of 1995, I had the privilege of touring the Necropolis ("City of the Dead") under St. Peter's Basilica in the Vatican City. The excavations leave little doubt that Peter was buried beneath the dome of St. Peter's, which was at the time Vatican Hill near Nero's Circus. For more information, see *Guide to the Vatican Necropolis*, by Michele Basso (Fabbrica di S. Pietro in Vaticano, 1968), which carefully describes the mausoleums beneath St. Peter's. Also see John Evangelist Walsh, *The Bones of St. Peter* (Garden City, N.Y.: Image Books, 1985), which gives a full description of the thirty-year excavations under the Vatican and the discovery and authentication of the bones of St. Peter. Oscar Cullmann concludes his section on the excavations by saying, "The excavations speak in favour of the report that *the execution of Peter took place in the Vatican district*" (*Peter*, 152, ital. in original).

silica."[27] We read further on the topic: "Most [scholars] would agree at the very least, however, that the excavations reveal that some Roman Christians of the early 3rd century believed that Peter's grave was on that site. This adds further weight to the already weighty tradition of Peter's presence at Rome—a tradition attested to by several important pieces of literary evidence from c. 96 onward, emanating from Africa and Asia Minor as well as from Rome itself, challenged by no rival tradition and contested by no contemporary witness."[28]

Second, let's examine a passage from Protestant Oscar Cullmann's book *Peter*: "In the following period the denial of the Roman tradition about Peter was almost universally abandoned. A man like Ernest Renan assumed as a fact Peter's stay in Rome, and in the year 1897 it was the Protestant theologian and historian A. Harnack who wrote the notable sentence that the denial of the Roman stay of Peter is 'an error which today is clear to every scholar who is not blind.' So one had the impression that the tradition was finally confirmed. Harnack was of the opinion that 'the martyr death of Peter at Rome was once contested by reason of tendentious Protestant prejudices, and then by reason of tendentious critical prejudices.' " After listing primary critics since Harnack against Peter's stay in Rome, Cullmann concludes that even among Protestants "the general tendency, even with regard to the literary witnesses, seems indeed to be moving in the direction of accepting the Roman stay of Peter."[29] After surveying the whole of the debate through the centuries, Cullmann concludes his historical survey in this manner, "In summary of our entire historical section, to the end of which we now have come, we must say that during the life time of Peter he held a pre-eminent position among the disciples; that after Christ's death he presided over the church at Jerusalem in the first years; that he then became the leader of the Jewish Christian mission; that, in this capacity, at a time which cannot be more closely determined but probably occurred at the end of his life, he came to Rome and there, after a very short work, died as a martyr under Nero."[30]

---

[27] "Peter the Apostle, Saint", in *The New Encyclopedia Britannica* (Chicago, Ill.: Encyclopedia Britannica, 1981), 14:156.

[28] "Papacy", in ibid., 13:955.

[29] Cullmann, *Peter*, 74, 77.

[30] Ibid., 152.

And finally, Protestant scholar F. F. Bruce, in his conclusion that Peter had indeed been martyred in Rome, states, "This event [the death of Peter in Rome] may justly be called indubitable because, in Hans Lietzmann's words: 'All the early sources about the year 100 A.D. become clear and easily intelligible, and agree with their historical context and with each other, if we accept what they plainly suggest to us—namely, that Peter sojourned in Rome and died a martyr there. Any other hypothesis regarding Peter's death piles difficulty upon difficulty and cannot be supported by a single document.' "[31]

---

[31] Hans Lietzmann, *Petrus und Paulus in Rome* (Berlin, 1927), 238, quoted by Bruce in *Peter, Stephen, James and John* (Grand Rapids, Mich.: Eerdmans, 1979), 46.

PART TWO

THE PRIMACY OF PETER
IN THE SEE OF ROME

OLDEST DOCUMENTS
Earliest Christian Documents Reveal the Primacy of Peter in the See of Rome

As the saying goes, the closer one gets to the source of a spring, the clearer, purer, and cooler the water. In history as well, it is helpful to read original sources and discover how contemporaries understood the events and beliefs of the time. When we read the earliest documents of the Church, we find the primacy of Rome and papal supremacy to be deeply embedded and thoroughly understood in the life of the primitive Church. This understanding has been vociferously contested in some quarters, but we will allow the ancient Church to speak for herself.

What do we mean by saying that the primacy of Rome was at the heart of the primitive Church? Protestants often chide that the Papacy of today little resembles the leadership of the first-century Church—and to a degree this is true. I remember watching television clips of the Pope riding through the throngs of his adoring fans, safely ensconced in his very expensive "Pope-mobile", protecting him from the people. I used to watch with contempt, thinking, "Why are all those millions of 'Catholic faithful' so duped by all this 'pomp and circumstance'? Can you imagine Peter or, worse yet, Jesus, riding in one of those protective vehicles?"[1]

So, I watched and chuckled until I did finally step out of my "cloistered" Evangelical tradition and began to read history, study the Fathers, search the Scriptures, and understand the implications of one holy, catholic, and apostolic Church. Was the

---

[1] I remembered later that Peter and Paul often were in similar situations. Throngs of adoring and curious people flocked to see and touch these men of God. Handkerchiefs and aprons that had been close to Paul "were carried away from his body to the sick" (Acts 19:12), and people threw themselves at Peter, so that "at least his shadow might fall on some of them" (Acts 5:15). They often needed protection, though it was usually the civil government that acted as the first-century "Pope-mobile" (Acts 21:30ff.). Even Jesus had to take shelter from the crowd, getting into a boat and pushing off from the shore "lest they should crush him" (Mk 3:9).

Catholic Church of today to be identified, organically, with the Church of the first centuries? How would a small group of illegal sectarians gathering around an uneducated group of fishermen and tax collectors change or develop as it grew? How would that group—if it maintained its organic unity, its universal and structural cohesiveness—look in twenty years? In fifty years? When it became a legal entity? When it spread to other lands? When it grew to a billion strong? How would the demands of the Petrine office change? How would the leadership of this burgeoning household develop over time to handle the growth, the responsibilities, Judaism, Gnosticism, heresies, persecutions, the pressures of paganism, imperial Rome, schism, barbarism, Islam, the Enlightenment, the Reformation, Modernism, Communism, secular humanism, internal and external dissent? The office of Peter, the See of Rome, the Pope in all his glory—or as a bloodied martyr of the faith—has remained and flourished as the longest existing Western institution. It stands as the ideal contradiction: the weakest of men (Peter, for example) with no military might or soldiers in arms, yet outlasting the mightiest of kings and the strongest of empires. I rejoice that I stepped out of my comfort zone.

No one professes to find in the primitive communities an exact duplicate of every practice or a "literal transcript of the present situation. What, then, do we ourselves mean when we say that the papal *régime* was in existence in the earliest beginnings of Christianity? The question really is as to whether the alleged counterpart in the early Church differs from its successor in the present, in substance, in principle, in essential features. Is the difference, for instance, between the papal *régime* of today and the position of the Papacy in the first four centuries of the Christian era more than between the oak and the acorn?[2] Does the difference be-

---

[2] "It would be as foolish to imagine the first Pope carried on a *sedia gestatoria* [portable throne], attended by *flabelli* [ostrich feather fans], as to conceive of King Merovic seated on a throne, surrounded by a throng of courtiers and ceremonies, such as were customary at the court of Louis XIV. The first of the Sovereign Pontiffs was in no way distinguishable by his dress from the laity and priests around him. The title of Pope was applied exclusively to his successors only in the sixth century. The Bishop, the *Episcopus* of Rome, lived as the heads of other Christian communities, sharing everything in common with the poor. . . . Nor were the religious duties of the Bishop of Rome in any way different

tween the two argue a dissimilarity of constituent elements, or is it merely the necessary difference between various stages of normal growth?" [3] Is the acorn of today not clearly represented by the oak of tomorrow? Do they appear exactly the same at first glance? No. Yet would any deny that what the oak is, in its substance and organic nature, the acorn is as well? The oak is in the acorn and is the result of organic and necessary development.

What about the outward appearance of the egg and sperm, the zygote, the fetus, the newborn, the infant, the toddler, the child, the pubescent, the adolescent, the adult, and finally the aged? Are they the same in identity and substance? When an elderly gentleman shows a friend his baby picture, does his friend scoff and say, "That couldn't be you, there is no resemblance!" Is it hard to believe that both accurately portray the same person? Is the mature corporation, with thousands of employees, an intricate hierarchy, and multiple locations, essentially different in nature and identity from the fledgling company that got its start in the owner's dining room? Are not the differences merely the necessary changes demanded by growth and development?

The Church began with twelve inadequate men scattering in fear at the assassination of their rabbi (Mk 14:50), who regathered with 120 people, huddled, again in fear, in an upper room (Acts 1:15). The Holy Spirit descended (Acts 2), and Peter spoke, explaining and defining God's New Covenant and opening the door of the Church to the Jewish nation. For roughly the first decade,

---

from those of the other bishops. In the early days, the meetings of the faithful took place in the Synagogues, but very soon they came to be held in private houses, such as the house of Aquila or Prisca [and later in church buildings]" (F. Mourret, *The Papacy*, trans. Robert Eaton, Catholic Library of Religious Knowledge, vol. 18 [St. Louis, Mo.: B. Herder Book Co., 1931], 7–8). Interestingly enough, we find believers meeting in private homes, but never do we find the use of "church" buildings in the New Testament. Development has occurred, and even Protestants have gladly benefited from it. How many, for instance, still worship in the temple (Acts 5:12) or hold worship in private homes as a non-negotiable Bible requirement? Just as one would not expect Peter to ride in a "Pope-mobile", so one would not expect to see William Bradford, a leader of the *Mayflower*'s Pilgrims, seated in front of the United States Congress presenting a State of the Union Address, or the anointed boy David surrounded by all the regalia of King Solomon's final days.

[3] Luke Rivington, *The Primitive Church and the See of Peter* (London: Longmans, Green and Co., 1894), xix.

the Church was made up of exclusively Jewish converts (Acts 10:44–48). As a result of Pentecost, there were three thousand Jewish converts added that day (Acts 2:5, 41).

The Church already looked different from what she looked like only a few days earlier. Are we sure she was the same Church? Over the next weeks and months, "the Lord was adding to their number day by day those who were being saved" (Act 2:47). All things were held in common; private property was sold and shared with those who were in need. The office of deacon was established (even invented, one could say), not based on any recorded decree or suggestion of Jesus, but out of the need for structure as the organism grew (Acts 6:1–6; 1 Tim 3:8). Bishops are first mentioned as Church leaders in Philippians 1:1 and Acts 20:28, a good thirty years after the gift of the Holy Spirit was poured out.[4] Why did the early Church have to introduce bishops? When would this ecclesiastical development cease? About a decade after Pentecost, the face of the Church altered as she received the first Gentile converts, the household of Cornelius, the Roman centurion (Acts 10). Gentiles were received into the Church without the need of prior circumcision. Many of the Jewish believers were scandalized—the Church was not what she *was*, she had gone awry. Change upon change, development upon development, organic growth and adaptations were spreading in every direction.

The "baby" Church grew larger, even spreading out of her geographical confines to cities in other countries, such as Antioch (Acts 11:19–26). But the Church also grew from within, organically; and, before the end of the first century, the newborn developed into an infant and then into a toddler. No longer limited to the Jewish temple for worship, it now moved into private homes (Rom 16:5; 1 Cor 16:19), taking on a distinctive liturgy separate from temple worship. Should a red flag have gone up when they moved out of Solomon's portico in the temple?[5] In Paul's earlier epistles, he was concerned with the salvation of the Gentiles through faith apart from circumcision and the law, but in his later epistles it is clear he is concerned about the hierarchical structure

---

[4] The only possible exception is Acts 1:20, in which Matthias takes over the "office" of Judas Iscariot. This office is that of bishop but applied here only to a position within the Twelve, not to a general office outside the original witnesses to the life, death, and Resurrection of Jesus.

[5] Acts 3:11; 5:12.

of the young Church. He, along with the other apostles, began to set up the second generation of leadership, to carry the tradition and sound teaching into the third generation (2 Tim 2:2; Acts 20:28; 1 Tim 3:2; Titus 1:5–9, and so on). Bishops (overseers) were appointed to stand in the place of the apostles (Titus 1:5). Who authorized this development away from the simple organization of the first years? Why do we hear so much now of bishops, deacons, and the like? And who gave the apostles and elders authority to dictate how the Gentiles were to act, live, and eat (Acts 15:1–29)? It is one thing for the apostles to exercise spiritual and judicial authority over the believers, but where do we find Jesus authorizing "elders" (πρεσβύτεροι) to rule in the Church? Is this not a red flag warning believers of a shift away from the simplicity of the early days?

Preaching marked the first days of the infant Church. In fact, there is no record of writing being stressed, either by Jesus or by his apostles. Preaching was the primary means of relaying the truth of God to the people of God (1 Th 2:13). The word preached and the practices taught came to form a tradition that was binding upon the believers. This happened well before the "teaching" was put into any written format. Paul tells the believers to obey and to adhere to the tradition he left with them.[6] The writings of the apostles soon took on an authoritative cast and were equated with or supplemented the oral tradition.[7] And not until several centuries later were these apostolic writings collected and canonized, recognized as inspired and infallible texts, equal in authority to those of the Old Testament Scriptures. What a development, especially when there was no promise from Jesus or any other reason to believe that such a "book" would emerge!

The Church spread throughout the Empire, and the word "Church" gained an adjective, *catholic*,[8] to describe her—a word

---

[6] 1 Cor 11:2: "I commend you because you remember me in everything and maintain the traditions even as I have delivered them to you." And: 2 Th 3:6: "Now we command you, brethren, in the name of our Lord Jesus Christ, that you keep away from any brother who is living in idleness and not in accord with the tradition that you received from us."

[7] 2 Th 2:15: "So then, brethren, stand firm and hold to the traditions which you were taught by us, either by word of mouth or by letter." See also 2 Pet 3:15.

[8] "Let that be deemed a proper Eucharist, which is [administered] either by the bishop, or by one to whom he has entrusted it. Wherever the bishop shall

that simply meant universal, for she embraced all peoples, in all lands, for all times. She was already the "one, holy, catholic, and apostolic Church", as the Nicene Creed would declare two centuries later. The organic development has continued to blossom from within; and, like the small mustard seed, she has grown strong and stout, quite different in appearance, but now, like a mustard tree, able to accommodate all the birds of the air (Mt 13:31–32).

And so the Church developed as she grew but did not change her organic nature or her Christ-established essence. The growth did not contradict what had gone before but rather complemented it in an essential unity with the Church's past stages of development. Under the pressure of increasing size, theological deviations, and persecution in the first century, leadership solidified and became layered, as is essential for the growth of any organization. This process was first developed and set in motion during the life of the apostles. It was a process of maturation that was fundamental to the organism and vital to its growth. The result of that growth in our age is still known as the Catholic Church and is essentially the same as the acorn planted two thousand years ago. The body is now in adulthood and bears the same marks as it did in the first century: oneness, holiness, catholicity, and apostolicity—in short, the Catholic Church. The development of the Church and of doctrine and leadership is simply part of the expected growth of her organic structure.[9]

---

appear, there let the multitude [of the people] also be; even as, wherever Jesus Christ is, there is the Catholic Church" (St. Ignatius of Antioch, *Epistle to the Smyrnaeans* 8, written c. A.D. 106, ANF 1:89–90).

[9] Regarding the organic and proper development of the papal office, we have the wisdom of Thomas Allies: "It follows, from what has just been said, that while 'the Apostolic Principate received by Peter from the Lord' was the root and womb of the whole hierarchy, not only in principle but in historic fact, the exercise of that Primacy was during these three centuries—as it has continued to be in every succeeding century—proportionate to the state and condition of the Church. Its action during the ages of persecution will be different from its action in a subsequent age, when the Roman State has acknowledged the Church; or again, from another period, when the whole order of civil government has been interfered with by the wandering of the nations. Not everything which follows from the idea of the Primacy was actually drawn out in the first centuries, just as not every work which the Church was to do had then been actually done. An Episcopate in which the three great Sees of Peter exercised a

In this section of our study on Peter and the See of Rome, we will look at two of the very first documents of the Christian era outside the New Testament documents. The "infant" Church seen in these early writings displays the essential characteristics of the later "adult" Church. According to the Fathers, both of the writers we will analyze were contemporaries of the apostles, and both of them were acquainted with them to varying degrees. Early tradition informs us that the Apostle Peter personally ordained these two men himself.[10]

---

sort of triumvirate in the Church was sufficient for the needs of those times. Until the emperor had bowed his head to the Church there was no danger of bishops dwelling at his court, entering into intrigues for his favour, countenancing the introduction of spiritual privileges for the exaltation of a particular church which was not grounded on descent from Peter, but on proximity to the emperor. The Primacy grew with the Church. Nor were the Popes themselves careful to draw out all that was contained in their Primacy before the time which needed each particular exertion of it. In the great order of government, at the head of which they stood, the bishops throughout the world had, as a rule, been constant in their faith. Penetrated as they were with the sense of the divine origin of the magistracy which each of them administered, they were not tempted to encroach upon the territory of their brethren. They had enough to do to live in any peace with the pagan empire. The rules of their forefathers were scrupulously followed by them" (*The Throne of the Fisherman* [London: Burns & Oates, 1887], 97–98). For an excellent discussion of the biblical basis and necessity of doctrinal development, especially regarding the Papacy, read *An Essay on the Development of Christian Doctrine*, by John Henry Cardinal Newman.

[10] Regarding the ordination of Clement, Tertullian states, "Clement was ordained by Peter" to succeed him as bishop of Rome (*Demurrer against the Heretics* 32, 1–3, in William A. Jurgens, *The Faith of the Early Fathers* [Collegeville, Minn.: Liturgical Press, 1970], 1:122). Some question arises as to whether Clement succeeded Peter directly or was third in line of succession after Peter. Since tradition tells us Clement was ordained by Peter himself (though we are not told the details), it seems likely that Clement, though ordained by Peter, declined the episcopal office for twenty-four years, deferring the position of bishop to Linus, only to take up the office later for a period of nine years. For an in-depth discussion, see "Clement" in *The Catholic Encyclopedia* (New York: Robert Appleton Co., 1908), 4:12f.

Regarding the ordination of St. Ignatius, Chrysostom wrote, in a homily honoring the saint, "that he [Ignatius] obtained this office from those saints, and that the hands of the blessed apostles touched his sacred head. . . . But since I have mentioned Peter, [Ignatius] is that man [who] succeeded to the office after [Peter in Antioch]" (*Homily on S. Ignatius*, NPNF1, 9:136, 138).

The two ancient documents we now approach, the first by Clement of Rome and the second by Ignatius of Antioch, both bishops in the Catholic Church, were written at the turn of the first century. At least one of the authors, though probably both, was martyred for his faith. Both men are highly esteemed by all Christian traditions, Catholic, Orthodox, and Protestant alike, for their orthodoxy and their passionate love of God and the Church.

Clement of Rome (fl. A.D. 96), our first witness, was probably a Gentile and a Roman—the third bishop of Rome after Peter and an associate of the same. The Apostle Paul writes, "And I ask you also, true yokefellow, help these women, for they have labored side by side with me in the gospel together with Clement and the rest of my fellow workers, whose names are in the book of life."[11] Clement was the bishop of Rome during the lifetime of the Apostle John[12] and wrote *The First Epistle of Clement to the Corinthians* in the name of the Roman Church in A.D. 96.

With a little imagination you can envision Clement strolling down the crowded and dirty streets of ancient Rome with the large fisherman, robes flowing in the breeze as they minister to the poor, preach the gospel, visit the sick, and serve the Lord Jesus in his Church. You can almost see them celebrating the Eucharist together behind locked doors to avoid detection. You can imagine them along the banks of the Tiber, baptizing new converts, initiat-

---

[11] Phil 4:3. There is some dispute as to whether this Clement is to be identified with the Clement of Rome. There is no reason to believe the two are not the same; in fact, writers in the early Church affirm that they were. "Writers of the 3rd and 4th centuries, like Origen, Eusebius, and Jerome, equate him, perhaps correctly, with the Clement whom St. Paul mentions (Phil 4:3) as a fellow-worker" (J. N. D. Kelly, *The Oxford Dictionary of the Popes* [New York: Oxford Univ. Press, 1986], 7). A. Cleveland Coxe writes, "He seems to have been at Philippi with St. Paul (A.D. 57) when the first-born of the Western churches was passing through great trials of faith. There, with the holy women and others, he ministered to the apostles and to the saints. . . . From the apostle [Paul], and his companion, St. Luke, he had no doubt learned the use of the Septuagint [Greek Old Testament], in which his knowledge of the Greek tongue soon rendered him an adept. . . . A co-presbyter with Linus and Cletus, he succeeded them in the government of the Roman Church" (ANF 1:1).

[12] We are told that John the Apostle lived to be about one hundred years old. Irenaeus (disciple of Polycarp, John's follower) writes that John lived until the reign of Trajan, which was the period between A.D. 98 and 117 (*Against Heresies* 2, 22). John was buried in Ephesus, where he had written his Gospel.

ing them into the mysteries of the Christian faith—Peter training his acolyte to be a bishop someday, to lead the Church, and to suffer for the sake of Christ. Clement was an interpreter of the apostolic teaching and a "codifier" of the apostolic ordinances.

Next, we will visit Ignatius of Antioch (c. A.D. 35–c. 107), bishop of Antioch in Syria, second in line of succession in Antioch after Peter,[13] as he is dragged from city to city across the Roman Empire, chained to Roman guards on his way to meet the jaws of wild beasts. The ignominious bondage and public display, even the freedom to receive delegations from the various Churches, were no doubt calculated to defeat Bishop Ignatius, to terrify other Christians to the point of complete passivity, and to stifle any outbreaks of religious fanaticism among this new "sect". Under these humiliating conditions, Ignatius wrote at least seven letters as he was transported in chains to Rome by Roman guards. In his letters he clearly reveals his great desire for martyrdom by the jaws of lions.[14] It is possible, considering what we know of his life, that the young Ignatius sat under the catechetical teaching of Peter in Antioch. Early tradition suggests he may have been the small child Jesus took upon his knee (Mt 18:2). Polycarp, who was a disciple of the Apostle John, was also a fellow bishop with Ignatius—we have extant correspondence between them. With our mind's eye we can see Ignatius, as he prays with furrowed brow for his brothers in Christ and writes to the churches along his route, imploring the saints to hold fast to their bishops and eschew divisions. Visiting the huge Coliseum in Rome causes our imagination to withdraw in horror and empathy at the hideous death he endured there. Yet it was this very martyrdom, this condemnation to an ignominious death, that brought Ignatius to Rome, willing as he was, though in chains, to seal his love for the Savior.

---

[13] After the persecution in Jerusalem, in which the Apostle James was martyred (Acts 12:1–2) and Peter was imprisoned (Acts 12:3–19), Peter left probably for Antioch, after being released from prison by an angel, and spent considerable time there (Gal 2:11). Early Christian tradition informs us that Peter was the bishop of Antioch for some time before going to Rome to found the Church there and become her first bishop and leader (see Eusebius, *History of the Church*, III, 36, 2).

[14] In his *Epistle to the Romans*, 4, Ignatius writes, "Suffer me to become food for the wild beasts, through whose instrumentality it will be granted me to attain to God. I am the wheat of God, and let me be ground by the teeth of the wild beasts, that I may be found the pure bread of Christ" (ANF 1:75).

The writings of both men clearly display a reverence for the Roman Church and recognition of her primacy in the Christian world. Clement, as the bishop of Rome, exercises the authority that accompanied the office; and Ignatius, writing to Rome, clearly defers to the Roman Church and honors her primacy.

We will look at Clement first, since his epistle is earlier in origin (A.D. 96, probably about the same time John wrote his Gospel); and then we will study Ignatius, who wrote about ten years later, during the lifetime of Polycarp. For the purpose of our study we will concentrate on the passages that relate to Peter and the primacy of Rome.

The Christians in Corinth were experiencing serious problems. Unity was being attacked by several who had arrogantly taken charge and opposed the ordained clergy, referred to in Clement's epistle as "that shameful and detestable sedition, utterly abhorrent to the elect of God, which a few rash and self-confident persons have kindled to such a pitch of frenzy, that your venerable and illustrious name, worthy to be universally loved, has suffered grievous injury." [15] Clement wrote a lengthy letter castigating the offenders and exhorting the Church to unity. Irenaeus writes, "In the time of this Clement, no small dissension having occurred among the brethren at Corinth, the Church in Rome dispatched a most powerful letter to the Corinthians, exhorting them to peace, renewing their faith, and declaring the tradition which it had lately received from the apostles." [16] Clement's exhortation was well received. Corinth did not contest the epistle, nor did they challenge the tone of authority woven throughout. We know from later writers that it accomplished the intended goal and was read regularly in the Corinthian Church for centuries, and in many other churches as well.[17]

At the time of Clement's *First Epistle to the Corinthians*, the Apostle John was presumably still living and presiding over the Asian Churches only 240 miles from Corinth. Why was John not consulted to correct the problem in Corinth? Why was the task assumed to be the responsibility of Rome, which was well over six hundred miles away? Here we find the occupant of the See of

---

[15] *1 Clement* 1, ANF 1:5.

[16] *Against Heresies* 3, 3, 3, ANF 1:416.

[17] Eusebius, *Church History* 3, 16, NPNF2, 147.

Rome in the first century speaking in the name of his Church and settling a disturbance in a region closer to a living apostle than to the Church of Rome.

In some circles, until the third or fourth century, Clement's epistle was considered an inspired writing, equal to Scripture.[18] One of the most important documents from the apostolic age, the letter is the earliest piece of Christian literature outside the New Testament for which the name, position, and date of the author are historically attested. The letter is a valuable source of information about the life, doctrine, and organization of the early Christian Church.

We have already quoted St. Irenaeus on this subject (see page 70, footnote 10).

Tertullian (c. A.D. 160–c. 225) informs us: "Moreover, if there be any [heresies] bold enough to plant themselves in the midst of the apostolic age, so that they might seem to have been handed down by the Apostles because they were from the time of the Apostles, we can say to them: let them show the origins of their Churches, let them unroll the order of their bishops, running down in succession from the beginning, so that their first bishop shall have for author and predecessor some one of the Apostles or of the apostolic men who continued steadfast with the Apostles. For this is the way in which the apostolic Churches transmit their lists: like the Church of the Smyrnaeans, which records that Polycarp was placed there by John; like the Church of the Romans where Clement was ordained by Peter. In just this same way the other Churches display those whom they have as sprouts from the apostolic seed, having been established in the episcopate by the Apostles."[19]

---

[18] "His namesake, Clement of Alexandria [c. A.D. 150–c. 215], and others thought so highly of his letter that they included it in the canon of the New Testament" (St. Clement and St. Ignatius, *The Epistles of St. Clement of Rome and St. Ignatius of Antioch*, trans. and annotated by James A. Kleist, Ancient Christian Writers [New York: Newman Press, 1946], 3–4). The British Museum houses the oldest complete Bible containing the Old and New Testaments, the Codex Alexandrinus, and bound among the pages of this ancient codex is the letter of Clement. "[Clement's letter] is one of the earliest, perhaps the very earliest, post-biblical works which we have. It was held in very high repute in the early Church, and in the Alexandrian codex it stands among the canonical books as part of the New Testament" (NPNF1, 1:147, n. 1).

[19] Tertullian, *The Demurrer against the Heretics* 32, 1–3, in Jurgens, *Faith of the Early Fathers*, 1:121–22.

What we see here and will continue to see as we proceed is what the Catholic Church has always taught: that the basic structure and hierarchy of the Catholic Church were in existence from the infancy of the Church and that the Catholic Church has the claim to continuity with the apostles and the early Fathers.

Is there just cause for claiming this organic and hierarchical identity with the Church of the apostles and the Fathers? "It seems established, therefore, that from primitive times, at all events by the second century, the whole Church recognized that Rome possessed a primacy relating simultaneously to doctrine and control. When in 1924 the German Protestant historian Harnack completed the great work he had begun at the end of the nineteenth century, he made the following assertion, which, coming from so great a scholar, has considerable weight: 'Twenty-two years ago, in my capacity as a Protestant historian, I exposed the fact that *Roman* equals *Catholic* in my *Manual of the History of Dogmas*, albeit with certain reservations. But since then this thesis has been strengthened, and Protestant historians should no longer be shocked by this proposition: that the basic elements of Catholicism go back to the apostolic age. . . . Thus the link appears to be complete, and the concept which Catholics have of their history is triumphant.' " [20]

With this introduction behind us, we will now delve into Clement's letter, along with a few documents that demonstrate the significance and impact of his epistle in the first centuries. We will try to probe the minds of the first Christians, in order to learn more about life in the Church of that time and to understand their respect for Clement's hierarchical authority and their intense desire to maintain visible unity.

The First Epistle of Clement to the Corinthians (c. A.D. 96)

A. *Clement Speaks for the Church of Rome,*
    the See of Peter

"The Church of God which sojourns at Rome, to the Church of God sojourning at Corinth, to them that are called and sanctified

---

[20] Henri Daniel-Rops, *The Church of Apostles and Martyrs* (New York: E. P. Dutton & Co., 1960), 248–49.

by the will of God, through our Lord Jesus Christ: Grace to you, and peace, from Almighty God through Jesus Christ, be multiplied."[21]

B. *Clement Apologizes to the Corinthians*

"Owing to the suddenly bursting and rapidly succeeding calamities and untoward experiences that have befallen us,[22] we have been somewhat tardy, we think, in giving our attention to the subjects of dispute in your community, beloved."[23]

---

[21] *1 Clement* 1, ANF 1:5. Some go to great lengths to point out that Clement does not call himself Pope in his epistle, implying that he did not assume any special authority as the bishop of Rome. Or that, since he speaks not in his own name but in the "plural" name of the Church of Rome, he is denying papal authority. This is a serious misconception. According to Luke Rivington, "The very doctrine of Papal Infallibility implies that he never can act apart from the general teaching of the Church. . . . When, then, the Popes used the plural 'we,' they were not only using the majestic plural, but they had gathered into their utterances with a special closeness a portion of that great whole [the Church] in whose name they were justified in speaking. . . . The supremacy which belongs strictly to the Bishop of Rome, as the successor of St. Peter, is often attributed, not to the Bishop of Rome, but to the Church of Rome. In the later history of the Church we constantly meet with the supremacy of the bishop spoken of as though it belonged to the *Church* of Rome" (*Primitive Church*, 3, 4). It should also be noted that Paul frequently used the plural "we" without ever placing his individual authority in question (e.g., 1 Cor 1:23; 4:10; 2 Cor 1:24; 8:1; Gal 1:8).

[22] The Papacy of Clement was during the reign of Emperor Domitian (reigned A.D. 51–96), who instigated a cruel persecution of the Church at the end of his reign. He arrogated despotic powers to himself and demanded public worship of himself as *Dominus et Deus* [Lord and God]. It is thought that Domitian persecuted and murdered both Jews and Christians. It was probably under the reign of Emperor Domitian that the Apostle John was exiled to the Isle of Patmos.

[23] *Clement to the Corinthians* 1, in Clement and Ignatius, *Epistles*, 1:9. There is no evidence of an appeal by the Corinthian Church to Rome for help, raising the likelihood that Clement, as bishop of the Roman Church, had heard of the strife and understood it as his responsibility to exercise apostolic authority and take care of the divisions. Some (e.g., Rivington) argue that Corinth had appealed to Rome for assistance, but either scenario delivers the same results. The bishop of Rome considered it his responsibility to step in to address the matter and even apologized for his inability to address it in a more timely manner. Here we see the primacy and jurisdiction of the Roman Church within the universal Church, even over an apostolic Church in another part of the Empire. Clement did not apologize for writing the letter; rather, he apologized for not writing to correct their abuses sooner, as was his duty.

C. *Clement Speaks of Apostolic Succession*

"The Apostles preached to us the Gospel received from Jesus Christ, and Jesus Christ was God's Ambassador. Christ, in other words, comes with a message from God and the Apostles with a message from Christ. Both of these orderly arrangements, therefore, originate from the will of God. And so, after receiving their instructions and being fully assured through the Resurrection of our Lord Jesus Christ, as well as confirmed in faith by the word of God, they went forth. . . . From land to land, accordingly, and from city to city they preached, and from their earliest converts appointed men whom they had tested by the Spirit to act as bishops and deacons for the future believers.[24] And this was no innovation, for, a long time before the Scripture had spoken about bishops and deacons; for somewhere it says: 'I will establish their overseers in observance of the law and their ministers in fidelity.' Our Apostles, too, were given to understand by our Lord Jesus Christ that the office of the bishop would give rise to intrigues. For this reason, equipped as they were with perfect foreknowledge, they appointed the men mentioned before, and afterwards laid down a rule once for all to this effect: when these men die, other approved men shall succeed to their sacred ministry. Consequently, we deem it an injustice to eject from the sacred ministry the persons who were appointed either by them, or later, with the consent of the whole Church, by other men in high repute."[25]

---

[24] This follows Paul's command to Timothy, who was appointed a bishop by Paul, as is apparent from the two Pauline epistles written to him. Paul commands Timothy, "And what you have heard from me before many witnesses entrust to faithful men, who will be able to teach others also" (2 Tim 2:2). Five generations are represented: Paul received it from others and told Timothy; Timothy is to teach faithful men, who will in turn teach others. Tradition thus passes on through five generations.

[25] *Clement* 42, 44, in Johannes Quasten, *Patrology* (Westminster, Md.: Christian Classics, 1993), 1:45–46. Who would better understand the intentions of the apostles, especially those of Peter, to whom the Lord Jesus had given the keys of the kingdom of heaven, than those who were personally trained and ordained by the apostles? Peter ordained Clement to succeed him in the authority of Christ, as the bishop of Rome. Those who knew the apostles understood that the apostolic authority (charism) would be passed on through the generations. As Quasten comments, "The document is precious from the dogmatic viewpoint. It may be called the manifesto of ecclesiastical jurisdiction. Here for the first time we find a clear and explicit declaration of the doctrine of apostolic succession.

D. *Clement Speaks with Authority from God*

"Receive our counsel, and ye shall have no occasion of regret. For as God liveth, and the Lord Jesus Christ liveth, and the Holy Spirit, . . . so surely shall he, who with lowliness of mind and instant in gentleness hath without regretfulness performed the ordinances and commands that are given by God [through us], be enrolled and have a name among the number of them that are saved through Jesus Christ. . . . But if certain persons should be disobedient unto the words spoken by Him [Jesus Christ] through us, let them understand that they will entangle themselves in no slight transgression and danger; but we shall be guiltless of this sin."[26]

The fact is stressed that the presbyters cannot be deposed by the members of the community because authority is not bestowed by them. The right to rule derives from the Apostles, who exercised their power in obedience to Christ, who in turn was sent by God" (*Patrology*, 1:45). Warren Carroll writes, "Almost as significant in the letter of Clement as this clear-cut assertion of the Roman primacy in the church is its statement about the apostolic succession of bishops. The letter of Clement falls within the period of the primitive church, by any reasonable definition of that term; likewise it clearly falls within the Apostolic Age. . . . It [along with Ignatius' epistles] supplies proof of the existence in that primitive Christian church, in the Apostolic Age, of a well-developed episcopate in direct succession from the Apostles" (*The Founding of Christendom* [Front Royal, Va.: Christendom College Press, 1985], 451).

Another early reference to apostolic succession near the time of Clement comes from a Gnostic heretic who attempts to validate his theology by claiming "we too" have succession. Ptolemaeus writes in his *Letter to Flora*, "For, if God permit, you will later learn about their origin and generation, when you are judged worthy of the apostolic tradition which we too have received by succession" (James F. McCue, *Papal Primacy and the Universal Church: Lutherans and Catholics in Dialogue V* [Minneapolis: Augsburg Pub., 1974], 57). McCue comments that this quotation from Ptolemaeus "is the earliest extant work after *1 Clement* to make significant use of apostolic succession ideas, and it is the earliest (except perhaps for the Pastorals) to connect apostolic succession with the handing on of teaching. . . . Lest this too easily be taken to show that apostolic succession in teaching is a gnostic creation that was subsequently taken over by the orthodoxy [*sic*] . . . it should be noted that the *kai hēmeis*—'we too'—indicates that Ptolemaeus is countering an already advanced orthodox claim that the orthodox doctrine goes back through succession to the apostles. Thus wherever the idea originated, it presumably existed in orthodox writers or bishops prior to Ptolemaeus" (*Papal Primacy*, 57).

[26] *Clement* 58, 59, in J. B. Lightfoot, *The Apostolic Fathers* (Grand Rapids, Mich.: Baker Book House, 1984), 82. These are very authoritative words. If one were to view Clement as "just another Christian" writing to other fellow Christians, they

E. *Clement Requires Obedience to His Epistle*

"For ye will give us great joy and gladness, if ye render obedience unto the things written by us through the Holy Spirit, and root out the unrighteous anger of your jealousy, according to the entreaty which we have made for peace and concord in this letter."[27]

F. *Clement and the Church of Rome Send Legates[28] to Corinth*

"Make haste and send our messengers, Claudius Ephebus, Valerius Vito, and Fortunatus[29] back to us in peace and joy;[30] so that

---

would sound extremely presumptuous. These are words of authority, words that assume God himself is speaking through Clement and the Church of Rome. To disobey Clement's exhortation would be sin. Clement, in discharging his duty as Pope, will be guiltless of their sin if they choose to disobey. The primacy of the Roman See is undeniably assumed in this epistle. Clement and the Church of Rome speak to the Church of Corinth as a superior speaks to his subjects. As Quasten says, "Such an authoritative tone cannot be adequately accounted for on the ground of the close cultural relations existing between Corinth and Rome. The writer [Clement] is convinced that his actions are prompted by the Holy Spirit" (*Patrology*, 1:47).

[27] *Clement* 63, in Lightfoot, *Apostolic Fathers*, 84. Again in this passage, Clement and the Church of Rome claim to speak with the authority of the Holy Spirit of God. Clement exhorts the Corinthians to accept his words as the words of God, which is reminiscent of Paul's claims in 1 Thessalonians 2:13 and the authority of the Roman Pontiff today. Lightfoot calls it "the first step towards Papal domination" (J. B. Lightfoot, *The Apostolic Fathers*, 2d ed. [Peabody, Mass.: Hendrickson, 1989], 2:70). What it really is, is the first recorded post-biblical exercise of papal primacy toward a distant Church. "There was no protest [from anyone]; on the contrary, St. Irenaeus and St. Ignatius praised it, and Corinth treasured the letter and read it at Divine service on the Lord's Day for years to come" (Rivington, *Primitive Church*, 9). It is a letter "in which the writer claims to speak with the authority of God. The least that can be said of this first disclosure of Rome's position in the Church is that it fits in with her present position in Roman Catholic Christendom. . . . The reasonable explanation [for Clement's assertion of divine authority] is that he spoke as successor of St. Peter, the Prince of the Apostles. The first recorded utterance of a Christian bishop in uninspired literature speaks in the name of his Church with the voice of infallibility, and that Church is the Church of Rome" (Rivington, *Primitive Church*, 10, 11).

[28] Legates are personal representatives of the Holy See who have been entrusted with its authority. Throughout the first centuries of the Church, it was the custom of the Church for the bishop of Rome to send legates to represent the papal office. It was a practice first initiated by the apostles (1 Cor 4:17; 2 Cor

news of the truce and the unity for which we are praying and longing may reach us the more speedily, and we may the sooner rejoice over your return to order. The grace of our Lord Jesus Christ be with you, and with each and all everywhere whom God has called by Him; and through Him be glory and honour to God, with might, majesty, and everlasting dominion from all ages now and to eternity. Amen." [31]

G. *Hermas Comments on Clement's Duty* [32]

"Brethren, a revelation was made to me in my sleep by an exceedingly beautiful young man, who said 'Who, do you think, is the

---

9:3; 2 Tim 4:12, etc.) and then carried on by their successors. Roman civil authorities also used legates.

[29] "It has been conjectured that these two elderly envoys may have been the members of 'Caesar's household' mentioned by St. Paul in *Philippians* IV:22" (*Early Christian Writings*, trans. Maxwell Staniforth [Harmondsworth, Middlesex, England: Penguin Books, 1968], 51, n. 24).

[30] Lutheran writer Max Lackmann says, "The use of the expression 'send back' in this sentence is not merely a special kind of biblical phrase but also a form of Roman imperial command. The Roman judge in a province of the empire 'sent back' a messenger or a packet of documents to the imperial capital or to the court of the emperor (Acts 25:21). Clement of Rome doubtless also knew this administrative terminology of the imperial government and used it effectively" (*The Unfinished Reformation*, ed. Hans Asmussen [Notre Dame, Ind.: Fides Pub., 1961], 213).

[31] *Clement*, 65, 1, in Staniforth, *Early Christian Writings*, 49. Clement not only writes an authoritative epistle to the Corinthians, but he also sends three legates to represent him. These legates would undoubtedly have authority—as representatives of Rome—to exhort, correct, and chastise those in error. After the ecclesiastical order had been restored and division healed, the legates returned to the Church of Rome with a report of their mission and supporting documents.

"Now it must be remembered that the Church of Rome, always peculiarly exposed to persecution, was at this period under, or just recovering from, 'sudden and repeated dangers and calamities,' and that St. John, the Apostle, was at this very time, most probably, living either at Patmos or Ephesus. Taking these, and other similar circumstances, into account, may not the embassy and letter sent, in the midst of such trials, by St. Clement, then Bishop of Rome, be considered as pointing to a recognized superiority in the Church over which he presided?" (Joseph Berington and John Kirk, comps., *The Faith of Catholics*, ed. T. J. Capel, [New York: F. Pustet & Co., 1884], 2:60).

[32] Hermas (fl. A.D. 140) was an apostolic Father and a Christian writer noted for his vivid description of early Christianity. According to his own testimony,

elderly lady from whom you took the book?' 'The Sibyl,' I said. 'No,' he said, 'you are mistaken.' 'Who is she, then?' I said. 'The Church,' he said. 'Why is she elderly?' I asked. 'Because she was created before all things,' he said. 'For this reason she is elderly and for Her sake the world was erected.' After this I had a vision in my house. The elderly lady came and asked me whether I had already given the book to the Presbyters. I said that I had not. 'That is well,' she said, 'for I have remarks to add. So, when I shall complete all the words, with your help they will be made known to all the elect. Write, then, two small booklets, one for Clement and one for Grapte. Clement will then send it to the cities abroad since this is his duty, and Grapte will instruct the widows and orphans. But you shall read it to this city together with the Presbyters, who are in charge of the church." [33]

Hermas was sold into slavery as a boy and sent to Rome. In Rome he was purchased by a woman called Rhoda, who set him free. Hermas himself says that he is a contemporary of St. Clement of Rome; but the Muratorian Canon (c. 180) attributes the *Shepherd* to a brother of Pope Pius (d. c. 154), while Origen believes the Hermas mentioned in Romans 16:14 to be its author. "A great number of modern scholars . . . accept the view of the Muratorian Canon, which would suggest a date between 140 and 155. . . . In the Greek Church of the 2nd and 3rd centuries the work was widely regarded as Scripture, e.g. by St. Irenaeus, Clement of Alexandria, also by Tertullian. . . . It was, however, greatly esteemed for its moral value and served as a textbook for catechumens, as is testified by St. Athanasius. In the Codex Sinaiticus it comes after the New Testament. . . . In the Latin Church it was valued far less highly; the Muratorian Canon denies its inspiration" (*Oxford Dictionary of the Christian Church*, ed. F. L. Cross and E. A. Livingstone [New York: Oxford Univ. Press, 1989], 640–41). Hermas' book, *The Shepherd*, is a series of revelations granted to him through two heavenly figures, an old woman and an angel who assumed the form of a shepherd.

[33] *The Shepherd of Hermas*, Visions 2, 4, in *The Apostolic Fathers*, trans. Francis X. Glimm, Gerald G. Walsh, S.J., and Joseph M.-F. Marique, S.J., The Fathers of the Church, vol. 1 (Washington, D.C.: Catholic Univ. of America Press, 1981), 241–42. Hermas demonstrates that the early Church viewed the bishop of Rome as having a responsibility for the well-being and unity of the universal Christian community. He was a successor of Peter and fulfilled the role of pastor of the Church. "Hermas states that it is Clement's task to write to cities abroad (Vis. 2:4.3). . . . While we have only the reference in the *Shepherd* to the duty of one bishop of the Roman community, it is none the less significant that it is an overseer [bishop] who has this task. This reference supports a view which sees a distinct group of leaders taking on increasingly defined functions" (Harry O. Maier, *The Social Setting of the Ministry as Reflected in the Writings of Hermas, Clement*

H. *Dionysius and the Continuing Importance of Clement's Letter* [34]

"In the same letter he [Dionysius] refers to Clement's *Epistle to the Corinthians,* proving that from the very first it had been customary to read it in church. He says: 'Today being the Lord's Day, we kept it as a holy day and read your epistle, which we shall read frequently for its valuable advice, like the earlier epistle which Clement wrote on your behalf.'" [35]

I. *Eusebius Relates the Importance and Weight of St. Clement's Epistle*

"In the twelfth year of the same reign Clement succeeded Anencletus after the latter had been bishop of the church of Rome for

---

and Ignatius [Waterloo, Ontario, Canada: Wilfrid Laurier Univ. Press, 1991], 104).

"According to a passage in the second vision (4, 3) Hermas receives the command from the Church to make two copies of the revelation, one of which he is to turn over to Clement, who will send it to distant cities. The Clement indicated is undoubtedly Pope Clement of Rome, who wrote his Epistle to the Corinthians about 96 A.D." (Quasten, *Patrology,* 1:92).

[34] Dionysius (fl. A.D. 170) was the bishop of Corinth, and some of his writings are preserved in Eusebius. One of his letters was written to Soter, the bishop of Rome (c. A.D. 166–c. 174), thanking the Church of Rome for recent correspondence and informing Soter that Clement's epistle, which had been sent about sixty or seventy years earlier, was routinely read in the Corinthian Church.

[35] Eusebius, *The History of the Church* 4, 23, trans. G. A. Williamson (Harmondsworth, Middlesex, England: Penguin Books, 1965), 132. Eusebius provides a quotation from Dionysius, bishop of Corinth, to Pope Soter, bishop of Rome, written toward the end of the second century. In the words of Orthodox theologian Nicholas Afanassieff, "Apparently Rome [Clement] had no doubt that its priority would be accepted without argument. The only apology made is for not having sent a letter to the Church of Corinth earlier, so as to restore order there, the delay being due to persecution. We do not know if the Corinthian Church followed Rome's advice, but we may fairly suppose that the voice of the Roman Church was heard. Anyhow, Clement's epistle was held in high esteem at Corinth thereafter" (*The Primacy of Peter,* ed. John Meyendorff et al. [Crestwood, N.Y.: St. Vladimir's Seminary Press, 1992], 126). Dionysius makes the interesting comment that the letter from Clement had been sent "on your behalf", which could only mean "on behalf of the Church of Rome". The comment shows a continuing state of Roman primacy and superiority in Dionysius' mind, which would indicate the attitude of the widely dispersed bishops toward the authority and responsibility of Rome.

twelve years. The apostle in his Epistle to the Philippians informs us that this Clement was his fellow-worker. His words are as follows: 'With Clement and the rest of my fellow-laborers whose names are in the book of life' [Phil 4:3]. There is extant an epistle of this Clement which is acknowledged to be genuine and is of considerable length and of remarkable merit. He wrote it in the name of the church of Rome to the church of Corinth, when a sedition had arisen in the latter church. We know that this epistle also has been publicly used in a great many churches both in former times and in our own. And of the fact that a sedition did take place in the church of Corinth at the time referred to Hegesippus is a trustworthy witness."[36]

The importance of Clement in the understanding of early Christianity is inestimable. To summarize our discussion of Clement's epistle, a passage from Protestant historian Philip Schaff seems appropriate. He writes, "The first example of the exercise of a sort of papal authority is found towards the close of the first century in the letter of the Roman bishop Clement. . . . It can hardly be denied that the document reveals the sense of a certain superiority over all ordinary congregations. The Roman church here, without being asked (as far as it appears), gives advice, with superior administrative wisdom, to an important church in the East, dispatches messengers to her, and exhorts her to order and unity in a tone of calm dignity and authority, as the organ of God and the Holy Spirit. This is all the more surprising if St. John, as is probable, was then still living in Ephesus, which was nearer to Corinth than Rome."[37]

The Epistle of Ignatius to the Romans (c. A.D. 106)

The letters of Ignatius are also invaluable for a glimpse of the first-century Christian community. Behind the veil of time, we can peer into the structure and practices of the apostolic Churches across Asia Minor and the East. Since the time of the Protestant Reformation, many have challenged the authenticity of these Ignatian documents. It was difficult to believe that the office of monarchical

---

[36] Eusebius, *Church History* 3, 15–16, NPNF2, 1:147.
[37] Philip Schaff, *History of the Christian Church* (Grand Rapids, Mich.: Eerdmans, 1980), 2:157–58.

bishop was so uniformly established—unchallenged and taken for granted—in the Churches during the apostolic period. However, scholarship, most notably that of J. B. Lightfoot in his magisterial five-volume *Apostolic Fathers,* has established the genuineness of these letters beyond doubt. Those who dislike the hierarchical structure of the Church, therefore, are left to grapple with the historical reality as transmitted down through the ages by a disciple of the apostles.[38] Ignatius' epistles illuminate the history of the primitive Christian communities like a blast of sunlight. In so doing, they stand as a solid witness to the hierarchical structure and visible unity of the Church—which Ignatius called the Catholic Church.

Two passages from Eusebius give witness to Ignatius' importance at the turn of the first century. First, we read, "And at the same time Papias, bishop of the parish of Hierapolis, became well known, as did also Ignatius, who was chosen bishop of Antioch, second in succession to Peter, and whose fame is still celebrated by a great many. Report says that he was sent from Syria to Rome, and became food for wild beasts on account of his testimony to Christ. And as he made the journey through Asia under the strictest military surveillance, he fortified the parishes in the various cities where he stopped by oral homilies and exhortations, and warned them above all to be especially on their guard against the heresies that were then beginning to prevail, and exhorted them to hold fast to the tradition of the apostles. . . . So much concerning Ignatius. But he was succeeded by Heros in the episcopate of the church of Antioch."[39]

---

[38] "Calvin, who, however, knew only the spurious and worthless longer recension, calls the Ignatian Epistles abominable trash (*Inst.* 1.1, c. 13, §29); Dr. W. D. Killen, who ought to know better, from strong anti-prelatic feeling, speaks of Ignatius, even according to the shorter Syriac recension, as an 'anti-evangelical formalist, a puerile boaster, a mystic dreamer and crazy fanatic' (*Ancient Church,* 1859, p. 414). Neander is far more moderate, yet cannot conceive that a martyr so near the apostolic age should have nothing more important to say than 'such things about obedience to the bishops' (*Ch. H.* I. 192, note, Bost. ed.). Baur and the Tübingen critics reject the entire Ignatian literature as a forgery. Rothe on the other hand is favorably impressed with the martyr-enthusiasm of the Epistles, and Zahn (an orthodox Lutheran) thinks the Ignatian epistles in the shorter Greek recension worthy of a comparison with the epistles of Paul" (Schaff, *History of the Christian Church,* 2:660, n. 1).

[39] Eusebius, *Church History* 3, 36, NPNF2, 1:166–69. Philip Schaff, in his *History of the Christian Church,* states that "Ignatius, surnamed Theophorus, stood

Second, we read in Eusebius, "At this time Ignatius was known as the second bishop of Antioch, Evodius having been the first. Symeon likewise was at that time the second ruler of the church of Jerusalem, the brother of our Saviour having been the first. At that time the apostle and evangelist John, the one whom Jesus loved, was still living in Asia, and governing the churches of that region, having returned after the death of Domitian from his exile on the island." [40] Church historian Warren Carroll tells us that Ignatius was "at least thirty years a bishop, probably trained by the Apostle John, and was apparently at this time the most venerated living member of the whole Church". [41]

To understand Ignatius a little better, to gain some insight into his personality, his deep spirituality, and his love for the Lord Jesus, it is appropriate to cite one last passage from his epistle to the Romans: "Only request in my behalf both inward and outward strength, that I may not only speak, but [truly] will; and that I may not merely be called a Christian, but really be found to be one. . . . I write to all the Churches, and impress on them all, that I shall willingly die for God. . . . Suffer me to become food for the wild beasts, through whose instrumentality it will be granted me to attain to God. I am the wheat of God, and let me be ground by the teeth of the wild beasts, that I may be found the pure bread of Christ. . . . Let fire and the cross; let the crowds of wild beasts; let tearings, breakings, and dislocations of bones; let cutting off of members; let shatterings of the whole body; and let all the dreadful torments of the devil come upon me: only let me attain to Jesus Christ. . . . All the pleasures of the world, and all the kingdoms of this earth, shall profit me nothing. It is better for me to die in behalf of Jesus Christ, than to reign over all the ends of the earth. 'For what shall a man be profited, if he gain the whole world, but lose his own soul?' Him

---

at the head of the Church of Antioch at the close of the first century and the beginning of the second. . . . The church of Antioch was the mother-church of Gentile Christianity; and the city was the second city of the Roman empire. Great numbers of Christians and a host of heretical tendencies were collected there, and pushed the development of doctrine and organization with great rapidity" (2:653–54). Ignatius was an extremely important figure in the period following that of the ministry of the apostles.

[40] Eusebius, *Church History* 3, 22–23, NPNF2, 1:149–50.
[41] Carroll, *Founding of Christendom*, 455.

I seek, who died for us: Him I desire, who rose again for our sake."[42]

The marvelous letters of Ignatius are invaluable in helping us to understand the early Christian community. Patrick Hamell informs us, "The *importance* of the Letters is evident. The position of the *bishop* has already been noted. He is one and in supreme authority. He is first, the priests second, deacons third. The bishop has duties as well as rights. *Rome's privileges* are stressed. *Christ* is the centre of all St. Ignatius's teaching."[43] Did Ignatius perceive Rome as holding a place of priority and superiority? Let us take a look at the clues he offers in his epistle to the Romans.

A. *The Preface*[44]

"Ignatius, also called Theophorus, to the Church that has found mercy in the transcendent Majesty of the Most High Father and of Jesus Christ, His only Son; the church by the will of Him who willed all things that exist, beloved and illuminated through the faith and love of Jesus Christ our God; which also presides in the chief place of the Roman territory;[45] a church worthy of God,

---

[42] *Epistle to the Romans* 3–6, ANF 1:74–76.

[43] Patrick Hamell, *Handbook of Patrology* (Staten Island, N.Y.: Alba House, 1968), 30.

[44] Ignatius' laudatory opening words in the epistle to the Romans have no parallels in his addresses to the other Churches. His other introductions show a clear distinction, a much more subdued tone, without the grand praises heaped upon the Roman Church. There is no doubt he held the Roman Church in much higher regard than other Churches. "Again no doubt we may explain all this away: the aged saint is enthusiastic for the city which is to see his desired martyrdom, and for the Church of Peter and Paul. But parallels, not much later, suggest that we should understand more than this, that Rome has a real presidency and a special gift of indefectible faith" (John Chapman, in *The Papacy*, ed. C. Lattey [London: Burns, Oates & Washbourne, 1923], 27). Why was the Church in Rome held in such high regard? Because she was the Church founded and built by the Apostles Peter and Paul. Rome is where St. Peter, with the keys of authority from Christ, spent the last years of his life. The first- and second-century believers respected the primacy of Peter and the superiority of the Roman Church.

[45] According to H. G. Liddell, *An Intermediate Greek Lexicon*, abridged from Liddell and Scott's *Greek–English Lexicon* (Oxford: Oxford Univ. Press, published in electronic form by Logos Research Systems, 1996), the word "preside" (προκάθημαι) means "to be seated before; ... and so, to protect, defend; to

worthy of honor, worthy of felicitation, worthy of praise, worthy of success, worthy of sanctification, and presiding in love,[46] maintain-

---

preside over". Ignatius uses it again in *Magnesians* 6, 1, regarding the local "bishop *presiding* after the likeness of God". Ignatius, though from a city in the East over thirteen hundred miles away, recognizes the primacy of the Roman Church over the whole Roman territory, using "preside" twice in his introduction. The Roman territory extended to the reaches of the Empire. Of Ignatius' wording, Luke Rivington says it is "an expression which indicates not the extent, but the centre of her presiding authority" (*Primitive Church*, 33). The ecclesiastical authority proclaimed here is inescapable. An alternate rendering, provided in Glimm et al., *Apostolic Fathers*, 107, is, "the Church in the place of the country of the Romans which holds the primacy". In one dismissive brush stroke, William Webster attempts to discard Ignatius' recognition of Rome's "presidency" with the words, "Ignatius of Antioch . . . wrote letters to different churches, including the church of Rome, rebuking, exhorting and giving instruction. Does this mean that Ignatius had a right of jurisdiction over these churches? Surely not, for that would mean that he had a right of jurisdiction over the church of Rome itself" (*The Church of Rome at the Bar of History* [Carlisle, Pa.: Banner of Truth Trust, 1995], 57). As we will see later, Ignatius does not exhort Rome, and his encouragement to other Churches does not ipso facto assume authority over the Roman Church; quite the opposite, he is entirely submissive to Rome and acknowledges her as the one who "presides".

[46] This phrase has attracted the attention of many scholars. Some claim the phrase simply refers to the love that the Roman Church lavishes on all other Churches—she was generous, loving, and helpful. However, the phrase "presiding in love" seems to imply more. As mentioned earlier, Ignatius also uses the word "preside" in his *Epistle to the Magnesians*, where he says, "Let the bishop preside in the place of God, and his clergy in place of the apostolic conclave" (6, 1). The word would seem, then, strongly to suggest a position of authority and leadership. The phrase "presiding in love" can also be translated as "presiding over the bond of [the] love". The Greek article "the" stands before the word "love", making it an articular Greek construction that points to a specific object. "It has been well argued by F. X. Funk that the word *agápe*, 'love' has often the meaning in St. Ignatius of 'the community.' The Greek verb *prokáthemai*, 'I preside over,' is always found followed, as in Plato (*Laws* 758 D), by some such word as 'city' and never by a merely abstract noun like 'love.' Whether St. Ignatius has in mind a pre-eminence of authority or charity, the context seems to imply that he means a universal not merely a local pre-eminence" (Glimm et al., *Apostolic Fathers*, 107, n. 2). The phrase implies that Rome is the guardian of the faith and presides over the covenant of divine love. According to Quasten, others have lately put forth a convincing case that the word *agape* has a broader meaning and stands for the "totality of the supernatural life which Christ enkindled in us by his love. Then Ignatius would by the phrase 'presiding in love' assign to the Roman Church authority to guide and lead in that which consti-

ing the law of Christ,[47] and bearer of the Father's name: her do I therefore salute in the name of Jesus Christ, the Son of the Father. Heartiest good wishes for unimpaired joy in Jesus Christ our God, to those who are united in flesh and spirit by every commandment of His; who imperturbably enjoy the full measure of God's grace and have every foreign stain filtered out of them."[48]

---

tutes the essence of Christianity and of the new order brought into the world by Christ's divine love for men" (Quasten, *Patrology*, 1:70). There is no question that the Churches throughout the world held the Roman Church in this high regard; and Ignatius' epistle "taken in its entirety, shows beyond cavil that the position of honor accorded the Roman Church is acknowledged by Ignatius as her due, and is founded not on the extent of her charitable influence but on her inherent right to universal ecclesiastical supremacy" (Quasten, *Patrology*, 1:70). Cardinal Newman renders the same passage very acceptably as "the Church, which has in dignity the first seat" (John Henry Cardinal Newman, *An Essay on the Development of Christian Doctrine*, in *Conscience, Consensus, and the Development of Doctrine* [New York: Image Books, Doubleday, 1992], 163).

We learn from J. Michael Miller, "Though probably not intending to signify any legal precedence for the Roman community, it could mean that the Roman church presides over the 'whole Church'. The term 'in love' is *agape*, which elsewhere refers to the universal Church. A good argument can therefore be made, and John Paul II makes it, that the phrase 'having the chief place in love' expresses 'the primacy in that communion of charity which is the Church, and necessarily the service of authority, the *ministerium Petrinum*' " (*The Shepherd and the Rock* [Huntington, Ind.: Our Sunday Visitor, 1995], 76).

[47] The Church of Rome is viewed by Ignatius, and probably by all of Christendom, as the "maintainer" of the law of Christ, not only in her own city, but in the Churches throughout the "whole Roman territory" (remembering especially the *Epistle of Clement to the Corinthians*), in recognition that the Church of Rome is the defender of true Christian doctrine, which through the centuries she certainly has been.

[48] Ignatius, *Epistle to the Romans*, preface, in Clement and Ignatius, *Epistles*, 80. The phrase means literally "filtered out", as used in Matthew 23:24, "straining out a gnat and swallowing a camel", in which a technical term is used, meaning straining a drink, such as wine. Ignatius uses it again in *Philadelphians* 3. Throughout history, the Roman Church has been respected and honored for her freedom from heresy. To some, she holds the primacy because she has avoided heresy; to the Catholic, she has avoided heresy because she holds the primacy and the promise of Christ's protection. Even when other Churches, especially in the East, were saturated with heresy (e.g., Arianism, Docetism, etc.), the Roman Church always remained free of such stains, so that throughout history other Churches have appealed to Rome to confirm doctrine, to refute heresy, to respond to problems, and to adjudicate finally in matters of controversy and practice. Jaroslav Pelikan writes, "Rome had been on the side that

B.   *The Church of Rome Presides in Love over Antioch* [49]

"Remember in your prayers the Church in Syria which now has God for her Shepherd in my stead. Jesus Christ alone will be her Bishop, together with your love." [50]

C.   *Ignatius Dares Not Issue Orders to the Roman Church*

"Petition Christ in my behalf that through these instruments I may prove God's sacrifice. Not like Peter and Paul do I issue any orders

---

emerged victorious from one controversy after another, and eventually it became clear that the side which Rome chose was the one that would emerge victorious. In the two dogmatic issues [of] . . . the doctrine of the person of Christ and the question of images in the church, the orthodoxy of Rome was a prominent element, in the first of these perhaps the decisive element, so that when the relation of East and West itself became a matter of debate, the Latin case could draw support from the record established not only in the early centuries but in the immediate past. Those who argued against the Latin case were not entirely bereft of documentation for their counterclaim that Rome had not been absolutely right every single time, but the weight of the evidence for the astonishingly high average accumulated by the see of Peter sometimes proved to be all but overwhelming" (*The Spirit of Eastern Christendom* [Chicago: Univ. of Chicago Press, 1974], 150).

[49] Now that Ignatius had been plucked from his diocese under order of the Roman Emperor, the Church in Antioch was left without a bishop. Ignatius appealed to the Church of Rome to shepherd his flock even though she was more than thirteen hundred miles away.

[50] Ignatius, *Epistle to the Romans* 9, 1, in Clement and Ignatius, *Epistles*, 84. Though Ignatius tells us he is done with the world and seeks a heavenly city, yet he is very concerned about his flock back in Antioch. He was probably whisked away by Roman troops before a bishop had been chosen as his successor. Ignatius now submits his flock to others, with the words: "Jesus Christ alone will be her Bishop, together with your love." He appeals to the Roman Church, not only to pray for his Syrian Church, but also to preside over her in love. Again we have the word ἀγάπη, which has been understood by many scholars to mean "community". "It has been conjectured that 'your love (charity, affection)' should be . . . substituted by 'you who are united by Christian charity', 'your brotherhood', 'your community' " (Clement and Ignatius, *Epistles*, 135, n. 6, 27). "[Perler] points out that the Roman Church alone, among those addressed in Ignatius's extant letters, is expected to have 'oversight' or 'care' for the distant Church of Antioch—just as the same Roman Church had shown maternal concern for the Church of Corinth in its distress" (B. C. Butler, *The Church and Infallibility: A Reply to the Abridged "Salmon"* [New York: Sheed and Ward, 1954], 131).

to you. They were Apostles, I am a convict; they were free, I am until this moment a slave."[51]

D. *The Church of Rome Is a Teacher of Others*

"You have never grudged any man. You have taught others. All I want is that the lessons you inculcate in initiating disciples remain in force [in my case]."[52]

E. *Eusebius Comments on the Importance of Ignatius*

Eusebius was writing very close to the time of the early Fathers and mentions Ignatius several times in his history of the Church. "At this time [from September 18, A.D. 96, to January 27, 98] Ignatius was known as the second bishop of Antioch, Evodius having been the first."[53] He also emphasizes the respect afforded Ignatius by other godly men. "And at the same time Papias, bishop of the parish of Hierapolis, became well known, as did also Ignatius, who

---

[51] Ignatius, *Epistle to the Romans* 4, in Clement and Ignatius, *Epistles*, 82. Ignatius makes many demands of the other Churches—he exhorts and orders them in numerous ways: "Obey your bishop", "partake of one Eucharist", "never allow yourselves to be led astray by false teaching", "avoid schism", etc. However, he gives no such commands to the Romans. He refuses to "issue any orders" to them. They have the pure word already, handed down by the very Prince of the Apostles. Even Ignatius, the bishop of the largest Church in the Roman Empire except for Rome itself, and himself a disciple of the apostles, does not presume to issue orders to the Church of Rome.

[52] Ignatius, *Epistle to the Romans* 3, 2, in Clement and Ignatius, *Epistles*, 81. Ignatius recalls that Rome has taught others (perhaps referring to Clement's letters). He is about to be martyred and reminds them that they have never begrudged anyone a successful martyrdom. He asks that they do not hinder him by saving his life. The Roman Church, the See of Peter and of Paul, was well known for having been a teacher and example of true Christian doctrine. "This pre-eminence of Rome accords well with other indications in the letter. The church is said to have 'taught others' (3:1), which is all the more remarkable since it received the gospel from the East. In addition, Ignatius does not address to Rome the exhortations to unity and obedience which are the common theme of the other epistles" (Michael M. Winter, *Saint Peter and the Popes* [Baltimore, Md.: Helicon Press, 1960], 124). Antioch, the home of Ignatius, was the early center of Christianity, following the severe persecution in Jerusalem and its subsequent destruction. Yet, the bishop of the great Church of Antioch does not instruct Rome but rather praises her for teaching others.

[53] Eusebius, *Church History* 3, 22, in NPNF2, 1:149.

was chosen bishop of Antioch, second in succession to Peter, and whose fame is still celebrated by a great many. . . . Irenaeus also knew of [Ignatius'] martyrdom and mentions his epistles. . . . Polycarp also mentions these letters in the epistle to the Philippians which is ascribed to him. [Polycarp's] words are as follows: 'I exhort all of you, therefore, to be obedient and to practice all patience such as ye saw with your own eyes not only in the blessed Ignatius and Rufus and Zosimus, but also in others from among yourselves as well as in Paul himself and the rest of the apostles; being persuaded that all these ran not in vain, but in faith and righteousness, and that they are gone to their rightful place beside the Lord, with whom also they suffered. For they loved not the present world, but him that died for our sakes and was raised by God for us. . . . The epistles of Ignatius which were sent to us by him and the others which we had with us we sent to you as you gave charge. They are appended to this epistle, and from them you will be able to derive great advantage. For they comprise faith and patience, and every kind of edification that pertaineth to our Lord.' So much concerning Ignatius. But he was succeeded by Heros in the episcopate of the church of Antioch."[54] The Christians of the primitive Church had tremendous respect and honor for Ignatius, both for the holiness of his life as well as for his orthodox teaching and loyalty to Jesus Christ.

F.   *St. Chrysostom Pays Tribute to Ignatius and*
     His Apostolic Ordination

"[Ignatius] presided over the Church among us nobly, and with such carefulness as Christ desires. . . . He held true converse with the apostles and drank of spiritual fountains. What kind of person then is it likely that he was who had been reared, and who had everywhere held converse with them, and had shared with them truths both lawful and unlawful to utter, and who seemed to them of so great a dignity? . . . For I do not wonder . . . that he [Ignatius] seemed to be worthy of so great an office, but that he obtained this office from those saints, and that the hands of the blessed apostles touched his sacred head. . . . But since I have mentioned Peter, this is that man [who] succeeded to the office

---

[54] Ibid., 3, 36, NPNF2, 1:166–69.

after him [in Antioch]. For just as any one taking a great stone from a foundation hastens by all means to introduce an equivalent to it, lest he should shake the whole building, and make it more unsound, so, accordingly, when Peter was about to depart from here, the grace of the Spirit introduced another teacher equivalent to Peter, so that the building already completed should not be made more unsound by the insignificance of the successor."[55]

"We may compare with the conclusions of the Catholic professor Perler the earlier pronouncement of the liberal Protestant Harnack: 'Ignatius is our first external witness in regard to the Roman church. After making all allowances for exaggerations of language in his letter to the Romans, it remains clear that Ignatius assigns a *de facto* primacy to the Roman church among its sister churches, and that he knew of an energetic *and habitual* activity of this church in protecting *and instructing* other churches' (*Dogmengeschichte*, 4th ed., p. 486). It is interesting to observe that independent scholars like Harnack tend to agree with Catholic scholarship, in their estimate of the position of the Roman Church in the earliest centuries, against those Anglican scholars who naturally desire to find a historical basis for a 'non-Roman Catholicism' such as this early history does not record."[56]

There is no clear statement in either Clement or Ignatius, in the form of a dogmatic pronouncement of Rome's primacy, but, as Winter says, "Nevertheless certain passages are intelligible only on the assumption that Ignatius was aware that Rome possessed some kind of superiority over the other churches."[57] Within these two ancient documents written by Clement and Ignatius, we see something of a widely accepted primacy of Rome, both from within the Roman Church and from other Churches.

Orthodox theologians recognize this primacy in the first centuries, though they may debate the actual form it took. In *The Primacy of Peter*, Nicholas Afanassieff writes, "He [Ignatius] pictured

---

[55] *Homilies on S. Ignatius and S. Babylas*, NPNF1, 9:136, 138. This homily was preached by St. John Chrysostom (c. A.D. 347–407) and is an excellent commentary on the life and work of St. Ignatius of Antioch. That the apostles (notably Peter and Paul, both in Antioch prior to founding the Church in Rome) laid hands on Ignatius to ordain him to the episcopacy was confidently known and taught in the early Church.

[56] Butler, *Church and Infallibility*, 132, n. 2; emphasis his.

[57] Winter, *Saint Peter*, 124.

the local churches grouped, as it were, in a eucharistic assembly, with every church in its special place, and the Church of Rome in the chair, sitting in the 'first place.' So, says Ignatius, the Church of Rome indeed has the priority in the whole company of churches united by concord. We are not told by Ignatius (or Clement, either) why the Church of Rome should preside, and not some other church. To Ignatius it must have seemed self-evident, and proofs a waste of time. In his period no other church laid claim to the role, which belonged to the Church of Rome."[58] He then goes on to limit carefully what this priority means; but the fact remains, there was a priority, or "church-in-priority", as he frequently refers to it. Timothy Ware explains the Orthodox position: "Orthodox believe that among the five Patriarchs a special place belongs to the Pope. The Orthodox Church does not accept the doctrine of Papal authority set forth in the decrees of the Vatican Council of 1870, and taught today in the Roman Catholic Church; but at the same time Orthodoxy does not deny to the Holy and Apostolic See of Rome a *primacy of honour*, together with the right (under certain conditions) to hear appeals from all parts of Christendom.[59] Note that we have used the word 'primacy', not 'supremacy'. Orthodox regard the Pope as the bishop 'who presides in love', to adapt a phrase of St Ignatius: Rome's mistake—so Orthodox believe—has been to turn this primacy or 'presidency of love' into a supremacy of external power and jurisdiction."[60] The Protestant, however, has to conclude that these texts from the first centuries show *no* primacy and that all churches were independent congregations or denominations.[61]

---

[58] Meyendorff, *Primacy of Peter*, 127.

[59] For more on "the primacy of honor" see Brian Daley, "Position and Patronage in the Early Church: The Original Meaning of 'Primacy of Honour'", *Theological Studies*, vol. 44, no. 2 (1993), 529–53.

[60] Timothy Ware, *The Orthodox Church* (New York: Penguin Books, 1993), 27.

[61] Referring to Clement's letter, as well as that of Ignatius by implication, William Webster disregards the obvious primacy displayed and asserts that their letters are simply "an example of the overall concern which individual churches took for the well being and care of one another" (*Church of Rome*, 57). Baptists, and others evolving from the sixteenth-century Anabaptist tradition, repudiate *any* episcopal authority or superiority among churches. "Each particular and individual Church is actually and absolutely independent in the exercise of its churchly rights, privileges, and prerogatives; independent of all other churches, individuals, and bodies of men whatever, and is under law to Christ alone. . . .

The Catholic and the Orthodox hold much in common regarding the hierarchical nature of the Church and the authority of bishops within the Church, even the primacy of the Roman bishop in his relation to all of Christendom. We will study the differences between them as we look to the writings and actions of the Fathers through the first five centuries of the Church.

G. *The Importance of St. Ignatius for Understanding Apostolic Teaching*

"It is scarcely possible to exaggerate the importance of the testimony which the Ignatian letters offer to the dogmatic character of Apostolic Christianity. The martyred Bishop of Antioch constitutes a most important link between the Apostles and the Fathers and the early Church. Receiving from the Apostles themselves, whose auditor he was, not only the substance of revelation, but also their own inspired interpretation of it; dwelling, as it were, at the very fountain-head of Gospel truth, his testimony must necessarily carry with it the greatest weight and demand the most serious consideration. Cardinal Newman did not exaggerate the matter when he said ('The Theology of the Seven Epistles of St. Ignatius', in *Historical Sketches*, I, London, 1890) that 'the whole system of Catholic doctrine may be discovered, at least in outline, not to say in parts filled up, in the course of his seven epistles.' "[62]

And finally, an observation regarding St. Ignatius and the Church of Rome at the end of the first century, by Protestant scholar J. N. D. Kelly: "Among the multiplicity of local bodies making up this community, he [Ignatius of Antioch] seems to suggest that the Roman church occupies a special position; he speaks of the church 'which has the primacy (προκάθηται) in the place of the region of the Romans'. This may be merely an elaborate way of defining the area of the authority of the congregation addressed, but something more appears to be implied since he

---

This statement is broad and comprehensive, and needs not defense, but explanation only. That Independency is the true form of Church government, as opposed to Prelacy [governing power in the hands of prelates or bishops] and Presbyterianism, will not now be argued, but is assumed, as accepted by all Baptists" (Edward T. Hiscox, *Principles and Practices for Baptist Churches* [Grand Rapids, Mich.: Kregel Pub., 1980], 145).

[62] *Catholic Encyclopedia*, 7:646.

goes on to salute the Roman church as possessing 'a primacy of love' (προκαθημένη τῆς ἀγάπης)—an expression which some have translated, rather forcedly, 'presiding over the love-community' (i.e., over the Church universal). What these early fathers were envisaging was almost always the empirical, visible society; they had little or no inkling of the distinction which was later to become important between a visible and an invisible Church."[63]

So we end this portion of the historical survey by finding that the very earliest authors, ordained by and fellow workers with the Apostles Peter and Paul, clearly portray in their epistles the special place that the Roman Church holds in the universal Church. Would not these two men, who lived and worked with the Lord's apostles, know the mind of the apostles and the early community better than we who are twenty centuries removed? And when it comes down to whom we will believe, do we choose to believe those who still had the very words of the apostles ringing in their ears or those with innovative ideas battling to secure their turf in the theological and ecclesiological battlefield—two millennia later?

---

[63] J. N. D. Kelly, *Early Christian Doctrines* (San Francisco: Harper & Row, 1978), 191.

THE FIRST FIVE CENTURIES
The Primacy of Rome in the Early Church

The history of the primitive Church is replete with the clear recognition of, and respect for, the primacy of Peter in the See of Rome. That this primacy is denied by various factions within the divided Christendom of today is obvious. There is a wide spectrum of teachings on the subject, from the Roman Catholic, which adhere to the primacy of Rome and the infallibility of the Pope, to the independent denominations and sects that hold to no authority whatever and consider Rome the whore of Babylon.

We are about to travel back in time again to meet the Church Fathers. We will consult the best minds of the Church. They speak to us through books transmitted through the long channel of time. The germ or outline of the doctrine of papal primacy can be seen in the Fathers long before necessity forced its full development. Just as a flower is forced by growth to bud forth and open magnificently before our eyes, so the primacy of Peter, prophesied by our Lord in the Gospels, grew out of the Lord's plant, his Church, and blossomed into a full-fledged flower. We will let the Fathers of the first centuries inform us—with their words we will see the fragile bud unfolding into a beautiful flower. Their voice still resounds with clarity and discernment.

Before we begin, we should review some of the main objections raised to papal primacy, so that we might keep them in mind as we read the Fathers in light of their historical and literary context. These matters have been debated for centuries, and the Fathers' words have been embellished, on the one hand, and "argued away", on the other. Opponents go to great lengths to dismiss this early witness. When the words of the Fathers pass in rapid succession before our gaze, however, century after century, the organic growth of the Church, with her doctrine, canon, and leadership, shines out clearly.

One key argument against papal infallibility claims it cannot be an apostolic doctrine since it was not dogmatically defined in the first century. Those who make this claim stop short of reaching the same conclusion when it is a question of the canon of the New Testament or the doctrine of the Blessed Trinity, though neither of these was clearly defined until the fourth century. Does the fact that Jesus and the apostles did not clearly define these latter two subjects in the written text of Scripture imply that the canon and the doctrine of the Trinity are unbiblical? Certainly not. They are in Scripture in embryo and needed only to grow and develop out of their organic source, to flower into their fullest expression. Thus it is with the stewardship of the kingdom, reinstituted by Christ and brought to full bloom by the Holy Spirit, as he waters and tends the tree of God, which grows from a seed to a massive tree spreading throughout the whole world (Mt 13:31–32). When we see the gradual development of doctrine and the Papacy, corresponding to the growth of the Church herself, we are left with a sense of God's hand on the Church of Rome and her bishop.

Other objections to papal primacy are in fact objections to the notion of authority itself. In secular society, businesses, families—alas, in all human institutions—this issue of authority is often at the root of contentions, quarrels, and factions; the history of the Church is no exception. Authority is challenged from all sides. Christ himself was challenged not only by the governmental authorities, including Herod, who attempted to murder him at birth, and Pilate, who sent him to the cross, but also by those who should have known better, those with the Scriptures and the prophesies of his arrival and mission. Even the common folk, though following Jesus for the multiple benefits of healing and bread, eventually turned their backs; and, sadly enough, before Jesus was crucified, even his own personal cadre of followers and confidants took off running. It should be no surprise, then, that the royal steward of the kingdom should also be opposed frequently and dismissed as an interloper who arrogates authority not granted. Yet we will see the continuous thread that began with Jesus' words to Peter at Caesarea Philippi and continues even until today. Each century the thread becomes more explicitly defined and visible, strengthened by God as the task increases and the demands of leadership multiply. As the flock grows, the shepherd has to rise to the occasion.

We will take an exciting journey back into the life of the infant Church in her formative years. We will look carefully at her understanding of authority and unity and how this was not only taught but practiced. These brothers and sisters in the Lord courageously endured severe persecution, torture, and martyrdom for the name of Christ and his Church. They resisted heresy and alien doctrine to the point of shedding their blood. They were also, with unanimous consent, steady in their appreciation for the primacy of Peter and his successors in Rome. The unity of the Church was paramount, and the unity had to be maintained.

Eastern Orthodox theologian Alexander Schmemann writes, "We do not need to go here into all details of this ecclesiology. The important point here is for us to see that in the light of this doctrine [of a universal Church] the need for and the reality of a universal head, i.e., the Bishop of Rome, can no longer be termed an exaggeration. It becomes not only acceptable but also necessary. If the Church is a universal organism, she must have at her head a universal bishop as the focus of her unity and the organ of supreme power. The idea, popular in Orthodox apologetics, that the Church can have no visible head, because Christ is her *invisible* head, is theological nonsense. If applied consistently, it should also eliminate the necessity for the visible head of each local church, i.e., the bishop.[1] Yet it is the basic assumption of a 'catholic' ecclesiology that the visible structure of the Church manifests and communicates its invisible nature. The invisible Christ is made present through the visible unity of the bishop and the people: the Head and the Body. To oppose the *visible* structure to the *invisible* Christ leads inescapably to the Protestant divorce between a visible and human Church which is contingent, relative and changing, and an invisible Church in heaven. We must simply admit that if the categories of organism and organic unity are to be applied primarily to the Church universal as the sum of all its component parts (i.e., local churches), then the one, supreme,

---

[1] Many Protestant groups, such as Fundamentalists and Evangelicals, often say, "The Catholic Church needs a visible head or vicar for its Church, but we don't, for we have the risen Christ as our head." But is that true? They still need a visible leader in the form of a pastor. But why do they need a pastor? Isn't Jesus Christ our Good Shepherd (Jn 10:11)? Isn't Jesus Christ the Shepherd (or *pastor*) and bishop of our souls (1 Pet 2:25)? Why do Protestants need a visible "man-shepherd" to lead their flocks? Cannot Christ do that? How is that different, in principle, from the Catholic Church having a pastor of the universal Church? And finally I would ask, if God is the head of our families (Eph 3:14–15), how is it that a husband can claim to be the head of his home? Isn't this an arrogation of God's authority and headship?

and universal power as well as its bearer becomes a self-evident necessity, because this unique visible organism must have a unique visible head. Thus the efforts of Roman Catholic theologians to justify Roman primacy not by mere historical contingencies but by divine institution appear as logical. Within a universal ecclesiology, primacy is of necessity *power* and, by the same necessity, a divinely instituted power; we have all this in a consistent form in the Roman Catholic doctrine of the Church."[2]

As we have seen, the primacy of Rome seems to be a given from the time of the apostles. As we will find in examining later documents, the understanding of this primacy grew and developed as an organic outgrowth of the apostolic Church well before it was defined in councils or decrees. As J. Michael Miller says, "The fact of Roman primacy emerged before its nature was explained and justified. Moreover, Rome never needed to demand recognition for its prerogatives; rather, it was peacefully accepted."[3] In rejecting this development of doctrine as unnecessary and unbiblical, some object that Christ is the *only* head of the *invisible* Church,[4] while denying that the Church needs a visible shepherd such as the Pope. In his classic work entitled *Principles and Practices for Baptist Churches*, Edward T. Hiscox states, "The religious cultivation of his Church and congregation constitutes the peculiar work of the pastor. It is the *shepherding* of the flock. He is not to be indifferent to their temporal interests, but their spiritual welfare is his special charge."[5] How is this different from the primacy of

[2] Alexander Schmemann, in *The Primacy of Peter*, ed. by John Meyendorff et al. (Crestwood, N.Y.: St. Vladimir's Seminary Press, 1992), 151. Schmemann holds to a eucharistic unity as opposed to a universal Church. However, he explains quite lucidly that if one accepts the doctrine or the idea of a universal Church, then the universal primacy is a *necessity* and the Catholic Church best represents the universal Church model.

[3] J. Michael Miller, *The Shepherd and the Rock* [Huntington, Ind.: Our Sunday Visitor, 1995], 88).

[4] The Westminster Catechism asks, "What is the invisible church?" to which it replies, "The invisible church is the whole number of the elect, that have been, are, or shall be gathered into one under Christ the head" (*The Westminster Larger Catechism* [Atlanta, Ga.: Committee for Christian Education & Publications, 1990], *Questions*, no. 64 in *Logos Library System Software* v.2.0c, Oak Harbor, Wash., 1996). However, Christ left a visible Church on earth to show the world the unity that proves that the Father sent the Son (Jn 17:20–21).

[5] Edward T. Hiscox, *Principles and Practices for Baptist Churches* (Grand Rapids, Mich.: Kregel Pub., 1980), 95.

Peter shepherding (pastoring) the universal flock, the one fold (Jn 10:16), the Church? The pastor of a Baptist church views himself as the shepherd of his flock, caring for real sheep in the name of the Chief Shepherd (1 Pet 5:2–4), Jesus Christ. He is to keep the unity and maintain "biblical teaching".

The Baptists realize that a flock without a shepherd is a flock unattended and scattered, even though in principle they would claim that Christ is their head. There is an inherent and even biblical mandate for a human shepherd to lead the flock, to be its visible head. How is this fundamentally different from the Catholic Church, which is worldwide, needing a shepherd for the worldwide or universal Church?

What Do the First Five Centuries Teach Us?

We have already taken a look at the biblical passages referring to Peter and his calling to shepherd the universal flock of Christ as the steward, representing the new and eternal King of the Davidic throne, Jesus Christ. We have established Peter's presence and martyrdom in Rome and the recognition of the Roman Church's special place in the first century. We saw this as we looked at the earliest documents of the Church outside the canonized documents of the New Testament.

Now, as we delve into the writings of the first five centuries of the Church, we should remember always as we read that the vast majority of the quotations and historical situations we will analyze are *prior to* the final collection and canonization of the New Testament. What an amazing fact—the primacy of Rome was established and recognized by the universal Church long before the New Testament canon was closed.

As the Church grew and spread throughout the known world, from India to Britain, from the northern European tribes to the depths of Africa, the responsibility to pastor and unite the Church fell to the bishops. When dissension and confusion arose, the local Churches turned to their bishops for unity; and eventually, the bishops turned to the Church of Rome. Cardinal Newman explains this very well:

St. Ignatius directed his doctrine according to the need. While Apostles were on earth, there was the display neither of bishop nor Pope; their power had no prominence, as being exercised by Apostles. In course of time, first the power of the bishop displayed itself, and then the power of the Pope. When the Apostles were taken away, Christianity did not at once break into portions; yet separate localities might begin to be the scene of internal dissensions, and a local arbiter in consequence would be wanted. . . . When the Church, then, was thrown upon her own resources, first local disturbances gave exercise to bishops, and next ecumenical disturbances [one Church with another] gave exercise to Popes; and whether communion with the Pope was necessary for Catholicity would not and could not be debated till a suspension of that communion had actually occurred. It is not a greater difficulty that St. Ignatius does not write to the Asian Greeks about Popes, than that St. Paul does not write to the Corinthians about bishops. And it is a less difficulty that the Papal supremacy was not formally acknowledged in the second century than that there was no formal acknowledgment on the part of the Church of the doctrine of the Holy Trinity till the fourth. No doctrine is defined till it is violated.

And, in like manner, it was natural for Christians to direct their course in matters of doctrine by the guidance of mere floating, and, as it were, endemic tradition, while it was fresh and strong; but in proportion as it languished, or was broken in particular places, did it become necessary to fall back upon its special homes, first the Apostolic sees, and then the See of St. Peter.[6]

Even those bishops who hesitated to acknowledge verbally the primacy of Rome in its fullness *practiced* the primacy of Peter by quickly appealing to Rome in theological and ecclesiastical matters. This will be demonstrated as we proceed.

That the early writers of the Church accepted the primacy of Rome from the turn of the first century is key to understanding how the apostles' disciples understood their mentors. Was this monarchical episcopate a novelty or invention devised by some slick salesmen trying to gain control, or was it the organic outgrowth of the apostolic tradition? "Was this short space of time [until the end of the first century] long enough to allow wholesale innovations to spread all over Asia Minor [and as far east as Syria] and take such firm root among the Christians [so] that Ignatius

---

[6] John Henry Cardinal Newman, *An Essay on the Development of Christian Doctrine* 4, 3, 2 and 4, in *Conscience, Consensus, and the Development of Doctrine* (New York: Doubleday, 1992), 157–58.

[and Clement] could appeal to them as the traditions of the Apostles?"[7]

So begins our journey through the first centuries of the one holy, catholic, and apostolic Church. By no means can we include every quotation available, for the citations are too many. Matthew 16 is a crucial passage establishing Peter's special prerogative. Since the objection is frequently raised that Matthew 16 is used by some Fathers in a manner confounding the Catholic understanding, we will look at the references to this passage with particular interest, beginning with its earliest appearance, in a text by Justin Martyr.

Biblical passages usually have only one literal meaning but can have several applications and interpretations. So, whereas the passage in Matthew 16 is literally and primarily to be understood in light of Jesus' commission of Peter and the investiture of stewardship, it can also be marshaled effectively in defense of the deity of Christ and the need for divine revelation. When the Fathers refer to the Rock as Christ, or Peter's confession, or Peter's faith, they are not denying the literal intent of the passage. They are simply utilizing all the riches of the passage for apologetical resources.

James Shotwell and Louise Loomis write:

> The name Peter would have little interest for history, if it had not been linked up with the interpretation given in full in the eighteenth verse of the sixteenth chapter of Matthew. . . . That interpretation, which has become the foundation text of the Papacy, has, however, been given varying interpretations itself. The orthodox Catholic view has been the simple and literal one,—that the rock was Peter (Kepha in both cases). But it was also held by some of the Fathers that it was the confession which Peter made—"thou art Christ, the son of the living God"—which was the corner-stone of the Church, since upon that belief the new religion was in reality based. This view was especially seized upon by the Fathers who were disputing with the bishop of Rome or with the heretics who denied the orthodox statement of Christ's divinity. Peter's confession, ratified so emphatically by Jesus, was the strongest text they had. In course of time, however, as the creed was settled the literal meaning became the common one, exalting the "fisherman's

---

[7] St. Clement and St. Ignatius, *The Epistles of St. Clement of Rome and St. Ignatius of Antioch*, trans. James A. Kleist, Ancient Christian Writers, vol. 1 (New York: Newman Press, 1946), 57.

chair" above the other apostolic foundations as the historical em-
bodiment of Christ's promise. This was not seriously challenged
until the Protestant theologians found the text, as commonly accepted, a stumbling block in their denial of papal claims. Most of
them fell back, then, to the interpretation first discussed, and
found support in the fact that some of the Fathers had once so
held.[8]

As we will see, Peter's commission can be understood and used in
various ways, but these useful applications do not negate the primary and literal interpretation of our Lord's words.

One further comment on the fact that various *applications* can
be gleaned from biblical passages, even though there is one *literal
interpretation* of this Matthean passage. John Lowe, an Anglican,
writes:

> The statement "Thou art Peter (*Kepha*) and upon this rock (*kepha*)
> I will build my church" must certainly be taken to refer to Peter
> personally. However true it may be that ultimately Christ himself is
> the rock, a truth proclaimed in Matthew 21:42 and in 1 Corin-
> thians 3:11, that is not said here. Nor is it at all natural to explain
> that the rock is the faith of Peter in virtue of which he has con-
> fessed that Jesus is Messiah. No doubt it is a legitimate homiletic
> application to make the point that the Lord's Messiahship and the
> faith represented in Peter's confession are both basic, but from the
> point of view of pure exegesis it is, I feel, impossible to claim that
> this meaning can be extracted from these words. Here the word-
> play does surely necessitate the identification of the rock with the
> man Peter. Reluctance to admit this, and there is a long history of
> such reluctance, has been due, consciously or unconsciously, to the
> supposed requirements of confessional [Protestant] controversy,
> to the fear that such an admission is to concede the claims of
> Rome. The authority of Luther, who in most of his thinking virtu-
> ally equates Peter and Pope, has dominated the reformed tradi-
> tion, and in the interests of the doctrine of justification by faith
> alone it has become almost a point of honour to explain away the
> reference to Peter in this passage—either that or to cut the knot by
> denying its authenticity. Thus has the critical and exegetical ques-
> tion been beclouded by polemical considerations. If we resolutely
> cut ourselves loose from the confusing influence of later contro-
> versies and look at the words themselves, we must, I think, agree

---

[8] James T. Shotwell and Louise Ropes Loomis, *The See of Peter* (1927; reprint,
New York: Columbia Univ. Press, 1991), 24.

that it is Peter himself personally who is here said to be the rock upon which the Church is to be built.[9]

We must always remember that the work of the Holy Spirit, working in and through the visible Church, did not cease to act when Luke laid down his pen at the end of his Acts of the Apostles. Nowhere do we find a "retirement clause" to inform us of the cessation of the Spirit's involvement or of a halt to ecclesiastical or theological development.[10] The organic Church continued to grow, develop, and flesh out the fullness of the faith. Having already discussed in some detail the earliest writers from the first century, *Clement of Rome*, *Ignatius of Antioch*, and *Hermas*, we will resume our survey at the time of St. John the Apostle's death and move right into the second century.

Justin Martyr (c. A.D. 100–c. 165)[11]

"For [Christ] called one of His disciples—previously known by the name of Simon—Peter; since he recognised Him to be Christ the Son of God, by the revelation of His Father: and since we find it

---

[9] John Lowe, *Saint Peter* (New York: Oxford Univ. Press, 1956), 55–56.

[10] The theological development of the trinitarian doctrines and the unfolding understanding and defining of the divinity of Christ in the first centuries are proof enough that the Holy Spirit did not cease to lead the Church and her councils infallibly. The final determination of the New Testament canon is another significant example. Even those who look upon Catholic tradition with suspicion and contempt depend upon the Spirit's work within the visible Catholic Church for the foundation of their doctrine and, interestingly enough, even for the New Testament itself.

[11] Justin Martyr was the outstanding apologist of the early Church. He was born of pagan parents in Flavia, Neapolis (twenty-one miles from Thessalonica and thirty-four miles from Philippi, visited by Paul [Acts 16:11]). After a long search for truth in the pagan philosophies, Justin at last embraced Christianity about A.D. 130. For a time he taught at Ephesus, and then he moved to Rome, where he opened a Christian school, having Tatian as one of his students. He and some of his disciples were denounced as Christians in 165 and, upon refusing to sacrifice to pagan gods, were scourged and beheaded. According to the *Oxford Dictionary of the Christian Church*, "the authentic record of their martyrdom ('*Martyrium SS. Iustini et Sociorum*'), based on an official court report, survives" (ed. F. L. Cross and E. A. Livingstone, rev. ed. [New York: Oxford Univ. Press, 1997], 915). Eusebius refers to Justin as "an ornament of our Faith soon after the Apostles' time" (*The History of the Church* 2, 13, trans. G. A. Williamson [Harmondsworth, Middlesex, England: Penguin Books, 1965], 47).

recorded in the memoirs of His apostles that He is the Son of God, and since we call Him the Son, we have understood that He proceeded before all creatures from the Father by His power and will . . . and that He became man by the Virgin." [12]

Polycarp (c. A.D. 69–c. 155)—Travels to Rome [13]

"And when the blessed Polycarp was at Rome in the time of [Pope] Anicetus, and they disagreed a little about certain other things, they immediately made peace with one another, not caring to

---

[12] *Dialogue with Trypho* 100, 4–5, ANF 1:249. This is the earliest allusion to Matthew 16 in the writings of the early Church. It is mentioned here to establish that this biblical passage has several applications, not the least of which is the primacy of Rome. However, this passage is also rightly used to teach other truths, which in no way minimizes or excludes its primary historical meaning: the unique prerogatives bestowed on Peter.

The orientation of the early Church was strongly influenced by the heresies that rose up against her. The heresies nearly all centered on the Person of Christ: Was he created or divine, unique or one in a series of emanations, etc. "The first of these heresies to cause serious anxiety to the church was Gnosticism, and it is in the anti-Gnostic writings that Matthew's Petrine text is first alluded to. . . . [St. Justin] was at pains to clarify the position of Christ, whose uniqueness had been obscured by Gnostic theory that there were many intermediaries bridging the gap between the Father and the world. Peter is then spoken of precisely because the Father had revealed to him the true nature of Christ. . . . It is evident from the wording that St. Justin had in mind Matthew 16. His understanding of it is by no means exhaustive, nor exclusive of other deductions, but its principal merit in Justin's eyes is its connection with the divinity of Christ" (Michael M. Winter, *Saint Peter and the Popes* [Baltimore, Md.: Helicon Press, 1960], 39). Confronting the Jew Trypho, Justin is also proving that Jesus is indeed the Christ and was revealed as such to Peter by God the Father himself. Using a passage such as this to emphasize the deity of Christ does not in any way detract from its other applications, such as that of establishing the primacy of Peter.

[13] Polycarp was a Christian since childhood and was given up to death by beasts, fire, and finally stabbing at the age of eighty-six. Irenaeus says, "Polycarp also was not only instructed by apostles and conversed with many who had seen Christ, but was also, by apostles in Asia, appointed bishop of the Church in Smyrna, whom I also saw in my early youth, for he tarried [on earth] a very long time, and when a very old man, gloriously and nobly suffering martyrdom, departed this life, having always taught the things which he had learned from the apostles, and which the Church has handed down, and which alone are true" (*Against Heresies* 3, 3, 4, ANF 1:416). Polycarp visited Rome a year or two before his martyrdom and met with Victor, the bishop of Rome.

quarrel over this matter. For neither could Anicetus persuade Polycarp not to observe what he had always observed with John the disciple of our Lord, and the other apostles with whom he had associated; neither could Polycarp persuade Anicetus to observe it [Easter], as he said that he ought to follow the customs of the presbyters that had preceded him.[14] But though matters were in this shape, they communed together, and Anicetus conceded the administration of the eucharist in the church to Polycarp, manifestly as a mark of respect. And they parted from each other in peace, both those who observed, and those who did not, maintaining the peace of the whole church."[15]

Soter, Bishop of Rome (c. A.D. 166–c. 174)[16]

"There is extant also another epistle written by Dionysius to the Romans, and addressed to Soter, who was bishop at that time. We

---

[14] The reoccurring cause of disturbance in the early Church revolved around the proper day to celebrate Easter. "It appears that by the middle of the second century the majority of the churches, including Rome, celebrated Easter on the Sunday which followed the fourteenth day of the Jewish month of Nisan. However, the churches of Asia observed the feast on the fourteenth day of Nisan, whether it happened to be a Sunday or not" (Winter, *Saint Peter*, 129).

[15] Irenaeus, letter to Victor of Rome, quoted in *Eusebius* 5, 24, 16–17, NPNF2, 1:243–44. Why is a man in his ninth decade of life traveling the treacherous journey of almost one thousand miles over rugged land and rough seas? Polycarp had been installed as bishop by apostles; why did he deem it necessary in his aged condition to travel such a distance? The records are fragmentary, and we are not explicitly told. However, we are told that he did two things while in Rome. First, he met with Pope Anicetus, discussing the Easter celebration, and he presided over the celebration of the Eucharist. John Farrow writes, "Polycarp, able bishop of Smyrna, tried to urge the latter usage on Rome but Anicetus remained steadfast to the custom that had begun with Peter. Great controversy was waged between bishop and pope but the pope did not make it a question of papal authority and the bishop had the good sense not to suggest or cause a schismatic break. The argument was to continue until finally settled, in favor of the Western Church [Rome], at the Council of Nicaea" (*Pageant of the Popes* [St. Paul, Minn.: Catechetical Guild Educational Society, 1955], 20). The problem was that both views seemed to have apostolic warrant. Rome stood strong in her conviction, and in short order the whole universal Church agreed with her.

[16] Soter was the eleventh Pope in succession from Peter. Most of what we know of his episcopacy comes from the remains of a letter addressed to him from Dionysius of Corinth.

cannot do better than to subjoin some passages from this epistle, in which he commends the practice of the Romans which has been retained down to the persecution in our own days. His words are as follows: 'For from the beginning it has been your practice to do good to all the brethren in various ways, and to send contributions to many churches in every city. Thus relieving the want of the needy, and making provision for the brethren in the mines by the gifts which you have sent from the beginning, you Romans keep up the hereditary customs of the Romans, which your blessed bishop Soter has not only maintained, but also added to, furnishing an abundance of supplies to the saints, and encouraging the brethren from abroad with blessed words, as a loving father his children.' "[17]

Pothinus of Lyons (A.D. 77–177)[18]

"We pray, father Eleutherus, that you may rejoice in God in all things and always. We have requested our brother and comrade

---

[17] Eusebius, *Church History* 4, 23, NPNF2, 1:201. Rome was generous and known for her plenteous support of other Churches. Rome was praised by the brethren from far and wide with blessed words, and her bishop was viewed by other Churches as a "loving father" caring for his children. J. N. D. Kelly comments, "Other letters of Dionysius have led scholars to suspect that Soter may have expressed disapproval of his [Dionysius'] lax attitude both to the ideal of sexual continence and to the restoration of penitent sinners to communion irrespective of the kind of sins they had committed, and that his obsequious reply may be an attempt to soothe the pope without yielding any point of principle" (J. N. D. Kelly, *The Oxford Dictionary of Popes* [New York: Oxford Univ. Press, 1986], 11). Soter, like his earlier predecessor Clement, had sent a pastoral letter to Corinth, probably exhorting Dionysius to correct laxity. The epistle was read aloud in the churches. The Pope of Rome continued to be viewed as a father of the Church, caring for, exhorting, and overseeing the universal Church.

[18] Pothinus was the bishop of Lyons in Gaul (modern-day France) and a disciple of Polycarp along with Irenaeus. The Church in Gaul was having trouble with the Montanists, and Pothinus sent a letter, carried by Irenaeus, to Pope Eleutherus in Rome. Pothinus died a horrible death under the persecution of Marcus Aurelius. Scores were killed in the most cruel and horrendous fashion. The account of the martyrdoms comes down to us in a letter that is "the pearl of the Christian literature of the second century" and is preserved in the pages of Eusebius. A short excerpt is provided: "The deacon Sanctus also endured cruel torments with unflinching courage. To all questions that were put to him, he only replied, 'I am a Christian.' When all the ordinary forms of torture had been exhausted, red-hot plates were applied to the tenderest parts

Irenaeus to carry this letter to you, and we ask you to hold him in esteem, as zealous for the covenant of Christ. For if we thought that office could confer righteousness upon any one, we should commend him among the first as a presbyter of the church, which is his position." [19]

Hegesippus of Syria
—written c. A.D. 180[20]

"And the church of Corinth continued in the true faith until

---

of his body until he appeared a shapeless mass of swollen flesh. Three days later, when he had revived, the same treatment was repeated. . . . Bishop Pothinus, in spite of his ninety years and manifold infirmities, was dragged before the tribunal amid the railing of the populace. . . . Thereupon he was beaten, kicked, and pelted until he was nearly insensible. Two days later he died in prison" (Alban Butler, *Butler's Lives of the Saints*, rev. Herbert J. Thurston and Donald Attwater [Allen, Tex.: Christian Classics, 1995], 2:455–56).

[19] Eusebius, *Church History* 5, 4, NPNF2, 1:219. Notice that Bishop Pothinus refers to the bishop of Rome as "father". This was of course, a title of honor and respect. Coxe, in his introductory note to the *Ante-Nicene Fathers*, 1:309, supposes the letter was a "letter of remonstrance" and that "Lyons checks the heretical tendencies of the bishop at Rome." In response, Dolan writes, "The statement of Dr. Coxe that the letters to Eleutherus which Irenaeus carried to Rome were 'letters of remonstrance' is purely gratuitous. It has not the merest semblance of historical foundation. . . . The statement of Eusebius that the Gallic martyrs sent an *orthodox* epistle [Eusebius 5, 3] to Eleutherus is perhaps sufficient proof that the letter from Lyons was an *appeal* to Rome against any toleration of the Montanist heresy. The Montanists appealed to the See of Peter, and we may assume, without doing violence to history, that the letter of the Gallic martyrs was a counter appeal. This letter is called by Eusebius πρέσβεία, which can never mean a simple communication, much less a letter of reproach, since the idea of reverence or honor is always included in the word. Incidentally we may remark, that this very πρέσβεία, indicates thus early a 'looking up to Rome'. . . . No historian suggests any infidelity on the part of that Pope" (Thomas S. Dolan, *The See of Peter and the Voice of Antiquity* [St. Louis, Mo.: B. Herder, 1908], 14–16). So, in the mid-second century, a bishop on the outskirts of the Empire refers to the Roman bishop with the title of "father" and sends a communication that could be interpreted as "looking up to Rome".

[20] St. Hegesippus (fl. A.D. 180), "who lived immediately after the apostles" (Eusebius, *Church History* 2, 23, 3, NPNF2, 1:125), was an early Church historian, born in the East, and probably a Hellenistic Jew. The date and occasion of his conversion from Judaism to Christianity are unknown. He wrote five books of *Memoirs* to refute the Gnostics. He visited Rome in the time of Pope St. Anicetus (A.D. 155–166). He is said to have made one of the first

Primus was bishop in Corinth.[21] I conversed with them on my way to Rome, and abode with the Corinthians many days, during which we were mutually refreshed in the true doctrine. And when I had come to Rome I remained there until Anicetus, whose deacon was Eleutherus. And Anicetus was succeeded by Soter, and he by Eleutherus. In every succession, and in every city that is held which is preached by the law and the prophets and the Lord." [22]

Eleutherus, Bishop of Rome (c. A.D. 174–189) [23]

"Where was Marcion *then*, that shipmaster of Pontus, the zealous student of Stoicism? Where was Valentinus *then*, the disciple of Platonism? For it is evident that those men [heretics] lived not so long ago,—in the reign of Antoninus, for the most part,—and that

---

"succession lists" of Roman bishops. In his *Memoirs* he tells of his journey to various centers of Christianity to gather information on the true doctrine of the apostles. He used the findings to resist Gnosticism better. Eusebius tells us, "that on a journey to Rome he met a great many bishops, and that he received the same doctrine from all" (*Church History* 4, 22, 1, NPNF2, 1:198). The time of his death is unknown.

[21] Earlier in his discourse he mentions that the Corinthians were still reading *The First Epistle of Clement to the Corinthians* almost one hundred years after it was originally written.

[22] Eusebius, *Church History* 4, 22, 2–3, NPNF2, 1:198–99. In Rome, Hegesippus collected the historical data necessary to reconstruct the succession of Popes from Peter down to his own day. Here it is clearly understood that there was a succession, not only in Rome, but also in each apostolic Church. It was in this succession that the true tradition and teaching of the apostles were preserved intact. The earliest records tell us that the apostles themselves set the doctrine of apostolic succession in motion (*1 Clem.* 44). Even William Webster, who has made a career of refuting the Papacy, admits that no father denies that Peter had a primacy or that there is a Petrine succession. Denial of apostolic succession is of recent origin. If apostolic succession were a false teaching, or contrary to the teachings of Christ and his apostles, orthodox writers would have opposed it ferociously from the beginning, as they did all other doctrinal deviations and heresies. But we have nary a word of dissent from this practice and teaching of the early Church; in fact, we have universal concurrence. The fact that Hegesippus researched the succession of many apostolic Churches in no way diminishes the primacy of the Roman Church; it only confirms that the bishops of the other Churches succeeded the apostles, but Peter's successors in Rome were always preeminent.

[23] Eleutherus was the twelfth bishop in succession after Peter. Eleutherus received a visit from Irenaeus regarding the Montanists.

they at first were believers in the doctrine of the Catholic Church, in the church of Rome under the episcopate of the blessed Eleutherus, until on account of their ever restless curiosity, with which they even infected the brethren, they were more than once expelled. Marcion, indeed, [went] with the two hundred sesterces which he had brought into the church, and, when banished at last to a permanent excommunication, they scattered abroad the poisons of their doctrines. Afterwards, it is true, Marcion professed repentance, and agreed to the conditions granted to him—that he should receive reconciliation if he restored to the church all the others whom he had been training for perdition: he was prevented, however, by death." [24]

Victor, Bishop of Rome (A.D. 189–198)
—continued dispute over the date of Easter [25]

"Synods and assemblies of bishops were held on this account [at the behest of Pope Victor], and all, with one consent, through

---

[24] Tertullian, *On Prescription against Heretics* 30, ANF 3:257. Tertullian reports the events that took place in Rome during the government of Eleutherus. Heretics began to preach in earnest and spread their heresies abroad. It fell to Eleutherus to condemn them. "Practically all the information we have about the Roman bishops of the latter half of the century concerns their relation to one or another of these early schisms and the measures that were being gradually devised to consolidate the Church against them. Eleutherus was confronted by at least two dilemmas, one created by the presence of the able Gnostic, Marcion, as a wealthy and influential member of his Roman congregation, and the other by the growth of the new puritan Montanist faction" (Shotwell and Loomis, *See of Peter*, 255). Marcion's money was returned, and he was expelled. Eleutherus initially cleared the Montanists until further information arrived from Praxeas and Irenaeus upon which the Montanists were disciplined and censured. Early on, the bishop of Rome is clearly taking a role of universal shepherd, in succession from Peter, overseeing the true doctrine and discipline throughout the universal Church, and both those who set up factions and those who resisted the heresies appealed to Rome for adjudication.

[25] Victor was the bishop of Rome, the thirteenth bishop after Peter. Many thought he was a man of strong personality, including probably Irenaeus of Lyons and Polycrates, bishop of Ephesus, who both opposed him regarding the day for celebrating Easter. "Though a general council was impossible, he paved the way for such councils by ordering local bishops everywhere to call synods to consider and, he hoped, condemn the quartodeciman Easter. The bishops obediently called their synods" (*The Popes: A Concise Biographical History*, ed. Eric John [London: Burns & Oates, 1964], 52). The synods all agreed with the

mutual correspondence drew up an ecclesiastical decree, that the mystery of the resurrection of the Lord should be celebrated on no other but the Lord's day, and that we should observe the close of the paschal fast on this day only. There is still extant a writing of those who were then assembled in Palestine, over whom Theophilus, bishop of Caesarea, and Narcissus, bishop of Jerusalem, presided. And there is also another writing extant of those who were assembled at Rome to consider the same question, which bears the name of Bishop Victor; also of the bishops in Pontus over whom Palmas, as the oldest, presided; and of the parishes in Gaul of which Irenaeus was bishop, and of those in Osrhoëne and the cities there; and a personal letter of Bacchylus, bishop of the church at Corinth, and of a great many others, who uttered the same opinion and judgment, and cast the same vote. And that which has been given above was their unanimous decision." [26]

" 'And how is it that they are not ashamed to speak thus falsely of Victor, knowing well that he cut off from communion Theodotus,

---

Roman Church, except the Churches of Asia Minor, which refused to abandon the practice established by St. John. Never do we see another Church making such a requirement of all the Churches everywhere. Only Rome practiced such authority.

[26] Letter from Polycrates to Pope Victor about A.D. 198, as recorded by Eusebius, *Church History* 5, 23, NPNF2, 1:241–42. The decision regarding the Easter celebration was unanimous except for the Churches of Asia Minor, of which Polycrates was the spokesman; and he said of himself, "I did not bear my gray hairs in vain, but had always governed my life by the Lord Jesus" (ibid., 5, 24, NPNF2, 1:242). The Catholic Church, at the request or command of Victor in Rome, held synods and assemblies of bishops to determine the mind of the Church. That Victor presided over, or at least ordered, the assemblies is clear from Polycrates' words, "I could mention the bishops who were present, whom I summoned at your desire" (ibid.). Coxe, in his footnotes to *The Nicene and Post-Nicene Fathers*, writes, "According to this, the Asiatic Council was summoned at the request of Victor of Rome, and in all probability this was the case with all the councils referred to in this last chapter [of Eusebius]" (NPNF2, 1:242, n. 11). Winter comments, "It is unlikely that all these synods would have met without some kind of central directive to do so, and in fact one of the letters is quite clear on the point. . . . It is reasonable to deduce from this indication that Victor had taken the initiative in arranging all the synods. . . . The sense of universal responsibility displayed in this request for synods is itself of relevance to the consideration of the power of the Bishop of Rome. However, the dramatic sequel to these synods is still more eloquent. Nearly all the churches declared that it had been their practice to celebrate Easter according to the Roman custom" (*St. Peter*, 130).

the cobbler, the leader and father of this God-denying apostasy, and the first to declare that Christ is mere man? For if Victor agreed with their opinions, as their slander affirms, how came he to cast out Theodotus, the inventor of this heresy?' So much in regard to Victor. His bishopric lasted ten years, and Zephyrinus was appointed his successor about the ninth year of the reign of [Emperor] Severus."[27]

Irenaeus
—written c. A.D. 180 [28]

"Thereupon Victor, head of the Roman church, attempted at one stroke to cut off from the common unity all the Asian dioceses, together with the neighboring churches, on the ground of heterodoxy, and pilloried them in letters in which he announced the

---

[27] Victor's actions as recorded in Eusebius, *Church History* 5, 28, NPNF2, 1:247. Many heretics made their way to Rome, as we will see later. The bishop of Rome made it his practice to preserve the true doctrine and excommunicate the heretics. "Among other incidents of Victor's pontificate were the deposition of the presbyter Florinus for defending Valentinian doctrines and the excommunication of the leather merchant, Theodotus, the founder of Dynamic Monarchianism" (Cross and Livingstone, *Oxford Dictionary*, 1437). According to Dr. Hergenröther, "Pope Victor I., in whose pontificate even Protestant authors 'have found combined all the agencies of the Papacy', excluded Theodotus of Byzantium from the Church, commanded Synods to be everywhere held upon the question of the paschal celebration, and menaced with excommunication the recalcitrant inhabitants of Asia Minor" (Joseph Hergenröther, *Anti-Janus: An Historico-Theological Criticism of the Work Entitled 'The Pope and the Council,' by Janus*, trans. J. B. Robertson [Dublin: W. B. Kelly, 1870], 110).

[28] Irenaeus' *Against Heresies* was written about A.D. 180. He reminisces in his treatise about how he heard the gospel of Christ in his youth from the preaching of St. Polycarp, a disciple of the Apostle John. (See also footnote 27, pp. 76–77, above.) Irenaeus was an early Father of the Church and was appointed bishop of Lyons in Gaul (now France) and converted many Gauls to the faith. He fought strongly against Gnosticism, confronting the error with great strength and clarity. He is mentioned as a martyr under Emperor Lucius Septimius Severus around A.D. 202. His profound writing against heresies, especially Gnosticism, is a wonderful historical source of information about the doctrine, life, and practice of the early Church. Before being appointed bishop of Gaul, Irenaeus made a trip to Rome, delivering a letter from his bishop, Pothinus, whom he later succeeded in the bishopric. Having had contact with and travels to Rome, Irenaeus would have intimate knowledge of the primacy of Rome and the orthodox teaching preserved in that great Church.

total excommunication of all his fellow-Christians there. But this was not to the taste of all the bishops: they replied with a request that he would turn his mind to the things that make for peace and for unity and love towards his neighbors. We still possess the words of these men, who very sternly rebuked Victor. Among them was Irenaeus, who wrote on behalf of the Christians for whom he was responsible in Gaul. While supporting the view that only on the Lord's Day might the mystery of the Lord's resurrection be celebrated, he gave Victor a great deal of excellent advice, in particular that he should not cut off entire churches of God because they observed the unbroken tradition of their predecessors." [29]

---

[29] Eusebius, *The History of the Church* 5, 23–25, trans. G. A. Williamson (Harmondsworth, Middlesex, England: Penguin Books, 1965), 172–73. After the synods on the celebration of Easter were concluded, all concurred with Rome except the Churches in Asia Minor, who through their spokesman, Polycrates, refused to follow Victor. Eusebius records the dispute between Pope Victor and the Asian bishops. Victor, though much younger and farther removed from the apostles than the Asian bishops, assumed his papal prerogatives and excommunicated the Asian Churches, not only from Rome, but also from the universal Church in general. The bishops felt free to challenge and even rebuke Victor, though in a very respectful manner. The amazing fact is that Victor assumed the authority to cut the Asian Churches off from the common unity, and *not one voice challenged his authority to do so.* Irenaeus writes to plead with Pope Victor. He takes the side of Victor against the teachers of his youth. He assumes the Pope can exercise this authority but urges him not to do so for the cause of peace. He challenged Victor's decision but not his rightful authority to make it.

As Rivington says, "He [Irenaeus] pleaded, as he had the right to do. . . . He therefore advised St. Victor with all becoming respect 'not to cut off whole Churches'. The Churches, therefore, were not, to the mind of St. Irenaeus, as yet excommunicated; but it was, according to the same saint, within the power of St. Victor to cut them off. . . . St. Irenaeus' advice as being to the effect 'that a rigorous right is not always to be used.' Not a hint is given all round that any one of the Churches disputed St. Victor's authority. Had any other portion of the Church talked of cutting off whole Churches from the common unity, it would only have made itself ridiculous. But when the threat comes from Rome the whole Church is astir; and there is one thing that no one says—neither St. Irenaeus nor the rest of the bishops said, 'It is ridiculous, you have no such authority;' but they exhort, and protest, and entreat him not to do so. . . . He [Victor] desisted from the final step, in accordance with the respectful remonstrance of St. Irenaeus. Eventually the Universal Church settled down to the Roman mode of observance. The whole incident discovers the actual center of Church life in that century" (*The Primitive Church and the See of Peter* [London: Longmans, Green and Co., 1894] 43–44). The prerogatives of leadership and primacy must already have been established and recognized for Victor to have

"Since, however, it would be very tedious in such a volume as this, to reckon up the successions of all the Churches, we do put to confusion all those who, in whatever manner, whether by an evil self-pleasing, by vainglory, or by blindness and perverse opinion, assemble in unauthorized meetings;[30] [we do this, I say,] by indicating that tradition derived from the apostles, of the very great, the very ancient, and universally known Church founded and organized at Rome by the two most glorious apostles, Peter and Paul; as also [by pointing out] the faith preached to men, which comes down to our time by means of the successions of the bishops. For it is a matter of necessity that every Church[31] should agree with this Church [of Rome], on account of its preeminent authority,[32] that is, the faithful everywhere, inasmuch as the apostolical

---

ventured such a universal requirement for synods and the subsequent edict without any protest denouncing his authority to do so. He did so, not as one vested with personal authority, but as one who recognizes the authority of the office of the bishop of Rome, and with such an office he was responsible in some way for the well-being of the universal Church.

[30] The primitive Church disregarded other "assemblies" that were outside the Catholic Church. Irenaeus refers to sects as those who "assemble where it is not proper". Ignatius of Antioch had earlier condemned the sectarians: "If any man follows him that makes a schism in the Church, he shall not inherit the kingdom of God" (*Epistle to the Philadelphians* 3, 2, ANF 1:80). Others referred to "unauthorized gatherings". The teachings of the Fathers are very clear in this matter, and they are certainly in harmony with the teachings of the apostles, who were always in the pursuit of unity.

[31] "Every Church" would mean every local Church around the world. Irenaeus recognizes the Roman Church as the standard of apostolic teaching and authenticity with which all other Churches in the world must agree. He defines the words himself when he says, "that is, the faithful everywhere".

[32] Coxe, in his footnotes to *The Ante-Nicene Fathers* (1:415, n. 3), shows his anti-Catholic bias when he chides the original editors, Alexander Roberts and James Donaldson. They had translated the Latin phrase *propter potiorem principalitatem* as "preeminent authority", which is how most scholars translate the words. In a footnote, Roberts and Donaldson write, "We are far from sure that the rendering given above is correct, but we have been unable to think of anything better." In response, and placed in brackets, Coxe, who revised the text notes, states, "A most extraordinary confession. It would be hard to find a worse [one]." The reason this translation is so nefarious in Coxe's eyes is that it supports the Roman Catholic interpretation. He as much as admits this in his *Elucidations* (ANF 1:460), "The authors of the Latin translation may have designed the ambiguity which gives the Ultramontane party an apparent advantage; but it is an advantage which disappears as soon as it is examined. . . . The Latin answers

tradition has been preserved continuously by those [faithful men] who exist everywhere." [33]

---

every purpose of the author's argument, and is fatal to the claims of the Papacy." Thomas Dolan, after responding to Coxe's assertions, concludes, "All this, I think, makes evident to the fair-minded reader, that the ideas of Dr. Coxe upon the famous testimony of St. Irenaeus, had no reality save as they floated about in the muddled waters of his [Coxe's] imagination" (*See of Peter,* 24).

The word "necessity" used by Irenaeus is a strong term, but agreement within the universal Church was essential for Irenaeus—the Church could not contradict herself—so a source of unity was necessary. "It is impossible to exaggerate the importance of this text, which comes from a bishop venerable among all others, from a man originally from Asia, a disciple of Polycarp and, through him, of St. John; the leader of a Church without close links with Rome, actuated only by a solicitude for the truth and for Christian unity. St. Irenaeus specifies that it is necessary to have recourse to the Roman Church and to be in agreement with it. This, according to him, is a moral, religious and, therefore, even a sacred necessity. It is not only a matter of convenience or utility; it is an obligation" (Wladimir d'Ormesson, *The Papacy,* trans. Michael Derrick. The Twentieth Century Encyclopedia of Catholicism, vol. 81 [New York: Hawthorn Books, 1962], 45).

The original Greek manuscript is no longer extant, but, whatever the original Greek words actually were, the reality is the same: Rome has a superior origin, has a more powerful preeminence, a preeminent authority, and a more powerful principality. After fifty-nine pages reviewing the two-thousand-year history of interpretation and the linguistic study of Irenaeus' passage concerning the *potiorem principalitatem* of Rome, Dominic J. Unger writes, "In conclusion, I think the traditional interpretation of this famous passage of Irenaeus remains the best proved and the correct one. All other interpretations are attempts to evade the obvious meaning concerning the Roman primacy or to solve the supposed contradiction in the last clause. Irenaeus, however, told the Gnostics of his day, and us too, that it is morally necessary for every Church, that is, for all the faithful, to agree with this, the Roman Church, in which, as by an instrumental cause, the tradition of the Apostles has always been preserved by those who are everywhere" ("Current Theology: St. Irenaeus and the Roman Primacy", *The Journal of Theological Studies* 44 (1993): 417.

[33] *Against Heresies* 3, 3, 2, ANF 1:415–16. Much discussion has revolved around this passage because of its great importance in the issue of Roman primacy. William Webster, in *The Church of Rome at the Bar of History* (Carlisle, Pa.: Banner of Truth Trust, 1995), as one would expect, ignores the pertinent points in the passage, dismissing them by pointing out that Irenaeus also mentions other Churches that have maintained the apostolic tradition. This is undenied, of course, but the fact that Irenaeus mentions other Churches proves nothing for two reasons. First, Irenaeus gives undeniable priority to Rome, especially through the use of unique terminology; and, secondly, the Catholic Church has always taught that bishops maintain the apostolic tradition through apostolic

"In the time of Clement, no small dissension having occurred among the brethren at Corinth, the Church in Rome dispatched a most powerful letter to the Corinthians, exhorting them to peace, renewing their faith, and declaring the tradition which it had lately received from the apostles. . . . From this document, whosoever chooses to do so, may learn that He, the Father of our Lord Jesus Christ, was preached by the Churches, and may also understand the apostolical tradition of the Church, since this Epistle is of older date than these men who are now propagating falsehood, and who conjure into existence another god beyond the Creator and the Maker of all existing things. To this Clement there succeeded Evaristus. Alexander followed Evaristus; then, sixth from the apostles, Sixtus was appointed; after him, Telephorus, who was gloriously martyred; then Hyginus; after him, Pius; then after him, Anicetus. Soter having succeeded Anicetus, Eleutherius does now, in the twelfth place from the apostles, hold the inheritance of the episcopate. In this order, and by this succession, the ecclesiastical tradition from the apostles, and the preaching of the truth, have come down to us. And this is most abundant proof that there is one and the same vivifying faith, which has been preserved in the Church from the apostles until now, and handed down in truth."[34]

---

succession. But, just as Peter was the leader of the other apostles, so the other Churches mentioned by Irenaeus are by his very context subordinate Churches to Rome. Webster proves nothing and only manages to evade the real meaning of the text as well as the obvious conclusion in favor of the Catholic Church.

In Meyendorff, *Primacy of Peter*, 131, Orthodox Church historian Nicholas Afanassieff struggles to dismiss this passage, even admitting that "our interpretations are just hypotheses, some plausible and others not." He tries too hard—the tension is palpable—to repudiate the obvious, and his attempt is thoroughly unconvincing. Irenaeus is *very* close to the apostles in time and *very* conservative in doctrine. He is not an innovator. He is not fabricating scenarios to baffle the heretics. Rather, he is standing on well-established doctrine and tradition. Rome was the safeguard of doctrine, because of her "superior origin". So, we see that Rome stands as the beacon, the center of unity, the safeguard of apostolic doctrine, and the Church of primacy for all believers throughout the world.

[34] *Against Heresies* 3, 3, 3, in ANF 1:416. There is no mistaking the apostolic succession and the authority and importance of the Church of Rome. "The apostolicity of the Roman church is preeminent in relation to that of the other churches because it goes back to the apostles. Here, on the grounds of its twofold apostolicity, a superiority over all the others is attributed to the Roman church" (Michael Schmaus, *The Church: Its Origin and Structure*, vol. 4 of *Dogma* [London: Sheed and Ward, 1972], 183). The basis of Irenaeus' defense against

"For our Lord never came to save Paul alone, nor is God so limited in means, that He should have but one apostle who knew the dispensation of His Son. . . . Or how could Peter have been in ignorance, to whom the Lord gave testimony, that flesh and blood had not revealed to him, but the Father, who is in heaven [Mt 16:17]? Just, then, as 'Paul [was] an apostle, not of men, neither by man, but by Jesus Christ, and God the Father,' [so with the rest;] the Son indeed leading them to the Father, but the Father revealing to them the Son. But that Paul acceded to [the request of] those who summoned him to the apostles, on account of the question [which had been raised], and went up to them, with Barnabas, to Jerusalem, not without reason, but that the liberty of the Gentiles might be confirmed by them, he does himself say." [35]

---

heresy was an exclusive appeal, not to Scripture, but to the Church. "In opposition to the various Gnostic tendencies of the second and third centuries, which stressed the deeper 'understanding of revelation' by individuals, especially charismatic interpreters, the Church realized the importance of the tradition and the magisterium of the Church, especially the magisterium of the bishops (Tertullian; Irenaeus)" (Johann Auer, *The Church: The Universal Sacrament of Salvation*, trans. M. Waldstein [Washington, D.C.: Catholic Univ. Press, 1993], 293). Here Rome is singled out as the preeminent, superior Church. Even though Irenaeus mentions others that have maintained the apostolic tradition through the apostolic succession, he singles out Rome with extraordinary and singular language that leaves no doubt as to Rome's unique and unrivaled position of authority.

[35] *Against Heresies* 3, 13, 1–3, ANF 1:436–37. Irenaeus uses Matthew's passage, not as an argument for the primacy of Rome, but to show that it was not only Paul who had been given revelation from God. The canon of the Marcionites consisted of Paul's epistles and an edited copy of St. Luke. Marcion taught that Paul alone understood the contrast of law and grace, the other apostles having been corrupted by Jewish influences. In response, Irenaeus argues that Peter *also* received revelation from the Father (Mt 16:17), before Paul, and thus was given special privileges from Christ. It is the standard fare of opponents to Catholicism to deny the biblical precedent in support of Peter's primacy by pointing to such passages as this from Irenaeus and commenting that all the apostles were equal, all had revelation from God, and that the Fathers sometimes do not utilize this passage to claim primacy for Peter. There are many teachings and truths that can be gleaned from Matthew's account, and the Church Fathers appropriated them all, depending on the purpose at hand. An application of one aspect of a passage does not negate an equally valid application in another situation. Michael Winter writes, "The same background of Gnosticism [as with Justin Martyr] must be borne in mind when examining . . . St. Irenaeus. His treatment of the matter is more developed, and he had

Clement of Alexandria
 —written between A.D. 190 and 210[36]

"Therefore on hearing those words, the blessed Peter, the chosen, the pre-eminent, the first of the disciples, for whom alone and Himself the Saviour paid tribute [Mt 17:27], quickly seized and comprehended the saying."[37]

---

to face the allegation that St. Paul alone had received the full revelation of Christ. . . . How could Peter be accused of ignorance, asks Irenaeus, when the Lord himself had declared that it was not from flesh and blood but from the Father that he had derived his knowledge. Although, . . . St. Irenaeus was aware of the Roman primacy, he himself does not say precisely how he connected it with the Apostle Peter" (*Saint Peter*, 39–40). Notice also the interesting observation by Irenaeus that Paul was summoned to Jerusalem and acceded to the request of those summoning, in order that his work could be confirmed by the "pillars of the Church". Thus Irenaeus refutes the claim that Paul was a singular apostle with insight superior to the others, since he was summoned to Jerusalem to give an account.

[36] Clement of Alexandria, whose full name was Titus Flavius Clemens, was a Greek theologian and an early Father of the Church. He was probably born in Athens and was educated at the catechetical school in Alexandria, Egypt, where he studied under the Christian philosopher St. Pantaenus (second century). Some time after Clement's conversion from paganism, he was ordained a presbyter. In about 190 he succeeded Pantaenus as head of the catechetical school, which became famous under his leadership. Origen, who later achieved distinction as a writer, teacher, and theologian, may have been one of Clement's pupils. During the persecution of the Christians in the reign of Lucius Septimius Severus, emperor of Rome, Clement moved from Alexandria to Caesarea in Cappadocia. Little is known of his subsequent activities.

[37] *Who Is the Rich Man That Shall Be Saved?* 21, ANF 2:597. Clement clearly sees Peter in a unique and leadership position among the band of apostles. Protestants, however, will cite another passage from Clement in an attempt to deny that he held a high view of Peter. In the sixth book of his *Hypotyposes*, Clement writes, "For they say that Peter and James and John after the ascension of our Saviour, as if also preferred by our Lord, strove not after honor, but chose James the Just bishop of Jerusalem" (Eusebius, *Church History* 2, 1, 3, NPNF2, 1:104). This in no way relegates Peter to a lesser stature, quite the contrary; Peter, along with James and John, chose James to succeed them in the leadership of the Church in Jerusalem so that Peter could fulfill his responsibilities to the universal Church and as the apostle of the circumcised around the world. D'Ormesson writes, "So, I come to the second Protestant objection, about the replacement of Peter by James at the head of the Church of Jerusalem. The answer here is clear. If Peter yielded the government of the Church of Jerusalem to James, it was in order to dedicate himself exclusively to his missionary activity; it was to obey his Master's first commandment, to 'go out, making disciples' " (*Papacy*, 25). Peter

Epitaph of Abercius
    —cemetery inscription c. A.D. 200 [38]

"The citizen of a prominent city, I erected this
While I lived, that I might have a resting place for my body.
Abercius is my name, a disciple of the chaste shepherd [Jesus]. . . .
He sent me to Rome to contemplate a kingdom,
And to behold a queen in a golden robe and golden sandals. . . .
            . . . Everywhere faith led the way
and everywhere set food before me,—fish from the fountain
Mighty and pure, which the chaste virgin caught,—
And gave this to friends to eat, always
Having good wine, giving mixed wine with bread.
Standing by, I, Abercius, ordered this to be inscribed;
Truly, I was in my seventy-second year.
May everyone who is in accord with this and who
        understands it pray for Abercius." [39]

Tertullian (c. A.D. 160–c. 225)
    —quotations from his orthodox period, 197–206. [40]

"Was anything withheld from the knowledge of Peter, who is called
'the rock on which the church should be built,' who also obtained

---

went throughout Syria, Asia, and Greece, and eventually to Rome, where the
center of Christianity and the Church would reside, in order to obey more fully
his Lord in preaching the gospel to "the ends of the earth".

[38] Abercius composed his own epitaph. He was the bishop of Hieropolis in
Phrygia Salutaris. It was inscribed between A.D. 180 and 200. The two fragments
were discovered near Hieropolis in 1883 and are currently preserved in the
Lateran Museum in Rome.

[39] William Jurgens, *The Faith of the Early Fathers* (Collegeville, Minn.: Liturgical
Press, 1970), 1:78. The inscription of Abercius is an account of his travels
written in literary and poetic form. He refers to Christ as the "Chaste Shepherd"
and the Eucharist with the words "good wine and bread" for his "friends to eat".
Abercius says Christ sent him to Rome, and he gives us a graphic description of
the kingdom and the queen, the Church, as dressed royally in "golden robe and
golden sandals". It is difficult not to recognize in this inscription a testimony to
the supreme position of the Roman Church, dressed in the gold of royalty and
purity.

[40] Tertullian was a very early writer and, at the beginning of his career, an able
defender of orthodox doctrine. He had available to him many manuscripts no
longer available to modern scholars. He was born about sixty years after the
death of the Apostle John. He was an eloquent and powerful spokesman for the

'the keys of the kingdom of heaven,' with the power of 'loosing and binding in heaven and on earth'?"[41]

"Moreover, if Peter was reproached [by Paul] because, after having lived with the gentiles, he later separated himself from their company out of respect for persons, the fault certainly was one of procedure and not of doctrine."[42]

---

teaching of the early Church and the apostolic tradition. However, toward the end of his career he joined the Montanists, who were a group censored for heresy. Tertullian's writings fall into three categories: his orthodox period (197–206); his semi-Montanist period (206–212), in which he wavers in his orthodoxy (during these years, he is virtually a Montanist but not yet disassociated from the Catholic Church); and finally the period of his full, anti-clerical Montanism, during the years 213–220 (see ibid., 1:111–12). As we will see, those opposed to the Catholic Church and the primacy of Rome quote freely from Tertullian's Montanist period but fail to acknowledge his loyalty to Rome in his orthodox years.

[41] *On Prescription against Heretics* 22, ANF 3:253. There are those who say that the early Church never understood the "rock" to be Peter; that the term only referred to his confession or his faith. Here we have one of the first recorded references to Matthew 16, and it is used quite clearly to proclaim Peter as the "rock" or foundation of the Church. There is no hint here that the rock referred to Christ, the confession, or Peter's faith, to the exclusion of Peter—it is Peter the man who is the rock.

[42] *On Prescription against the Heretics* 23, in Jurgens, *Faith of the Early Fathers*, 1:121. Many Protestants and Orthodox use Galatians 2:11–12, referred to here by Tertullian, in an attempt to disprove papal infallibility. As we have already pointed out (see n. 77, pp. 56–57), papal infallibility refers to the office of the Papacy and does not assume the person himself to be impeccable. Peter's doctrine, moreover, is clearly defined in his preaching, especially at the Jerusalem Council in Acts 15. Infallibility is the "inability to err in teaching the truth. In theology, it refers to: 1) the Church, in that she preserves and teaches the deposit of truth as revealed by Christ; 2) the Roman Pontiff, when he teaches *ex cathedra* in matters of faith or morals, and indicates that the doctrine is to be believed by all the faithful; and 3) the college of bishops, when speaking in union with the Pope in matters of faith and morals, agreeing that a doctrine must be held by the universal Church, and the doctrine is promulgated by the Pontiff" (Peter M. J. Stravinskas, *Our Sunday Visitor's Catholic Dictionary* on diskette [Huntington, Ind.: Our Sunday Visitor, 1994]).

The emissaries from Jerusalem must either have exceeded their powers or abused them. It was presumably for the sake of peace and to avoid serious friction that Peter withdrew gradually from taking meals with the Gentile converts in Antioch. Peter's authority led the rest of the Jewish Christians and even Paul's own lieutenant, Barnabas, to follow his example. Peter's action was not in conformity with his convictions, and Paul reproached Peter, not with a doctrinal error, but with not holding firm to the principle he held and taught. Paul's use

"Afterwards, as he himself [Paul] narrates, 'he went up to Jerusalem for the purpose of seeing Peter,' [Gal 1:18] because of his office, no doubt, and by right of a common belief and preaching."[43]

"Come now, if you would indulge a better curiosity in the business of your salvation, run through the apostolic Churches in which the very thrones [*cathedrae*] of the Apostles remain still in place; in which their own authentic writings are read, giving sound to the voice and recalling the faces of each. Achaia is near you, so you have Corinth. If you are not far from Macedonia, you have Philippi. If you can cross into Asia, you have Ephesus. But if you are near to Italy, you have Rome, whence also our authority derives. How happy is that Church, on which Apostles poured out their whole doctrine along with their blood, where Peter endured a passion like that of the Lord, where Paul was crowned in a death like John's [the Baptist], where the Apostle John, after being immersed in boiling oil and suffering no hurt, was exiled to an island."[44]

---

of "Cephas" in Galatians shows he was fully aware of Peter's position as the Rock. There is nothing here to diminish the authority or preeminent position of Peter; in fact, we know that earlier Paul came first to Peter and stayed with him for fifteen days (Gal 1:18) and later submitted his gospel to the apostles to make sure he was not "running in vain" and that later he was given the right hand of fellowship to preach to the uncircumcised (Gal 2:2, 9).

[43] *On Prescription against the Heretics* 23, ANF 3:254. Tertullian acknowledges here that Paul, sometime after his conversion, went up to see Peter "because of his office, no doubt". What office? The office mentioned by Paul a few paragraphs earlier. Paul refers to Peter as "Cephas", indicated by Jesus to be the "Rock". Peter holds the office of steward (Is 22; Mt 16), the shepherd or pastor of the Church. Paul later visits the apostles in Jerusalem and has this to say about the encounter: "I laid before them (but privately before those who were of repute) the gospel which I preach among the Gentiles, lest somehow I should be running or had run in vain" (Gal 2:2). Paul, though called by revelation from God, did not function independently of Peter and the Eleven; rather he met with Peter in private, submitted his gospel to the leaders in Jerusalem, and then accepted their decrees at the Jerusalem Council. He had a call from God but recognized the office of Cephas.

[44] *On Prescription against the Heretics* 36, 1, in Jurgens, *Faith of the Early Fathers*, 1:122. Where does one find the authentic teaching and authority? Earlier Tertullian argues, "For this reason we should not appeal merely to the Scriptures nor fight our battle on ground where victory is either impossible or uncertain or improbable. For a resort to the Scriptures would but result in

Tertullian
—quotations from his semi-Montanist period, 206–212

"For though you think heaven still shut, remember that the Lord left here to Peter and through him to the Church, the keys of it, which every one who has been here put to the question, and also made confession, will carry with him."[45]

---

placing both parties on an equal footing, whereas the natural order of procedure requires one question to be asked first, which is the only one now that should be discussed. 'Who are the guardians of the real faith? To whom do the Scriptures belong? By whom and through whom and when and to whom was committed the doctrine that makes us Christians? For wherever the truth of Christian doctrine and faith clearly abide, there will be also the true Scriptures and the true interpretations and all the true Christian traditions" (Shotwell and Loomis, *See of Peter*, 289). Tertullian then presents the true doctrine and the repository of this doctrine—the apostolic Churches, especially Rome. He reminds his readers, the heretics, that each apostolic Church had the apostles' chair (*cathedra*) still prominently in its place. Next, he reminds them of Rome's singular position, from where "our authority derives". He is not necessarily referring to any type of governmental authority here but to the authority of the true gospel. Rome has the final word as to correct teaching and apostolic authority. Did the primacy of Rome begin late in the history of the Church? No. The universal acceptance of Rome's primacy in the first centuries is simply a fact of history.

[45] *Scorpiace* 10, ANF 3:643, written about 211 or 212. The Montanist tendencies can be seen in his description of Peter and the keys. During this phase of his life, Tertullian was turning his back on the orthodox teaching of the Church. However, in understanding this quotation we need not dismiss it entirely as "Montanist", but we can understand the context and the point Tertullian is making. Knowledge of the opponent and the argument waged help to interpret a passage properly. Tertullian is defending the heroism of confession and martyrdom against the lax opinions of certain Gnostics. Was heaven closed? Was confession to be made later in the heavenly levels but not here on earth? Certainly heaven was open, for Christ had given the keys to Peter because of his confession, and he then passed the keys on within the Church. Can confession of faith (even to death) be avoided on earth and reserved for the heavens after death, thus eliminating the need for martyrdom, or is it required by God that we make confession even to death here on earth, prior to death? Peter made confession on earth and thus was given the key to open heaven; Christians will also have the key to open heaven when they confess as Peter did. Tertullian refutes the errors of Gnostics. This is certainly a proper use of a Scripture passage to refute such errors. Does Tertullian's deeper application of the passage on "the keys" negate the literal interpretation of the passage? No, it is an application in the heat of a battle, and a good application to defuse the Gnostic heresy. Does Tertullian's use of Matthew 16 indicate a denial of Rome's primacy?

"Again, He changes the name of Simon to Peter, inasmuch as the Creator also altered the names of Abram, and Sarai, and Oshea, by calling the latter Joshua, and adding a syllable to each of the former. But why *Peter*? If it was because of the vigour of his faith, there were many solid materials which might lend a name from their strength. Was it because Christ was both a rock and a stone? For we read of His being placed 'for a stone of stumbling and for a rock of offence.' I omit the rest of the passage. Therefore He would fain impart to the dearest of His disciples a name which was suggested by one of His own especial designations in figure; because it was, I suppose, more peculiarly fit than a name which might have been derived from no figurative description of Himself."[46]

Tertullian
—from documents written after A.D. 213, as a Montanist

"Peter alone [among the apostles] do I find married, and through mention of his mother-in-law. I presume he was a monogamist; for the Church, built upon him, would for the future appoint to every degree of orders none but monogamists. As for the rest, since I do not find them married, I must presume they were either eunuchs or continent."[47]

Not at all; and anyone who argues thus does so from silence and theological bias. As Thomas S. Dolan writes, responding to A. Cleveland Coxe, "Dr. Coxe together with a number of his coreligionists allow special prerogatives to Peter (though just what these prerogatives were it is difficult to discover), but deny them to his successors" (*See of Peter*, 32). The keys were given to Peter; yes, but Tertullian understands that through Peter the keys were passed on "through him to the Church" in the apostolic succession.

[46] *Against Marcion* 13, ANF 3:365. Why would Jesus bestow on Simon a name drawn especially from the figures or qualities associated with himself? Because the name relates Peter closely to Jesus; he partakes in Christ's "rockness". We do not find here the common anti-papal objection: "The rock is *either* Christ *or* Peter"; rather, for Tertullian, "The rock is *both* Christ *and* Peter." Tertullian finds no reason to set them at odds, to compartmentalize them. That Christ is the primary rock and associates Peter with himself is no problem for Catholic thought. Again, this passage shows the singularly prominent place of Peter in the economy of Christ and his Church.

[47] *Monogamy* 8, 4, in Jurgens, *Faith of the Early Fathers*, 1:158. Even during his heretical Montanist period, Tertullian verifies that the early Church accepted the interpretation of Matthew 16, which declared Peter as the rock and the

"For after the Bishop of Rome [probably Victor] had acknowledged the prophetic gifts of Montanus, Prisca, and Maximilla, and, in consequence of the acknowledgment, had bestowed his peace[48] on the churches of Asia and Phrygia, *he* [Praxeas][49] by importunately urging false accusations against the prophets themselves and their churches, and insisting on the authority of the bishop's predecessors in the see, compelled him to recall the pacific letter which he had [earlier] issued, as well as to desist from his purpose of acknowledging the *said* gifts."[50]

---

foundation of the Church. It was not contested; in fact, Tertullian uses it as a *given* in his argument. Had the interpretation not been a given, his argument would have fallen flat. That Tertullian says the Church was built upon Peter is not as significant as the manner in which he says it. *He states it, not as a point to prove, but as a proof for his point.* The early Church was extremely conservative and held tenaciously to the teaching passed down from the apostles, both written, oral, and in practice. Tertullian, even as a Montanist, makes this statement confidently, knowing that all those who heard or read his statement would agree without question, since it was the clear understanding of the whole of Christendom. The Church, built upon a monogamist, would not later promote multiple marriages. The Church would continue to carry the organic qualities of her foundation. Peter and the apostles were monogamists, eunuchs, or continent.

[48] Or, "*admitted them to communion*".

[49] Though condemned as a heretic by Tertullian, "There is little reason for thinking that Praxeas was a heresiarch. . . . He was very likely merely an adversary of the Montanists who used some quasi-Monarchian expressions when at Carthage, but afterwards withdrew them when he saw they might be misunderstood" ("Praxeas", in *The Catholic Encyclopedia* [New York: Robert Appleton Co., 1911], 12:344). Praxeas came to Rome and provided information to the Pope about the Montanist movement. Irenaeus arrived later to inform the Pope of the heretical nature of Montanus and his group. The Pope withdrew his approval, and Tertullian hated Praxeas and the Pope for censuring the Montanists.

[50] *Against Praxeas* 1, ANF 3:597. Tertullian, as a Montanist and opponent of the Church and Rome, demonstrates clearly the authority of the Roman bishop in the early third century. It was common and accepted practice for the bishop of Rome to accept or reject various groups or teachings, to determine what was orthodox and what was heretical. We do not find teachers going to just *any* bishop for doctrinal approval—it is always to the bishop of Rome. When the Pope received further information about Montanist teaching, he no longer accepted the Montanists, excommunicating them from fellowship with the universal Church—again affirming the papal authority even at this early date. The fact that an earlier papal letter had "brought peace" to Asia demonstrates again how much depended upon papal sanction.

"I hear that there has even been an edict set forth, and a peremptory one too. *The Pontifex Maximus*—that is, the bishop of bishops—issues an edict: 'I remit, to such as have discharged (the requirements of) repentance, the sins both of adultery and of fornication.' "[51]

" 'But,' you say, '*the Church* has the power of forgiving sins.' This I acknowledge and adjudge more (than you; I) who have the Paraclete Himself in the persons of the new prophets,[52] saying, 'The Church has the power to forgive sins; but I will not do it, lest they commit others withal.[53] . . . If, because the Lord has said to Peter, 'Upon this rock will I build My Church,' 'to thee have I given the keys of the heavenly kingdom;' or, 'Whatsoever thou shalt have bound or loosed in earth, shall be bound or loosed in the heavens,' you therefore presume that the power of binding and loosing has derived to you, that is, to every Church akin to Peter, what sort of man are you, subverting and wholly changing the manifest intention of the Lord, conferring (as that intention did) this (gift) personally upon Peter?[54] '*On thee*,' He says, 'will I

---

[51] *On Modesty* 1, written about A.D. 220, ANF 4:74. Tertullian, as a Montanist, is ridiculing the bishop of Rome for readmitting certain penitents into communion. "Pope Callistus (A.D. 217–222) had decided that the rigid discipline which had hitherto prevailed in many Churches must be in a large measure relaxed. Tertullian, now lapsed into heresy, fiercely attacks the 'peremptory edict'. . . . The words are intended as sarcasm: but none the less they indicate clearly the position of authority claimed by Rome. And the opposition comes, not from a [orthodox] Catholic bishop, but from a Montanist heretic" ("Pope", in *Catholic Encyclopedia*, 12:264). Tertullian taught that there was no forgiveness after baptism for the sins for idolatry, fornication, and murder. That the Church forgave such sins led Tertullian to chastise her. Protestants, of course, would disagree with Tertullian on this point and side with the Catholic Church.

[52] Tertullian adopted the Montanist belief that the Church no longer had the Paraclete, the Holy Spirit. The gift now resided in the "new prophets", who received direct revelation from God through trances and ecstatic encounters with the Spirit.

[53] As a member of the heretical sect of Montanists, Tertullian seems to agree that the Church *does* have the authority to forgive sins but that the Paraclete speaking through the "new prophets" declares that even though the Church has the power to forgive, he, the Spirit, refuses to forgive sins because the sins may be repeated through laxity. Note that this is not a denial of the Church's authority; it is rather that God has closed his heart to forgiveness for fear that the sinners may repeat their sin if forgiveness is so easily attained.

[54] "The church of Rome must at that time [217–222] have already numbered some thousands, and it is easy to understand how the severe discipline of the

build My Church;' and, 'I will give *to thee* the keys,' not *to the Church*;[55] and, 'Whatsoever *thou shalt have loosed or bound*,' not what *they* shall have loosed or bound. For so withal the result teaches. In (Peter) himself the Church was reared; that is, *through* (Peter) himself; (Peter) himself essayed the key; you see *what* (key): 'Men of Israel, let what I say sink into your ears: Jesus the Nazarene, a man destined by God for you,' and so forth. (Peter) himself, therefore, was the first to unbar, in Christ's baptism, the entrance to the heavenly kingdom, in which (kingdom) are 'loosed' the sins that were beforetime 'bound;' and those which have not been 'loosed' are 'bound.' "[56]

Primitive Church, which expelled grievous sinners from the ranks of the faithful, relaxed by degrees. [Pope] Calixtus took an important step by admitting the principle that, after due penance done, even infringements of the sixth commandment should not involve permanent excommunication from the Church. He based this arbitrary decision upon his 'power of the keys,' i.e., upon the judicial authority bestowed by the Lord on the apostles, and in particular on St. Peter. He encountered lively opposition in the matter. Part of his congregation elected a rival bishop, the presbyter Hippolytus, in opposition to him, and in a passionate lampoon the Carthaginian Tertullian attacked with his biting sarcasm the Roman bishop's claims to supremacy. Thus for the first time was the promise to St. Peter brought into ecclesiastical controversy" (Gustav Krüger, *The Papacy*, trans. F. M. S. Batchelor and C. A. Miles [London: T. Fisher Unwin, 1909], 20).

[55] "Vainly he [Tertullian] tried to undo the effect of the fateful quotation from Matthew, by pointing out that the gift of authority to Peter was a special reward for an individual act of loyalty, not the perquisite of an office, and that if it were of such a nature as to be transmitted to anyone it must be to those who merited it spiritually, as Peter did" (Shotwell and Loomis, *See of Peter*, 297).

[56] *On Modesty* 21, ANF 4:99. This treatise was written in 220, at the peak of Tertullian's Montanist period. He was in a sect that would have been extremely odious to Protestants and Orthodox today. He scorned the orthodox teaching of the Church and depended upon the ecstatic trances and revelations of two women prophets: Prisca and Maximilla. Interestingly enough, this is the only quotation from Tertullian that William Webster refers to in his book *The Church of Rome at the Bar of History*—a book with the intent of discrediting the Catholic Church. Webster writes, "Tertullian, at the beginning of the third century, was the first to identify the 'rock' of Matthew 16:18 with Peter in his treatise *On Modesty*. But what he means by this identification is not that Peter is the rock in the sense that the Church is built on him, but that it is built through him as he preaches the gospel" (48–49). He then quotes the above passage in its entirety. Whether Webster is being dishonest by withholding pertinent information, or whether he failed to research the issue thoroughly, is not certain; but there are two severe problems with his assertion. First, he does not tell us that there is

Origen (c. A.D. 185–c. 254) [57]

"Peter, upon whom is built the Church of Christ, against which the
gates of hell shall not prevail, left only one Epistle of acknowl-

---

actually a reference to Peter as the "rock" twenty years earlier, made *by
Tertullian himself while in his orthodox period.* We read it a few pages back: "Was
anything withheld from the knowledge of Peter, who is called 'the rock on
which the church should be built,' who also obtained 'the keys of the kingdom
of heaven,' with the power of 'loosing and binding in heaven and on earth'?"
We also find Tertullian referring to the Church as "built upon him [Peter]".
Why does Webster not inform his readers of Tertullian's earlier orthodox
teaching? Second, Webster neglects to alert his reader to the fact that the
passage cited is from the depths of Tertullian's Montanist period—his descent
into heresy. Webster himself would recoil at Montanist extremes and would
shun Montanist theology, especially the expectation of the imminent descent
of the heavenly Jerusalem, coming down from the sky to settle near Pepuza in
Phrygia. Is it not curious that Webster, in rejecting the orthodox teaching of
the early Church on Peter's primacy (as reflected in Tertullian's orthodox
writings), sides with the heretical Tertullian in the interpretation of this Scripture passage?

It should be remembered that Tertullian had turned his back on the Church
and was writing in indignation—with all the acrimony he could muster—to
repudiate the Church and her foundations. All the orthodox theologians of the
time condemned him and his Montanist theology. Tertullian's indictment of the
Church's understanding of Matthew 16, however, only serves to prove beyond a
shadow of doubt that the Church *did* teach that Matthew 16 referred to Peter as
the Rock and that that office and authority had been passed on to the Church.
If the Church had not assumed this foundational understanding, and overtly
taught it, why else would Tertullian strike out vindictively to subvert the accepted interpretation?

[57] Origen was a highly esteemed theologian in the early Church—a gifted
teacher who lived shortly after the time of the apostles. He was born in Alexandria, Egypt; as a young man, he watched his father suffer as a martyr for his faith.
While running to join his father in death, he was restrained by his mother, who
hid his clothing to save his life. According to standard Church histories, he was
a student of Clement of Alexandria. Origen taught in Alexandria for about
twenty-eight years, instructing Christians and pagans alike. He visited Palestine
in A.D. 216, where he was asked to teach the Scriptures in the churches. Origen
settled at Caesarea and founded a school of literature, philosophy, and theology.
During the persecutions of the Christians in 250 under Emperor Decius,
Origen was imprisoned and tortured. Released in 251, but weakened by inju-
ries, he died about 254, probably in Tyre. Origen may well have been the most
accomplished biblical scholar of the early Church. His accomplishments as an
exegete and student of the Old Testament were outstanding. He was a volumi-
nous writer, whose works include letters, treatises in dogmatic and practical
theology, apologetics, exegeses, and textual criticism.

edged genuinity. Let us concede also a second, which however, is doubtful." [58]

"Look at the great foundation of the Church, that most solid of rocks, upon whom Christ built the Church! And what does the Lord say to him? 'O you of little faith,' He says, 'why did you doubt!'" [59]

"Although there are many who believe that they themselves hold to the teachings of Christ, there are yet some among them

---

[58] *Commentaries on John* 5, 3, written by Origen between 226 and 232, in Jurgens, *Faith of the Early Fathers*, 1:202. Can anyone claim that the Fathers attributed Jesus' words recorded in Matthew's Gospel, "You are Peter [Rock] and upon this rock I will build my Church" (Mt 16:18), to Peter's confession alone and not to Peter himself?

[59] *Homilies on Exodus* 5, 4, in Jurgens, *Faith of the Early Fathers*, 1:205. William Webster writes, "Chrysostom followed the teaching of Origen that the rock is to be interpreted as Peter's confession of faith and this exegesis became standard for the Eastern Church and theologians as a whole throughout the centuries" (*Church of Rome*, 51). However, we see in this quote from Origen that the confession of Peter is not even mentioned; rather, the foundation of the Church is Peter himself. Webster continues, "On the one hand the Eastern Fathers and theologians held very high views of the status of the apostle Peter but they did not transfer that status to the bishops of Rome" (ibid.). We will provide plenty of evidence to disprove Webster's assertion later in our study; but here is a single reference to put the lie to Webster's claim. Methodius (c. 815–885), the famous Eastern Father and "apostle to the Slavs", or one of his disciples, wrote, "It is not true, as this Canon states, that the holy Fathers gave the primacy to old Rome because it was the capital of the Empire; it is from on high, from divine grace, that this primacy drew its origin. Because of the intensity of his faith Peter, the first of the Apostles, was addressed in these words by our Lord Jesus Christ himself: 'Peter, lovest thou me? Feed my sheep'. That is why in hierarchical order Rome holds the pre-eminent place and is the first See. That is why the privileges of old Rome are eternally immovable, and that is the view of all the churches" (N. Brian-Chaninov, *The Russian Church* [1931], 46; cited by Butler, *Church and Infallibility*, 210). J. Michael Miller writes, "The apostles to the Slavs, Sts. Cyril (†869) and Methodius (†885), were evangelizing while controversy raged between the patriarch and the pope. Belonging to the ecclesiastical tradition of the Christian East, the two brothers were subject to the patriarch of Constantinople under whose aegis they had begun their mission. Even so, they considered it their duty to give an account of their missionary labor to the pope, asking him to confirm their work. The two brothers submitted to the pope's judgment 'in order to obtain his approval for the doctrine which they professed and taught, the liturgical books which they had written in the Slavonic language and the methods which they were using in evangelizing those peoples'" (*Shepherd and the Rock* [Huntington, Ind.: Our Sunday Visitor, 1995], 128).

who think differently from their predecessors. The teaching of the Church has indeed been handed down through an order of succession from the Apostles, and remains in the Churches even to the present time. That alone is to be believed as the truth which is in no way at variance with ecclesiastical and apostolic tradition." [60]

"He [Origen] wrote also to Fabianus, bishop of Rome, and to many other rulers of the churches concerning his orthodoxy." [61]

"And perhaps that which Simon Peter answered and said, '*Thou art the Christ, the Son of the living God,*' if we say it as Peter, not by flesh

---

[60] *The Fundamental Doctrines* 1, preface, 2, written between 220 and 230, in Jurgens, *Faith of the Early Fathers*, 1:190. Cleveland Coxe, in his "Elucidations" to *The Ante-Nicene Fathers*, comments on Origen's phrases "the faith of the Church" and "the teaching of the Church" in the following manner: "It is noteworthy how frequently our author [Origen] employs this expression . . . 'a clearly defined teaching.' He shows what the Church's teaching 'has laid down' touching demons and angels. Touching the origin of the world, he again asserts the Church's teaching, and then concedes, that, over and above what he maintains, there is 'no clear statement regarding it'. . . . Elsewhere he speaks of 'the faith of the Church,' and all this as something accepted by all Christians recognised as orthodox or Catholics" (ANF 4:382). Origen, around 220 (still almost two hundred years before the final collection of the canon of Scripture), speaks of a "teaching" and "faith" of the Church that is held safely in the tradition of the Church, and we know from the Christian activity at the time that the main protector of this truth was the See of Rome.

[61] Eusebius, *Church History* 6, 36, 4, NPNF2, 1:279. Fabianus (Pope St. Fabian) (A.D. 236–250) was elected bishop of Rome under unusual circumstances. A dove flew into the room and alighted upon his head. Those assembled assumed it was a sign from God, and he was chosen Pope. An Alexandrian synod convened in 231 or 232 condemned Origen for insubordination, self-mutilation, and heterodoxy. Asian Christians protested, but Rome, under the government of Pontianus (A.D. 230–235), upheld the decision. When Fabianus succeeded to the government of the See of Rome, the issue was still hot. Origen then wrote a letter to Pope Fabianus, seeking either to obtain a reversal or to ease his mind regarding new charges. Jerome tells us, "Origen himself, in the letter which he writes to Fabianus, bishop of the city of Rome, professes his penitence for writing such things and lays the blame of indiscretion on Ambrosius because he had published a private composition" (Epistle 84, in Shotwell and Loomis, *See of Peter*, 315). Eusebius seems to set up two categories here: first, the bishop of Rome, ruler of the Church, and second, the "other rulers of the churches". In any case, the fact that Origen felt compelled to write a letter of apology and explanation to the distant and remote bishop of Rome, mentioned apart from and emphasized over the "other rulers of the churches", professing his penitence, is significant and again implies, if not clearly demonstrates, the respect that the Eastern Christians had for the Roman Church and her bishop.

and blood revealing it unto us, but by the light from the Father in heaven shining in our heart, we too become as Peter, being pronounced blessed as he was, because that the grounds on which he was pronounced blessed apply also to us, by reason of the fact that flesh and blood have not revealed to us with regard to Jesus that He is Christ, the Son of the living God, but the Father in heaven, from the very heavens, that our citizenship may be in heaven, revealing to us the revelation which carries up to heaven those who take away every veil from the heart, and receive 'the spirit of the wisdom and revelation' of God. And if we too have said like Peter, 'Thou art the Christ, the Son of the living God,' not as if flesh and blood had revealed it unto us, but by light from the Father in heaven having shone in our heart, we become a Peter, and to us there might be said by the Word, 'Thou art Peter,' etc.[62] For a rock is every disciple of Christ of whom those drank who drank of the spiritual rock which followed them, and upon every such rock is built every word of the church, and the polity in accordance with it; for in each of the perfect, who have the combination of words and deeds and thoughts which fill up the blessedness, is the church built by God. . . . Are the keys of the kingdom of heaven given by the Lord to Peter only, and will no other of the blessed receive them? But if this promise, 'I will give unto thee the keys of the kingdom of heaven,' be common to the others, how shall not all the things previously spoken of, and the things which are subjoined as having been addressed to Peter, be common to them?"[63]

---

[62] Regarding Origen and Matthew 16, Winter writes, "It is most natural to seek [Origen's] study on St. Peter in the commentary which he wrote on the Gospel of St. Matthew, bearing in mind, of course, that in these biblical commentaries he was concerned with the mystical rather than the literal sense. The Petrine text of Matthew 16 interests him chiefly on account of its seventeenth verse: 'It is not flesh and blood, it is my Father in heaven that has revealed this to thee.' Thence his whole interest is focused on the heavenly enlightenment which Peter has received. . . . The passages in question have often been invoked in an anti-Petrine and anti-papal sense. Batiffol has cast doubts on the correctness of such an interpretation. The whole problem is complicated by such factors as Origen's *penchant* for departing from the literal sense, as well as by the down-to-earth factor of the loss of so many of his exegetical works [a small fraction of his prodigious output remains]. Undeniably his theory of St. Peter is perplexing and it is significant that it did not command any notable following in the subsequent patristic tradition" (Winter, *Saint Peter*, 51, 52).

[63] *Origen's Commentary on Matthew* 12, 10–11, ANF 9:455–56. Protestants often use Origen's Gospel commentary on Matthew 16 in an attempt to defuse the

Cyprian of Carthage (d. A.D. 258) [64]

"The Lord says to Peter: 'I say to you,' He says, 'that you are Peter, and upon this rock I will build my Church, and the gates of hell

---

Catholic understanding of Matthew 16. We have already established that Origen accepted the *literal* and *historical* intent of this passage by the fact that he clearly states that Peter *is* the rock upon which the Church is built. So, why does Origen seem to contradict this later in life? There could be several reasons. Origen viewed the Scriptures as a chest full of spiritual treasures, the preserve of a few privileged Christians. "If the apparent sense of a given passage contradicts the necessary convictions of morality or the nature of God [or the understanding of the reader], there must be some deeper lesson underneath the surface of the passage. This conviction led Origen into what we usually call the 'allegorical interpretation of Scripture'. He held that there are three levels of meaning in the Bible: the literal sense; the moral application to the soul; and the allegorical or spiritual sense" (Bruce L. Shelley, *Church History in Plain Language* [Waco, Tex.: Word Books, 1982], 100). Does Origen intend to slight the *literal* sense of Matthew 16? Intentionally or unintentionally, through his allegorizing, he does not address the literal and historical sense of the passage but "digs deeper" for a personal and spiritual application. Although Catholics approve and acknowledge the necessity of "spiritual exegesis" of Scripture, it must be noted that it can be taken to unhelpful extremes. In a classic Protestant textbook we read, "This method of interpretation has done much harm to the cause of correct interpretation of the Scriptures and has resulted in absurd and, often, unbiblical theological ideas" (Earle E. Cairns, *Christianity through the Centuries*, 2d rev. ed. [Grand Rapids, Mich.: Zondervan, 1981], 120). Too often Protestant theologians will denigrate the methods used by Origen, yet will utilize this section of his commentary to refute the Catholic teaching. Another historian writes, "[A former Jew] had told Origen how Scripture was like a house full of locked rooms: God, he said, had confused the keys, and it was up to his heirs to fit the right key to each lock. Origen considered this view a 'beautiful tradition' and showed himself an inventive opener of some very secret doors. His allegories were totally false to the plain meaning of Scripture. . . . In his own commentaries, we find Origen taking a similar view" (Robin Lane Fox, *Pagans and Christians* [New York: Alfred A. Knopf, 1987], 524). W. H. C. Frend agrees, "Although Origen often had useful things to say about the texts he was studying, . . . nevertheless he was not primarily interested in historical data" (*The Rise of Christianity* [Philadelphia: Fortress Press, 1984], 378–79). We can understand Origen to be simply "spiritualizing the text".

[64] Cyprian was a saint and bishop whose full name was Thascius Caecilianus Cyprianus. He was a leading bishop in the Catholic Church in Africa. He was of noble origin, and when he became a Christian (c. A.D. 246), he gave the greater part of his fortune to the poor. Only two years after his conversion, he was chosen bishop of Carthage. During the Decian persecution many Christians denied the faith through fear of death. When the persecution ended, sometime after 251, opinions in the Church were divided about how to treat those who

will not overcome it. And to you I will give the keys of the kingdom of heaven: and whatever things you bind on earth shall be bound also in heaven, and whatever you loose on earth, they shall be loosed also in heaven.' And again He says to him after His resurrection: 'Feed my sheep.' On him He builds the Church, and to him He gives the command to feed the sheep; and although He assigns a like power to all the Apostles, yet He founded a single chair, and He established by His own authority a source and an intrinsic reason for that unity.[65] Indeed, the others were that also which Peter was; but a primacy is given to Peter,[66]

---

had denied the faith and also those who had been baptized by heretics. On the former question, Cyprian was inclined toward leniency (opposing Novatianism), but he was adamant against accepting those baptized by heretics. He insisted they be rebaptized. On this point, Cyprian was in marked disagreement with Pope Stephen (r. 254–257), and the controversy between the two became sharp. There is good reason to believe that the controversy influenced Cyprian's full submission to Roman primacy. By 257, when Stephen was martyred, Cyprian appears to have accepted the Roman bishop's decision on baptism, which was subsequently confirmed by the Council of Arles (314) as the official teaching of the Church. During a new wave of persecution, conducted under the Roman emperor Valerian, Cyprian was tried and martyred by beheading.

[65] Interestingly enough, Nicholas Afanassieff, who was professor of canon law and Church history at the Orthodox Theological Institute in Paris, writes, "To posterity [Cyprian] has left an ideal picture of 'the Bishop' which shines so brightly and clearly that our minds really see it; he has left us a literary heritage broken by frequent self-contradiction, which has been a matter for controversy from then until the present day.... According to [Cyprian's] doctrine there should have really been one single bishop at the head of the Universal Church. He was unwilling to place the Bishop of Rome outside the *concors numerositas* of bishops, and yet the place given by him to the Roman Church did raise it above the 'harmonious multitude.' The ideal 'Peter's throne' occupied by the whole episcopate became confused in Cyprian's mind with the actual throne occupied by the Bishop of Rome. According to Cyprian, every bishop occupies Peter's throne (the Bishop of Rome among others), but the See of Peter is Peter's throne *par excellence*. The Bishop of Rome is the direct heir of Peter, whereas the others are heirs only indirectly, and sometimes only by the mediation of Rome. Hence Cyprian's insistence that the Church of Rome is the root and matrix of the Catholic Church. The subject is treated in so many of Cyprian's passages that there is no doubt: to him, the See of Rome was *ecclesia principalis unde unitas sacerdotalis exorta est*" ("The Church which Presides in Love", in Meyendorff, *Primacy of Peter*, 98–99).

[66] Earle Cairns, professor of church history at Wheaton College from 1943 to 1977, writes, "The Roman church has insisted from earliest times that Christ gave to Peter a special rank as the first bishop of Rome and the leader of the

whereby it is made clear that there is but one Church and one chair.[67] So too, all are shepherds, and the flock is shown to be one, fed by all the Apostles in single-minded accord. If someone does not hold fast to this unity of Peter, can he imagine that he still holds the faith? If he desert the chair of Peter upon whom the Church was built, can he still be confident that he is in the Church?"[68]

---

apostles. Cyprian [not from Rome] and Jerome did the most to advance this position by their assertion of the primacy of the Roman see to the other ecclesiastical seats of authority" (*Christianity through the Centuries*, 116). Philip Schaff writes, "Cyprian is clearest, both in his advocacy of the fundamental idea of the papacy, and in his protest against the mode of its application in a given case. Starting from the superiority of Peter, upon whom the Lord built his church, and to whom he entrusted the feeding of his sheep, in order to represent thereby the unity in the college of the apostles, Cyprian transferred the same superiority to the Bishop of Rome, as the successor of Peter, and accordingly called the Roman church the chair of Peter, and the fountain of priestly unity, the root, also, and mother of the catholic church" (*History of the Christian Church* [Grand Rapids, Mich.: Eerdmans, 1980], 2:161). And finally, Jaroslav Pelikan, Sterling Professor of History at Yale University, writes, "No passage in Cyprian's writings has received more detailed attention than the two versions of the exegesis of these words in chapter 4 of his *Unity of the Church* [on Mt 16]: one version seems to assert the primacy of Peter as prerequisite to unity among the bishops, while the other seems to treat the primacy of Peter as only representative of that unity" (*The Emergence of the Catholic Tradition (100–600)*, vol. 1 of *A History of the Development of Doctrine* [Chicago: Univ. of Chicago Press, 1971], 159).

[67] The early Church held a different concept of Church unity from the one that is accepted by most Protestant denominations today.

[68] *The Unity of the Catholic Church* 4, written between A.D. 251 and 256, in Jurgens, *Faith of the Early Fathers*, 1:220. Few selections from the Fathers have been as heatedly debated as these words of Cyprian. Certain ambiguities in Cyprian's writings cause partisans to claim him for their individual "causes". After verbal altercations with Pope Stephen over baptism, Cyprian toned down his treatise in a later revised version, possibly because "Rome was making more of his words than he had intended" (Pelikan, *Emergence of the Catholic Tradition*, 159), especially now that he was in theological disagreement with Rome. Bévenot summarizes the situation, "At Rome, where there were no doubts about its Bishop's authority over the whole Church, Cyprian's original text could not fail to be read as a recognition of that fact. If, in the course of the baptismal controversy this was, as it were, thrown in his teeth, he will have exclaimed, quite truthfully: 'But I never meant *that!*'—and so he 'toned it down' in his revised version. He did not, then, repudiate what he had formerly held. He had never held that the Pope possessed universal jurisdiction. But he had never denied it either; in truth he had never asked himself the question where the final authority in the Church might be. . . . We have in Cyprian's *De ecclesiae catholicae unitate*

Cyprian of Carthage to Pope Cornelius of Rome
  —written c. A.D. 252

"With a false bishop appointed for themselves by heretics, they dare even to set sail and carry letters from schismatics and blasphemers to the chair of Peter and to the principal[69] Church, in which sacerdotal unity has its source; nor did they take thought that these are Romans, whose faith was praised by the preaching Apostle, and among whom it is not possible for perfidy to have entrance."[70]

---

a good example of what a dogma can look like while still in an early stage of development. The reality (in this case, the Primacy of Rome) is there all the time: it may be recognized by some; by others it may even be denied, and that though much of what they say or do unconsciously implies it. . . . Cyprian is a standing example of what we mean when we speak of the Papal Primacy being 'implicit' in the early Church" (Cyprian, *The Lapsed; The Unity of the Catholic Church*, trans. Maurice Bévenot, Ancient Christian Writers, 25:7–8, quoted in Jurgens, *Faith of the Early Fathers*, 1:220). Cyprian seems to have adopted a modified view of primacy after Cornelius, possibly as a result of his disagreements with Stephen, the bishop of Rome. The modified conception leveled the office of bishop and, in theory anyway, perceived the government of the Church to be an "aristocracy of equal bishops", each accountable to God alone. Instead of seeing Peter as invested with a dynastic office, Cyprian seems to have modified his view to perceive Peter alone as the recipient of the keys so as to *symbolize* the unity of the episcopate and the Church. However, even in his own lifetime, he saw the impossibility of unity on this unrealistic basis, which is demonstrated by his frequent appeal to Rome for theological and practical determinations. Dom John Chapman, whose book should be read by anyone wanting to understand Cyprian's attitude toward Rome, wrote, "I fear it was the shortness of his experience which made it possible to put forward a theory which no one has ever held before or since. This is why I think 'St. Cyprian's theory of the episcopate' is of no importance except for his own biography" (*Studies on the Early Papacy* [1928; reprint, Port Washington, N.Y.: Kennikat Press, 1971], 44).

[69] The same word used to describe the primacy of Rome by St. Irenaeus about seventy years earlier.

[70] *Letter of Cyprian to Cornelius of Rome* 59, 14, in Jurgens, *Faith of the Early Fathers*, 1:232. Heretics and schismatics, in an attempt to get their heresies and innovations sanctioned, knew that they had to receive the approval of Rome. Heretics traveled from around the Empire for the bishop of Rome's blessing and approval. However, as Cyprian wrote, they were going to the Romans "whose faith was praised by the preaching Apostle, and among whom it is not possible for perfidy to have entrance". William Webster, who mentions only the passages he considers harmful to the Catholic Church, fails, of course, to mention this quotation and others from Cyprian in his *The Church of Rome at the Bar of History* and *Peter and the Rock* because it does not fit his "proof-texting" agenda.

Cyprian of Carthage to Antonianus of Numidia
    —written about A.D. 252

"You wrote also, that I should forward to Cornelius [bishop of Rome], our colleague, a copy of your letter, so that he might put aside any anxiety and know immediately that you are in communion with him, that is, with the Catholic Church."[71]

"When the persecution was quieted, and opportunity of meeting was afforded; a large number of bishops . . . met together. . . .

In his book *Peter and the Rock* (Battle Ground, Wash.: Christian Resources, 1996), Webster attempts to prove that Cyprian had no concept of Roman primacy and says that the citations he provides "reveal a consensus of scholarly opinion on Cyprian's teaching effectively demonstrating the incompatibility of Cyprian's views with those espoused by Vatican I" (39). His comments seem to betray an ignorance of scholars who disagree with him. His imagined "consensus" is one built upon selective proof-texting. He quite blithely dismisses a *complete* modern consensus that cuts across Protestant, Catholic, and even secular (as well as conservative and liberal) lines with respect to the identification of Peter and the Rock in Matthew 16:18. Instead, he points to Protestant apologists who often cite modernist Catholic theologians—those who have abandoned the historic teachings of the Church—to try to show that "our own" scholars have rejected our position but then refuse even to acknowledge their own Evangelical Protestant scholars who disagree with their position. This amounts to a huge double standard that needs to be exposed for what it is. Scholars who do not fit Webster's "consensus" include B. C. Butler, John Chapman, E. Giles, A. H. Cullen, William Barry, and Warren Carroll, to mention only a few.

Webster's section on St. Cyprian also demonstrates his unwillingness to represent fairly the process and necessity of doctrinal development within the Church. As we have demonstrated earlier in this book: the oak tree has grown and looks perceptibly different from the fragile sprout that cracked the original acorn, yet the organic essence and identity remain the same. Do the words of the very first Christians contain the full-blown understanding of the Papacy as expressed in Vatican I? No, they do not, as Webster correctly observes. But then, neither do the words of the first Christians present the fully developed understanding of the Trinity and the divinity of Christ (or the canon of the New Testament, for that matter) as expounded and practiced by later generations of the Church. One must be careful not to read too much into the early centuries—but one must also be careful not to ignore the obvious doctrinal substance contained and practiced by our forebears, which was simply developed and implemented as the need arose throughout subsequent centuries.

[71] *Letter of Cyprian to Antonianus, a Bishop in Numidia* 55 (52), 1, written between 251 and 252, in Jurgens, *Faith of the Early Fathers*, 1:230. If you want to be in communion with the whole Catholic Church, you must be in immediate communion with the bishop of Rome. This was the assurance of orthodoxy, unity, and communion.

And lest perchance the number of bishops in Africa should seem unsatisfactory, we also wrote to Rome, to Cornelius our colleague, concerning this thing, who himself also holding a council with very many bishops, concurred in the same opinion as we had held." [72]

"Cornelius was made bishop [of Rome] by the decision of God and of His Christ, by the testimony of almost all the clergy, by the applause of the people then present, by the college of venerable priests and good men, . . . which is the place of Peter, the dignity of the sacerdotal chair. . . . Since it has been occupied both at the will of God and with the ratified consent of all of us, whoever wishes now to become bishop must do so outside. For he cannot have ecclesiastical rank who does not hold to the unity of the Church." [73]

Pope Cornelius to Cyprian of Carthage (A.D. 251—253) [74]

"Cornelius to Cyprian his brother, greeting. . . . Urbanus and Sidonius the confessors came to our presbyters, affirming that Maximus the confessor and presbyter, equally with themselves, desired to return into the Church. . . . The whole of this transaction therefore being brought before me. . . . There was one voice from all, giving thanks to God; all were expressing the joy of their heart by tears, embracing them as if they had this day been set free

---

[72] *Letter of Cyprian to Antonianus, a Bishop in Numidia* 51, 6, written 252, ANF 5:328. Why was it necessary to write to Rome? If Cyprian believed in the universal equality of all bishops, why was it necessary to acquire Rome's approval? Why was it necessary to relieve a doubt as to the insufficiency of the "large number" of African bishops by appealing to Rome? These letters of Cyprian demonstrate his practical, day-to-day recognition of the primacy of the Roman bishop, which belies some of the theoretical modifications he seems to have made later in his bishopric.

[73] *Letter of Cyprian to Antonianus, a Bishop in Numidia* 55 (52), 8, written between 251 and 252, in Jurgens, *Faith of the Early Fathers*, 1:230. The Chair of Peter is called the "sacerdotal chair", which is "the place of Peter". This certainly argues against the notion that for Cyprian the "chair of Peter" refers only to the episcopacy as a whole and not to the seat of Peter as a singular authority.

[74] The pontificate of Cornelius (251–253) is, though short, important for the history of discipline in the Church and because of the Novatian schism. Most of Cornelius' letters deal with these two questions. In his difficulties he found a loyal supporter in Cyprian of Carthage, to whom he sent no less than seven epistles. Two letters from their correspondence have survived, Epistles 49 and 50.

from the penalty of the dungeon. And to quote their very own words,—'We,' they say, 'know that Cornelius is bishop of the most holy Catholic Church elected by Almighty God, and by Christ our Lord. . . . For although we seemed . . . to have held a kind of communion with a man who was a schismatic and a heretic, yet our mind was always sincere in the Church. For we are not ignorant that there is one God; that there is one Christ the Lord whom we have confessed, and one Holy Spirit; and that in the Catholic Church there ought to be one bishop.' " [75]

Cyprian to Pope Stephen
   —written between A.D. 254 and 257

"Cyprian to his brother [Pope] Stephen, greeting. . . . It behoves you to write a very copious letter to our fellow-bishops appointed in Gaul, not to suffer any longer that Marcian . . . because he does not yet seem to be excommunicated by us. . . . Let letters be directed by you into the province and to the people abiding at Arles, by which, Marcian being excommunicated, another may be substituted in his place. . . . For the glorious honour of our predecessors, the blessed martyrs [Popes] Cornelius and Lucius, must be maintained, whose memory as we hold in honour, much more ought you, dearest brother, to honour and cherish with your weight and authority, since you have become their vicar and successor. . . . Intimate plainly to us who has been substituted at Arles in the place of Marcian, that we may know to whom to direct our brethren, and to whom we ought to write." [76]

---

[75] *Cornelius [Pope] to Cyprian, on the Return of the Confessors to Unity* [Epistle 49, 2 (45 in Coxe)], ANF 5:323. Many had followed the heretic Novatian; and when they repented and confessed the truth, Pope Cornelius received them back into communion with the Church. He quotes verbatim their words of repentance in this letter. Cornelius informs Cyprian of the solemn return of the Roman confessors who had been deceived and alienated from the Church by the craft and malice of Novatian. It is clear again, even at this early age of the Church, that the primacy of Rome was the safeguard and gateway of orthodox teaching.

[76] *To Father [Pope] Stephenus, concerning Marcianus of Arles, who had joined himself to Novatian; Epistle LXVI,* ANF 5:367–69. If Cyprian held to the equality of all bishops, is it not a bit strange that he would write to Pope Stephen requesting that *he* excommunicate Marcion, the bishop of Arles? Even Cyprian, whom many hold up as a Father opposing the Papacy, appealed to Rome to exercise its

Cyprian to All His People
 —written in A.D. 251

"There is one God and one Christ, and one Church, and one Chair founded on Peter by the word of the Lord. It is not possible to set up another altar or for there to be another priesthood besides that one altar and that one priesthood. Whoever has gathered elsewhere is scattering."[77]

---

jurisdiction over the universal Church. Is this a primacy of honor only, or one also of jurisdiction?

As we have seen, William Webster asserts that the consensus of scholars denies any Roman primacy in Cyprian's writings. He is incorrect in his assessment, both of the consensus of scholars and of the respect of Cyprian for the Roman primacy, as even a casual reading has demonstrated. Another example of a scholar who exposes the seeming disingenuousness of Webster's conclusions is the nineteenth-century German Protestant historian and theologian Adolf von Harnack, who according to Jaroslav Pelikan was a scholar of Eastern Orthodoxy and "carried out in his lifetime the most ambitious critical edition ever undertaken of the sources for Eastern Christianity" (*Christian Doctrine and Modern Culture (since 1700)* [Chicago: Univ. of Chicago Press, 1989], 5:304). S. Herbert Scott quotes Harnack, who is just another voice among many: "[In St. Cyprian's concept of the primacy], a special importance attaches itself to the Roman see, because it is the seat of the apostle to whom Christ first granted apostolic authority in order to show with unmistakable plainness the unity of these powers and the correspondency of the Church that rests on them; and further because, from her historical origin, the Church of this see had become the mother and root of the Catholic Church spread over the earth. In a severe crisis which Cyprian had to pass through in his own diocese he appealed to the Roman Church (the Roman bishop) in a manner which made it appear as if communion with that Church was in itself the guarantee of faith" (*The Eastern Churches and the Papacy* [London: Sheed & Ward, 1928], 50). As C. Lattey concludes, "It has repeatedly been demonstrated—and without any difficulty—that St. Cyprian held a peculiar theory of the episcopate—every bishop is independent, and can act as he pleases, and cannot be interfered with in his diocese. It is easy to prove this by his words—yet it is a theory which is belied by everything we know of his actions, and by a great many of his other words. The fact is that he had only a working theory, which was anything but rigid. He was always concerned to establish his own authority. . . . Many moderns 'in appealing to Cyprian neglect his main doctrine, the necessity of one Church, and appeal to his error, with the Donatists and Luciferians' " (*The Papacy* [London: Burns, Oates & Washbourne, 1923], 34–35).

[77] *Letter of Cyprian to All His People* [43 (40), 5], in Jurgens, *Faith of the Early Fathers*, 1:229.

Firmilian of Caesarea (d. c. A.D. 268)[78]

"But what is his error, and how great his blindness, who says that the remission of sins can be given in the synagogues of the heretics, and who does not remain on the foundation of the one Church which was founded upon the rock by Christ, can be learned from this, which Christ said to Peter alone: 'Whatever things you shall bind on earth shall be bound also in heaven; and whatever you loose on earth, they shall be loosed in heaven;' and by this, again in the gospel, when Christ breathed upon the Apostles alone, saying to them: 'Receive the Holy Spirit: if you forgive any man his sins, they shall be forgiven; and if you retain any man's sins, they shall be retained.' Therefore, the power of forgiving sins was given to the Apostles and to the Churches which these men, sent by Christ, established; and to the bishops who succeeded them by being ordained in their place."[79]

"And in this respect I am justly indignant at this so open and manifest folly of Stephen, that he who so boasts of the place of his episcopate, and contends that he holds the succession from Peter,[80]

---

[78] Firmilian of Caesarea, who sympathized with Cyprian in the matter of rebaptism, was angry that Pope Stephen had censured the practice of rebaptizing those who came into the Church from heretical sects. He provides us with an invaluable testimony to a pre-Nicene Pope's concept of his own position and authority. Even though sarcastic and dissenting, he gives a clear testimony to the claim of the bishop of Rome to a "succession from Peter on whom the foundations of the Church were laid", a "succession to the throne of Peter", and the "authority of the Apostles".

[79] *Letter to Cyprian* 75, 16, written about 255/256, in Jurgens, *Faith of the Early Fathers*, 1:245. This passage confirms that Firmilian bases his whole concept of the Church on apostolic succession, the visible hierarchy of the Church, and the power of the bishops to forgive sins. He also confirms the early Church's understanding that Peter held a place of primacy in the Church and that he was the rock upon which Christ built his Church.

[80] A footnote in *The Ante-Nicene Fathers* admits that the place and succession of Peter are conceded in Firmilian's argument (5:394). Also, J. Michael Miller writes, "[Pope] Stephen [254–257] was also the first bishop of Rome [recorded] to cite the Matthew text to justify his authority. Rome possessed a superior authority, according to Stephen, because its bishop was heir to the unique prerogatives Jesus gave Peter" (*Shepherd and the Rock* [Huntington, Ind.: Our Sunday Visitor, 1995], 81–82). The inclusion of the word "recorded" is very important, for much was said and written in the first centuries that is no longer available. The lack of a recorded prior use of Matthew 16 by a bishop of Rome is no proof that Stephen was the first to use the argument.

on whom the foundations of the Church were laid, should introduce many other rocks [heretics and schismatics] and establish
new buildings of many churches; maintaining that there is baptism
in them by his authority. . . . Stephen, who announces that he
holds by succession the throne of Peter, is stirred with no zeal
against heretics."[81]

Pope Dionysius (d. 268, bishop of Rome from 259)
—as related in a letter by St. Athanasius[82]

"But a charge had been laid by some persons against the Bishop of
Alexandria before the Bishop of Rome, as if he had said that the

---

[81] *Letter to Cyprian* 74, 17, ANF 5:394. As we have seen, there was a debate
raging as to whether a person baptized by heretics, or while in schism, was validly
baptized. Firmilian was supporting Cyprian of Carthage as Cyprian argued the
matter with then Pope Stephen I (r. A.D. 254–257). Stephen said that any person
properly baptized was validly baptized, even if the baptism was by a heretic.
Cyprian and Firmilian said baptism was valid only if it occurred inside the Catholic Church. Stephen's decree is the teaching of the Catholic Church today.

To summarize St. Firmilian: "In these words Firmilian, carried away by passion, unjustly attacks S. Stephen for his letter to S. Cyprian: whereupon we make
the following remarks: The letter of S. Stephen has not, indeed, come down to
us; but it is evident that he must have written to S. Cyprian with great authority,
deciding as Pope, and as he who *holds the succession of Peter upon whom the
foundations of the Church were laid*, what from ancient tradition was the course to
be taken with regard to converted heretics. And thus we see that S. Stephen
asserted, as a fact beyond dispute, S. Peter's Roman Episcopate and his own
succession, no less emphatically and solemnly than did S. Leo two centuries
later in his well-known Sermons. Firmilian could not but recognize that herein
lay the foundation of Stephen's authority; yet how displeasing to him were the
Pontiff's words is evident enough from the bitter way in which he repeats them.
Were he able to deny or call in question the Roman Episcopate of Peter and
Stephen's succession therefrom, this certainly would have been the readiest and
most efficacious means of breaking the force of that authority; and, from the
bitter vehemence with which he asperses S. Stephen, it is only reasonable to
suppose that, had he been able, he would have made use even of that means. But
this he does not do: he neither denies, nor calls in question, S. Peter's Roman
Episcopate and Stephen's succession. And hence it is clear that here was a fact
universally held as certain. The cutting expressions of Firmilian prove only how
deeply wounded he felt at the words used by Stephen in setting forth his authority as S. Peter's successor in the Roman See" (T. Livius, *S. Peter, Bishop of Rome*
[London: Burns & Oates, 1888], 20–21; italics his).

[82] Dionysius assumed the office of bishop of Rome after the violent persecution of Emperor Valerian (A.D. 253–260), who called for the execution of all

Son was made, and not coessential with the Father. And, the synod at Rome being indignant, the Bishop of Rome expressed their united sentiments in a letter to his namesake. And so the latter [Dionysius of Alexandria], in defence, wrote a book with the title 'of Refutation and Defence;' and thus he writes to the other [Dionysius of Rome]: '. . . And my Letter, as I said before, owing to present circumstances, I am unable to produce, or I would have sent you the very words I used, or rather a copy of it all; which, if I have an opportunity, I will do still.' "[83]

Eusebius
   —an appeal to Emperor Aurelian against the heretic
      Paul of Samosata[84]

"As Paul had fallen from the episcopate, as well as from the ortho-dox faith, Domnus, as has been said, became bishop of the church

---

clergy. Sixtus II, bishop before Dionysius, and all seven deacons of the Roman Church were executed. Lawrence was the last of the seven to die. Dionysius had been a presbyter under Sixtus II; and after the persecution waned, he was elected Pope.

[83] *Councils of Ariminum and Seleucia* 3, 43, NPNF2, 4:473. If the doctrines of the Churches were outside the jurisdiction of the See of Rome, why is it that Dionysius of Rome could authoritatively write to the bishop of Alexandria demanding an accounting of his doctrine? And why is it that the bishop of Alexandria quickly and respectfully responds to the Pope, acknowledging his authority to oversee the doctrine in Alexandria and saying, "*I should have sent you the very words I used.*" Dionysius of Rome vindicated Dionysius of Alexandria after discovering the facts. Why, also, did St. Athanasius consider the imposition of Rome's jurisdiction on the Alexandrian bishop, demanding an accounting, as acceptable practice and the exercise of lawful authority? "This is evidence of capital importance. Those Egyptians [in the See of Alexandria, Egypt] felt no doubt at all. Their Bishop was a considerable personage, the see of Alexandria one of the most ancient in the Church; but they did not hesitate. They knew that there existed a sovereign arbiter in disputes which might arise within the Church, and that that supreme arbiter was the Bishop of Rome. . . . [Dionysius of Rome wrote to Alexandria, and] in the following century Athanasius quoted this letter as an unanswerable document. The head of the Church of Rome there speaks, in fact, as a teacher who decides and not as a theologian who discusses. He transmits the apostolic teaching of which he has the sovereign custody" (d'Ormesson, *Papacy*, 48–49). See also Dolan, *See of Peter*, 40–42.

[84] Paul of Samosata (between A.D. 200 and 300) was a heretical bishop of Antioch appointed in about 260. He taught that God was a closely knit Father, Wisdom, and Word that was one single person until creation. He taught that

at Antioch. But as Paul refused to surrender the church building,[85] the Emperor Aurelian was petitioned; and he decided the matter most equitably, ordering the building to be given to those to whom the bishops of Italy and of the city of Rome should adjudge it."[86]

Poem against the Marcionites
    —written before A.D. 325 [87]

"In this chair in which he himself had sat, Peter,
In mighty Rome, commanded Linus, the first elected, to sit down.
After him, Cletus too accepted the flock of the fold.[88]

Christ was just a man, like a prophet, but that the Word rested upon the human Jesus; in this way he denied the divinity of Christ. It took the authority of the emperor to dislodge the heretic and to install Domnus, an orthodox bishop. Why was this not done by the Pope himself? Simply because the heretic had already rejected the authority of the Pope, which is natural for heretics, and because the Pope had no military might, only the moral authority of the Church, an authority that is not enforced with weapons of the flesh.

[85] The Catholic Church had already judged Paul of Samosata a heretic and excommunicated him. When force was required to remove him from the church building, the emperor (civil authority) had to be called in.

[86] Eusebius, *Church History* 7, 30, NPNF2, 1:316. The civil authority was summoned to remove the heretic from the church building. He refused to leave. The emperor removed Paul of Samosata by force and gave the church building to those approved by Rome. Remember, Antioch is in the East, about 1,330 miles from Rome as a crow flies and only three hundred miles north of Jerusalem. Is it not amazing that even the secular authorities knew who had jurisdiction over the universal Church? Why not give the church building to the bishop of Jerusalem or another nearby patriarch? Why put the church in the hands of the Roman Church? Not only the Church leaders but also the civil authorities recognized the primacy of Rome's jurisdiction over the universal Church. Only the heretics and schismatics dissented—dissented even though they recognized the Roman prerogatives.

[87] There is some discussion as to the exact date that the *Poem against the Marcionites* was composed; however, according to William Jurgens, the latest scholarship places it prior to the Nicene Council in A.D. 325. An unknown author in Gaul probably composed it, though it is preserved as a work of Tertullian and originally entitled *Adversus Marcionem libri Quinque* (see Jurgens, *Faith of the Early Fathers*, 1:390).

[88] Reference to John 10:16: "And I have other sheep, that are not of this fold; I must bring them also, and they will heed my voice. So there shall be one flock, one shepherd."

As his successor, Anacletus was elected by lot.
Clement follows him, well-known to apostolic men.
After him Evaristus ruled the flock without crime.
Alexander, sixth in succession, commends the fold to Sixtus.
After his illustrious times were completed, he passed it on to
Telesphorus. He was excellent, a faithful martyr.
After him, learned of the law and a sure teacher. . . .
Hyginus, in the ninth place, now accepted the chair.
Then Pius, after him, whose blood-brother was Hermas,
An angelic shepherd, because he spoke the words delivered
    to him;
And Anicetus accepted his lot in pious succession." [89]

Aphraates (or Aphrahat) the Persian Sage (c. A.D. 280–d. after 345)
—first of the Syrian Church Fathers [90]

"David received the kingdom of Saul his persecutor; and Jesus
received the kingdom of Israel His persecutor. . . . David handed
over the kingdom to Solomon, and was gathered to his people;
and Jesus handed over the keys to Simon, and ascended and
returned to Him who sent Him." [91]

---

[89] *Poem against the Marcionites*, 3, 276–96, in Jurgens, *Faith of the Early Fathers*,
1:390. The means of opposing heresy in the early Church was not to appeal to
Scripture primarily but to appeal to the apostolic succession and apostolic
Churches. Paul tells us that the Church is the "pillar and bulwark of the truth"
(2 Tim 3:15). The Christians of the first centuries, the primitive Church, appealed to the apostolic Churches and ultimately to the "chair of Peter" in Rome
to determine true doctrine and to root out heresy.

[90] Little is known about Aphraates other than that he was an important figure
in the Syrian Church, probably a bishop. He was an ascetic and lived through
the persecution of the Sassanid king, Shapur II (310–379). Our knowledge of
him comes from his twenty-three *Treatises*, where he is seen to be an orthodox
Christian.

[91] *Select Demonstrations of Aphrahat* 21, 13, NPNF2, 13:398, written between 336
and 345 by Aphraates the Persian Sage, who was one of the first Fathers of the
Syrian Church. If it were not an already well-established fact, he would have no
reason to promote the primacy of Peter or the Roman See, since he was at the
extreme eastern frontier of the Roman Empire. This particular line in Aphraates
is referring to the position of steward. In the Near Eastern kingdoms, including
that of Israel, the king would delegate the keys (authority) of his kingdom to his
steward, who was often his son, who would then exercise the authority of the king
in his absence. The steward acted for the king (Mt 16:19; Is 22:22).

Jacob of Nisibis (d. A.D. 338) [92]

"And Simon the head of the Apostles, he who denied Christ . . . our Lord received him, and made him the foundation, and called him the rock of the edifice of the Church." [93]

---

[92] Jacob of Nisibis, called "Moses of Mesopotamia", was bishop of Nisibis in Persia. He had a great reputation in the East for learning, ability, and holiness. He was present at the Council of Nicaea and stood firm for the orthodox faith, strongly opposing Arius (see Cross and Livingstone, *Oxford Dictionary*, 856).

[93] *Orat.* 7, *De Poenit.* 6, 57, in Joseph Berington and John Kirk, comps., *The Faith of Catholics*, ed. T. J. Capel (New York: Pustet & Co., 1885), 2:13–14. To William Webster's credit, he included this passage from Jacob of Nisibis along with another, which reads "Our Lord Jesus Christ is the firm and true foundation; and upon this rock our faith is established. Therefore, when any one has come to faith, he is set upon a firm rock. . . . And Simon, who was called a rock, was deservedly called a rock because of his faith", and another referring to "Simon the rock of faith". However, Webster concludes by saying that "James, like Eusebius and Augustine, states that the rock of the Church is Christ. He alone is the true and unique foundation. However, Peter is also called a rock and foundation of the Church but only because of his faith. The Church is built upon Christ as the foundation, not upon Peter. It can be said to be built upon Peter only in the sense that it is built upon his faith which points to Christ" (Webster, *Peter and the Rock*, 100). Why does Webster have to work so hard to establish the *either-or* dichotomy? Why not accept the *both-and* position of the Fathers and the Catholic Church? The beautifully written and profound *Catechism of the Catholic Church* is able to fathom the whole depth of the matter without petty distinctions and is quite willing to proclaim the merits of Peter's faith: "Moved by the grace of the Holy Spirit and drawn by the Father, we believe in Jesus and confess: 'You are the Christ, the Son of the living God.' On the rock of this faith confessed by St. Peter, Christ built his Church" (CCC 424). The Catechism also teaches that *Christ* is the foundation of the Church, in harmony with 1 Corinthians 3:11, "Often, too, the Church is called the *building* of God. The Lord compared himself to the stone which the builders rejected, but which was made into the corner-stone. On this foundation [of Christ] the Church is built by the apostles and from it the Church receives solidity and unity" (CCC 756). One must remember the principle established in the beginning of our study: mixing metaphors does damage to the text and intent of biblical passages. For example, in Matthew 16 we find Peter the foundation, Christ the builder, and believers the building stones. In 1 Corinthians 3, Christ is the foundation (not the builder), the apostles are the builders, and the building material is good or worthless works. The first deals with the Church as a whole, whereas the second deals with the individual Christian. One must not mix metaphors, for in doing so one is wrongly dividing the word of truth.

St. Ephraim (c. A.D. 306–373)[94]

"Simon, My follower, I have made you the foundation of the holy Church.[95] I betimes called you Peter [Kēfâ, or *Rock*, in the original text], because you will support all its buildings. You are the inspector of those who will build on earth a Church for Me.[96] If they should wish to build what is false, you, the foundation, will condemn them. You are the head of the fountain from which My teaching flows, you are the chief of My disciples. Through you I will give drink to all peoples.[97] Yours is that life-giving sweet-

---

[94] St. Ephraim is referred to as the *Lyre of the Holy Spirit* and is the great classic author and biblical exegete of the Syrian Church. He was born in Nisibis, Syria, probably to Christian parents. He was ordained a deacon of the Catholic Church before A.D. 338. His works are almost all in poetic form, and they are a storehouse of treasures. He was famous for his sanctity and learning.

[95] Interestingly enough, and true to form as well, William Webster fails to mention this passage from St. Ephraim. He does quote two other passages in an attempt to prove that St. Ephraim would never have considered Peter to be the rock or foundation upon which the Church is built. He intends these two passages to damage the Catholic position (*Peter and the Rock*, 108–9). The first is from *Hymns for the Feast of the Epiphany* 2, 14, which reads, "It [Mount Sinai] saw against its Lord—stones taken up: but He [the Lord] took stones [as the builder, not the foundation]—to build the Church upon the Rock [Peter]; blessed *be* His building!" (NPNF2, 13:267). This would certainly be the correct interpretation, especially in light of our current passage. How does Webster possibly come to the conclusion that the "Rock" is Christ exclusively and not Peter? In Matthew 16, Christ is the builder and Peter the rock, which fits perfectly with what St. Ephraim says here. Secondly, Webster cites the hymn *The Pearl* 2, 2, which reads, "Shadowed forth in thy beauty is the beauty of the Son, . . . And if they showed no pity upon thee, neither did they love thee: still suffer as thou mightest, thou hast come to reign! Simon Peter [ed. note: 'Cephas; i.e., Rock'] showed pity on the Rock" (ibid., 13:295). Even the editor makes it clear that Peter is pointed out to be the Rock [Cephas] in the sense of Matthew 16:18 and John 1:42, whereas Christ is pointed out to be the rock in the sense of 1 Corinthians 3, where Christ is referred to as a foundation, but not as the rock. It seems obvious that St. Ephraim is *not* setting up an *either-or* dichotomy.

[96] In order to be the "*inspector*", or overseer, of the universal Church over all time and the entire world, succession was necessary; and those who succeeded Peter in the See of Rome have overseen the building of the Church throughout the centuries.

[97] This would appear to be an allusion to 1 Corinthians 10:1–4, where we see Christ as the Rock in the wilderness from whom the Israelites received water. Christ, though he himself is the Rock in this passage, is seen by St. Ephraim as sharing his "rockness" with Peter, or appointing Peter as a mediator of the grace and life that will flow from Christ through his Church.

ness which I dispense. I have chosen you to be, as it were, the first-born in My institution, and so that, as the heir, you may be executor of my treasures. I have given you the keys of my kingdom. Behold, I have given you authority over all my treasures![98]

Council of Nicaea (325)[99]

"Let the ancient custom which is followed in Egypt and Libya and the Pentapolis remain in force, by which the Bishop of Alexandria has the supervision of all those places, since this is also the custom[100] of the Bishop of Rome."[101]

---

[98] *Homilies* (*Ephraim's Memre*) 4, 1, written between A.D. 338 and 373, in Jurgens, *Faith of the Early Fathers*, 1:311. This poem was written very close to the Nicene Council, before the final canonization of Scripture and while the battle over the divinity of Christ and the Holy Spirit still raged. St. Ephraim was from the East, a deacon in the Syrian Church. He was not a Western Christian, so Western bias may not be invoked to explain his understanding of the Petrine prerogatives. We see here of course the understanding of Peter as the royal steward of Christ's kingdom—insofar as he is referred to as "first-born in My institution", "heir", "executor of my treasures", and with the keys of the kingdom Peter has "authority over all my [Jesus'] treasures". Remember at this point that even though the man dies, the office continues and successors fill the vacancy. There is virtually no doubt that St. Ephraim has the dynastic succession of royal steward in mind.

[99] The Council of Nicaea was a definitive council, in which 318 bishops from around the Empire, many maimed and deformed by persecutions for the faith, assembled primarily to combat Arianism and establish the orthodox teaching on the divinity of Christ. From the Council flowed the Nicene Creed, which is recited throughout the Catholic Church. It is of interest that in the Creed the Church proclaims: "We believe in one holy, catholic, and apostolic Church." This implies trust in a certain and recognizable institutional authority, as opposed to many informal Protestant credos, which tend to proclaim "We believe in the 'Bible-only' and not in any visible institution or society." The early Church trusted the Church and said so in her Creed.

[100] This phrase could be understood in two ways. First, it is the custom of Rome to have jurisdiction over the bishops of surrounding territories, providing a justification for Alexandria to do so as well. Second, it is the custom of Rome to acknowledge the prerogatives of the Alexandrian bishop, giving the council the precedent for doing so. Either way, it shows Rome as the primary model and the basis for the determination of the other Churches.

[101] These were the opening words from the Nicene Council, canon 6, as read by the Roman legates at the Council of Chalcedon (A.D. 451), in Jurgens, *Faith of the Early Fathers*, 283. There is no record of anyone arguing with their rendering. At the Council of Chalcedon the Greeks present followed the papal legates

Council of Sardica (c. 343) [102]

"But if any bishop loses the judgment in some case, and still believes that he has not a bad but a good case, in order that the

---

by reading their version, and it is often argued that they did so to refute the Latin text. There is no evidence for this. All the acts of the Council say is that the Greeks read theirs, which did not have any words about the primacy. There is great discussion as to the actual words of the canons of the Council of Nicaea. There is little information about the actual Acts of the Council, possibly destroyed by the Arians. Papal legates attended the Council of Nicaea, and their names were first in the list of signatories. The Arabic canons, attributed to the Council of Nicaea, decree, "The patriarch must consider what things are done by the archbishops and bishops in their provinces, . . . just as he who occupies the chair of Rome, is the head and prince of all patriarchs; since he is the first, as was Peter, to whom power is given over all Christian princes, and over all their peoples, as he who is the Vicar of Christ our Lord, over all peoples and over the whole Christian Church, and whosoever shall gainsay this is excommunicated by the Synod" (Labbe & Cossart, *Concilia*, as quoted by Dolan, *See of Peter*, 48–49). Dolan comments: "I am perfectly aware that there has been a very long and as yet unsettled controversy, as to the exact number of canons promulgated by the Council of Nice. I am aware also that *perhaps* the more critical view seems to point to only twenty canons, whereas the Arabic manuscript translated into Latin by Father Romanus S.J. points to eighty. The antiquity of the Arabic [manuscript] however is not to be called into question, and the fact that it proceeds from an oriental source, makes it valuable in this connection" (ibid., 49). According to Luke Rivington, "This whole contention will be greatly strengthened if we consider the probability that his canon had for its heading, or rather, for its first sentence, the works read by the Roman legates at the Council of Chalcedon, viz. 'The Church of Rome has always held [or, Let the Church of Rome always hold] the primacy [author's note: The full reading is very likely 'let the ancient custom remain that the Church of Rome should,' &c.]. . . . The imperial commissioners, in summing up, decided that from all that had gone before it was clear that Rome held the primacy" (*Primitive Church*, 170, 171). In an excellent article written by James F. Loughlin, we read, "Now it is plain that . . . the Synod made no enactment of any kind in regard to the Roman Pontiff. This canon neither grants new privileges to the Apostolic See, nor concerns any existing ones. For some reason or other, the Council did not think it necessary to legislate upon the Bishop of Rome. It strengthened the hands of the Patriarchs of Alexandria and Antioch, and of the Exarchs of Pontus, Asia, and Thrace. In Canon VII it conceded a Patriarchate of Honor to the Bishop of the Holy City; but it did not DARE exercise, in any way, a legislative authority over the city of St. Peter" ("The Sixth Nicene Canon and the Papacy", *American Catholic Quarterly Review* 5 [1880]: 220–39).

[102] The Emperors Constans and Constantius called the Council of Sardica to settle the widespread contention regarding the orthodoxy of St. Athanasius. St. Athanasius is called the Father of Orthodoxy and almost single-handedly

case may be judged anew let us honor the memory of the Apostle Peter, by having those who gave the judgment write to Julius, Bishop of Rome, so that, if it seem proper, he may himself send arbiters, and judgment may be made again by the bishops of a neighboring province." [103]

---

defended the deity of Christ against the Arians, who claimed Christ was a created being and not coeternal with the Father. The intention was to have an ecumenical council; but Eastern bishops refused to attend because St. Athanasius, whom the Eastern bishops had deposed, was present and considered a proper member of the council. The council confirmed the restoration of Athanasius and is famous for acknowledging the bishop of Rome as a court of appeals for accused bishops from other geographical areas.

[103] Council of Sardica, canon 3, in Jurgens, *Faith of the Early Fathers*, 1:308. The Abbé Vladimir Guettée, who left the Catholic Church to receive "communion in both kinds at the hands of the Greeks, in the Church of the Russian Embassy in Paris" (Abbé Vladimir Guettée, *The Papacy* (1866; reprint, Blanco, Tex.: New Sarov Press, n.d.], v.), goes into great detail, attempting to strip the Council of Sardica of any hint of Roman primacy or jurisdiction. He writes, "It is these bishops that the council refers, in the last resort, to *Julius, Bishop of Rome*. It does not refer them to the Bishop of Rome generally, but to Julius. Nor does it make this rule *obligatory*; the appeal is purely optional; and lastly, the council proposes to *honour the memory of St. Peter by granting to a Bishop of Rome* a prerogative which it considers new and exceptional" (ibid., 126). As we see, Guettée, insists that the judicial authority is not granted at Sardica to the bishop of Rome as an office but only to the particular bishop at the time, Julius. Though there is some debate as to the degree and extent of the Roman authority acknowledged, it is still clear that Roman primacy was both recognized and extended.

To cite only a few examples of scholarly opinion that dismiss the claims of Guettée and others who attempt to minimize the decrees of the Council of Sardica, the non-partisan *Encyclopedia of Early Christianity* (ed. Everett Ferguson [New York: Garland Pub., 1990], 832), informs us that "The council confirmed the orthodoxy of Athanasius. . . . More significantly, the council upheld the right of bishops to appeal to Rome, thus advancing the jurisdictional authority of the papacy in opposition to imperial intervention in ecclesiastical controversies." Another non-partisan source informs us, "Canons 3–5 of this council were of great historical importance. They invested the Roman bishop with a prerogative, which was the first legal recognition [first time clearly defined in a council] of the bishop of Rome's jurisdiction over the other sees and was, therefore, the basis for the further development of his primacy as pope" ("Sardica, Council of", in *Encyclopedia Britannica* [Chicago: Encyclopedia Britannica, Inc., 1981], 8:900). And finally, "Episcopal right of appeal to the Holy See was guaranteed, and the papal prerogative of ultimate decision in case of a bishop's deposition explicitly acknowledged" (Newman C. Eberhardt, *A Summary of Catholic History* [St. Louis, Mo.: B. Herder, 1961], 1:196. For a decidedly Catholic perspective, see Rivington, *Primitive Church*, 173–84.)

"Bishop Gaudentius said: If it pleases you, it is necessary to make an addition to this decree which the fullness of Your Unalloyed Charity has proposed, so that if some bishop be deposed by the judgment of the bishops sitting in the neighborhood, and if he declare that he will seek further redress, another should not be appointed to his see until the bishop of Rome can be acquainted with the case and render a judgment."[104]

"If anyone demands that his case be heard again, and by his own entreaty he wishes the bishop of the Romans to send priests as his personal legates to judge the case, it is in the power of the bishop [of Rome] to do whatever seems right to him; and if he decides that he ought to send them, and that they are to have the authority of him that sent them when they render judgment along with the bishops, this too must be allowed. But if he considers that the judgment of the case and the decision rendered upon the bishop is already sufficient, he will do whatever seems best to him in his most prudent counsel. The bishops responded: the matters so stated are approved."[105]

---

[104] Council of Sardica, canon 4, in Jurgens, *Faith of the Early Fathers*, 1:308. "The history of the Arians of the fourth century has sometimes been written with the Pope almost left out. St. Athanasius appealed to the Pope, obeyed the Pope's summons, and was acquitted by the Pope. The Eusebians used flattery and guile; they pretended to appeal to Pope Julius, and evaded obedience. The Pope quashed their council of Tyre. The great council of Sardica instituted a new system under which metropolitans or bishops of the East, who wished to appeal to the Pope, need not appear in person in Rome, as had been till then the law; the Pope can order a new trial to be held in the province, appointing the judges himself; no successor to an accused bishop can be appointed, until Rome has given a final decision. If, on the other hand, a bishop actually goes to Rome, the Pope can have the matter settled by the comprovincials on the spot, if he prefers this course, or he can send a legate *a latere* to sit with them, or can appoint other judges, at his will. This is new canon law. It was understood that the Pope would not leave Rome, even to preside at great councils of the Empire, such as Aries and Nicaea, and Sardica itself. But until now his decisions had always been made at Rome with the help of a local council. To the Catholic bishops from all parts of the world assembled at Sardica under the leadership of Hosius and Athanasius and the papal legates, it seemed that the great hope for the Nicene faith lay in this novel idea of making Roman authority no longer a distant court of appeal, but a working reality in the most distant provinces" (Lattey, *Papacy*, 35–36).

[105] Council of Sardica, canon 5, in Jurgens, *Faith of the Early Fathers*, 1:308. Jurgens comments, "The point of this part of the canon is that judgment is to be rendered first by the bishops of the province in which the difficulty arises. The

Athanasius (c. A.D. 296–373)
—defending his own orthodoxy and quoting Pope Julius[106]

"Why was nothing said to us [Pope Julius and the Roman Church] concerning the Church of the Alexandrians in particular? Are you ignorant that the custom has been for word to be written first to us [Rome], and then for a just decision to be passed from this place? If then any such suspicion rested upon the Bishop there, notice thereof ought to have been sent to the Church of this place [Rome]; whereas, after neglecting to inform us, and proceeding on their own authority as they pleased, now they desire to obtain our concurrence in their decisions, though we never condemned him. Not so have the constitutions of Paul, not so have the traditions of the Fathers directed; this is another form of procedure, a novel practice. I beseech you, readily bear with me: what I write is for the common good. For what we have received from the blessed Apostle Peter, that I signify to you; and I should not have written

---

next part of the canon provides for appeal to Rome, if the first judgment is not accepted" (ibid., n. 1). Just as the Supreme Court of the United States retains the final authority in matters of law in our country, after lower court remedies have been expended, so the bishop of Rome held jurisdiction over issues of faith and morals, exerting oversight to the "lower courts", for example, local councils. Protestants frequently claim that the early Church had no hierarchical leaders who exercised authority over the universal Church. Those especially of the Baptist tradition claim that every Church was an independent congregation with no external control or hierarchy. The Eastern Orthodox usually claim that the bishops were all equal and the bishop of Rome had no special place of jurisdictional authority, only a primacy of honor. It is clear from this council of the Church that, not only was the bishopric of Rome considered the See of Peter, but also it had authority to make binding judgments in regards to the bishops of other geographical areas. This council took place only eighteen years after the opening of the Council of Nicaea and fifty years before the final collection of the New Testament canon.

[106] The unbending character and unswerving orthodox theology of Athanasius were the main reason the correct doctrine of the divinity of Christ finally prevailed in the East. As a deacon he accompanied the bishop of Alexandria to the Council of Nicaea. Three years later he became the bishop of Alexandria. In his early twenties he wrote two treatises, one of which is the famous *De Incarnatione* (On the Incarnation). He was exiled numerous times and hid in caves while defending the divinity of Christ against the heretics. He was also relentless in his defense of the divinity of the Holy Spirit and the full manhood of Christ. We owe an eternal debt of gratitude to Athanasius for standing against all odds to defend orthodox Christianity.

this, as deeming that these things were manifest unto all men, had
not these proceedings so disturbed us. . . . Thus wrote the Council
of Rome by Julius, Bishop of Rome." [107]

"When Ursacius and Valens saw all this, they forthwith condemned themselves for what they had done, and going up to
Rome, confessed their crime, declared themselves penitent, and
sought forgiveness, addressing the following letters to Julius,
Bishop of ancient Rome, and to ourselves. Copies of them were
sent to me from Paulinus, Bishop of Treveri. [108]

"Ursacius and Valens to the most blessed lord, pope Julius.

---

[107] *Defence against the Arians* 2, 35, NPNF2, 4:118–19. The above quotation is
an excerpt from Pope Julian's letter included in Athanasius' correspondence as
proof of his orthodoxy and as authority for his restoration as bishop. The Arian
heretics repeatedly deposed Athanasius from his position as bishop of Alexandria. He was forced to flee to Rome, where he made close associations. Rome
continued to defend him and his orthodox doctrine throughout his life. The
Eastern bishops, steeped in Arianism, deposed Athanasius and said he had no
grounds for appeal since a council of bishops had condemned him under
imperial leave.

"It was on this point that the Roman Pontiff at once joined issue in his
celebrated letter preserved by St. Athanasius. In the course of that letter he
accuses these bishops of violating the discipline of the Church. They had condemned the Bishop of Alexandria, St. Athanasius. . . . It was, then, according to
St. Julius, a novel practice in the middle of the fourth century for a council of
bishops to proceed to censure the second Petrine See, that of Alexandria, on
their own authority, *instead of obtaining a just sentence from Rome*. The latter, he
says, was the usual course, sanctioned by antiquity. And the authority thus to
decide was, he adds, derived to Rome from 'that which we have received from
the blessed Apostle Peter.' And this was under the very shadow of the Nicene
Council" (Rivington, *Primitive Church*, 177). Athanasius was cleared in Rome
and, with a signature from Pope Julius, was reinstated to his bishopric in Alexandria, Egypt. "Rome was not only the place to seek answers; after they were given,
after decisions received the Petrine solidity, no further appeal was possible. . . .
The greatest threat to the Church was mutability, but Rome provided stability. . . . Earlier Rome alone defended those unjustly persecuted in the East:
Athanasius, Chrysostom, Flavian. In these cases the acquittal granted by Rome
alone outweighed all the Eastern condemnations. By what right did they call
Rome to judgment? Rome could judge the whole Church and no one could
dispute its judgment. Just as 'what the first see did not approve, could not stand,
so what it judged, the whole church accepted'" (Robert Eno, "Pre-History of
Papal Infallibility", in *Teaching Authority and Infallibility in the Church: Lutherans
and Catholics in Dialogue VI*, ed. Paul C. Empie, T. Austin Murphy, and Joseph
Burgess [Minneapolis: Augsburg Pub. House, 1980], 245–46).

[108] *Defence against the Arians* 1, 4, 58, NPNF2, 4:130.

"Whereas it is well known that we have heretofore in letters laid many grievous charges against the Bishop Athanasius, and whereas, when we were corrected by the letters of your Goodness, we were unable to render an account of the statement we had made; we do now confess before your Goodness. . . . Wherefore we earnestly desire communion with the aforesaid Athanasius, especially since your Piety, with your characteristic generosity, has vouchsafed to pardon our error. But we also declare, that if at any time the Eastern Bishops, or even Athanasius himself, ungenerously should wish to bring us to judgment for this matter, we will not depart contrary to your judgment. . . . I Ursacius subscribed this my confession in person; and likewise I Valens." [109]

"When I left Alexandria, I did not go to your brother's headquarters, or to any other persons, but only to Rome; and having laid my case before the Church (for this was my only concern), I spent my time in the public worship." [110]

Hilary of Poitiers (c. A.D. 315–367/368) [111]

"Peter believeth the first, and is the prince of the apostleship." [112]

---

[109] Ibid., 130–31. This passage of Athanasius' *Defence* relates the repentance of two heretics and speaks quite eloquently for itself. Notice the request of pardon from Rome and the conviction that the bishop of Rome's judicial determination stands supreme, even over their own Eastern bishops.

[110] *Defence before Constantius* 4, NPNF2, 4:239, Athanasius writing to Emperor Constantius. This passage seems to present the equation: Rome = Church. It is interesting that the orthodox bishops looked to and took refuge in Rome. It was the heretics and schismatics, not those of orthodox faith, who opposed Rome's primacy. As Michael Winter says, "The East had undergone many changes in less than half a century. Caesaropapism [supreme authority over the Church exercised by a secular monarch; in other words, the regime in which Caesar would be Pope] had appeared, Arianism was going from strength to strength, and opposition to the Pope was following in its train. . . . The latter half of the fourth century would see the restoration of Nicene orthodoxy [in the East], and the first half of the fifth century would witness the re-establishment of the Pope's authority. The third evil of the Eastern church, caesaropapism, was never remedied" (*Saint Peter*, 191).

[111] St. Hilary of Poitiers, the "Athanasius of the West", an archbishop and Doctor of the Church, was born in Poitiers, France. Of pagan parentage, Hilary was a convert to Christianity. About 353 he was elected bishop of Poitiers and immediately began a rigorous suppression of the heresy of Arianism in his diocese. Although his Arian opponents secured his banishment to Phrygia in

"Blessed Simon, who after his confession of the mystery was set to be the foundation-stone of the Church, and received the keys of the kingdom of heaven".[113]

356, Hilary attended the Synod of Seleucia in 359, where he delivered a scholarly and vigorous defense of orthodoxy. He returned to Poitiers in 361, where he continued his battle against Arianism until his death.

[112] *Commentary in Matthew*, 7, 6, in Berington and Kirk, *Faith of Catholics*, 2:15.

[113] *On the Trinity* 6, 20, NPNF2, 9:105. This passage is of particular interest in light of James White's book *The Roman Catholic Controversy* (Minneapolis: Bethany House, 1996). White asserts that the Fathers did not understand the "Petrine texts" as the Catholic Church currently understands them. He writes, "Remember that Vatican I tells us that the Catholic Church has *always* understood these passages, specifically Matthew 16 and John 21, in the way presented by Rome today. This is manifestly untrue. The existence of different interpretations . . . refutes the Roman contention" (119). He then provides a quotation from Hilary to prove his point: "This faith it is which is the foundation of the Church; through this faith the gates of hell cannot prevail against her. This is the faith which has the keys of the kingdom of heaven [*On the Trinity* 6, 37, 121]." The point White is making is that it is Peter's *faith* that is the foundation, not Peter *himself*. In other words, the foundation is *either* Peter *or* his faith. Hilary, just a few chapters earlier in this same work (as we have cited here) refutes White. Why does White not inform his readers that Hilary, *in the same treatise*, refers to blessed Simon as the foundation stone of the Church? Is Hilary confused? Is it Peter *or* his faith? Does Hilary see these two applications of the passage as mutually exclusive, as Protestants like White are wont to do, forcing them into two, separate, water-tight compartments. Why is it so difficult for opponents of the Papacy to see that there is no conflict here? Even Pope John Paul II, in his book *Crossing the Threshold of Hope* (New York: Alfred A. Knopf, 1994), refers to the *rock* of Matthew 16 as Peter *and* as Christ: "He [Peter] became the 'rock,' even if as a man, perhaps, he was nothing more than shifting sand. *Christ Himself is the rock*, and Christ builds His Church on Peter—on Peter, Paul, and the apostles. *The Church is apostolic* in virtue of Christ. . . . In the Church—built on the rock that is Christ—Peter, the apostles, and their successors are witnesses of God crucified and risen in Christ" (9, 11).

Paragraph 552 of the *Catechism of the Catholic Church*, moreover, refers clearly to Peter as the "Rock" by stating: "Simon Peter holds the first place in the college of the Twelve; Jesus entrusted a unique mission to him. Through a revelation from the Father, Peter had confessed: 'You are the Christ, the Son of the living God.' Our Lord then declared to him: 'You are Peter, and on this rock I will build my Church, and the gates of Hades will not prevail against it.' Christ, the 'living stone,' thus assures *his Church, built on Peter*, of victory over the powers of death. Because of the faith he *confessed Peter will remain the unshakeable rock of the Church*" (Vatican City: Libreria Editrice Vaticana, 1994; emphasis added). But the Catechism earlier asserts that the "rock" is Peter's *faith*! "Moved by the grace of the Holy Spirit and drawn by the Father, we believe in Jesus and confess: 'You are the Christ, the Son of the living God.' On the rock of this faith confessed by

"The fear excited in the Apostles by the lowliness of the Passion (so that even the firm rock upon which the Church was to be built trembled), after the death and resurrection of the Lord ceased."[114]

"He [Jesus] took up Peter—to whom He had just before given *the keys of the kingdom* of heaven, upon whom He was about to build the Church, *against which the gates of hell should not* in any way *prevail,* who *whatsoever* he should *bind or loose on earth,* that should abide *bound or loosed in heaven*—this same Peter . . . the first confessor of the Son of God, the foundation of the Church, the doorkeeper of the heavenly kingdom, and in his judgment on earth a judge of heaven."[115]

"And in sooth Peter's confession obtained a worthy recompense. . . . Oh, in thy designation by a new name, happy foundation of the Church, and a rock worthy of the building up of that which was to scatter the infernal laws, and the gates of hell, and all the bars of death! O blessed keeper of the gate of heaven, to whose disposal are delivered the keys of the entrance into eternity; whose judgment on earth is an authority prejudged in heaven, so that the things that are either loosed or bound on earth, acquire in heaven too a like state of settlement."[116]

St. Peter, Christ built his Church" (CCC 424). The Fathers used Matthew 16 in many ways—as does the Catholic Church today.

[114] *Tract. in Ps.* 141, 8, in Berington and Kirk, *Faith of Catholics,* 2:15.

[115] *Tract. in Ps.* 131, 8, in ibid., 2:14–15. A statement like this provides a strong patristic affirmation of the Church's teaching on the primacy of Peter and makes the opposition pale in comparison. It should be noted: there is a vast difference between applying a passage in several ways to meet the need of the moment (e.g., the "rock" being Peter, Christ, Peter's faith or confession, etc.) and a denial that Peter is the rock. We find many Fathers using Matthew 16 for multiple purposes, as is freely done today, but not one of them denies or rebukes the universal and literal understanding that Peter is the foundation of the Church. Since this was, as we see, so commonly taught, the orthodox Christians would have soundly condemned a denial of this interpretation of Matthew 16:18. Firmilian argues with the exercise of the Roman primacy but not with the theological and biblical basis for it. Heretics resisted the authority, but orthodox Christians supported the teaching that Peter is the rock upon which the Church is built and also the primacy of the bishop of Rome as Peter's successor. It is interesting that those who oppose the primacy of Rome today find themselves lined up with the heretics and schismatics of old.

[116] *Commentary on Matthew* 7, 6, in ibid., 2:15. The implications of this passage from Hilary are very profound, as it touches on the infallibility of Peter and the

"And you [Pope Julius], most dearly loved brother, though absent from us in body, were present in mind concordant, and will. . . . For this will be seen to be best, and by far the most befitting thing, if to the head, that is to the see of the Apostle Peter, the priests of the Lord report (or, refer) from every one of the provinces." [117]

Macarius of Egypt (c. A.D. 300–c. 390) [118]

"For of old Moses and Aaron, when this priesthood was theirs, suffered much; and Caiphas, when he had their chair, persecuted and condemned the Lord. . . . Afterwards Moses was succeeded by Peter, who had committed to his hands the new Church of Christ, and the true priesthood." [119]

Church. Peter's judgment is ratified in heaven and acquires "in heaven too a like state of settlement".

[117] *Fragment 2 ex opere Historico* (*ex Epistle Sardic. Concil. ad Julium*) n. 9, p. 629, in ibid., 2:68–69. The visible head of the universal Church is acknowledged by Hilary, as well as the need of all "priests of the Lord" to report to the See of Peter "from every one of the provinces". Hilary demonstrates that Peter's prerogatives were successive and passed on to the bishop of Rome. To deny Petrine succession, along with "Peter's keys" of stewardship, is to deny the evidence.

[118] Mark the Evangelist, who accompanied Peter and wrote the Gospel that bears his name, introduced Christianity into Egypt in the first century. The largest church in Cairo today is named the Church of St. Mark in commemoration of his evangelistic mission. Many of the early Christians fled to the deserts of Egypt to escape persecution and to develop a deeper spiritual life through monasticism. St. Athanasius frequented these Egyptian desert regions when in exile and visited St. Macarius. We learn from Abuna Matta el-Meskin, the current spiritual director of the Monastery of St. Macarius, that, "Since his early youth, St. Macarius had shown a high degree of wisdom, and his friends dubbed him 'the youth endowed with the wisdom of the old'. . . . St. Macarius' face shone with the grace so remarkably that many fathers witnessed that it shone in the dark, and thus called him 'the shining lamp' " (Matta el-Meskin, *Coptic Monasticism and the Monastery of St. Macarius* [Cairo, Egypt: Monastery of St. Macarius, 1984], 27).

[119] *Homily* 26, in Berington and Kirk, *Faith of Catholics*, 2:22. St. Macarius is of special interest to me, since I have spent time in Egypt, especially at the Monastery of St. Macarius in the desert outside Alexandria. We were treated to the most gracious hospitality of Matta el-Meskin and the monks. Matthew the Poor, for that is his common name, was writing a commentary on the Gospel of St. Matthew during our short stay, and we spent several hours discussing the matter of Peter and the primacy, Protestantism, the Holy Spirit, and other topics. As a

Optatus of Milevis
  —written about A.D. 367
  —a defender of the faith against the Donatist schism[120]

"You cannot deny that you are aware that in the city of Rome the episcopal chair was given first to Peter; the chair in which Peter sat, the same who was head—that is why he is also called Cephas—of all the Apostles;[121] the one chair in which unity is maintained by all. Neither do other Apostles proceed individually on their own; and anyone who would set up another chair in opposition to that single chair would, by that very fact, be a schismatic and a sinner. It was Peter, then, who first occupied that chair, the foremost of his endowed gifts. He was succeeded by Linus, Linus was succeeded by Clement . . . Damasus by Siricius, our present incumbent. . . . I but ask you to recall the origins of your chair, you who wish to claim for yourselves the title of holy Church."[122]

Coptic monk, he rejects the special prerogatives of Peter and the See of Rome, though he has great respect for Pope John Paul II.

St. Macarius draws a very interesting parallel in our current selection, which we develop further in our appendix *An Old Testament Basis for the Primacy and Succession of St. Peter.* He shows that Moses was given a special teaching office, the chair, or seat, of Moses, and that Peter inherited that chair. As the old congregation of Israel was given into the hands of Moses and his successors, so the new congregation, the Church, was given into the hands of Peter and his successors. Also placed in Peter's hands was the "new priesthood".

[120] Optatus of Milevis was the bishop of Milevis in North Africa. We know little about Optatus save what we can glean from his treatise *Against Parmenian the Donatist.*

[121] "As Christ is the head of the body of the Church so that all members live only through him and receive their functions from him, so all power and authority in the Church come from the pope who represents Christ the head. . . . This in turn is derived from a strange etymology (not a new one, for it is found in the work of Optatus of Mileve at the beginning of the fifth century): According to John 1:42, Peter was called 'Cephas', which in Hebrew means 'rock', but in Greek corresponds to *kephalē*, 'head' " (Klaus Schatz, *Papal Primacy* [Collegeville, Minn.: Liturgical Press, 1996], 92).

[122] *The Schism of the Donatists* 2, 2, in Jurgens, *Faith of the Early Fathers,* 2:140. A man named Parmenian had written a work entitled *Against the Church of the Apostates.* It was written in defense of the Donatists in A.D. 363. The Donatists were heretics in the African Church in the fourth and fifth centuries. Starting about A.D. 367, Optatus of Milevis wrote a six-volume work against them entitled *The Schism of the Donatists.* St. Augustine developed his refutation of Donatism based on St. Optatus' work.

Basil the Great (C. A.D. 330–379) [123]

"When we hear the name of Peter, that name does not cause our minds to dwell on his substance, but we figure to our minds the properties that are connected with him. For we at once, on hearing that name, think of the son of him that came from Bethsaida, Andrew's brother; him that was called from amongst fishermen unto the ministry of the Apostleship; him who on account of the pre-eminence of his faith received upon himself the building of the Church." [124]

"One also of these mountains was Peter, upon which rock the Lord promised to build His Church." [125]

Notice the first line of this passage. He starts with a truth, a very basic truth, which any Christian or heretic had to acknowledge and no one denied—earlier in the treatise he ridicules anyone who would even consider a denial. The argument in support of this truth, according to Optatus, is quite certain, based on apostolic succession and the primacy of Peter. We learn from Berington and Kirk, *Faith of Catholics*, and from Henri de Lubac, that Optatus viewed Rome as the center of unity, not only of the Church, but also of the whole universe. Optatus writes in *The Schism of the Donatists* 2, 2, "Thanks to an exchange of official letters, the entire universe agrees and becomes one with the bishop of Rome in a society of communion" (Henri de Lubac, *The Motherhood of the Church*, trans. Sr. Sergia Englund [San Francisco: Ignatius Press, 1982], 292).

[123] St. Basil the Great is a Father and Doctor of the Church who was born of wealthy parents in Caesarea Mazaca, modern-day Turkey, and educated in Athens and Constantinople. He traveled out to the deserts to visit well-known hermits in Egypt and Syria, and he gave up an administrative career and settled as a hermit himself along the river Iris in Neo-Caesarea. Noted for his brilliance, he was called upon by the bishop of Caesarea to defend Christian doctrine against the heretical attacks of the Arians. In A.D. 370 he was elected bishop of Caesarea, a post he held until his death on January 1, 379. Basil, his brother St. Gregory of Nyssa, and his friend St. Gregory Nazianzen are known collectively as the Cappadocian Fathers. Basil's grandmother Macrina, his parents, Basil and Emmelia, his sister Macrina, and his younger brothers Gregory and Peter of Sebaste are all venerated as saints.

[124] *Adv. Eunom.* 4, in Berington and Kirk, *Faith of Catholics*, 2:22.

[125] *Comm. in Esai* 2, 66, in ibid., 2:22. Webster brings this passage to the fore and comments that Peter had no exclusive status or office but that "the Church is built upon all the apostles and prophets equally, not just upon Peter. All of them are the foundation of the Church. He [Basil] states that Peter is only one of the foundations" (*Peter and the Rock*, 97). Webster draws this conclusion from the full context, which says, "Now the foundations of this Church are on the holy mountains, since it is built upon the foundation of the apostles and prophets. One of these mountains was indeed Peter, upon which rock the Lord promised

"It has seemed to me to be desirable to send a letter to the bishop of Rome, begging him to examine[126] our condition, and since there are difficulties in the way of representatives being sent from the West by a general synodical decree, to advise him [the bishop of Rome] to exercise his own personal authority in the matter by choosing suitable persons to sustain the labours of a journey,—suitable, too, by gentleness and firmness of character, to correct the unruly among us here."[127]

---

to build his Church" (*Peter and the Rock*, 97). First, this is nothing new, since Paul tells us in Ephesians 2:20 that the apostles and prophets comprise the foundation of the Church. Again we have various metaphors used to explain various aspects of the Church, yet this does not negate the special prerogatives of Peter. In our two citations from Basil, he mentions Peter by name, specifically to show that he does have a special place. With Basil we do not see the typical Protestant and Orthodox formula: *either* Peter *or* Christ; *either* Peter *or* all the other apostles. Basil sees the matter as *both* Peter *and* the other apostles without doing injustice to either metaphor. *Basil's wording incorporates two of the three predominant metaphors used in Scripture to illuminate the teaching about the establishment of the Church.* In one metaphor Christ alone is the foundation with God as the builder (1 Cor 3:11); in another Peter is the foundation and Christ is the builder (Mt 16:18); and in the third the "apostles and prophets" are the foundation (Eph 2:20; Rev 21:14), with Christ as the cornerstone and the Holy Spirit the builder. I am not suggesting that Basil would have jumped up at Vatican I and been the first to endorse the teaching of papal infallibility, saying "We've always taught the Pope's infallibility, and in those exact words." The doctrine was not yet fully developed in Basil's day; yet, we see St. Basil single out Peter by name twice as the "rock [on which] the Lord promised to build His Church", and we will also highlight the actual circumstances in which Basil called upon the special prerogatives of Rome. Webster fails, unfortunately, to give his readers access to Basil's specific appeals to Rome's bishop for intervention and adjudication for problems in the East—based upon Rome's unique authority. He thus does exactly what he accuses others of doing throughout his book—being selective with his proof texts.

[126] We learn from Luke Rivington that in the original Greek, the word "examine" is "the verb of which *bishop* is the substantive form" (*Primitive Church*, 213). The word "bishop" derives from the Greek word for "oversee".

[127] *Letter* 69, *to Athanasius*, NPNF2, 8:165. We have 366 letters written by Basil to a wide variety of persons. This letter was written about A.D. 371. The Eastern churches were in dismal condition due to heresy and schism, caused especially by Arianism. Basil confides in Athanasius that the only way out of the situation, in his estimation, is to appeal to the bishop of Rome. He tells Athanasius that he has appealed to the bishop of Rome to "*act on his own authority in the matter*". Basil must have understood the Roman Church to have superior authority and the right to exercise it in the Eastern churches. He knows that if the bishop of Rome

"It is these that we implore your diligence[128] to denounce publicly to all the Churches of the East. . . . I am constrained to mention them by name, in order that you may yourselves recognise those who are stirring up disturbance here, and may make them known to our Churches. . . . You, however, have all the more credit with the people, in proportion to the distance that separates your home from theirs, besides the fact that you are gifted with God's grace to help[129] those who are distressed." [130]

---

speaks, those in contention will have to submit. He does not expect anyone to oppose the decision on technical grounds, by claiming that Rome has no authority to make such a determination. Basil accepted Rome's authority and must have been assured that the other bishops of the East would accept it as well. Rivington comments, "The relation of Rome to the East must have been recognized by St. Basil as that of a superior authority, and he must have been well assured that his Eastern co-prelates held the same view" (*Primitive Church*, 214). Ray Ryland writes, "All the significant heresies of the early centuries of the Church arose and flourished in the East. Often these heresies were espoused by the emperor of the East. At one time or another, and in some instances frequently, the Eastern patriarchal sees were occupied by heretics. Easterners were adept at creating heresies, but lacked dominical authority to resolve them. In every single instance, it was the papacy that had to come to the rescue" ("Papal Primacy and the Council of Nicaea", *This Rock*, June 1997, 26–27).

[128] Basil writes the letter to the "Westerns", which was not a loose confederation of various Christians. The "West" was ordinarily represented by the Roman Synod. To appeal to this body, headed by the bishop of Rome, was the long-standing custom of the Churches.

[129] Or "the grace of God conferred on you for the oversight of those in trouble."

[130] *Letter* 263, 2, *To the Westerns*, NPNF2, 8:302, written in A.D. 377. The heresies of Arius, Apollinarius, Paulinus, and others had overtaken the Eastern Churches, and Basil, the bishop of Caesarea, appeals to the West for immediate assistance in the form of a letter condemning the heretics. Basil refers to the "grace of God conferred on you for the oversight of those in trouble", which can hardly be seen as anything other than Rome's possession of a special charism, beyond a mere primacy of honor. Basil sees Rome as the caretaker of the troubled Eastern Churches.

Later in the letter Basil mentions a heretic who lied to and misled the Roman bishop and who was thus reinstated by returning with a letter from Pope Liberius and "showing it". This is a clear indication, not only that heretics and deceitful bishops saw Rome as having jurisdictional authority over the East, but also that the orthodox bishops shared that view, since a letter from the bishop of Rome was enough to reinstate a deposed bishop. As J. Michael Miller writes, "By the end of the fourth century, many Byzantines admitted that the Roman bishop received from God the grace to uphold and pass on undefiled the truth of the

"Nearly all the East (I include under this name all the regions from Illyricum to Egypt) is being agitated, right honourable father [Pope Damasus], by a terrible storm and tempest. The old heresy, sown by Arius the enemy of the truth, has now boldly and unblushingly reappeared. Like some sour root, it is producing its deadly fruit and is prevailing. The reason of this is, that in every district the champions of right doctrine have been exiled from their Churches by calumny and outrage, and the control of affairs has been handed over to men who are leading captive the souls of the simpler brethren. I have looked upon the visit of your mercifulness as the only possible solution of our difficulties. . . . I have been constrained to beseech you by letter to be moved to help us. . . . In this I am by no means making any novel request, but am only asking what has been customary in the case of men who, before our own day, were blessed and dear to God, and conspicuously in your own case. For I well remember learning from the answers made by our fathers when asked, and from documents still preserved among us, that the illustrious and blessed bishop [Pope] Dionysius, conspicuous in your see as well for soundness of faith as for all other virtues, visited by letter my Church of Caesarea, and by letter exhorted our fathers, and sent men to ransom our brethren from captivity." [131]

gospel. . . . The East recognized that the Roman Church had been spared, compared to itself, from the inroads of heresy. This nearly spotless record of doctrinal orthodoxy provided the Easterners with a reason for accepting Rome's special role within the *koinonia*. . . . Due to this dissension in the East, the leaders of both orthodox and heterodox factions sought the support and approbation of the Roman see. According to Shotwell and Loomis, during these crises, the Orientals were ready to admit that Rome 'had received from God through Peter the priceless gift which the Eastern prelates as a body seemed to lack, namely, the power to hold fast to the truth and transmit it undefiled to posterity' " (Miller, *Shepherd and the Rock*, 124–25).

[131] *Letter* 70, NPNF2, 8:166. The letter has no official address, though it is obviously addressed to Pope Damasus (r. A.D. 366–384). Again previous practice and ancient custom acknowledge the special place of the Roman bishop. Basil remarks elsewhere that certain men were "carrying about letters from the westerns, handing over the bishopric of Antioch to them" (NPNF2, 8:253). What right had Rome to hand over Eastern bishoprics to anyone? How could Rome prove its primacy in any stronger terms than to hand the Antiochean bishopric over to someone of its own choosing? Obviously Rome had the right and duty of overseeing such ecclesiastical matters, and Basil recognized this authority.

Gregory of Nyssa (c. a.d. 330–c. 395)[132]

"Peter, with his whole soul, associates himself with the Lamb; and, by means of the change of his name, he is changed by the Lord into something more divine; instead of Simon being both called and having become a rock (Peter). [He gives other instances of names changed by the Almighty, and continues:] The great Peter did not by advancing by little and little attain unto this grace, but at once he listened to his brother, believed in the Lamb, and was through faith perfected, and, having cleaved to the rock, became [Rock] Peter."[133]

But we must be clear and not say more than can be rightly said. Understanding the authority of bishops and patriarchs over their particular sees, the East considered their bishops able to function without constant input, so to speak, from Rome, though Rome did have final jurisdiction. Timothy Ware reminds us of what he and the Orthodox believe: "Orthodox believe that among the five Patriarchs a special place belongs to the Pope. The Orthodox Church does not accept the doctrine of Papal authority set forth in the decrees of the Vatican Council of 1870, and taught today in the Roman Catholic Church; but at the same time Orthodoxy does not deny to the Holy and Apostolic See of Rome a *primacy of honour*, together with the right (under certain conditions) to hear appeals from all parts of Christendom. . . . But as with Patriarchs, so with the Pope: the primacy assigned to Rome does not overthrow the essential equality of all bishops. The Pope is the first bishop in the Church—but he is the *first among equals*" (*The Orthodox Church* [New York: Penguin Books, 1993], 27, 28). The Orthodox place the supreme authority of the Church in the ecumenical council (of which they accept the first seven), yet we have shown repeatedly that the authority of the Roman bishop was not only exercised in the East as needed but was the sure source of apostolic teaching as early as Clement in the first century.

[132] St. Gregory was an Eastern father and a younger brother of St. Basil, who was last consulted in our study. His brother Basil ordained Gregory as bishop of Nyssa in Cappadocia (modern-day Turkey, mentioned by Peter in 1 Peter 1:1). According to the *Oxford Dictionary of the Christian Church*, Gregory "was a thinker and theologian of originality and learning, acquainted especially with Platonist speculation, as well as an outstanding exegete, orator, and ascetical author. . . . He was an ardent defender of the Nicene dogma of the Trinity, and distinguished carefully between the generation of the Son and the procession of the Holy Spirit. The Second Person of the Trinity was incarnate in the womb of Mary, who therefore is truly θεοτόκος [God-bearer], for Christ is one Person in two natures" (Cross and Livingstone, 712). "He had come to be regarded as 'the common mainstay of the Church', and to be on Gregory's side was considered in his day as a proof of orthodoxy" (*Butler's Lives of the Saints*, 1:535).

[133] *Homily* 15, in Berington and Kirk, *Faith of Catholics*, 2:20–21.

"The memory of Peter, the head of the Apostles, is celebrated; and magnified indeed with him are the other members of the Church; but (upon him) is the Church of God firmly established. For he is, agreeably to the gift conferred upon him by the Lord, that unbroken and most firm rock upon which the Lord built His Church." [134]

Gregory Nazianzen (c. A.D. 329–389) [135]

"Seest thou that of the disciples of Christ, all of whom were great and deserving of the choice, one is called a rock, and is entrusted with the foundations of the Church; whilst another is the beloved,

---

[134] *Alt. Or. De S. Steph. Galland*, in ibid., 2:21. In *The Papacy*, the study "that led Fr. Vladimir, the Abbé Guettée, to enter into the fullness of the Orthodox Church", the Abbé Guettée supposedly gives a literal translation from the Greek, which he presumes diminishes the import of the passage, yet even in his text it still reads, "He [Peter] is the firm and *most* solid rock upon which the Saviour has constructed the Church" (167). He italicizes the word "most" to make it appear that Gregory is proclaiming that Peter is the *most* solid of all the other solid rocks. This is stretching credulity. There is nothing in the context to suggest that he is comparing Peter to any other rocks. The Abbé Guettée then attempts to substantiate his claim by quoting another passage, as is the habit of Webster and others, to show that it was the *faith* of Peter that was the "rock". Forgetting, it seems, that Paul referred to all the "apostles and prophets" as foundations of the Church in a different metaphor, he then goes on with the same old tired and artificial dichotomy between Peter and his faith by concluding, "It is, therefore, not the person of Peter that is the rock of the Church, but the faith he confessed" (ibid., 168–69). This starts to sound all too familiar—papal antagonists creating artificial distinctions and mixing metaphors to conform to their own anti-papal traditions. The Catholic Church, as we have seen in the Catechism, sees no contradiction and views Peter and his faith as inseparable.

[135] During the raging scourge of Arianism, St. Gregory "opened a small chapel in the house of a friend, consoling himself with the reflection that if the Arians were the stronger party his was the better cause; though they had the churches and the people, God and the angels were with him. In that small chapel he preached the famous *orations* on the Trinity that won him the title of 'Theologian' which he shares with St. John the Apostle" (Augustine Kalberer, *Lives of the Saints* [Chicago: Franciscan Herald Press, 1975], 3). He was the son of the bishop of Nazianzus (also named Gregory), and he studied at the University of Athens. He was a contemporary of St. Basil and, with him, one of the three Cappadocian Fathers. Gregory was ordained a priest about A.D. 362 and later was called to Constantinople to subdue heresy and restore the faith of the Nicene Creed. He was a major figure in the final establishment of the Nicene Creed at the Council of Constantinople in 381. He was appointed

and reposes on the breast of Jesus; and the rest bear with the prior honor (thus bestowed)."[136]

"Neither does a man know, though he be the parent of an evil like unto Judas, whether his offspring shall be called the godlike Paul, or be like unto Peter,—Peter who became the unbroken rock, and who had the keys delivered to him."[137]

Pope Damasus I (c. A.D. 304–384)[138]

"Although all the Catholic Churches spread abroad through the world comprise but one bridal chamber of Christ, nevertheless, the holy Roman Church has been placed at the forefront not by the conciliar decisions of other Churches, but has received the primacy by the evangelic voice of our Lord and Savior, who says: 'You are Peter, and upon this rock I will build My Church, and the gates of hell will not prevail against it; and I will give to you the keys of the kingdom of heaven, and whatever you shall have bound on earth will be bound in heaven, and whatever you shall have loosed on earth shall be loosed in heaven.' . . . The first see, therefore, is that of Peter the Apostle, that of the Roman Church, which has neither stain nor blemish nor anything like it. The second see, however, is that at Alexandria, consecrated in behalf of blessed Peter by Mark, his disciple and an evangelist, who was sent to Egypt by the Apostle Peter, where he preached the word

---

bishop of Constantinople. He also wrote against the heresy of Apollinarianism (which held to the full divinity of Christ but denied his full manhood).

[136] *Oration* 26, in Berington and Kirk, *Faith of Catholics*, 2:21. Each apostle was given honor. Peter was given a special honor, that of being the foundation rock of the Church; John, that of being the beloved disciple.

[137] *Carm.* 2, in Berington and Kirk, *Faith of Catholics*, 2:21. "We have already seen the reunion of 380, under [Emperor] Gratian. His edict obliges all to embrace the faith delivered to the Romans by St. Peter. The East breathed again, and was free to be at peace and Catholic. St. Gregory Nazianzen, who led the bishops to reunion at the council of Constantinople in the following year, expressed the feelings of the orthodox in a poem: 'The faith [of Rome] was of old, and is still, in the straight path, binding together the whole West with her saving word, as is right for her who presides over all.' In the next year again that troubled council concluded its sittings by writing to the Pope and his Roman council, calling themselves his 'members,' and [Pope] Damasus replied to them as most honoured sons, saying that they conferred the greatest honour on themselves by paying due reverence to the Apostolic Chair" (Lattey, *Papacy*, 46).

[138] St. Damasus was bishop of Rome from A.D. 366 to 384.

of truth and finished his glorious martyrdom. The third honorable see, indeed, is that at Antioch, which belonged to the most blessed Apostle Peter, where first he dwelt before he came to Rome, and where the name *Christians* was first applied, as to a new people." [139]

Jerome to Pope Damasus
—written between A.D. 374 and 379 [140]

"Since the East, shattered as it is by the longstanding feuds, subsisting between its peoples, is bit by bit tearing into shreds the seamless vest of the Lord, . . . I think it my duty to consult the chair of Peter, and to turn to a church whose faith has been praised by Paul. I appeal for spiritual food to the church whence I have received the garb of Christ. The wide space of sea and land that lies between us cannot deter me from searching for 'the pearl of great price.'. . . Though your greatness terrifies me, your kindness attracts me. From the priest I demand the safe-keeping of the victim, from the shepherd the protection due to the sheep. Away with all that is

---

[139] *The Decree of Damasus* 3, written in A.D. 382, in Jurgens, *Faith of the Early Fathers*, 1:406–7. This passage needs no comment other than to say we have no record of anyone from East or West disputing this expression of the primacy of Peter in the See of Rome; in fact, even the Churches of the East appealed to Pope Damasus for doctrinal and disciplinary determinations. This gives a clear perspective of the primacy that the bishop of Rome held in the mid-fourth century, not only in official teaching, but also in actual practice, not only in the West, but also in the East.

[140] St. Jerome is a Father and Doctor of the Church who also has the distinction of being respected by many as the greatest biblical scholar of the early Church and whose most important work was a translation of the Bible into Latin. His translation is called the Vulgate. Jerome was born in Stridon, on the border of the Roman provinces of Dalmatia and Pannonia. After studying in Rome, he journeyed to the desert, where he lived as an ascetic and pursued the study of Scripture. In 379 he was ordained a priest. He then spent three years in Constantinople with the Eastern Church Father St. Gregory Nazianzen. In 382 he returned to Rome, where he became secretary to Pope Damasus I and gained much influence. Many persons placed themselves under his spiritual direction. Later he resided at Bethlehem in 386. In Bethlehem Jerome pursued his literary labors and engaged in controversy not only with the heretics Jovinian and Vigilantius and the adherents of Pelagianism but also with St. Augustine. Because of his conflict with the Pelagians, Jerome went into hiding for about two years. He died soon after his return to Bethlehem, in 419 or 420.

overweening; let the state of Roman majesty withdraw. My words are spoken to the successor of the fisherman, to the disciple of the cross. As I follow no leader save Christ, so I communicate with none but your blessedness, that is with the chair of Peter. For this, I know, is the rock on which the church is built! This is the house where alone the paschal lamb can be rightly eaten. This is the ark of Noah, and he who is not found in it shall perish when the flood prevails. But since by reason of my sins I have betaken myself to this desert which lies between Syria and the uncivilized waste, I cannot, owing to the great distance between us, always ask of your sanctity the holy thing of the Lord."[141]

"The Church here is split in three parts, each eager to seize me for its own. . . . Meanwhile I keep crying: 'He that is joined to the chair of Peter is accepted by me!'. . . Therefore I implore your Blessedness by the cross of the Lord, by the necessary glory of our faith, the Passion of Christ,—that as you follow the Apostles in dignity may you follow them also in worth,— . . . tell me by letter with whom it is that I should communicate in Syria. Despise not a soul for whom Christ died!"[142]

---

[141] *Letter of Jerome to Pope Damasus* 15, 2, written between A.D. 374 and 379, NPNF2, 6:18.

[142] *Letter of Jerome to Pope Damasus* 16, 2, written between A.D. 374 and 379, in Jurgens, *Faith of the Early Fathers*, 2:184. In the midst of great heresies and schisms in the East, Jerome hoists his flag with the See of Peter in Rome, proclaiming that to be with Rome is to be with Christ. He does not perceive Christ and the Roman bishop to be opposing loyalties. Quite the contrary; by following the bishop of Rome, one is sure of truly following Christ. He pledges loyalty to Rome, in honor of Peter, the rock on which the Church has been built. Interestingly enough, George Salmon has little to say about such a notable witness as Jerome and offhandedly dismisses Jerome's letters to Pope Damasus by suggesting they were merely comedic letters. Even though Jerome's epistles have no ring of sarcasm or humor, Salmon brushes them off with these words: "[Jerome's] amusing letter would not need much notice if this specimen of Western conceit were not frequently cited as truly illustrating Patristic opinion as to the rightful claims of Rome" (George Salmon, *Infallibility of the Church* [London: John Murray, 1914], 420). Salmon is frequently held aloft as the unrefuted champion of the anti-Roman forces; however, Salmon was rebutted by B. C. Butler (*The Church and Infallibility, A Reply to the Abridged "Salmon"* [New York: Sheed and Ward, 1954]) and also soundly discredited and refuted in a series of scholarly articles entitled "Dr. Salmon's 'Infallibility' ", in *The Irish Ecclesiastical Record* 9 (January to June 1901)–11 (January to June 1902).

Notice that Jerome, considered one of the greatest biblical scholars of all time, does not make all his decisions based on his own private judgment of

"The Church was founded upon Peter: although elsewhere the same is attributed to all the Apostles, and they all receive the keys of the kingdom of heaven, and the strength of the Church depends upon them all alike, yet one among the twelve is chosen so that when a head has been appointed, there may be no occasion for schism." [143]

"I think, therefore, that I ought to warn you, in all kindness and affection, to hold fast the faith of the saintly [Pope] Innocent, the spiritual son of Anastasius and his successor in the apostolic see; and not to receive any foreign doctrine, however wise and discerning you may take yourself to be." [144]

"What has Paul to do with Aristotle? or Peter with Plato? For as the latter was the prince of philosophers, so was the former chief of the Apostles: on him the Lord's Church was firmly founded, and neither rushing flood nor storm can shake it." [145]

Scripture but appeals to the living, visible head of the visible Church. Jerome's loyalties lie with those who cling to the chair of Peter, the bishop of Rome. He is writing to Pope Damasus to find out whom Rome accepts so he will know with whom to associate. This is not an innovation or a desperate move on Jerome's part. To appeal to Rome as the chair of Peter is the ancient custom of the Churches and of the Fathers from the earliest days.

[143] *Against Jovinianus* 1, 26, NPNF2, 6:366. Commenting on this passage, St. Alphonsus Liguori writes, "All the Apostles were commissioned by Jesus Christ to propagate the faith, with the power to make priests, bishops, and also to found Churches, in those first days when the new law needed to be firmly established. This power, however, which was conferred on the Apostles was a power always subordinate to that of S. Peter. It was, moreover, an extraordinary power which came to an end with the Apostles, whilst the power conferred upon S. Peter was absolute, and, so to say, ordinary—a power which was to pass to his successors. Hence S. Jerome says that although at first, when the faith needed to be propagated, all the Apostles had the same power, nevertheless on Peter alone was conferred the supreme power, in order that he might preside; over all the rest in quality of head" (*Venitá della Fede* 3, 7, as quoted in Livius, *St. Peter*, 258).

[144] *Letter* 130 *to Demetrias* (a Roman woman), NPNF2, 6:269. Jerome also refers frequently to Christ as the rock upon which the Church is built (1 Cor 3:11) and also as her cornerstone, resting upon the "foundation of the apostles and prophets" (Eph 2:20), concepts that have been dealt with at length (see his *Commentary on Matthew* 7, 25; *Epistle* 65, 15; *Commentary on Amos* 6, 12–13; *Commentary on Isaiah* 2, 2; *Epistle* 146, 1; etc.). As an experienced Scripture scholar, St. Jerome does not fall into the trap of setting up false divisions between differing metaphors.

[145] *Against the Pelagians* 1, 14a, NPNF2, 6:455.

"As Christ himself gave light to the apostles, that they might be called the light of the world, and as they obtained other names also from the Lord, so to Simon also, who believed in the rock Christ, He bestowed the name Peter; and according to the metaphor of a rock, it is rightly said of him 'I will build my church upon thee.'"[146]

"For what function, excepting ordination, belongs to a bishop that does not also belong to a presbyter? It is not the case that there is one church at Rome and another in all the world beside. Gaul and Britain, Africa and Persia, India and the East worship one Christ and observe one rule of truth. If you ask for authority, the world outweighs its capital. Wherever there is a bishop, whether it be at Rome or at Engubium, whether it be at Constantinople or at Rhegium, whether it be at Alexandria or at Zoan, his dignity is one and his priesthood is one. Neither the command of wealth nor the lowliness of poverty makes him more a bishop or less a bishop. All alike are successors of the apostles."[147]

---

[146] *Commentary on Matthew* 3, 16, 18, cited in Winter, *Saint Peter*, 63. "Of all the fathers it would appear that St. Jerome presents the clearest and most carefully thought out theory of St. Peter. In this matter he was helped by his thorough knowledge of the Biblical languages as well as a solicitude to establish the literal meaning of the text rather than any rhetorical or homiletic [or allegorical] elaborations. His testimonies to St. Peter are so numerous and so unequivocal that it is necessary only to select a few passages to give a just estimate of his thought. In the first place the identification of Peter as the 'rock' is abundantly clear [quoting then the above passage]. . . . Secondly, he is not confused by the passage in 1 Cor. 10:4 which refers to Christ as a rock. In Jerome's theory Peter derives his privilege from Christ in such a way that the titles of both harmonize without difficulty, as is expressed in his commentary on Jeremias: 'Christ is not alone in being the rock, for He granted to the apostle Peter that he should be called "Rock" ' [*Comm. on Jeremias* 3, 65]. Jerome also clarified the meaning of the 'gates of hell' and declared without hesitation that it referred to the church's security from heresy, rather than a promised immortality" (Winter, *Saint Peter*, 62–63).

[147] *Epistle* 144, 1 *to Evangelus*, NPNF2, 6:289. This passage from Jerome is often marshaled (e.g., Guettée, *Papacy*, 187–88) to "prove" that all bishops are of equal rank. First, the epistle is written to establish the distinction and superiority of bishops and presbyters over deacons. Some churches had begun to allow deacons to assume a more prestigious and authoritative role. He is not here arguing for the jurisdiction of one Church over another, but rather that the rank of bishop and presbyter exceeded that of deacon throughout the Church. The unusual example of Rome was used to prove that deacons exceeded the authority of bishops to which Jerome, without denigrating the primacy of Rome in the

Edict of the Three Emperors
—namely, Gratian, Valentinian, and Theodosius
—issued on February 28, A.D. 380

"[The emperors demand that all peoples remain] 'in the religion which the divine apostle Peter passed on to the Romans' [and which has flowered to this day of (Pope) Damasus]." [148]

Ambrose of Milan (c. A.D. 340–397) [149]

"We recognized in the letter of your holiness the vigilance of the good shepherd. You faithfully watch over the gate entrusted to

---

least, says that the whole Church practices the same custom: presbyters exceeded deacons in rank. The office of bishop is superior, "Wherever there is a bishop, whether it be at Constantinople or at Rhegium, whether it be at Alexandria or at Zoan, his dignity is one and his priesthood is one. . . . All alike are successors of the apostles" (ibid., 6:288). We read in Winter, "In this sentence there is a rebuttal of any implication that the Roman episcopate might be inferior to that elsewhere, and that the deacons were taking advantage of it to look down on the bishop of Rome. When viewed in its proper context, it can be seen that he had in mind the relative positions of the three orders from the point of view of their sacramental not jurisdictional powers. Without, for the moment, considering Rome, St. Jerome could not have been ignorant of the lack of equality which existed between the Bishop of Alexandria and the other bishops of Egypt" (*Saint Peter*, 163). I can see why Guettée would latch on to this passage in an attempt to use it to his advantage, even though to do so he had to wrench it from its context, both within the epistle and within the context of Jerome's whole corpus of writings.

[148] Johann Auer, *The Church: The Universal Sacrament of Salvation*, trans. M. Waldstein (Washington, D.C.: Catholic Univ. of America Press, 1993), 247. Roman emperors decreed the true religion to be that of Peter, deposited in the Church of Rome.

[149] St. Ambrose is one of the most celebrated Fathers of the Church and one of the four Doctors of the Latin Church, born in Trier (now in Germany) and educated in Rome. His father was prefect of Gaul. Ambrose studied law, entered the civil service, and about 370 was appointed a consular magistrate in upper Italy, with his headquarters at Milan. In this office his kindness and wisdom won the esteem and love of the people, who called him to be bishop of Milan in 374. As bishop, he defended the churches of Milan against the introduction of Arian doctrines and brought Theodosius I, emperor of Rome, to repentance and public penance for ordering the massacre of the rebellious Thessalonians. Ambrose is best known as the sympathizing friend of Monica, mother of St. Augustine, and as the one who received Augustine into the Church. He tirelessly defended the orthodox Christian faith.

you, and with pious solicitude you guard Christ's sheepfold [Jn 10:7ff.], you that are worthy to have the Lord's sheep hear and follow you. Since you know the sheep of Christ you will easily catch the wolves and confront them like a wary shepherd, lest they disperse the Lord's flock by their constant lack of faith and their bestial howling." [150]

"It is to Peter himself that He says, 'You are Peter, and upon this rock I will build My Church.' Where Peter is, there is the Church. And where the Church, no death is there, but life eternal." [151]

"In fine, Peter, after having been tempted by the devil [Lk 22:31–32], is set over the Church. The Lord, therefore, fore-showed what that was, that He afterwards chose him as the pastor of the Lord's flock. For to him He said, But thou when converted confirm thy brethren." [152]

"Yet was your clemency to be petitioned, not to suffer the head of the Roman empire (world), the Roman Church, to be thrown into confusion; for from her flow all the rights of venerable communion." [153]

"Christ is the Rock, 'For they drank of that spiritual Rock that followed them, and that Rock was Christ,' and He did not refuse to bestow the favour of this title even upon His disciple, so that he,

---

[150] *Synodal Letter of Ambrose, Sabinus, Bassian, and Others to Pope Siricius* 42, 1, written about A.D. 389, in Jurgens, *Faith of the Early Fathers*, 2:148. Ambrose equates the bishop of Rome with the shepherd of the universal flock of God. Bishops pastored the local Churches, whereas the Pope acted as the universal shepherd of all of Christ's sheep, following the Lord's commission to Peter to "feed my sheep" (Jn 21:15–17).

[151] *Commentaries on Twelve of David's Psalms* 40, 30, written by Ambrose between about A.D. 381 and 397, in ibid., 2:150. Peter is the rock upon which the Church is built. If one is with Peter, that is, the bishop of Rome, he is with the Church— all others are on the outside.

[152] *In Ps.* 43, n. 40, in Berington and Kirk, *Faith of Catholics*, 26. J. Michael Miller writes, "Peter was the chief, the head of the apostles. According to St. Ambrose, Peter was personally the rock upon which Christ built the Church. The bishop of Milan, convinced that the responsibility given to Peter was transmitted to his successors on the *cathedra* at Rome, was also the first to draw together coherently the three Petrine texts of Matthew, Luke, and John. By the middle of the fourth century, the see of Peter became more simply 'the apostolic see' without comparison—as if no others worth mentioning existed" (*Shepherd and the Rock*, 82).

[153] *Ep.* 11 *Concil. Aquil. Impp. Gratian. Valentin. et Theodos.* 4, in Berington and Kirk, *Faith of Catholics*, 2:73. Rome is said to be the source of "all the rights of venerable communion".

too, might be Peter [or, Rock], in that he has from the Rock a solid constancy, a firm faith." [154]

Ambrosiaster [155]

"Whereas the whole world is God's, yet is the Church said to be His house, of which [Pope] Damasus is at this day the ruler." [156]

John Chrysostom (c. A.D. 347–407) [157]

"[Jesus] saith unto him, 'Feed My sheep.' And why, having passed by the others, doth He speak with Peter on these matters? He was

---

[154] *Expos. in Luc.* in Colin Lindsay, *The Evidence for the Papacy* (London: Longman's, 1870), 37. This again shows the participatory nature of Christ's ministry. He is not selfish and jealous with his prerogatives. Jesus is the Good Shepherd, yet he calls men to share the ministry of pastoring; he is the Priest, yet he invites men to share the priesthood; he is the mediator, yet he expects us to intercede and to mediate the gospel to others; he is the Rock, yet he renames Simon "Rock" and causes him to participate uniquely in the foundation of the Church. When we participate in the body of Christ, in union with its Head, we partake of and are included in the ministries and offices of our Lord. We do this without in any way supplanting the unique work of the Savior.

[155] "[Ambrosiaster is] the name given to the author of a set of Latin commentaries on the [thirteen epistles] of St Paul, ascribed in all the MSS but one, and by most medieval writers, to Ambrose.... Their ascription to Ambrose ... is now universally denied" (Cross and Livingstone, *Oxford Dictionary*, 51).

[156] Ambrosiaster, in the *Commentary on the Epistle of First Timothy*, in *Cathedra Petri—The Titles and Prerogatives of St. Peter*, by Charles Allnatt, 2d ed. (London: Burns & Oates, 1879), 107. Obviously, Damasus was the bishop of Rome at the time.

[157] St. John Chrysostom is a Doctor and Father of the Church and was born in Antioch, Syria (now Antakya, Turkey). The surname Chrysostom (Greek for "golden-mouthed") was first used in the sixth century. At the age of eighteen he came under the influence of Meletius, bishop of Antioch, who directed him to a monastic school and baptized him soon afterward. After spending six years as a monk in the mountains near Antioch, John was ordained deacon in 381 by Meletius and ordained priest in 386 by Bishop Flavian I, who succeeded Meletius. The name "Chrysostom" was given to John because of his eloquence, earnestness, and the practical nature of his preaching—he had a reputation of being the greatest preacher of the early Church. In 398 Arcadius, emperor of the Eastern Roman Empire, named John patriarch of Constantinople. His preaching against vices excited the hatred of Theophilus (reigned 385–428), patriarch of Alexandria, and of Arcadius' empress, Eudoxia, who banished him from the capital in 403. John was soon recalled, only to be banished again, in

the chosen one of the Apostles, the mouth of the disciples, the leader of the band;[158] on this account also Paul went up upon a time to enquire of him rather than the others. And at the same time to show him that he must now be of good cheer, since the denial was done away, Jesus putteth into his hands the chief authority among the brethren; and He bringeth not forward the denial, nor reproacheth him with what had taken place, but saith, 'If thou lovest Me, preside over thy brethren." [159]

" 'And I say unto thee, thou art Peter, and upon this rock will I build my Church;' that is, on the faith of his confession. Hereby He signifies that many were now on the point of believing, and raises his spirit, and makes him a shepherd." [160]

"For what purpose did He shed His blood? It was that He might win these sheep which He entrusted to Peter and his successors.[161]

404, to the desert areas of the Taurus Mountains, where he attempted to convert the neighboring Persians and Goths to Christianity.

[158] The word *coryphaeus*, "Latin, leader, from Greek *koryphaios*, from *koryphē* summit" (Merriam-Webster's collegiate dictionary, 10th ed.) on the Logos Library System 2.1 CD-ROM [Oak Harbor, Wash.: Logos Research Systems, 1997]), means, first, the leader of a party or school of thought and, second, the leader of a chorus. According to Orthodox theologian John Meyendorff, it was evident to Byzantine theologians that "Peter is the 'coryphaeus' of the apostolic choir; he is the first disciple of Christ and speaks always on behalf of all. It is true that other apostles, John, James and Paul, are also called 'coryphaei' and 'primates,' but Peter alone is the 'rock of the Church.' His primacy has, therefore, not only a personal character, but bears an ecclesiological significance" ("St. Peter in Byzantine Theology", in Meyendorff, *Primacy of Peter*, 74). It is only fair to point out that Meyendorff also makes it clear that he does not believe the title *coryphaeus* or the teaching of the Eastern Orthodox Churches supports the Roman ecclesiology or Vatican I understanding of papal infallibility.

[159] *Homilies on John* 88, 1, NPNF1, 14:331. It is no small matter for St. John Chrysostom, an Eastern bishop, to teach that Peter was the universal teacher of the universal Church. I am aware that John Chrysostom is often used by papal antagonists to resist the Roman teaching on papal primacy, but passages like this make it less than likely that Chrysostom would have sided with the decidedly "anti-Roman" sentiment held by Protestants and Orthodox today.

[160] *Homilies on Matthew* 54, 3, NPNF1, 10:333. Michael Whelton (*Two Paths: Papal Monarchy—Collegial Tradition* [Salisbury, Mass.: Regina Orthodox Press, 1998], 29) marshals this quote from John Chrysostom and attempts to undermine Petrine primacy. He fails to inform his readers that, four paragraphs later, Chrysostom affirms that Jesus "entrusted the authority over all things in Heaven" to "a mortal man" and gave him, Peter, the keys of heaven.

[161] "There is indeed one passage which may be a categorical affirmation of the primacy of the pope. *De Sacerdotio*, 53: 'Why did Christ shed His Blood? To

Naturally then did Christ say, 'Who then is the faithful and wise servant, whom his lord shall make ruler over His household.' " [162]

"For the Father gave to Peter the revelation of the Son; but the Son gave him to sow that of the Father and that of Himself in every part of the world; and to a mortal man He entrusted the authority over all things in Heaven, giving him the keys; who extended the church to every part of the world, and declared it to be stronger than heaven. 'For heaven and earth shall pass away, but my word shall not pass away.' " [163]

"Peter himself the chief of the Apostles, the first in the Church, the friend of Christ, who received a revelation not from man, but from the Father, as the Lord bears witness to him, saying, 'Blessed are thou, Simon Bar-Jona, because flesh and blood hath not revealed it to thee, but my Father who is in heaven'; this very Peter,— and when I name Peter, I name that unbroken rock, that firm foundation, the great Apostle, the first of the disciples, the first called and the first who obeyed." [164]

---

purchase the sheep which *He confided to Peter and those who came after him.*' It may be urged that S. Chrysostom means no more by this than all those who have the cure of souls. On the other hand, there may be a reference to Peter only and to his personal commission: 'Feed my sheep'; and Chrysostom soon afterwards actually quotes these words. And when one recalls his comments on them given above, as meaning Peter's 'government' and 'ruling the brethren,' it is at least likely that here is a reference to Peter's successors in the see of Rome" (Scott, *Eastern Churches*, 133).

[162] *The Priesthood* 2, 1, NPNF1, 9:39. In this document St. John Chrysostom, an Eastern bishop, recognizes the primacy of Peter and the continued authority that would be carried out through Peter's successors. Peter and his successors were the shepherds who had been given authority over the whole flock, "one flock with one shepherd" (Jn 10:16). If the shepherd is commanded to govern the sheep, the obverse is also true: the sheep are commanded to follow and obey the shepherd. One may object that Chrysostom perceived the "successors" to refer to all bishops, not just the bishop of Rome, but if this had been the case, his actions would have given evidence of it. As Dr. Hergenröther reminds us, "Chrysostom sent epistles and deputies to Pope Innocent I., to obtain from him speedy correction of the acts done against him, and the annulling of his condemnation, as well as the chastisement of those who had violated all canonical law" (*Anti-Janus*, 130–31). This is another case where one's actions speak volumes.

[163] *Homilies on Matthew* 54, 3, NPNF1, 10:334.

[164] *Homily 3 de Poenit.* 4, in Berington and Kirk, *Faith of Catholics*, 2:31. Similar words by St. John Chrysostom, "Peter, the leader (coryphaeus) of the choir, that

"Again, consider the moderation of James. He it was who received the Bishopric of Jerusalem,[165] and here he says nothing.

---

mouth of the rest of the Apostles, that head of that brotherhood, that one set
over the entire universe, that foundation of the Church, that ardent lover of
Christ" (*In Illud, hoc scitote*, 4, in ibid., 2:32–33). One could not construct a more
appropriate set of phrases to describe Peter, or to describe the office of the
Papacy, especially when one looks at our current Pope John Paul II. However,
one must be honest about the overall situation in the East. There was no clear
consensus in the East about Peter and the jurisdictional primacy of Rome, just as
there was little consensus during these centuries about the full divinity of Christ.
As J. Michael Miller writes, "From Peter's prominence among the apostles,
Easterners drew different conclusions than Westerners did. Some Orientals
held that all believers were successors of Peter. Others limited Petrine succession only to bishops. Very few conceded that the bishop of Rome was the
successor of Peter in a unique sense" (*Shepherd and the Rock*, 116). The East was
in constant theological and political flux. When trials, heresies, and expulsions
afflicted orthodox Christians, however, it was to Rome that they made their
appeals; it was to Rome they went for letters of reinstatement and "certification"
of their orthodoxy. There are innumerable instances, as we have seen, in which
a Father who might have never lauded the "infallible" See of Rome or proclaimed her jurisdictional primacy in writing ran to her for protection, doctrinal
clarification, reinstatement, or to solicit from her a final and authoritative
doctrinal or judicial decree. Again, the old maxim holds true: "Actions speak
louder than words", and even in the East we are not short of teaching that
proclaims the unique authority of Peter and the unique primacy of the bishop
of Rome. Besides, we should not be surprised if the East was less enthusiastic
about subscribing to Roman jurisdiction than the Western Church. For the
Orientals, Rome was "way over there across land and sea", and it is never much
comfort to be subject to a "distant land". Nor had the development of Church
polity developed fully yet. The Church was growing, and so was the internal
structure—the framework and governance. One can see the development
throughout the New Testament (with the institution of the deaconate, appointment of bishops, etc.), and the progress continued throughout the first centuries of the Church. As the edifice grew, so the structure and the foundation
became ever more important. Just as when a corporation develops, or a tree
grows, or as a family expands, so does the need for unity, leadership, and a court
of final appeal.

[165] John Chrysostom comments elsewhere about the matter of James and the
"throne of Jerusalem". It is often contended that James took the first "throne" of
the Church with his appointment as bishop of Jerusalem; yet, Chrysostom and
the Fathers understood the See of Jerusalem to be an inferior position to the
ultimate call of Peter. Chrysostom writes, "And if any should say, 'How then did
James receive the chair at Jerusalem?' I would make this reply, that He appointed Peter teacher, not of the chair [of Jerusalem], but of the world" (*Homily*
88, 1 *on St. John*, NPNF1, 14:332). The "world" was thought of as a wheel, with

Mark also the great moderation of the other Apostles, how they concede the throne to him [Peter], and no longer dispute with each other.... [Peter says, 'Men and brethren'—Acts 1:15–16, etc.] Here is forethought for providing a teacher; here was the first who ordained a teacher. He did not say, 'We are sufficient.' So far was he beyond all vainglory, and he looked to one thing alone. *And yet he had the same power to ordain as they all collectively.*[166] But well might these things be done in this fashion, through the noble spirit of the man, and because prelacy then was not an affair of dignity, but of provident care for the governed. This neither made the elected to become elated, for it was to dangers that they were

---

Rome as its hub. How appropriate that it was in Rome that Peter spent his last days and suffered his martyrdom.

[166] John Chrysostom's understanding of the replacement of Judas by Matthias is interesting. Stanley Jaki writes, "While the twelve could tolerate the pre-eminence of three—Peter, James, and John—they could not bear the even greater prominence given to Peter. And, according to Chrysostom, part of Jesus' answer to their indignation was his choosing Peter for the miraculous catch of the fish with the tax coin in its mouth, and that the tax was to be paid only on behalf of himself and Peter. Chrysostom certainly did not notice anything de-rogatory to Peter's prominence in his handling the election of Matthias, the replacement of Judas. On the contrary, he saw in it the humility of a leader truly assured in his prominence. In order to cut off the possible charge of favoritism, Peter entrusted the outcome to lottery, although he had the power of constitut-ing an apostle. Reflecting on Chrysostom's interpretation, Erasmus noted that in Chrysostom's view Peter 'habet jus constituendi par omnibus [apostolic],' that is, Peter had a constitutional power equal to that of all the twelve taken together. Thus, according to Chrysostom, Peter did not have to call the council of Jerusalem; he alone could have settled all its business. Unlike many modern exegetes, Chrysostom did not overlook the fact that Peter spoke last at the council as the one who had the last word. In commenting on Paul's assertion of his right to take along a sister-woman, Chrysostom called attention to the order in which Paul referred to the similar procedures of the apostles, the brethren of the Lord, and Cephas. 'He [Paul] puts the leader [Peter] last, for in that position he places his most powerful point. For it was not so wonderful to list the others ... as it was to name the primate entrusted with the keys of heaven" (*The Keys of the Kingdom* [Chicago: Franciscan Herald Press, 1986], 88).

John Chapman comments, "I know no more emphatic testimony to the su-preme jurisdiction of St. Peter in any writer, ancient or modern, than the view taken in this homily of the election of St. Matthias, for I know of no jurisdiction in the Church more tremendous than the appointment of an apostle.... And, I ask, will anyone venture, after considering the last sentence of the passage quoted, to maintain that the apostles were excluded from the 'brethren' over whom Peter was told to rule" (*Studies on the Early Papacy*, 89).

called, nor those not elected to make a grievance of it, as if they were disgraced. But things are not done in this fashion now; nay, quite the contrary.—For observe, they were an hundred and twenty, and he asks for one out of the whole body with good right, as having been put in charge of them: for to him had Christ said, 'And when thou art converted, strengthen thy brethren.' " [167]

"What can be more lowly than such a soul [as Paul]? After such successes, wanting nothing of Peter, not even his assent, but being of equal dignity with him, (for at present I will say no more,) he comes to him as his [Paul's] elder and superior. And the only object of this journey was to visit Peter; thus he pays due respect to the Apostles, and esteems himself not only not their better but not their equal. . . . He says, 'to visit Peter;' he does not say to see, (ἰδεῖν,) but to visit and survey, (ἱστορῆσαι,) a word which those, who seek to become acquainted with great and splendid cities, apply to themselves. Worthy of such trouble did he consider the very sight of Peter; and this appears from the Acts of the Apostles also." [168]

Socrates Scholasticus (c. A.D. 380–450) [169]

"Neither was Julius, bishop of the great Rome, there, nor had he sent a substitute, although an ecclesiastical canon [Church law] commands that the churches shall not make any ordinances against the opinion of the bishop of Rome." [170]

---

[167] *Homily 3 in Acts*, NPNF1, 11:20; emphasis added. For a very thorough analysis of Chrysostom's thoughts and teachings on Peter and the primacy of Rome, see Scott, *Eastern Churches and the Papacy*, and Chapman, *Studies on the Early Papacy*, 89.

[168] *Commentary on Galatians* 1, 18, NPNF1, 13:12–13.

[169] Socrates Scholasticus was a Greek Church historian. He was native to Constantinople and wrote mainly of the Eastern Church, touching only on the West when it affected his narrative on the East. He would obviously have no reason to promote or exaggerate the Roman primacy.

[170] *The Ecclesiastical History* 2, 8, NPNF2, 2:38. This takes us back to the time of Athanasius and is quoted here because of the time period in which Socrates wrote his ecclesiastical history. This quotation and that of Sozomen show how two historians in the East perceived the Pope in the West. "Let it be well remembered that Zozomen [Sozomen] and Socrates are writing events which took place after Nice [Nicaea] and before Sardica; and as the canon above mentioned is not found among the commonly received twenty of Nice, it is only fair

"Athanasius, meanwhile, after a lengthened journey, at last reached Italy. . . . At the same time also Paul, bishop of Constantinople, Asclepas of Gaza, Marcellus of Ancyra . . . and Lucius of Adrianople, having been accused on various charges, and expelled from their several churches, arrived at the imperial city [Rome]. There each laid his case before Julius, bishop of Rome. He on his part, by virtue of the Church of Rome's peculiar privilege,[171] sent them back again into the East, fortifying them with commendatory letters; and at the same time restored to each his own place, and sharply rebuked those by whom they had been deposed. Relying on the signature of the bishop Julius, the bishops departed from Rome, and again took possession of their own churches, forwarding the letters to the parties to whom they were addressed." [172]

Sozomen (c. A.D. 370–d. after 439) [173]

"Athanasius, on leaving Alexandria, had fled to Rome. Paul, bishop of Constantinople, Marcellus, bishop of Ancyra, and

---

to conclude the Ante-nicene character of the enactment. And if the existence of a definite written law in the case is called into question, then the testimony of the two historians above mentioned is all sufficient to prove a generally acknowledged supremacy of Rome, and more so, since neither Socrates nor Zozomen faintly suggests that there was any controversy concerning the acknowledgment itself" (Dolan, *See of Peter*, 39–40).

[171] "Sozomen's word, which we translate 'oversight,' is κηδεμονία. Socrates' word, translated 'prerogative,' is προνομία" (Shotwell and Loomis, *See of Peter*, 505 n. 118).

[172] *The Ecclesiastical History* 2, 15, NPNF2, 2:42. Church historian Socrates makes it quite clear that Rome was the final court of appeal for any local Church determinations. Interestingly enough, only the heretical Arians refused to accept the doctrine of Rome, though they did not reject the Roman primacy. Socrates mentions not only the illustrious Eastern Father Athanasius but also other bishops from various Churches traveling to the central authority of Rome for a final ecclesiastical ruling. This shows not just a primacy of *honor* but a clearly understood primacy of *jurisdiction*. The bishop of Rome had the power to excommunicate bishops and put new bishops in place, overturn the decisions of local councils and reverse their decrees.

[173] Salaminius Hermias Sozomen (Salmaninius Hermias Sozomenus) was a lawyer from Palestine and undertook the task of writing a history of the Church, with the intention of continuing where Eusebius' *Church History* left off and updating the history. Commenting on his writings (and those of Socrates),

Asclepas, bishop of Gaza, repaired thither at the same time. Asclepas, who was opposed to the Arians and had therefore been deposed, after having been accused by some of the heterodox of having thrown down an altar; Quintianus had been appointed in his stead over the Church of Gaza. Lucius also, bishop of Adrianople, who had been deposed from the church under his care on another charge, was dwelling at this period in Rome. The Roman bishop, on learning the accusation against each individual, and on finding that they held the same sentiments about the Nicaean dogmas, admitted them to communion as of like orthodoxy; and as the care for all was fitting to the dignity of his see,[174] he restored them all to their own churches. He wrote to the bishops of the East, and rebuked them for having judged these bishops unjustly, and for harassing the Churches by abandoning the Nicaean doctrines. He summoned a few among them to appear before him on an appointed day, in order to account to him for the sentence they had passed, and threatened to bear with them no longer, unless they would cease to make innovations. This was the tenor of his letters. Athanasius and Paul were reinstated in their respective sees, and forwarded the letter of Julius to the bishops of the East."[175]

"The bishops of Egypt, having sent a declaration in writing that these allegations were false, and Julius having been apprised that Athanasius was far from being in safety in Egypt, sent for him to his own city. He replied at the same time to the letter of the bishops who were convened at Antioch, for just then he hap-

---

Philip Schaff writes, "Eusebius, without intending it, founded a school of church historians, who continued the thread of his story from Constantine the Great to the close of the sixth century, and, like him, limited themselves to a simple, credulous narration of external facts, and a collection of valuable documents, without an inkling of the critical sifting, philosophical mastery, and artistic reproduction of material, which we find in Thucydides and Tacitus among the classics, and in many a modern historian. . . . All of them combine ecclesiastical and political history, which after Constantine were inseparably interwoven in the East; and (with the exception of Philostorgius) all occupy essentially the same orthodox stand-point. They ignore the Western church, except where it comes in contact with the East" (*History of the Christian Church*, 3:880).

[174] In *Patrologia Graeca*, by J. P. Migne, the wording is as follows: "And inasmuch as the oversight of everyone belongs to him [Pope Julius], through the merit of his see" (PG 67:1049–56, in Shotwell and Loomis, *See of Peter*, 505).

[175] *The Ecclesiastical History of Sozomen* 3, 8, NPNF2, 2:287.

pened to have received their epistle, and accused them of having clandestinely introduced innovations contrary to the dogmas of the Nicene council, and of having violated the laws of the Church, by neglecting to invite him to join their Synod; for he alleged that there is a sacerdotal canon which declares that whatever is enacted contrary to the judgment of the bishop of Rome is null." [176]

Augustine of Hippo (A.D. 354–430) [177]

"For if the lineal succession of bishops is to be taken into account, with how much more certainty and benefit to the Church do we reckon back till we reach Peter himself, to whom, as bearing in a figure the whole Church, the Lord said: 'Upon this rock will I build my Church, and the gates of hell shall not prevail against it!' The successor of Peter was Linus, and his successors in unbroken

---

[176] *The Ecclesiastical History of Sozomen* 3, 10, NPNF2, 2:288–89. It is understood by Sozomen, and not contested, that there was an ecclesiastical law from Nicaea or earlier that states that Rome had the final authority to sanction or nullify the decrees of councils.

[177] St. Augustine's devoted Christian mother, Monica, followed him around the Roman Empire praying and working for his salvation. She is the patron saint of mothers because of her prayers and persistence, which were answered by God in the conversion of her gifted son. Augustine is considered the greatest of the Latin Fathers and one of the most eminent Western Doctors of the Church. Augustine was born on November 13, 354, in Tagaste, Numidia (Algeria). His father, Patricius, was a pagan (later converted to Christianity), but his mother, Monica, was a devout Christian, who labored untiringly for her son's conversion. Augustine became an earnest seeker after truth. He considered becoming a Christian but experimented with several philosophical systems before finally entering the Church. About 383 Augustine left Carthage for Rome, but a year later he went on to Milan as a teacher of rhetoric. There he met the bishop of Milan, St. Ambrose, then the most distinguished ecclesiastic in Italy. Augustine presently was attracted again to Christianity. At last one day, according to his own account, he seemed to hear a voice, like that of a child, repeating, "Take up and read." He interpreted this as a divine exhortation to open the Scriptures and read the first passage he happened to see, which was Romans 13:13–14. He immediately resolved to embrace Christianity. Along with his natural son, he was baptized by Ambrose on Easter Vigil in 387. His mother, who had rejoined him in Italy, rejoiced at this answer to her prayers and hopes. She died soon afterward in Ostia. He became bishop of Hippo in 395, an office he held until his death. John Calvin and Martin Luther, leaders of the Reformation, had a great respect for Augustine. Augustine died at Hippo, August 28, 430.

continuity were these:—Clement, Anacletus, Evaristus, Alexander, Sixtus, Telesphorus, Iginus, Anicetus, Pius, Soter, Eleutherius, Victor, Zephirinus, Calixtus, Urbanus, Pontianus, Antherus, Fabianus, Cornelius, Lucius, Stephanus, Xystus, Dionysius, Felix, Eutychianus, Gaius, Marcellinus, Marcellus, Eusebius, Miltiades, Sylvester, Marcus, Julius, Liberius, Damasus, and Siricius, whose successor is the present Bishop Anastasius. In this order of succession no Donatist bishop is found." [178]

[In a letter that treats of the condemnation of Caecilianus, bishop of Carthage, by schismatics, Augustine writes:] "That city (Carthage) had a bishop of no slight authority, who was able not to heed the multitude of enemies conspiring against him, when he saw himself united by letters of communion, both with the Roman Church, in which the primacy (principality) of the apostolic chair [*apostolicae cathedrae principatus*] has always been in force—and with other lands—whence the Gospel came into Africa itself, where he might be ready to plead his own cause, if his adversaries should attempt to alienate those churches from him." [179]

Pope Innocent I (d. A.D. 417) [180]

"In seeking the things of God, . . . following the example of ancient tradition, . . . you have strengthened . . . the vigor of your

---

[178] *Letters of St. Augustine* 53, 2, NPNF1, 1:298. Here we have a strong statement supporting the primacy of Rome, the special position of Peter, and the basis for refuting heretics: the tradition and succession of apostolic authority in the Catholic Church. St. Augustine was one of the greatest Christian minds of the early Church, and he demonstrates again the core of the visible Church— that Peter was given a primary authority and that authority flowed on in his successors in the Apostolic See. "Do the Donatists have any claim to the truth?", Augustine asks rhetorically. "No." Let us take a look and see. Can they claim apostolic succession back to Peter himself? No. Then they are not in the Church and have no claim to the apostles.

[179] *Epistle* 43, 7, in Berington and Kirk, *Faith of Catholics*, 2:81–82. In dealing with heresy in northern Africa, the bishops, including St. Augustine, bishop of Hippo, sent a letter to obtain the official confirmation of their councils from the "Apostolic See". Their letter starts out with "Because the Lord, by the special bounty of His grace, has placed you in the Apostolic See". There is no hint of opposition to the primacy of Rome. This is another case of actions speaking louder than words. Next we see the response from Pope Innocent.

[180] St. Innocent I was Pope from 401 to 417. "At a time when the western empire was crumbling under barbarian invasions, he seized every opportunity

religion with true reason, for you have acknowledged that judgement is to be referred to us, and have shown that you know what is
owed to the Apostolic See, if all of us placed in this position are to
desire to follow the Apostle himself from whom the episcopate
itself and the total authority of this name have emerged. Following
him, we know how to condemn evils just as well as we know how to
approve what is laudable. . . . [The Fathers] did not regard anything
as finished, even though it was the concern of distant and remote
provinces, until it had come to the notice of this See [Rome], so
that what was a just pronouncement might be confirmed by the
total authority of this See, and thence other Churches,—just as all
waters proceed from their own natal source and, through the various regions of the whole world, remain pure liquids of an uncor-
rupted head,—might take up what they ought to teach, whom they
ought to wash, whom the water worthy of clean bodies would shun
as being soiled with a filth incapable of being cleansed."[181]

---

to assert the primacy of the Roman see" (Kelly, *Oxford Dictionary*, 37). Though
there seems to be a bit of sarcasm in Kelly's tone, the fact is that Innocent was
obliged to consolidate power and unity in order to withstand the chaos brought
about by social upheaval. With the imminent collapse of the Roman Empire, it
was crucial that the Church consolidate her resources and solidify her unity to
withstand the onslaught of the barbarians. Because of the strength of the Church,
the barbarians were eventually converted to Christianity and Europe civilized.
Pope Innocent befriended and defended Chrysostom and Jerome in the East. He
used his authority as bishop of Rome to condemn the Pelagians (who taught
salvation could come through human efforts apart from the grace of God).
Because the papal councils under Pope Innocent I had condemned Pelagius, St.
Augustine spoke the famous words attributed to him, "Rome has spoken, the
matter is settled" (see p. 233, n. 187, below). Rome was sacked during Innocent's
pontificate, while he was away. He returned in 412 and died in 417.

[181] *Letter of Pope Innocent I to the Fathers of the Council of Carthage* on January 27,
A.D. 417, in Jurgens, *Faith of the Early Fathers*, 3:181–82. "The Popes themselves,
needless to say, upheld the primacy of St. Peter. Evidence of their views is to be
found principally in their letters, which reveal a uniform pattern of thought.
The text of Matthew 16 is the *locus classicus* on which they base their claims for
St. Peter, whose primacy is clearly appreciated, but in a way which shows little
advance on the position adopted by Pope Stephen in the third century" (Winter,
Saint Peter, 63). Luke Rivington makes a few pointed observations: "But the
important point is, Did the African bishops, did any African bishop, take exception to St. Innocent's definitions of the place occupied by Rome towards the rest
of the Church *as the See of Peter*? Did they throw out the remotest hint that, in
accepting the net result of St. Innocent's letters, they excepted the passages
about the authority with which it was done? Not one. Yet the letter was much

"If cases of greater importance are to be heard, they are, as the synod decrees and as happy custom requires, after episcopal judgement, to be referred to the Apostolic See [of Rome]."[182]

Augustine

"We determined that the judgment should stand which was issued by the venerable Bishop [Pope] Innocent from the See of the most blessed Peter."[183]

"[Pope Innocent] in reference to all things, wrote back to us in the same way in which it is lawful and the duty of the Apostolic See to write."[184]

---

before the world. . . . But what of St. Augustine himself? St. Augustine says that Innocent, 'in reference to all things, wrote back to us in the same way in which it was lawful and the duty of the Apostolic See to write'. I do not know how it would be possible for St. Augustine to set his signature to the Vatican decrees by anticipation in plainer terms. Of these two great letters of Pope Innocent he says, in another place, challenging the Pelagian bishop, Julian, 'Reply to him [i.e., Innocent], yea, rather to the Lord Himself, whose testimony that prelate used' " (*Primitive Church*, 290).

[182] *Letter of Pope Innocent I to Vitricius, Bishop of Rouen* 2, 3, 6, dated Feb. 15, A.D. 404, only eleven years after the Council of Hippo formalized the canon of the New Testament, in Jurgens, *Faith of the Early Fathers*, 3:179. "Pelagianism is a heresy which strikes at the very root of the Christian attitude to God and redemption. A provincial Council in proconsular Africa (A.D. 416) decreed that Pelagius and Caelestius should be anathematized 'unless they openly anathematize' their errors. But the Council wrote to Pope Innocent I 'in order that to the statutes of our littleness might be added the authority of the Apostolic See. . . . Augustine, preaching at Carthage in September 417 about the Pelagian trouble, says: 'On this matter [the findings of] two Councils have been sent to the Apostolic See, and answers have been received thence. The matter is ended: let us hope that the error [sc. the heresy] may soon be ended.' Thus Augustine, the great anti-Pelagian theologian, appears to agree with Innocent that the papal determination of a controversy about the faith is final" (Butler, *Church and Infallibility*, 169–70).

[183] These words are not Augustine's words per se but the words of the 214 African bishops, among whom Augustine was included, in response to Pope Innocent's decision.

[184] *Sermon* 186, n. 2, in Rivington, *Primitive Church*, 290. We find no hint in Augustine that he challenges or resents the authority over the sea in Rome. In Africa's receipt of Innocent's ruling and declaration of jurisdiction, without murmuring the bishops of Africa were "either the tamest and most hypocritical of all men, or they believed in the Papal supremacy. . . . No decree was received

"Reply to him [Pope Innocent I], yea, rather to the Lord Him-self, whose testimony that prelate used." [185]

"In this same period of my priesthood, I also wrote a book against a letter of Donatus who, after Majorinus, was the second bishop of the party of Donatus at Carthage. In this letter, he argues that the baptism of Christ is believed to be only in his communion. It is against this letter that we speak in this book. In a passage in this book, I said about the Apostle Peter: 'On him as on a rock the Church was built.' This idea is also expressed in song by the voice of many in the verses of the most blessed Ambrose where he says about the crowing of the cock: 'At its crowing he, this rock of the Church, washed away his guilt.' But I know that very frequently at a later time, I so explained what the Lord said: 'Thou art Peter, and upon this rock I will build my Church,' that it be understood as built upon Him whom Peter confessed saying: 'Thou art the Christ, the Son of the living God,' and so Peter, called after this rock, represented the person of the Church which is built upon this rock, and has received 'the keys of the kingdom of heaven.' For, 'Thou art Peter' and not 'Thou art the rock' was said to him. But 'the rock was Christ,' in confessing whom, as also the whole Church confesses, Simon was called Peter. But let the reader de-cide which of these two opinions is the more probable." [186]

---

in terms of more unqualified admiration by the Church of North Africa in the time of St. Augustine" (Rivington, *Primitive Church*, 288, 291). The words of Augustine bring to mind words of Hermas centuries earlier concerning Clem-ent, the bishop of Rome: "Write, then, two small booklets, one for Clement and one for Grapte. Clement will then send it to the cities abroad since this is his duty" (*The Shepherd of Hermas*, Visions 2, 4, in *The Apostolic Fathers*, trans. Francis X. Glimm, Gerald G. Walsh, and Joseph M.-F. Marique, The Fathers of the Church [Washington, D.C.: Catholic Univ. of America Press, 1981], 1:241–42).

[185] *Lib. i. c. Julian c. 4*, in Rivington, *Primitive Church*, 290. Pope Innocent I had spoken for God in this matter, and his word should be obeyed as the word of the Lord. These words remind us of the letter to the Corinthians sent by Clement in A.D. 96.

[186] *Retractationes* 1, 20, 1, in *Saint Augustine: The Retractations*, trans. Sister Mary Inez Bogan [Washington, D.C.: Catholic Univ. of America Press, 1968], 60:90–91. This passage has generated a lot of excitement in those who oppose the Papacy. They mistakenly think they have discovered a nail for the "coffin" of Catholic teaching, even though Augustine teaches here that it is perfectly valid to understand Peter, in Matthew 16, as the rock upon which Christ built his Church. St. Augustine denies neither the fact that the rock is Peter nor the visible reality of the Church and the primacy of Rome. James White, neglecting to mention

everything else in the Augustinian corpus that refutes his proof-texting, touts this passage as some kind of coup de grace (see *Roman Catholic Controversy*, 121–22). No one denies that the Fathers saw additional applications to Matthew's text (as we see in the *Catechism of the Catholic Church* 424, 442, 552), but White fails, unhappily, to represent properly St. Augustine, whose constant words and actions professed a thoroughly "Catholic" understanding of the Petrine primacy in the See of Rome. Even if, for the sake of argument, Augustine had said that Peter was definitely *not* the rock in Matthew 16 (which, by the way, no Father *ever* said), the Fathers taught and practiced what most Evangelicals fail to understand—that the Petrine succession was of apostolic origin and was an organic outgrowth of the Holy Spirit's leading and protection of the Church and would have been adhered to even if Matthew 16 had not existed. White also fails to factor in development of doctrine—the fact that Christian doctrine and practice develop over time as the need arises. If we apply White's methodology to the development of the New Testament, we would assert that since the early Christians did not define the canon of Scripture in the precise words of today's Evangelicals, then the New Testament is to be rejected today. It was not until the end of the fourth century that 2 Peter and Jude were universally accepted as canonical. Should we reject them now because the earliest Christians failed to define the canon definitively the way Evangelicals do today? Catholics understand that the earliest Christians may not have appreciated the ramifications of the primacy of St. Peter and his successors. Jesus' words to St. Peter can be seen as a "prophecy", in the words of Cardinal Newman. The full-blown understanding and implementation of the Papacy took time to develop, just as did the canon of the New Testament and the doctrine of the Trinity.

Let us apply White's principle, in his own words, concerning Peter and Matthew 16, to the issue of the canon's development. Regarding the development of the doctrine of the Papacy he writes, "Notice the huge movement in thought that has taken place between the early part of the fifth century and the latter part of the nineteenth" (*Roman Catholic Controversy*, 122). But, would not even White have to agree that in the case of the canon of the New Testament there is just such a huge movement in thought—from almost exclusive reliance on oral tradition and no defined New Testament canon, to a list of twenty-seven books that are non-negotiable and required for any Evangelical—which has taken place between the latter part of the first century and the latter part of the fifth? Why does White accept such development in the early Church's understanding of the canon but not in that of the Papacy? White recommends that we read further on the topic: "The reader is strongly encouraged to read the fine presentations available on this topic", and then he directs us to four sources, to all of which we have referred in this book. But here I would like to address his encouragement to read the *History of the Christian Church*, by Philip Schaff (*Roman Catholic Controversy*, 245). What Schaff tells us is what we already know but what James White denies: "Augustine, it is true, unquestionably understood by the church the visible Catholic church, descended from the apostles, especially from Peter, through the succession of bishops; and according to the usage of his time he called the Roman church by eminence the *sedes apostolica* [Apostolic Chair]" (*History of the Christian Church*, 3:307).

"Roma locuta est; causa finita est [Rome has spoken; the case is closed]." [187]

Fr. Stanley Jaki, in his excellent book on the "keys" of Matthew 16, writes, "[Against the Donatists Augustine emphasized] that Peter was first given the keys which later on were communicated to the others apostles. . . . The need to insist on the Church's power to forgive sins against Donatists and all their kindred 'spiritualists' made almost inevitable the insistence that all apostles and all their successors had the power of keys, as a power tied even in Matthew to the power of loosing and binding given to the twelve as well. Such a stretching of the meaning of the passage in Matthew could have led to anarchy in the Church if pivotal importance had not been attributed at the same time to the Roman succession. Only a deliberate oversight of this latter point can prompt one to rehash an old superficiality and make anti-Roman hay out of Augustine's ignorance of Greek (and Aramaic), which left him undecided whether Christ founded the Church on Peter or on his faith. Only ill-will can turn into a champion of a 'spiritualist' invisible church that Augustine who repeatedly greeted Rome's decision as a *rescriptum* or in Roman legal terminology a decision against which there was no further appeal. . . . For Augustine the twelve [apostles] were no more conceivable without their head, Peter, than the Church was conceivable without the chief apostolic see, Rome" (*Keys of the Kingdom*, 75, 76).

[187] *Sermons* 131, 10. These sermons were presented between 391 and 430. This sermon, however, was written subsequent to the Councils of Carthage and Milevis (A.D. 416). This popular, shortened version of Augustine's statement put to rest the contention caused by the Pelagian heretics. The full text of his statement—the exact equivalent of the shortened version above—is, "[On the matter of the Pelagians] two Councils have already been sent to the Apostolic See [Rome]; and from there rescripts [decrees from the Pope] have come. The matter is at an end [*causa finita est*]; would that the error too might sometime be at an end" (Jurgens, *Faith of the Early Fathers*, 3:28). "In matters of faith, [Augustine] says, it is the duty of all to have recourse to the Apostolic See and its pastoral ministry; for God specially directs the Pope in giving his decisions. It is true, the oft quoted phrase: 'Roma locuta est, causa finita est,' is not found verbally in any writings of Augustine; but its equivalents occur again and again. And this is all that is required to make him a staunch supporter of Papal infallibility" (Bernard J. Otten, *A Manual of the History of Dogmas* [St. Louis, Mo.: B. Herder, 1917], 1:336). Rome was the final appeal. In the mind of St. Augustine "[the authority of the Apostolic See] was an authority beyond and including the authority of local councils, which, when they had done their best, referred to it for approval and ratification of what they had done. No part of the Church was more autonomous than the African; yet when 130 bishops had met under the Primates of Carthage and Numidia, and were as sure as to the truth of the doctrinal statements which they opposed to error as bishops could be, St. Augustine himself being one of them, they did not think their labours concluded until they had sent their decrees to be ratified at Rome. St. Augustine described their

"Not to speak of that wisdom which you [the Manichaeans] do not believe to be in the Catholic Church, there are many other things which most justly keep me in her bosom. The consent of people and nations keeps me in the Church; so does her authority, inaugurated by miracles, nourished by hope, enlarged by love, established by age. The succession of priests keeps me, beginning from the very seat of Peter the Apostle, to whom the Lord after His resurrection gave it in charge to feed His sheep down to the present episcopate. And so lastly does the name itself of Catholic, which not without reason, amid so many heresies, that Church alone has so retained that, though all heretics wish to be called Catholics, yet when a stranger asks where the Catholic Church meets no heretic will venture to point to his own basilica or house. Since then so many and so great are the very precious ties belonging to the Christian name which rightly keep a man who is a believer in the Catholic Church ... no one shall move me from the faith which binds my mind with ties so many and so strong to the Christian religion. ... For my part I should not believe the gospel except the authority of the Catholic Church moved me."[188]

Theodoret (c. A.D. 393–c. 466) [189]

"This most holy See has preserved the supremacy over all Churches on the earth, for one especial reason among many

---

authority as being a rivulet when compared with the fountainhead" (Thomas W. Allies, *The Throne of the Fisherman* [London: Burns & Oates, 1887], 338).

[188] *Against the Epistle of Manichaeus* 5, 4–5, in *A Source Book for Ancient Church History*, by Joseph Cullen Ayer (New York: Charles Scribner's Sons, 1948), 454–55 (see also NPNF1, 4:130, 131). This is one of those classic texts that resound with ageless wisdom and common sense. It is the heartbeat of the early Church and the conviction of the Fathers. Augustine sums up the Fathers' view of the Church—the Catholic Church—as the visible entity in theological and hierarchical continuity with the Apostle Peter, and this traditional teaching remained virtually unchanged throughout the patristic period. One finds the same foundational principles in the current teaching of the Catholic Church. Such a statement and sentiment as Augustine's has brought many wayward Christians back to the Catholic Church, the Church of the Fathers.

[189] Theodoret was a native of Antioch, who, after committing his life to the gospel and his Savior, gave all his property to the poor and entered a monastery for prayer and study. He was consecrated bishop of Cyrrhus in Syria and governed his flock with wisdom and generosity. He battled paganism and heresy.

others; to wit, that it has remained intact from the defilement of heresy. No one has ever sat on that Chair, who has taught heretical doctrine; rather that See has ever preserved unstained the Apostolic grace."[190]

Council of Ephesus (431)
—the opening words of Philip, the papal legate

"There is no doubt, and in fact it has been known in all ages, that the holy and most blessed Peter, prince and head of the Apostles, pillar of the faith, and foundation of the Catholic Church, received the keys of the kingdom from our Lord Jesus Christ, the Savior and Redeemer of the human race, and that to him was given the power of loosing and binding sins: who down even to to-day and forever both lives and judges in his successors. The holy and most blessed pope Celestine, according to due order, is his successor and holds his place, and us he sent to supply his place in this holy synod, which the most humane and Christian Emperors have commanded to assemble, bearing in mind and continually watching over the Catholic faith. For they both have kept and are now keeping intact the apostolic doctrine handed down to them from their most pious and humane grandfathers and fathers of holy memory down to the present time."[191]

Pope Leo I
—written in July, A.D. 445[192]

"Our Lord Jesus Christ, Savior of the human race, so established the worship of divine religion, which He wanted to shine out by

---

His Christology was at one time in question, but he abandoned the questionable views by A.D. 451.

[190] *Epistle 116 to Renatus*, in Hergenröther, *Anti-Janus*, 67. An Eastern Father acknowledges the supremacy of Rome and the infallibility of those who have sat on the seat of Peter.

[191] *Council of Ephesus*, third session in *The First Seven Ecumenical Councils, 325–787*, by Leo Donald Davis (Minneapolis: Liturgical Press, 1990), 157.

[192] Saint Leo I, called the Great (c. A.D. 400–461), Pope from 440–461 and considered one of the greatest administrators of the ancient Church. History has only recognized two Roman bishops with the title "Great", and Leo was the first. Leo further developed the primacy of the bishop of Rome over the

God's grace unto all nations and peoples. . . . But the Lord desired that the sacrament of this gift should pertain to all the Apostles in such a way that it might be found principally in the most blessed Peter, the highest of all the Apostles. And He wanted His gifts to flow into the entire body from Peter himself, as if from the head, in such a way that anyone who had dared to separate himself from the solidarity of Peter would realize that he was himself no longer a sharer in the divine mystery. . . . The Apostolic See—out of reverence for it, I mean,—has on countless occasions been reported to in consultation by bishops even of your province. And through the appeal of various cases to this see, decisions already made have been either revoked or confirmed, as dictated by long-standing custom." [193]

---

universal Church, based on the teaching and practice of the previous Popes and the Fathers. Pope Leo was probably born in Tuscany, and he was active as a cleric in Rome long before his election to the Papacy. He was consecrated bishop of Rome on September 29, 440, at a time of political disintegration in the West. With the barbarian invasions threatening the West and the Church, he concentrated on creating a strong central government in the Church to maintain unity and suppress heresy. Leo persuaded Attila the Hun not to invade Rome in 452 and Gaiseric the Vandal not to sack the city in 455.

Leo was equally assertive in the East, where his greatest triumph was at the Council of Chalcedon (451), over which his own legates presided. The council was summoned to condemn the heresy of Eutychianism, a form of Monophysitism, a doctrine asserting that Christ has only one (divine) nature. Leo's definition of the "two natures" (divine and human) of Christ in his *Tome* (449), his doctrinal letter to the patriarch of Constantinople, was endorsed by the Council with the famous words "Peter has spoken this through Leo." He died in Rome on November 10, 461, and was proclaimed a Doctor of the Church in 1574. "Leo's contemporaries remembered him as the savior of Rome and Italy. For us his services to the papacy, and to the development of doctrine, are more important. He is the great champion, in the ancient Church, of a dynamic as opposed to a static concept of tradition. He left a papacy fully conscious of its prerogatives as the center and foundation of Church unity. As the remnants of Rome's Empire collapsed and Europe sank into what historians call the Dark Ages, it was the papacy alone which possessed the moral prestige and intellectual power to preserve the noble elements of ancient civilization and to exercise in the new world that was struggling to be born the Lord's command to the fisherman Peter: 'Feed my sheep' " (John Jay Hughes, *Pontiffs: Popes Who Shaped History* [Huntington, Ind.: Our Sunday Visitor, 1994], 46).

[193] *Letter of Pope Leo I to the Bishops of the Province of Vienne* 10, 1–2, written in July, A.D. 445, in Jurgens, *Faith of the Early Fathers*, 3:269.

"Let the entire matter, with a record of the proceedings, be referred to us. . . . Although bishops have a common dignity, they are not all of the same rank. Even among the most blessed Apostles, though they were alike in honor, there was a certain distinction of power.[194] All were equal in being chosen, but it was given to one to be preeminent over the others. . . . Through them [bishops with greater responsibility] the care of the universal Church would converge in the one See of Peter, and nothing should ever be at odds with this head."[195]

"From the whole world only one, Peter, is chosen to preside over the calling of all nations, and over all the other Apostles, and over the Fathers of the Church. Thus, although among the people of God there are many priests and many pastors, it is really Peter who rules them all, of whom, too, it is Christ who is their chief ruler."[196]

"For no one may venture upon anything in opposition to the enactments of the Fathers' canons which many long years ago in the city of Nicaea were founded upon the decrees of the Spirit, so that any one who wishes to pass any different decree injures

---

[194] Eastern Orthodox Christians tend to explain away the primacy in terms of *dignity* for Rome, but not *obedience* to it, *honor*, but not *jurisdiction*. Hans Urs von Balthasar comments rightly on this: "Thus, for all those who adhere to a real (sacramental) succession—Orthodox, Anglicans, Old Catholics—the primacy of Peter remains a goad against which they are always trying to kick. The attempt to soften it into an 'honorary primacy' is totally alien within the context of a Church that knows no other honor than that of the 'last place', of service rendered without thanks. This interpretation derives from the ideology of the Byzantine Empire. (We have already mentioned that Photius himself saw in the Roman 'preeminence' a legal right that should be exercised when requested and should never be a spontaneous reaction.) If there is any primacy, it is modeled on Peter's primacy within the college of the apostles; even if there were shown to be twelve patriarchal sees in apostolic succession, it would not change anything. The only real question is the *manner* in which the primacy of jurisdiction is exercised in actual Christian practice. The Eastern Church may be critical of this, but she should not forget that Pope Clement's exhortation [96 A.D.]—issued with truly ecclesial *agape* at the time of his intervention at Corinth—was far more than a gentle reminder of one of Christ's commandments: the function of government demands authority, even in Christian love, and this presupposes obedience" (*The Office of Peter and the Structure of the Church* [San Francisco: Ignatius Press, 1986], 77–78).

[195] *Letter of Pope Leo I to Anastasius, Bishop of Thessalonica* 14, 11, written about A.D. 446, in Jurgens, *Faith of the Early Fathers*, 3:270.

[196] *Sermons* 4, 2, written before A.D. 461, in Jurgens, *Faith of the Early Fathers*, 3:275.

himself rather than impairs them. And if all pontiffs will but keep them inviolate as they should, there will be perfect peace and complete harmony through all the churches. . . . But the bishops' assents, which are opposed to the regulations of the holy canons composed at Nicaea in conjunction with your faithful Grace, we do not recognize, and by the blessed Apostle Peter's authority we absolutely disannul in comprehensive terms." [197]

Council of Chalcedon (451) [198]

"Peter has spoken this through Leo." [199]

---

[197] *Epistle* 105, NPNF2, 12:76, 77. Those who received these words, nullifying the twenty-eighth canon of Chalcedon, did not resist them or oppose Leo and his decree. They did not accuse him of violating their rights or overextending his authority. As in the centuries before, back to Clement of the first century, the bishops of Rome exercised their prerogatives over other Churches, and though the decision may have been challenged, the authority to *make* the decision was not. Leo's words are lofty and authoritative, yet we do not find the bishops, even in the East, denying the Petrine authority. Many have tried to portray Leo as arrogant and jealous of his position, grasping for power, but history does not reveal this at all. "From the day of his first words as bishop of Rome, amid the splendid ceremonial of his consecration, until his death, his various utterances concerning the supremacy of the Roman bishopric, manifest a deep-seated consciousness, that the supremacy rested upon no other than a divine foundation" (Dolan, *See of Peter*, 86). Prominent Protestant scholar J. N. D. Kelly says, "His sermons, covering the liturgical year, reveal him as a pastor concerned to guide and instruct, watchful for heresy. . . . In Africa, traditionally jealous of its autonomy, his rulings on irregularities in elections and other scandals were eagerly sought and accepted. . . . [At the Council of Chalcedon Leo] affirmed the doctrine that Christ is one person in two natures" (*Oxford Dictionary*, 43–44).

[198] The Council of Chalcedon, the fourth ecumenical council, was summoned in A.D. 451 by the Eastern emperor Marcian at the behest of Pope Leo I. Some six hundred bishops, joined by two bishops from the province of Africa and two papal legates from Rome, attended the seventeen sessions held between October 8 and November 1. The council condemned Eutychianism. The Chalcedonian Definition, based on Pope Leo's formulation in his *Tome* to Flavian, the bishop of Constantinople, and the synodical letters of St. Cyril of Alexandria to Nestorius, established that Christ has both a divine and a human nature, which exist inseparably within him.

The Council also promulgated twenty-seven canons governing ecclesiastical discipline and hierarchy and clerical conduct—the Western Church accepted them all. A twenty-eighth canon, however, which would have granted the bishop of Constantinople the title of patriarch and status in the East equal to that of the

"And we further inform you that we have decided on other things also for the good management and stability of church matters, being persuaded that your holiness will accept and ratify them, when you are told. . . . Accordingly vouchsafe most holy and blessed father to accept as your own wish, and as conducing to good government the things which we have resolved on for the removal of all confusion and the confirmation of church order. . . . Accordingly, we entreat you, honour our decision by your assent, and as we have yielded to the head our agreement on things honourable, so may the head also fulfil for the children what is fitting. . . . But that you may know that we have done nothing for favour or in hatred, but as being guided by the Divine Will, we have made known to you the whole scope of our proceedings to strengthen our position and to ratify and establish what we have done." [200]

Pope in Rome, was rejected. The pronouncements made in Chalcedon were eventually accepted by the Eastern and Western Churches.

[199] Response to Pope Leo's *Tome* quoted in Hughes, *Pontiffs*, 46. The *Tome* was read at the Council of Chalcedon during the second session on October 10, reaffirming the two natures of Christ and condemning the heresy that stated Christ had only one nature. "When it was finally read at the second session of October 10, the minutes record seventeen affirmative acclamations. The most significant from the Pope's point of view was the cry: 'Peter has spoken this through Leo'—an exact echo of Leo's doctrine of the Pope as Peter's living voice" (ibid., 42).

[200] *Letter 98: From the Synod of Chalcedon to Leo*, NPNF2, 12:73. The council of Eastern bishops cannot be much clearer as to the authority of Leo, the bishop of Rome, even calling him "father" and "head", referring to themselves as "children". As Philip Hughes points out, "The bishops, in this letter, have dropped the language about the imperial importance of the new city [Constantinople], and about recognition of the pope's primacy as related to the like importance of Rome. It is to him as primate because Peter's successor that they address their plea—to the one sure concrete reality beneath their wealth of insinuating compliment" (*The Church in Crisis: A History of the General Councils, 325–1870* [Garden City, N.Y.: Doubleday, 1961], 90).

The situation with Anatolius, Patriarch of Constantinople (c. A.D. 400–458) is also instructive from this period. He had written to Leo to announce his consecration and await Leo's confirmation. He did not, however, send along a statement of his orthodox Catholic faith. "Consider now Leo's dealings with Anatolius. They signify a good deal and illustrate very plainly what the relations between the Eastern Churches and the see of Rome really were. And there is no word of protest, no question of Leo's right of interference or dictation. Anatolius had written to Leo to announce his consecration, and from Leo's

Cyril of Alexandria (A.D. 370–444) [201]

"He [Jesus] suffers him no longer to be called Simon, exercising authority and rule over him already, as having become His own. But by a title suitable to the thing, he changed his name into Peter, from the word *petra* (rock); for on him He was afterwards to found His Church." [202]

---

letter to the Emperor it is patent that Anatolius wrote, as was customary, to obtain Leo's confirmation. But the Declaration of Faith, which it was customary to send at the same time, he omitted to dispatch, and it is especially to be noted that Eutyches and his teaching had not been mentioned. And this is why Leo wrote to the Emperor asking the reason. It shows that Leo, like Celestine before him, had a great idea of his own importance; and it shows equally that that great importance was recognised.... To make a long story short, Leo requires Anatolius to sign his Tome, Cyril's Second Letter to Nestorius, and the patristic passages inserted in the Acts of the Council of Ephesus. And Pulcheria [the Catholic Empress] writes to Leo that 'Anatolius embraces the Apostolical confession of Your letters,' 'the letter of the Catholic Faith.' In reply Leo congratulates Anatolius 'that those who serve our God may rejoice that your peace has been concluded with the Apostolic See'" (Scott, *Eastern Churches and the Papacy*, 189–90). Hardly can a more extreme case be imagined: the bishop of Rome requiring an accounting from the patriarch of Constantinople, and the results simply refute any idea that the bishop of Rome was seen as anything less than the head, occupying the Apostolic See of the Blessed Peter.

[201] "As a youth, Cyril lived with monks and was later appointed as the patriarch of Alexandria in 412.... When Nestorius [the heretic] from Antioch became bishop of Constantinople in 428, he and Cyril soon clashed. Nestorius emphasized the humanity of Christ and refused to refer to Mary as 'Godbearer,' calling her 'Christ-bearer' instead, on the grounds that she gave birth only to a man, who then became both an instrument and a vessel of divinity. In Christ, Nestorius taught, the human person (Jesus) and the divine person ('the Word' of John 1:1) were united by such a close and sympathetic association as to be virtually indistinguishable. Cyril, on the other hand, argued that although Christ had two completely separate natures, divine and human, they were united 'hypostatically' (in a more intrinsic union)" (*Who's Who in Christian History*, ed. J. D. Douglas and Philip W. Comfort [Wheaton, Ill.: Tyndale House, 1992] on Logos Systems Library 2.1 CD-ROM). Cyril turned to Rome for clarification and authority in his fight against Nestorius.

[202] *Commentary on John*, in Berington and Kirk, *Faith of Catholics*, 2:46. Along with acknowledging in his writings that Christ is the foundation of the Church, Cyril of Alexandria sees no dichotomy or conflict with the fact that in another metaphor Peter is the foundation of the Church. Again, the Fathers did not find themselves in the *either-or* dilemma.

"They (the Apostles) strove to learn through one, that preeminent one, Peter."[203]

"We have not openly and publicly separated from communion with Nestorius before making known the whole matter to your Holiness. Be pleased then to prescribe what you think right to be done. Whether it behooves us to persevere in communion with him, or to declare openly that communion is impossible with one who fosters and teaches doctrines so erroneous."[204]

Peter Chrysologus (c. A.D. 400–450)[205]

"We exhort you in every respect, honorable brother, to heed obediently what has been written by the Most Blessed Pope of the City of Rome; for Blessed Peter, who lives and presides in his own see, provides the truth of faith to those who seek it. For we, by reason of

---

[203] Ibid.

[204] *In Conc. Ephes.* 1, 14, as quoted in *The Pope and the Church*, by Paul Bottalla (London: Burns, Oates and Co., 1868), 84. "No doctrine in the Church of Christ is so clearly deducible from the records of ecclesiastical history as that of the supremacy of the Apostolic See. To deny this doctrine is nothing less than to gainsay the clear testimony of indisputable facts and documents. It is surprising that so many Protestants who pretend to learning seem unaware of the existence of these historical evidences, or at least unable to appreciate their import. But it is yet more strange to see such men labour at drawing darkness from the clear light of history, and throwing into obscurity the fundamental doctrine upon which rests the divine economy of the whole Church. . . . St. Cyril, Patriarch of the most eminent see of the East, applied to Pope Celestine against Nestorius" (ibid., 81, 84). St Cyril's words demonstrate clearly his respect for the primacy of the Apostolic See. Pope Celestine wrote to St. Cyril, "In virtue of authority delegated to you by our See, and acting in our stead, and by our commission, you will execute our sentence with exact severity" (ibid., 85). According to Bottalla, "We cannot fail to recognize, in the words of Celestine, the language in which a superior addresses an inferior. The Pontiff, conscious of his full authority in the Church, passes a solemn sentence, and deputes, on the one hand, a Patriarch to see to its execution; on the other, he puts forth a confession of faith, and, under threat of excommunication, calls upon a second Patriarch to adhere to the doctrine so set forth. . . . We here find a plain evidence of Papal supremacy" (ibid., 86).

[205] St. Peter Chrysologus was bishop of Ravenna in Italy. All that remains of his work is a collection of his sermons. He was apparently named Chrysologus ("golden-worded") to make him the Western counterpart to John Chrysostom. He was declared a Doctor of the Church in 1729.

our pursuit of peace and faith, cannot try cases on the faith without the consent of the Bishop of the City of Rome." [206]

Flavian (Patriarch of Constantinople, d. A.D. 449)
  —to Pope Leo I [207]

"The whole question needs only your single decision and all will
be settled in peace and quietness. Your sacred letter will with
God's help completely suppress the heresy which has arisen and
the disturbance which it has caused; and so the convening of a
council which is in any case difficult will be rendered super-
fluous." [208]

---

[206] *Letter to Eutyches* 25, 2, written in A.D. 449, in Jurgens, *Faith of the Early Fathers*, 3:268.

[207] St. Flavian was patriarch of Constantinople and was noted for his holiness of life, which of course makes his testimony rather impressive. Flavian recom-mended moderation in the matter of Eutyches, who denied the two natures of Christ, but Flavian was eventually forced to pronounce a sentence of excommu-nication against Eutyches. Flavian forwarded the results of the council to Pope Leo I, who confirmed Flavian's decision. "Flavian and six bishops who had assisted at the previous synod were allowed no voice, being, as it were, on trial. Eutyches was absolved of heresy. . . . Flavian was condemned and deposed. In the violent scenes which ensued he was so ill-used that three days later he died in his place of exile. . . . St. Flavian was repeatedly vindicated by Pope Leo, whose epistle of commendation failed to reach him before his death. . . . At the Coun-cil of Chalcedon (451) . . . Flavian [was] eulogized as a martyr for the Faith" (*Catholic Encyclopedia*, 6:99).

[208] *Letter to Pope Leo* as cited by Vladimir Solovyev in *Russia and the Universal Church*, trans. H. Rees (London: Geoffrey Bles, 1948), 134. "Peter Chrysologus, though a Greek and writing to a Greek, was nevertheless bishop of Ravenna and therefore half Western. But a few pages further on we find the same doctrine [of papal primacy] from the representative of the metropolis of the East, Flavian, a saint and confessor of the Orthodox Church" (ibid.). Again we see that the East looked to Rome as the final arbiter and protector of the true faith, the court of last appeal, whose word was authoritative, even making an ecumenical council unnecessary.

PART THREE

CURRENT CHURCH TEACHING

We will now take a look at the current teachings of the Roman Catholic Church to see if that teaching is still faithful to the ancient tradition and custom of the Church—if it is still loyal to Peter's commission, given by the Lord himself. Those who spend their energies devising ingenious arguments against the Papacy and who even acknowledge, as we saw in the introduction, that "No father denies that Peter had a primacy or that there is a Petrine succession" ought to consider the ramifications of their stance. If all Christians in the early centuries, even those who learned at the feet of the apostles, believed in a primacy of Peter and a primacy of his successors, why is it there are Christians today who so categorically denounce that primacy? Why should I trust the teaching of such opponents of the Papacy when I can trust the teaching of the whole early Church, "who still had the preaching of the apostles ringing in their ears and the authentic tradition before their eyes"? The antagonists admit that the question at issue is not whether there *was* a primacy but how it was *interpreted.* Our study has shown it was interpreted very literally and very consistently—in line with the teaching of the Catholic Church today. In fact, what we find is that the Roman Catholic Church is the only Church still within the apostolic tradition and functioning according to the principles and customs of the Fathers.

Catechism of the Council of Trent (1566)

"The Church has but one ruler and one governor, the invisible one, Christ, whom the eternal Father *hath made head over all the Church, which is his body*; the visible one, the Pope, who, as legitimate successor of Peter, the Prince of the Apostles, fills the Apostolic chair. It is the unanimous teaching of the Fathers that this visible head is necessary to establish and preserve unity in the Church. This St. Jerome clearly perceived and as clearly expressed when . . . he wrote: "*One is elected that, by the appointment of a head, all occasion of schism may be removed.*" [1]

"Should anyone object that the Church is content with one Head and one Spouse, Jesus Christ, and requires no other, the

---

[1] *The Catechism of the Council of Trent*, 2d rev. ed., trans. J. A. MacHugh and C. J. Cullan (1923; reprint, Rockford, Ill.: TAN Books, 1982), 103. The original was issued by order of Pope Pius V in 1566.

answer is obvious. For as we deem Christ not only the author of all
the Sacraments, but also their invisible minister—He it is who
baptizes, He it is who absolves, although men are appointed by
Him the external ministers of the Sacraments—so has He placed
over His Church, which He governs by His invisible Spirit, a man
to be His vicar and the minister of His power. A visible Church
requires a visible head; therefore the Saviour appointed Peter
head and pastor of all the faithful, when He committed to his care
the feeding of all His sheep, in such ample terms that He willed
the very same power of ruling and governing the entire Church to
descend to Peter's successors." [2]

First Vatican Council (1869–1870)

"And so We, adhering faithfully to the tradition received from the
beginning of the Christian faith, to the glory of God, our Savior,
the elevation of the Catholic religion and the salvation of Christian
peoples, with the approbation of the sacred Council, teach and
explain that the dogma has been divinely revealed: that the Roman
Pontiff, when he speaks *ex cathedra* [i.e., 'from the chair'], that is,
when carrying out the duty of the pastor and teacher of all Christians in accord with his supreme apostolic authority he explains a
doctrine of faith or morals to be held by the universal Church,
through the divine assistance promised him in blessed Peter, oper-
ates with that infallibility with which the divine Redeemer wished
that His church be instructed in defining doctrine on faith and
morals; and so such definitions of the Roman Pontiff from himself,
but not from the consensus of the Church, are unalterable.

"[Canon.] But if anyone presumes to contradict this definition
of Ours, which may God forbid: let him be anathema ['cut off', cf.
Mt 18:17; Gal 1:8–9; 1 Cor 16:22]." [3]

---

[2] Ibid., 104.

[3] Session 4, chap. 4, DS 1839–40, in *The Sources of Catholic Dogma*, by Henry
Denzinger, trans. Roy Deferrari [St. Louis, Mo.: B. Herder, 1957], 457. This is
the famous definition of the dogma of infallibility. Though the two documents
are seventeen centuries apart, recall and notice the similarity to the words of
Clement, bishop of Rome, to the Corinthians in A.D. 96. "For ye will give us great
joy and gladness, if ye render obedience unto the things written by us through
the Holy Spirit" (chap. 73) and "Receive our counsel, and ye shall have no
occasion of regret. . . . But if certain persons should be disobedient unto the

Second Vatican Council (1962–1965)

"The Roman Pontiff, as the successor of Peter, is the perpetual and visible source and foundation of the unity both of the bishops and the whole company of the faithful. The individual bishops are the visible source and foundation of unity in their own particular Churches, which are constituted after the model of the universal Church; it is in these and formed out of them that the one and unique Catholic Church exists. And for that reason precisely each bishop represents his own Church, whereas all, together with the pope, represent the whole Church in a bond of peace, love and unity." [4]

"In the Church of Christ the Roman Pontiff, as the successor of Peter, to whom Christ entrusted the care of his sheep and lambs, has been granted by God supreme, full, immediate and universal power in the care of souls. As pastor of all the faithful his mission is to promote the common good of the universal Church and the particular good of all the churches." [5]

Catechism of the Catholic Church (1994) [6]

"When Christ instituted the Twelve, 'he constituted [them] in the form of a college or permanent assembly, at the head of which he placed Peter, chosen from among them.' Just as 'by the Lord's institution, St. Peter and the rest of the apostles constitute a single apostolic college, so in like fashion the Roman Pontiff, Peter's successor, and the bishops, the successors of the apostles, are related with and united to one another.' " [7]

---

words spoken by Him [Jesus Christ] through us, let them understand that they will entangle themselves in no slight transgression and danger; but we shall be guiltless of this sin" (chaps. 58, 59, in Lightfoot and Harmon, *Apostolic Fathers*).

[4] *Lumen gentium,* no. 14, in *Vatican Council II,* ed. Austin Flannery, O.P., vol. 1, new rev. ed. (Collegeville, Minn.: Liturgical Press, 1992), 365–66.

[5] *Christus Dominus,* no. 2, in ibid., 564.

[6] *Catechism of the Catholic Church* (Vatican City: Libreria Editrice Vaticana, 1994). This is the first universal catechism in four hundred years. It was released in English in June 1994. It is a wonderfully lucid book, easy to read, completely faithful to the teaching of Scripture and the tradition of the Church as received by the apostles and expounded by the Fathers.

[7] CCC 880.

"The Lord made Simon alone, whom he named Peter, the 'rock' of his Church. He gave him the keys of his Church and instituted him shepherd of the whole flock. 'The office of binding and loosing which was given to Peter was also assigned to the college of apostles united to its head.' This pastoral office of Peter and the other apostles belongs to the Church's very foundation and is continued by the bishops under the primacy of the Pope."[8]

"The *Pope*, Bishop of Rome and Peter's successor, 'is the perpetual and visible source and foundation of the unity both of the bishops and of the whole company of the faithful.' 'For the Roman Pontiff, by reason of his office as Vicar of Christ, and as pastor of the entire Church has full, supreme, and universal power over the whole Church, a power which he can always exercise unhindered."[9]

Summary

When we read the pages of the past and hear the voices full of godly wisdom and apostolic fervor, we see clearly how our forefathers in the faith maintained the unity of the Church in the bond of peace. We have glimpses, like historical snapshots, of how they put into practice the words of our Lord Jesus in the Gospels, and we must ask ourselves: Where is that Church today? Is there a Church in modern times that still adheres to the teachings and practices of the Fathers of the first centuries? Can anyone claim an organic continuity with the Church of the Fathers? Are there any today that have the same form of government and that adhere loyally to the forms and principles of the early Church? Are there any that still acknowledge and obey the primacy of Peter in the See of Rome as the source of organizational unity and orthodox theology?

The answer is Yes, and that church is, as we have seen, the Roman Catholic Church—the only one that still fits the criteria of the Fathers and puts into practice the teachings of the ancient Church. She covers the whole earth with her teaching and jurisdiction, speaking and preserving the word of God—not one square inch of land is without a Catholic bishop, ruling in collegi-

---

[8] CCC 881.
[9] CCC 882.

ality with, and obedience to, the bishop of Rome, the See of Peter. It should cause all believers in our Lord Jesus Christ to sit up and take notice. In the first century, St. Paul could confidently state, "But if any one is disposed to be contentious, we recognize no other practice, nor do the churches of God" (1 Cor 11:16). The Churches were not free to "do as they please", so to speak.[10] The apostles and their successors, the bishops, ruled in the Church to maintain true doctrine and unity.[11]

The Catholic Church has always held to the necessity of a physical head of the Church in order to preserve unity of faith and spirit. Jesus chose Peter and named him *Rock* in order to set one shepherd in front of the universal flock to tend and feed the sheep. Sheep without a shepherd tend to scatter. Fundamentalists like to claim, "We don't need a pope because we have the risen Lord as the head of our Church." Is this true, in the sense that a "risen Christ" eliminates the need for a man to be a visible leader? Of course not. Do they have a pastor? Does he lead the congregation? Does he protect the flock from errors in doctrine? Does he endeavor to teach the truth and feed his sheep? Does he strive to maintain the unity of peace and the unity of faith?

And, if the "visible" pastor leaves his church to accept a pastorate or similar position elsewhere, what does the congregation do? They immediately appoint a "search committee" to find a new "visible head" for their church, a shepherd to lead and minister to their flock.[12]

---

[10] "For though you have countless guides in Christ, you do not have many fathers. For I became your father in Christ Jesus through the gospel. I urge you, then, be imitators of me. Therefore I sent to you Timothy, my beloved and faithful child in the Lord, to remind you of my ways in Christ, as I teach them everywhere in every church. Some are arrogant, as though I were not coming to you. But I will come to you soon, if the Lord wills, and I will find out not the talk of these arrogant people but their power. For the kingdom of God does not consist in talk but in power. What do you wish? Shall I come to you with a rod, or with love in a spirit of gentleness?" (1 Cor 4:15–21).

[11] Acts 1:20; 20:28; Phil 1:1; 1 Tim 3:1–2; 5:17; Titus 1:7.

[12] For example, we read the following from a guide for Baptist churches: "Every form of organized society, whether civil, social or religious, is supposed to have officers, duly constituted to execute the laws, administer the government, and secure the ends contemplated by the organization. The Church is a commonwealth, a society, a family, and has its officers as leaders and administrators of its affairs. . . . It was a Church before it had officers, and supplied these

As a young boy in a Baptist church, I remember how agitated my father became when the pastor would go on vacation. My father, a member of the deacon board, worried that he was "canvassing" for a better position at another Baptist church. That always meant another search for a new pastor, and that always brought about the possibilities of dividing the church. Finding a new pastor was never an easy or pleasant job.

I also remember the six-year stint my wife and I had with a small "non-denominational church" in the 1970s, where we met and were married. Our church proudly boasted of a unique situation: we were a "New Testament church" without a paid pastor, based upon the "pattern" we "discovered" from the pages of the New Testament. Watchman Nee was our "patron saint", so to speak. We were not an "organized" church; we deplored organized churches. How could Christ be the literal Head of a church if a paid pastor governed it? We boasted that Christ was our *literal* Head, not merely the *figurehead* of the organized churches. But, how did this work out in practice? The elders ruled the congregation, to the point that they intruded into the privacy of homes and personal lives and expected to be involved in all private and corporate decisions. Doctrine and practice were strictly enforced according to the new tradition they had established. I recall one Sunday evening when the "head elder" actually announced he had the authority to legislate how often people changed their undergarments. I was young at the time, but not too young to recognize that this was an obvious abuse of pastoral authority, bordering on authoritarianism. At that point we moved on to the next Protestant group that most resembled *my* determination of what a church should be.

But the point is this: Even our "New Testament church", which had no "head" but Christ himself, actually became more dictatorial and controlling than churches admitting that they have human headship. Protestant churches have pastors, visible heads, leaders, even vicars.[13] How is this different in principle from the

administrative functionaries from among its own members. And should they all resign, or be removed, the Church would still survive, and supply the deficiency by the election of others to fill their places" (Edward T. Hiscox, *Principles and Practices for Baptist Churches* [Grand Rapids, Mich.: Kregel Pub., 1980], 83).

[13] Vicar simply means one serving as a substitute or agent of another; specifically: an administrative deputy. A pastor or elder in a Protestant church

Catholic Church having a pastor for the worldwide universal Church? Should the Church with over one billion faithful be without a visible head, a shepherd, while the small congregation of fifty or a hundred needs a pastor—a spiritual leader, counselor, visible head, definer of doctrine, teacher of truth, source of unity, arbiter of differences? Why should the Protestant denominations be allowed a pastor but not the Catholic Church?

The amazing thing, now that I look back on our years of "church-hopping", was that we *never* considered the apostolic and Church Fathers of the first centuries; we always thought we could go to the Bible alone to recreate the Church for our generation. Why did we take Watchman Nee's "twentieth-century ecclesiology" as the final word, without considering the ecclesiology of those who actually knew and lived in the shadow of the apostles? We ignored the Catholic Church, which can trace her pedigree and continuity back to the very first Church, the real New Testament Church, the Church of the apostles and the Fathers.

Jesus appointed Peter as the shepherd to tend, pastor, and feed his flock (Jn 21:15–17). We have already given ample reason to believe that he did so, based on biblical exegesis and historical evidence. Peter, in turn, appointed a shepherd to fill his shoes in the event of the martyrdom Jesus had foretold for him (Jn 21:18–19). We also learn from St. Clement of Rome, disciple of St. Peter and St. Paul, that "[the apostles] having received perfect foreknowledge, [so] they appointed those who have already been mentioned, and afterwards added the further provision that, if they should die, other approved men should succeed to their ministry." [14] The apostles knew that the Church needed a recognizable shepherd, and shepherds. Peter described our Lord Jesus as the shepherd (Greek: *poimen*) of our souls (1 Pet 2:25); but earlier, had Jesus not told Peter to "shepherd" his sheep, and did Paul not say Christ had appointed *pastors* (Greek: *poimen*) for the Church? Again, the Catholic Church has, under the guidance of the Holy Spirit, been faithful to the calling of her Lord and Master

---

stands in for the chief pastor, administering, governing, promoting the will and desires of the one he represents.

[14] *First Epistle of Clement to the Corinthians* 44, 2, written in A.D. 96, in W. A. Jurgens, *The Faith of the Early Fathers* (Collegeville, Minn.: Liturgical Press, 1970), 1:10.

and has preserved the unity of the Church during tumultuous centuries through the See of Rome and primacy of blessed Peter.

Local churches needed a bishop, as acknowledged by Paul in his Pastoral Epistles;[15] before the dawn of the second century, monarchical bishops were already in place throughout Christendom. As we have seen affirmed by Clement and Ignatius, the universal Church already had a universal shepherd to be the guarantor of unity and orthodox teaching.

Even the Eastern Orthodox Churches are willing to admit that if we accept the concept of a universal Church (which, however and unhappily, they deny), there is then a definite need for a universal pastor. According to Eastern Orthodox Church historian Nicholas Afanassieff, "Cyprian did not succeed in constructing his system without some idea of primacy, and this shows that if a universal theory of the church is adhered to, the doctrine of primacy will somehow be a necessary concomitant. A single body must be crowned by a single head, showing in his own person the unity of the whole system. If we take the universal theory of the Church, we cannot refute the doctrine of universal primacy just by saying that the Church has Christ as Head; that is an indisputable truth, and supporters of primacy do not themselves oppose it. The real question is: If the Church has an invisible Head (Christ), can she, or can she not, also have a visible head? If not, then why can a local church have a single head in the person of its bishop [or pastor, elder, or minister]? In other words, why can one part of the Universal Church have a single head, while the entire Universal Church is deprived of one?"[16]

The need for a real unity and a visible leadership did not cease with the Ascension of Christ, nor did it end with the death of Peter and the apostles. Shepherds are needed to ensure doctrinal purity, unification, and leadership. Even the Protestant admits and practices this principle. Throughout the history of God's covenant

---

[15] We see a development of doctrine and emphasis in Paul's writings. In the beginning of his ministry, his emphasis is on preaching and converting the Gentiles to Christ, whereas we see a new emphasis begin to emerge toward the end of his life, when he knew his death was imminent. In his last three epistles, to Timothy and Titus, we see a real concern for the government of the churches that will enable them to resist heresy and continue into the next century.

[16] "The Church which Presides in Love", in John Meyendorff et al., *The Primacy of Peter* (Crestwood, N.Y.: St. Vladimir's Seminary Press, 1992), 99–100.

people, from the Old Testament right on through the New Testament and into the primitive Church of the first centuries, right up to our day, there has always been a visible head of God's covenant people.[17] Christ never intended his people to be divided into fragmented little groups, each with its self-appointed pastor, conflicting in teachings and competing for sheep. This is the end result of sheep who reject a visible shepherd. Jesus wishes his Church to be one, as he and the Father are one (Jn 17:21, 22), perfected in unity. He announced that his goal was to bring the various sheep together, "so there shall be one flock, one shepherd" (Jn 10:16).[18]

---

[17] The Old Covenant consisted of the Torah (written law), the Prophets, the Writings, and other oral traditions that were held as binding; the teaching authority of Moses was passed on through succession and exemplified by the seat of Moses (Mt 23:2). A continuation and expansion of the grace of God, through a worldwide, all-encompassing New Covenant, took place, as explained in the New Testament Scriptures and the Sacred Tradition, taught and preserved in the Catholic Church, through the college of bishops and the chair of Peter.

[18] Some Protestants assume that denominational division does not negate the unity Christ willed for his followers. As evangelical scholar R. C. Sproul writes, "The church is one. Though fragmented by denominations, the elect are united by one Lord, one faith, and one baptism" (*Essential Truths of the Christian Faith* [Wheaton, Ill.: Tyndale House Pub., 1992], 217). But consider that as a mathematical equation: fragmented + divided = one and unity. Rather than accept the concept of a fragmented Church as being normal or inevitable, we should remember the words of St. Paul, which reflect the desire for unity expressed by Jesus: "I appeal to you, brethren, by the name of our Lord Jesus Christ, that all of you agree and that there be no dissensions among you, but that you be united in the same mind and the same judgment. For it has been reported to me by Chloe's people that there is quarreling among you, my brethren. What I mean is that each one of you says, 'I belong to Paul,' or 'I belong to Apollos,' or 'I belong to Cephas,' or 'I belong to Christ.' Is Christ divided?" (1 Cor 1:11–13; see also 1 Cor 11:18; 12:25 [Greek word for *schism*]; Jude 19; 1 Jn 2:19; Acts 20:30; Jn 10:16; 17:11, 21–23). Ignatius of Antioch writes, "See that ye all follow the bishop, even as Jesus Christ does the Father, and the presbytery as ye would the apostles; and reverence the deacons, as being the institution of God. Let no man do anything connected with the Church without the bishop. Let that be deemed a proper Eucharist, which is [administered] either by the bishop, or by one to whom he has entrusted it. Wherever the bishop shall appear, there let the multitude [of the people] also be; even as, wherever Jesus Christ is, there is the Catholic Church" (*Epistle of Ignatius to the Smyrnaeans* 8, ANF 1:89–90.)

On the other hand, whatever does have the bishop's sanction can be sure of God's approval too. The early Fathers of the Church would have been aghast at

From the first days of the Church, Peter and his successors, all 264 of them, including John Paul II, have faithfully carried out our Lord's mandate, shepherding the worldwide and universal Church. Those who reject the Church and her shepherd do so to their own detriment.

We will close with the wisdom of Cardinal Wiseman: "Thus you see, my brethren, that [the Papacy] is no new doctrine, but that all antiquity supports us in the belief, that our Blessed Saviour gave to Peter a headship and primacy over his Church, and that it was continued, through the following ages, in the persons of his successors, the Bishops of Rome. We find these exercising acts of decided authority over the highest dignitaries of the Eastern Church; we see them acknowledged as supreme by the most learned fathers; we have recorded, in strong terms, the deference and submission even of general Councils to their decisions and decrees. And if all this suffice not to prove the belief of those ages in the Papal Supremacy, I know not how we can ever arrive at a knowledge of what they held on any subject."[19]

May God bless his Church, and may the Spirit continue to breathe into us the life of springtime and renewal.

---

the condition of Christendom today. The concept of a fragmented Church is something that Jesus, the apostles, and the early Church would *never* have tolerated or promoted!

[19] Nicholas Cardinal Wiseman, *Lectures on the Principal Doctrines and Practices of the Catholic Church* (New York: P. O'Shea, Pub., 1843), 1:245.

APPENDIX A
The Chronological List of the Popes

Source: Annuario Pontificio.[1] The table below lists the year of accession of each Pope. The Apostle Peter, the first bishop of Rome, is acknowledged as the founder of the Church in Rome. He arrived in Rome about A.D. 42, was martyred there about A.D. 67, and was raised to sainthood and venerated as the pastor of the Church, whose successors rule in the name of the Lord Jesus Christ.

The Pope's temporal title is Sovereign of the State of Vatican City.

The Pope's spiritual titles are Bishop of Rome, Vicar of Jesus Christ, Successor of St. Peter, Prince of the Apostles, Supreme Pontiff of the Universal Church, Patriarch of the West, Primate of Italy, Archbishop and Metropolitan of the Roman Province.

(1)   St. Peter, d. c. 64 or 67
(2)   St. Linus, 67–76
(3)   St. Anacletus, 76–88
(4)   St. Clement I, 88–97
(5)   St. Evaristus, 97–105
(6)   St. Alexander 1, 105–115
(7)   St. Sixtus (Xystus) I, 115–125
(8)   St. Telesphorus, 125–136
(9)   St. Hyginus, 136–140
(10) St. Pius I, 140–155
(11) St. Anicetus, 155–166
(12) St. Soter, 166–175
(13) St. Eleutherius, 175–189
(14) St. Victor I, 189–199
(15) St. Zephyrinus, 199–217
(16) St. Callistus I, 217–222
(17) St. Urban I, 222–230

---

[1] Reprinted from *The Catholic Almanac 1999* (Huntington, Ind.: Our Sunday Visitor, 1999), 125–29. The permission to reproduce copyrighted materials was extended by Our Sunday Visitor, Inc., 200 Noll Plaza, Huntington, Ind., 1–800–348–2440. No other use of this material is authorized.

(18)   St. Pontian, 230–235
(19)   St. Anterus, 235–236
(20)   St. Fabian, 236–250
(21)   St. Cornelius, 251–253
(22)   St. Lucius I, 253–254
(23)   St. Stephen I, 254–257
(24)   St. Sixtus (Xystus) II, 257–258
(25)   St. Dionysius, 259–268
(26)   St. Felix I, 269–274
(27)   St. Eutychian, 275–283
(28)   St. Caius, 283–296
(29)   St. Marcellinus, 296–304
(30)   St. Marcellus I, 308–309
(31)   St. Eusebius, 309 (310)
(32)   St. Melchiades (Miltiades), 311–314
(33)   St. Sylvester I, 314–335
(34)   St. Marcus, 336
(35)   St. Julius I, 337–352
(36)   Liberius, 352–366
(37)   St. Damasus I, 366–384
(38)   St. Siricius, 384–399
(39)   St. Anastasius I, 399–401
(40)   St. Innocent I, 401–417
(41)   St. Zosimus, 417–418
(42)   St. Boniface I, 418–422
(43)   St. Celestine I, 422–432
(44)   St. Sixtus III, 432–440
(45)   St. Leo I (the Great), 440–461
(46)   St. Hilary, 461–468
(47)   St. Simplicius, 468–483
(48)   St. Felix III (II), 483–492
(49)   St. Gelasius I, 492–496
(50)   Anastasius II, 496–498
(51)   St. Symmachus, 498–514
(52)   St. Hormisdas, 514–523
(53)   St. John I, 523–526
(54)   St. Felix IV/III, 526–530
(55)   Boniface II, 530–532
(56)   John II, 533–535
(57)   St. Agapitus I, 535–536

(58)   St. Silverius, 536–537
(59)   Vigilius, 537–555
(60)   Pelagius I, 556–561
(61)   John III, 561–574
(62)   Benedict I, 575–579
(63)   Pelagius II, 579–590
(64)   St. Gregory I, 590–604
(65)   Sabinian, 604–606
(66)   Boniface III, 607
(67)   St. Boniface IV, 608–615
(68)   St. Deusdedit, 615–618
(69)   Boniface V, 619–625
(70)   Honorius I, 625–638
(71)   Severinus, 640
(72)   John IV, 640–642
(73)   Theodore I, 642–649
(74)   St. Martin I, 649–655
(75)   St. Eugene I, 654–657
(76)   St. Vitalian, 657–672
(77)   Adeodatus, 672–676
(78)   Donus, 676–678
(79)   St. Agatho, 678–681
(80)   St. Leo II, 682–683
(81)   St. Benedict II, 684–685
(82)   John V, 685–686
(83)   Conon, 686–687
(84)   St. Sergius I, 687–701
(85)   John VI, 701–705
(86)   John VII, 705–707
(87)   Sisinnius, 708
(88)   Constantine, 708–715
(89)   St. Gregory II, 715–731
(90)   St. Gregory III, 731–741
(91)   St. Zachary, 741–752
        Stephen II, 752 (elected but died before his consecration)
(92)   Stephen II (III), 752–757
(93)   St. Paul I, 757–767
(94)   Stephen III (IV), 768–772
(95)   Adrian I, 772–795
(96)   St. Leo III, 795–816

(97)   Stephen IV (V), 816–817
(98)   St. Paschal I, 817–824
(99)   Eugene II, 824–827
(100)   Valentine, 827
(101)   Gregory IV, 827–844
(102)   Sergius II, 844–847
(103)   St. Leo IV, 847–855
(104)   Benedict III, 855–858
(105)   St. Nicholas I (the Great), 858–867
(106)   Adrian II, 867–872
(107)   John VIII, 872–882
(108)   Marinus I (Martin II), 882–884
(109)   St. Adrian III, 884–885
(110)   Stephen V (VI), 885–891
(111)   Formosus, 891–896
(112)   Boniface VI, 896
(113)   Stephen VI (VII), 896–897
(114)   Romanus, 897
(115)   Theodore II, 897
(116)   John IX, 898–900
(117)   Benedict IV, 900–903
(118)   Leo V, 903
(119)   Sergius III, 904–911
(120)   Anastasius III, 911–913
(121)   Landus, 913–914
(122)   John X, 914–928
(123)   Leo VI, 928
(124)   Stephen VII (VIII), 928–931
(125)   John XI, 931–935
(126)   Leo VII, 936–939
(127)   Stephen VIII (IX), 939–942
(128)   Marinus II (Martin III), 942–946
(129)   Agapitus II, 946–955
(130)   John XII, 955–964
(131)   Leo VIII, 963–965
(132)   Benedict V, 964–966
(133)   John XIII, 965–972
(134)   Benedict VI, 973–974
(135)   Benedict VII, 974–983
(136)   John XIV, 983–984

(137) John XV, 985–996

(138) Gregory V, 996–999

(139) Silvester II, 999–1003

(140) John XVII, June 1003 to Dec. 1003

(141) John XVIII, Jan. 1004 to July 1009

(142) Sergius IV, July 31, 1009, to May 12, 1012

(143) Benedict VIII, May 18, 1012, to Apr. 9, 1024

(144) John XIX, Apr. (May) 1024 to 1032

(145) Benedict IX,[2] 1032–1044

(146) Silvester III, Jan. 20 to Feb. 10, 1045

(147) Benedict IX,[2] 1045

(148) Gregory VI, May 5, 1045, to Dec. 20, 1046

(149) Clement II, Dec. 24, 1046, to Oct. 9, 1047

(150) Benedict IX,[2] Nov. 8, 1047, to July 17, 1048

(151) Damasus II, July 17 to Aug. 9, 1048

(152) St. Leo IX, Feb. 12, 1049, to Apr. 19, 1054

(153) Victor II, Apr. 16, 1055, to July 28, 1057

(154) Stephen IX (X), Aug. 3, 1057, to Mar. 29, 1058

(155) Nicholas II, Jan. 24, 1059, to July 27, 1061

(156) Alexander II, Oct. 1, 1061, to Apr. 21, 1073

(157) St. Gregory VII, Apr. 22, 1073, to May 25, 1085

(158) Bl. Victor III, May 24, 1086, to Sept. 16, 1087

(159) Bl. Urban II, Mar. 12, 1088, to July 29, 1099

(160) Paschal II, Aug. 13, 1099, to Jan. 21, 1118

(161) Gelasius II, Jan. 24, 1118, to Jan. 28, 1119

(162) Callistus II, Feb. 2, 1119, to Dec. 13, 1124

(163) Honorius II, Dec. 15, 1124, to Feb. 13, 1130

(164) Innocent II, Feb. 14, 1130, to Sept. 24, 1143

(165) Celestine II, Sept. 26, 1143, to Mar. 8, 1144

(166) Lucius II, Mar. 12, 1144 (cons.), to Feb. 15, 1145

(167) Bl. Eugene III, Feb. 15, 1145, to July 8, 1153

(168) Anastasius IV, July 12, 1153 (cons.), to Dec. 3, 1154

(169) Adrian IV, Dec. 4, 1154, to Sept. 1, 1159

(170) Alexander III, Sept. 7, 1159, to Aug. 30, 1181

(171) Lucius III, Sept. 1, 1181, to Sept. 25, 1185

(172) Urban III, Nov. 25, 1185, to Oct. 20, 1187

---

[2] The situation of Benedict IX is confusing. He was forcibly removed from office in 1044; he resigned in 1045; and he was again removed from office at the synod of December 1046. If those actions were not legitimate, Sylvester III, Gregory VI, and Clement II were antipopes.

(173) Gregory VIII, Oct. 21 to Dec. 17, 1187
(174) Clement III, Dec. 19, 1187, to Mar. 1191
(175) Celestine III, Mar. 30, 1191, to Jan. 8, 1198
(176) Innocent III, Jan. 8, 1198, to July 16, 1216
(177) Honorius III, July 18, 1216, to Mar. 18, 1227
(178) Gregory IX, Mar. 19, 1227, to Aug. 22, 1241
(179) Celestine IV, Oct. 25 to Nov. 10, 1241
(180) Innocent IV, June 25, 1243, to Dec. 7, 1254
(181) Alexander IV, Dec. 12, 1254, to May 25, 1261
(182) Urban IV, Aug. 29, 1261, to Oct. 2, 1264
(183) Clement IV, Feb. 5, 1265, to Nov. 29, 1268
(184) Bl. Gregory X, Sept. 1, 1271, to Jan. 10, 1276
(185) Bl. Innocent V, Jan. 21 to June 22, 1276
(186) Adrian V, July 11 to Aug. 18, 1276
(187) John XXI, Sept. 8, 1276, to May 20, 1277
(188) Nicholas III, Nov. 25, 1277, to Aug. 22, 1280
(189) Martin IV, Feb. 22, 1281, to Mar. 28, 1285
(190) Honorius IV, Apr. 2, 1285, to Apr. 3, 1287
(191) Nicholas IV, Feb. 22, 1288, to Apr. 4, 1292
(192) St. Celestine V, July 5 to Dec. 13, 1294
(193) Boniface VIII, Dec. 24, 1294, to Oct. 11, 1303
(194) Bl. Benedict XI, Oct. 22, 1303, to July 7, 1304
(195) Clement V, June 5, 1305, to Apr. 20, 1314
(196) John XXII, Aug. 7, 1316, to Dec. 4, 1334
(197) Benedict XII, Dec. 20, 1334, to Apr. 25, 1342
(198) Clement VI, May 7, 1342, to Dec. 6, 1352
(199) Innocent VI, Dec. 18, 1352, to Sept. 12, 1362
(200) Bl. Urban V, Sept. 28, 1362 (cons.), to Dec. 19, 1370
(201) Gregory XI, Dec. 30, 1370, to Mar. 26, 1378
(202) Urban VI, Apr. 8, 1378, to Oct. 15, 1389
(203) Boniface IX, Nov. 2, 1389, to Oct. 1, 1404
(204) Innocent VII, Oct. 17, 1404, to Nov. 6, 1406
(205) Gregory XII, Nov. 30, 1406, to July 4, 1415
(206) Martin V, Nov. 11, 1417, to Feb. 20, 1431
(207) Eugene IV, Mar. 3, 1431, to Feb. 23, 1447
(208) Nicholas V, Mar. 6, 1447, to Mar. 24, 1455
(209) Callistus III, Apr. 8, 1455, to Aug. 6, 1458
(210) Pius II, Aug. 19, 1458, to Aug. 14, 1464
(211) Paul II, Aug. 30, 1464, to July 26, 1471
(212) Sixtus IV, Aug. 9, 1471, to Aug. 12, 1484

(213) Innocent VIII, Aug. 29, 1484, to July 25, 1492

(214) Alexander VI, Aug. 11, 1492, to Aug. 18, 1503

(215) Pius III, Sept. 22 to Oct. 18, 1503

(216) Julius II, Oct. 31, 1503, to Feb. 21, 1513

(217) Leo X, Mar. 9, 1513, to Dec. 1, 1521

(218) Adrian VI, Jan. 9, 1522, to Sept. 14, 1523

(219) Clement VII, Nov. 19, 1523, to Sept. 25, 1534

(220) Paul III, Oct. 13, 1534, to Nov. 10, 1549

(221) Julius III, Feb. 7, 1550, to Mar. 23, 1555

(222) Marcellus II, Apr. 9 to May 1, 1555

(223) Paul IV, May 23, 1555, to Aug. 18, 1559

(224) Pius IV, Dec. 25, 1559, to Dec. 9, 1565

(225) St. Pius V, Jan. 7, 1566, to May 1, 1572

(226) Gregory XIII, May 13, 1572, to Apr. 10, 1585

(227) Sixtus V, Apr. 24, 1585, to Aug. 27, 1590

(228) Urban VII, Sept. 15 to 27, 1590

(229) Gregory XIV, Dec. 5, 1590, to Oct. 16, 1591

(230) Innocent IX, Oct. 29 to Dec. 30, 1591

(231) Clement VIII, Jan. 30, 1592, to Mar. 3, 1605

(232) Leo XI, Apr. 1 to 27, 1605

(233) Paul V, May 16, 1605, to Jan. 28, 1621

(234) Gregory XV, Feb. 9, 1621, to July 8, 1623

(235) Urban VIII, Aug. 6, 1623, to July 29, 1644

(236) Innocent X, Sept. 15, 1644, to Jan. 7, 1655

(237) Alexander VII, Apr. 7, 1655, to May 22, 1667

(238) Clement IX, June 20, 1667, to Dec. 9, 1669

(239) Clement X, Apr. 29, 1670, to July 22, 1676

(240) Bl. Innocent XI, Sept. 21, 1676, to Aug. 12, 1689

(241) Alexander VIII, Oct. 6, 1689, to Feb. 1, 1691

(242) Innocent XII, July 12, 1691, to Sept. 27, 1700

(243) Clement XI, Nov. 23, 1700, to Mar. 19, 1721

(244) Innocent XIII, May 8, 1721, to Mar. 7, 1724

(245) Benedict XIII, May 29, 1724, to Feb. 21, 1730

(246) Clement XII, July 12, 1730, to Feb. 6, 1740

(247) Benedict XIV, Aug. 17, 1740, to May 3, 1758

(248) Clement XIII, July 6, 1758, to Feb. 2, 1769

(249) Clement XIV, May 19, 1769, to Sept. 22, 1774

(250) Pius VI, Feb. 15, 1775, to Aug. 29, 1799

(251) Pius VII, Mar. 14, 1800, to Aug. 20, 1823

(252) Leo XII, Sept. 28, 1823, to Feb. 10, 1829

(253) Pius VIII, Mar. 31, 1829, to Nov. 30, 1830
(254) Gregory XVI, Feb. 2, 1831, to June 1, 1846
(255) Pius IX, June 16, 1846, to Feb. 7, 1878
(256) Leo XIII, Feb. 20, 1878, to July 20, 1903
(257) St. Pius X, Aug. 4, 1903, to Aug. 20, 1914
(258) Benedict XV, Sept. 3, 1914, to Jan. 22, 1922
(259) Pius XI, Feb. 6, 1922, to Feb. 10, 1939
(260) Pius XII, Mar. 2, 1939, to Oct. 9, 1958
(261) John XXIII, Oct. 28, 1958, to June 3, 1963
(262) Paul VI, June 21, 1963, to Aug. 6, 1978
(263) John Paul I, Aug. 26 to Sept. 28, 1978
(264) John Paul II, Oct. 16, 1978, to

Antipopes

Antipopes were illegitimate claimants of or pretenders to the papal throne.

St. Hippolytus (217–235) was reconciled before his death; Novatian (251); Felix II (355–365); Ursinus (366–367); Eulalius (418–419); Lawrence (498; 501–505); Dioscorus (530); Theodore (687); Paschal (687); Constantine (767–769); Philip (768); John (844); Anastasius (855); Christopher (903–904); Boniface VII (974; 984–985); John XVI (997–998); Gregory (1012); Benedict X (1058–1059); Honorius II (1061–1072); Clement III (1080–1100); Theodoric (1100); Albert (1102); Sylvester IV (1105–1111); Gregory VIII (1118–1121); Celestine II (1124); Anacletus II (1130–1138); Victor IV (1138); Victor IV (1159–1164) did not recognize his predecessor; Paschal III (1164–1168); Callistus III (1168–1178); Innocent III (1179–1180); Nicholas V (1328–1330); *Antipopes of the Western Schism include:* Clement VII (1378–1394); Benedict XIII (1394–1423); Alexander V (1409–1410); John XXIII (1410–1415); Felix V (1439–1449).

APPENDIX B

An Old Testament Basis for the Primacy and Succession of St. Peter: A Study of Jesus' Words to Peter in Matthew 16

GENERAL OUTLINE

I. Scripture Interprets Scripture

The "Protestant principle" of Scripture interpreting Scripture,[1] is not a Protestant innovation at all. It has been taught and practiced

---

[1] In his *Commentary on the Psalms*, Martin Luther wrote, "Scriptura sui ipsius interpres", or, in English, "The Bible is its own interpreter." Well-known Evangelical theologian R. C. Sproul echoes Luther when he writes, "The chief rule of biblical interpretation is 'sacred Scripture is its own interpreter.' This principle

from the earliest years in the Catholic Church, as a short review of the Church Fathers' writings and the subsequent teachings of the Church clearly demonstrates. We will continue applying this principle—Scripture interpreting Scripture—in researching the primacy of Peter. After having already explored the New Testament references, we will now turn to the Old Testament. Knowledge of the culture and society of ancient Israel and its monarchical view of government will help us understand the "big picture" and how Peter's primacy is solidly rooted in the Jews' understanding of the kingdom of God.

We will begin with the profound passage in Matthew 16, in which Jesus appoints Peter the vice-regent, or steward, of his kingdom. To understand this passage in all its glory, one must first have a grasp of the Old Testament and Jewish world view. Understanding the biblical precedents will shed valuable light on Peter and the papal office. What do the Scriptures and history have to say about the "keys of the kingdom" and, especially, about the steward who carries them?[2]

---

means that the Bible is to be interpreted by the Bible" (*Essential Truths of the Christian Faith* [Wheaton, Ill.: Tyndale House Pub., 1992], 25). The Catholic Church of course has understood and taught this from the time of the Fathers. The *Catechism of the Catholic Church* (Vatican City: Libreria Editrice Vaticana, 1994), teaches this as one of the three criteria for interpreting Scripture in accordance with the Spirit who inspired it: "*Be especially attentive 'to the content and unity of the whole Scripture.'* Different as the books which comprise it may be, Scripture is a unity by reason of the unity of God's plan" (CCC 112).

[2] Since Matthew 16:13–20 is dealing with Jesus' kingship and his delegation of authority to Peter through the "power of the keys", it is not surprising that Matthew is the book where, according to Fundamentalist W. Graham Scroggie, the key word is "sovereignty", and the key phrase is "Behold thy King." Scroggie says it is the Gospel of *power* written for the Jews. "Internal evidence shows that he wrote mainly for his own countrymen, the Jews. Evidence is found in his references to Jerusalem, to David, to the Kingdom; in his sixty-five references to the Old Testament. . . . The object of the writer seems to have been to connect the Law with the Gospel; to show the relation of the Old Dispensation to the New. . . . Though not the first of the Four [Gospels] to be written, it is placed first as being most intimately connected with the Old Testament" (*Know Your Bible* [Old Tappan, N.J.: Fleming H. Revell, 1974], 2:35, 37). This analysis supports the idea that Jesus is acting as king, delegating authority to his "head of the house", and relating the whole event back to the Old Testament, which was one of the purposes of Matthew. Old and New are intimately related, and Matthew shows that to understand the New, one must be intimately familiar with the Old.

II. Jesus Appoints Peter as Royal Steward of His Kingdom

A. *Peter Chosen by Divine Revelation*

Let us take a look at the passage in question (Mt 16:13–20) before delving into the Old Testament. Jesus quizzes his disciples: "Now when Jesus came into the district of Caesarea Philippi, he asked his disciples, 'Who do men say that the Son of man is?' And they said, 'Some say John the Baptist, others say Elijah, and others Jeremiah or one of the prophets.' " Then Jesus puts them on the spot by asking, "But who do you say that I am?" Peter, with his characteristic impetuosity, states, "You are the Christ, the Son of the living God." Peter's singular response elicits an immediate and amazing declaration from Jesus, a declaration that, as we have seen, became one of the most hotly debated passages of the New Testament.

This dialogue between Jesus and his disciples cannot be taken lightly, for it is recorded prominently in the Gospel. All attempts to prove that the passage was inserted at a later date have failed. Even many critical scholars acknowledge that our Lord's response in Matthew's Gospel is authentic and historically accurate. Jesus' words, therefore, cannot be brushed aside or "explained away". They are of great importance for several reasons. For one thing, this is the first of only two recorded times that Jesus mentions the word "Church". Also, Jesus and his Father are seemingly in intimate cooperation in this remarkable announcement to Peter, since it was the Father in heaven who actually initiated the whole event. It appears that the Father had chosen Peter for this honor and "pointed out his choice" by revealing the truth of Jesus' identity to him. The Father's words were revealed—even "mediated"— through the person of Peter, and Jesus acknowledges them and their divine source. Based on this interaction, certain promises were made to Peter *alone*, for Peter alone received the revelation. This touches on the matter of infallibility, which we will discuss briefly later.

The fisherman's response is not a result of his intellectual prowess or erudition. In fact, Peter is acknowledged later on to be an uneducated, even an ignorant man.[3] God the Father had

---

[3] Acts 4:13: "Now when they saw the boldness of Peter and John, and perceived that they were uneducated, common men, they wondered; and they recognized that they had been with Jesus."

intervened at this moment in space and time and had given Peter a revelation. Jesus acknowledges this supernatural event with the words, "Blessed are you, Simon Bar-Jona! For flesh and blood has not revealed this to you, but my Father who is in heaven" (Mt 16:17). The poetic and prophetic words of Jesus that follow Peter's declaration are truly amazing. Because of Peter's revelation from God, he is separated out from the group, and specific appointments and promises are made to him alone from the mouth of Jesus himself.

B. *Definition of "Steward", "Over the House", "Vizier", and "Majordomo"*

Let us look at the actual declaration of Jesus, pregnant with meaning and based on a common experience of governments and kingdoms that was clearly understood by those who heard his words. We will not analyze each clause of the pronouncement but only those that are applicable to this study of Peter's stewardship. After stating that Peter has seen something unique and revealed directly by God, Jesus says to Simon, "And I tell you, you are Peter [Rock], and on this rock I will build my church, and the powers of death shall not prevail against it. I will give you [singular] the keys of the kingdom of heaven, and whatever you [singular] bind on earth shall be bound in heaven, and whatever you [singular] loose on earth shall be loosed in heaven" (Mt 16:18–19).

There is much we could discuss at this point, but the words I want to focus on are those in which Jesus promises to confer on Simon, newly named Peter, the keys of the kingdom of heaven. This is an act of investiture, and in the Greek it is stated in the future tense, singular. Why the future? While still on earth, Jesus was establishing the kingdom of God, and through his death and Resurrection he was given all authority in heaven and on earth (Mt 28:18). In the Eastern kingdoms, the sovereign king of the realm would delegate the authority and administration of his kingdom to a steward, who managed the kingdom—virtually ruling for the king—especially in his absence. This promise is directed to Peter alone. As we will see, Jesus had chosen Peter to be the steward of his kingdom—"over the house", the head vizier, the majordomo. Once the work of redemption had been completed and all authority had been given to Jesus, he passed the keys of authority over to Peter to administer the kingdom as a visible steward in his "absence".[4]

These words, rather, this governmental position in the Eastern kingdoms is at the core of our discussion, so it is important to take a few minutes to understand the terms *steward*, *"over the house"*, *vizier*, and *majordomo*. These terms were in common usage during biblical times, not only in Israel, but also in the surrounding kingdoms. "Steward" and "over the house" are technical terms, "the name given to an office of state of great importance in both kingdoms (1 Ki 4:6; 18:3), in fact the highest office of all and one so vastly superior to all others (Is 36:3, 37:2), that it was sometimes filled by the heir to the throne (2 Chron 26:21). . . . The person 'who was over the house' had the whole of the domestic affairs of the sovereign under his superintendence, and was therefore also called the *socēn* or administrator, as standing nearest the king."[5] We learn a bit more from Baptist professor John Watts, "[Eliakim the steward] served as chief of ministers in the royal government. He made decisions which carried royal authority and could not be appealed."[6]

"Vizier" is a title for a high officer in a Moslem government, especially during the Ottoman Empire, where the title designated the highest official in the administrative hierarchy. A vizier was the king's "right hand", literally running the kingdom on his behalf. The famous "Step Pyramid" in Saqqara, near Cairo, Egypt, was built for King Djoser (Third Dynasty) by the vizier Imhotep around 2630 B.C. Joseph, whom we will discuss in some detail later, was the grand vizier of Pharaoh's kingdom. "Majordomo" is a common designation for one who is the chief of the house. In the palace of a king, a majordomo is the one who rules the palace and kingly affairs for the king. It is a delegated and powerful position. These terms are all synonyms, and their importance will

---

[4] Jesus announced to his disciples in advance that he would be leaving them. See John 13:33, 36; 14:1, 2; Acts 1:9–11. His visible and physical presence would be removed. His kingdom would remain and flourish. He left a steward in charge and promised to send the Holy Spirit, the Comforter.

[5] C. F. Keil and F. Delitzsch, *Isaiah*, vol. 7 of *Commentary on the Old Testament* (Grand Rapids, Mich.: Eerdmans, 1978), 398.

[6] *Isaiah 1–33*, Word Biblical Commentary, vol. 24 (Waco, Tex.: Word Books, 1985), 292.

be seen as we continue to look at the biblical basis for the primacy of Peter in the kingdom of God.

C. *Jesus Gives Peter the Keys of the Kingdom*

We learn from Revelation 3:7 that Jesus is "the holy one, the true one, who has the key of David, who opens and no one shall shut, who shuts and no one opens." These words are obviously based on Isaiah 22 (which we will study in a later section). Jesus is the "son of David", the royal heir to the Davidic Kingdom.[7] The angel Gabriel said to Mary, "Do not be afraid, Mary, for you have found favor with God. And behold, you will conceive in your womb and bear a son, and you shall call his name Jesus. He will be great, and will be called the Son of the Most High; and the Lord God will give to him the throne of his father David, and he will reign over the house of Jacob for ever" (Lk 1:30–31). The key of David, the key of God's kingdom, belongs to Jesus. He has come to restore the throne of David. He has no challengers to the throne. He is the king; he is the sovereign.

God binds himself to his people with covenants. God made a covenant with David that his throne would be forever.[8] The kings of the Davidic covenant were the proud possessors of the "keys of David", signifying unquestioned royal authority. Jesus possesses these keys as the heir to David's throne. But Jesus went one step farther. He established a new covenant, an eternal covenant,[9] and it was to be catholic, or universal. It was not limited to the Jews or to the nation of Israel. The new covenant was for all men. It was an establishment of the kingdom of God. Each king has a kingdom, and each king has an "official over the house". We will see that this is the case with all the Eastern kingdoms. The keys are the sign of authority, and they belong exclusively to the king. Kings, however, would delegate the keys to the stewards or viziers of their kingdom. Jesus ascended the throne of David and then, through his

---

[7] Ps 89:3ff.; Is 9:6–7; 11:1–2; Mt 1:1, etc.

[8] 2 Sam 7:12–13: "When your days are fulfilled and you lie down with your fathers, I will raise up your offspring after you, who shall come forth from your body, and I will establish his kingdom. He shall build a house for my name, and I will establish the throne of his kingdom for ever."

[9] 1 Cor 11:25; Heb 13:20.

death and Resurrection, expanded the covenant to *all* men, not just to the Jews. God gave him all authority in heaven and earth; he was now the king of the eternal kingdom of God. He was the proud possessor of the royal keys of God's kingdom. What did he do with the "keys of kingdom"?

He delegated the keys to Peter. *Simon the fisherman became Peter the royal steward.* Next we are told that the keys gave Peter the authority to "bind and loose". As a Protestant I argued that the keys simply gave Peter the job of initially unlocking the door of the kingdom so that Gentiles might be saved. But what about the authority to "bind"? If the keys allowed Peter to open the door, what was meant by his authority to close or bind?[10] Let us take a closer look at these two terms, "binding" and "loosing"—the power of the keys—before we delve into the Old Testament precedents for the primacy of Peter.

D. *The Authority to Bind and Loose*

The authority delegated to Peter by his investiture and possession of the keys includes the power to bind and loose. This terminology had *profound* meaning for the first-century Jews. The disciples of Jesus would not have misunderstood the delegation of the keys and the authority to bind and loose, as we will clearly see. Kingdoms in the East, including Egypt, Persia, Assyria, Israel, and Judah, had well-established governmental positions within their hierarchy, just as well known then as the positions of president and vice-president are today in our own American society. Jesus uses terminology based on those positions within the Eastern kingdoms and the teaching of the Jewish rabbis in order to assure clarity in the minds of his followers. As we learn from Protestant

---

[10] Anglican scholar R. T. France writes, "These terms [binding and loosing] thus refer to a teaching function, and more specifically one of making halakhic [legal or relating to custom and tradition] pronouncements which are to be binding on the people of God. In that case Peter's 'power of the keys' declared in [Matthew] 16:19 is not so much that of the doorkeeper, who decides who may or may not be admitted to the kingdom of heaven, but that of the steward (as in Is 22:22, generally regarded as the Old Testament background to the metaphor of the keys here), whose keys of office enable him to regulate the affairs of the household" (*Matthew: Evangelist and Teacher* [Grand Rapids, Mich.: Zondervan, 1989], 247).

scholar Marvin Vincent, "No other terms were in more constant use in Rabbinic canon-law than those of *binding* and *loosing*. They represented the *legislative* and *judicial* powers of the Rabbinic office. These powers Christ now transferred . . . in their reality, to his apostles; the first, here to Peter."[11] The early Jewish converts would not have been confused or uncertain about what Jesus meant by these words, especially when they had the history of the Jewish monarchy behind them and the Rabbinic teaching and prerogatives at the forefront of their religious worship and society. They would have also seen this prerogative being exercised in the first years of the Church as they observed Peter's exercise of authority, especially in the first Church council recorded in Acts 15.

To show the common usage of the terms "bind and loose" I quote from Jewish historian Flavius Josephus (c. A.D. 37–c. 100), who wrote, "[The] Pharisees artfully insinuated themselves into her [Alexandra's] favour by little and little, and became themselves the real administrators of the public affairs: they banished and reduced whom they pleased; they bound and loosed (men) at their pleasure; and, to say all at once, they had the enjoyment of the royal authority."[12] The Pharisees under Queen Alexandra had

---

[11] *Word Studies in the New Testament* (1887; reprint, Grand Rapids, Mich.: Eerdmans, 1980), 1:96. Those opposed to the Catholic Church often try to reduce "binding" and "loosing" simply to the opening of the gates of heaven to the Gentiles. However, in so doing they ignore the meaning of the words within the culture at the time of Jesus. These words are defined in *The Illustrated Bible Dictionary* as "rabbinic terms used in Mt. 16:19 of Peter's doctrinal authority to declare things forbidden or permitted; and in Mt. 18:18 of the disciples' disciplinary authority to condemn and absolve" (J. D. Douglas, ed. [Wheaton, Ill.: InterVarsity Press and Tyndale House Pub., 1980], 1:199).

Aramaic biblical scholar George Lamsa writes of binding and loosing: " 'He has the key,' means he can declare certain things to be lawful and others unlawful; that is to bind or to loose, or to prohibit or to permit, or to forgive" (*Old Testament Light* [San Francisco: Harper & Row, 1964], 657). William Barclay informs us that "*To loose* and *bind* were very common Jewish phrases. They were used especially of the decisions of the great teachers and the great Rabbis. Their regular sense which any Jew would recognize was *to allow* and *to forbid*. To *bind* something was *to declare it forbidden; to loose* was *to declare it allowed*. These were the regular phrases for taking decisions in regard to the law. That is in fact the only thing these phrases in such a context would mean" (*The Gospel of Matthew* [Philadelphia: Westminster Press, 1975], 2:145–46).

[12] *Wars of the Jews* 1, 5, 2, in *Josephus: Complete Works*, trans. William Whiston (Grand Rapids, Mich.: Kregel Pub., 1980), 434. We also learn from Alfred Eders-

been granted royal authority and were therefore able to bind and to loose men from obligations, to punish and absolve, to make actions lawful or unlawful, and so on. So we see that these were not obscure terms in the first century but were widely used to describe religious, legislative, and judicial authority. This was the context of Jesus' delegation of authority to Peter in the kingdom of God.

"Disputes among [the Rabbis] were so numerous in Jesus' time as to let the expression 'to loose and to bind' become a standard reference to the endless disagreements that raged a little earlier between the two main rabbinical authorities, Shamma and Hillel. What the one loosed, the saying went, the other bound, and vice versa. [Referring to the above quotation] Flavius Josephus did not hint at anything novel in referring to the power of binding and loosing."[13] Jesus put an end to the disputes and the question of who has the *real* authority to bind and loose. Who has the *real* authority? He does! He delegated the royal authority to Peter, the steward and vizier of his new kingdom, and promised to ratify in heaven what Peter bound or loosed on earth. This also introduces the issue of infallibility, for Jesus could not promise to ratify Peter's earthly decisions in heaven if he were not certain of Peter's declarations. Jesus would have to protect Peter's teaching and judgments in order to make such a sweeping promise. Now to the heart of our study. Why did Jesus use the symbolism of the "keys" and "binding and loosing"? Is there an Old Testament precedent for the use of such phrases? Is there Jewish precedent for the idea of Peter being the royal steward of the palace?

III. Governmental Mind-Set of the Jews

Matthew, the only evangelist to record the discourse about the rock, the keys, the gates of hell, and the power to loose and bind,

---

heim (*The Life and Times of Jesus the Messiah* [Grand Rapids, Mich.: Eerdmans, 1972], 2:645) that "the power of 'loosing' and 'binding' referred to the legislative authority claimed by, and conceded to, the Rabbinic College. . . . In the true sense, therefore, this is rather administrative, disciplinary power, 'the power of the keys' . . . the power of admission and exclusion, of the authoritative declaration of the forgiveness of sins, in the exercise of which power (as it seems to the present writer [Edersheim]) the authority for the administration of the Holy Sacraments is also involved."

[13] Stanley L. Jaki, *The Keys of the Kingdom* (Chicago: Franciscan Herald Press, 1986), 43.

was a Jew writing to Jews. In order to place these amazing words of Jesus in their full proper context and to help us understand the cultural, biblical, and social background that caused the words to ring with meaning in the ears of the listeners, we must go to several Old Testament passages, allowing Scripture to interpret Scripture. Matthew was presenting Jesus as the king of the new kingdom of God, and he drew heavily on history and the Old Testament Scriptures, in which his listeners were steeped. They longed for the day when the Messiah, the son of David, would free them from the tyranny of Rome and reestablish the earthly kingdom. The words Jesus used would have immediately brought such things to mind. Keys represented royal authority; binding and loosing represented judicial authority. Old Testament history, the prophetic words of Isaiah, the teaching authority of the rabbis, and the whole monarchical structure of the Eastern kingdoms suggest this.

Today we are far removed from the ancient Jewish mind-set. We think like democracy-loving Americans, not like first-century Jews. We have contempt for hierarchies and monarchies. We threw off such antiquated systems long ago and revel in our egalitarian and "level" society. Not only do we dislike hierarchical governments, but we have even forgotten how to understand or relate to them. The Jews of Jesus' day had centuries of monarchical government behind them and were then ruled by an Empire under the Caesars of Rome. Jesus was not speaking to his followers about the coming "*democracy* of God"; rather, he spoke of the *kingdom* of God, a hierarchy, the kind of government that the ancient Eastern cultures understood plainly. Democracy was not within their range of experience. These people thought in terms of hierarchies, kings and kingdoms, authorities, ruling officials, and obedience. Let us look first at a passage from Isaiah 22 for a better understanding of this.

IV. Eliakim, the Royal Steward "Over the House" (Is 22)

Speaking for God, Isaiah proclaims, "And I will place on his [Eliakim's] shoulder the key of the house of David; he shall open, and none shall shut; and he shall shut, and none shall open" (Is 22:22). King Hezekiah ascended the throne of David in 715 B.C. and ruled the land of Judah. The key of David was on the shoulder of Shebna, the royal steward.[14] Isaiah prophesies that Shebna will be removed from his office and the key of David will be given to Eliakim, his successor. Not a Jew alive, at least no one who had been to the synagogue for the reading of the law and the Prophets, would have missed the implication of Jesus' utterance. Jesus' statement did not recall this passage in Isaiah without reason— Jesus always had profound reasons for saying what he said and for using the Old Testament passages he selected. He targeted this eight-hundred-year-old prophecy because of the governmental office that Isaiah was addressing and the parallel context Jesus was addressing. Both involved kingdoms; both involved delegated authority; both involved the appointment of royal stewards. Both situations had to do with royal appointments, and both would have decisive impacts on the respective kingdoms. Let us look at the passage from Isaiah in its entirety:

> Thus says the Lord God of hosts, "Come, go to this steward, to Shebna, who is over the household, and say to him: What have you to do here and whom have you here, that you have hewn here a tomb for yourself, you who hew a tomb on the height, and carve a habitation for yourself in the rock? . . . I will thrust you from your office, and you will be cast down from your station. In that day I will call my servant Eliakim the son of Hilkiah, and I will clothe him with your robe, and will bind your girdle on him, and will commit your authority to his hand; and he shall be a father to the inhabitants of Jerusalem and to the house of Judah. *And I will place on his shoulder the key of the house of David; he shall open, and none shall shut; and he shall shut, and none shall open.* And I will fasten him like a peg in a sure place, and he will become a throne of honor to his father's house. And they will hang on him the whole weight of his father's house, the offspring and issue, every small vessel, from the cups to all the flagons" (Is 22:15–16, 19–24, emphasis added).

Jesus is intentionally drawing attention to the context of Isaiah's prophecy—a new steward is being placed over the kingdom of

---

[14] Until roughly the time of the Romans, keys were very large, usually nine inches or longer, and made of wood embedded with metal spikes. These keys were hung over the shoulder due to their size and as a demonstration of the authority possessed by the one who carried them. For more information on keys and their history, see John L. McKenzie, *Dictionary of the Bible* (New York: Simon & Schuster, 1995), 472–73, and for more detailed information, especially in relation to scriptural references, see Jaki, *Keys of the Kingdom.*

Judah—as the backdrop for his current appointment of Peter as steward over *his* kingdom. Jesus ascends the throne of David as the heir and successor of the kings of Israel and Judah, and he too, according to custom and legal precedent, appoints a royal steward over his kingdom. Notice the words used to describe the steward: he has an "office"; he is "over the household [vizier]"; "authority" is committed into his hand; he shall be a "father" to the people of God; he is given the "keys" of authority; he has the unquestioned supremacy to open and shut so that no one can oppose him; he is fastened firmly as a peg; he will "become a throne of honor to his father's house"; and on him will hang the weight of everything in the king's house, including the offspring and issue and every small thing. This is really an amazing passage. Was it by chance that Jesus drew his listeners' ears to this prophecy? Was it by coincidence that Matthew drew his reader's eyes to this prophetic passage?

V. Comparing Eliakim and Peter

The parallels between Peter and Eliakim are striking. The physical kingdom of Israel has been superseded by the spiritual kingdom of God. The office of steward in the old economy is now superseded by the Petrine office with the delegation and handing on of the keys. The office of steward was successive, and so is the Petrine office in the new kingdom. Interestingly enough, James White refers to this obvious correlation as a "novel attempt by Roman Catholic apologists to apply Isaiah 22 and the key to the house of David to Peter himself in Matthew 16. Such an attempted connection is logically necessary for the Roman position, for there must be some effort made to establish succession in this passage, for Matthew's words make no mention of it." [15] Going against the stream of current scholarship, Catholic and Protestant alike, White attempts to make a distinction between the keys mentioned in Isaiah and those mentioned by Jesus. He quotes Revelation 3:7 [16] and makes the argument that key is *singular* in Isaiah and

---

[15] James White, *The Roman Catholic Controversy* (Minneapolis: Bethany, 1996), 249.

[16] "The words of the holy one, the true one, who has the key of David, who opens and no one shall shut, who shuts and no one opens."

Revelation while *plural,* "keys", in Matthew, therefore negating the possibility that the "keys" of Matthew could have any relation to the "key" of Isaiah and Revelation.[17] Even though the overwhelming consensus of scholars, historians, and commentators espouses the correlation between Isaiah and Matthew, let us take a quick look at White's objections. He sees a correlation only between Isaiah and Revelation and excludes Matthew from the equation; yet, White's reasoning in support of this position actually works against him. The passages in Isaiah and Revelation seem to refer to different keys: the latter to the "key of David", the former to "the key of *the house of David* ". Is White sure *these* are the same keys? We also find other keys mentioned in Revelation: "the keys of Death and Hades" (1:18), "the key of the shaft of the bottomless pit" (9:1), and "the key of the bottomless pit" (20:1). (Is it not interesting, with these last three passages in mind, that after Jesus gives Peter the keys, he mentions "the gates of hell"?) Would it be incorrect to consider all these keys, and not *just* the key of David, as belonging to our Lord? We find more than one key possessed by the Eternal King—keys in the plural. Add the "key of David" to these others keys, and we now see more than one key for sure— "keys". But, in reality, "keys" are not used literally in the New Testament, in the singular or the plural; rather, they are symbolic.[18] They symbolize governmental supremacy and judicial

---

[17] According to J. Jeremias, in his article "κλεις" [keys], "Materially, then, the keys of the kingdom of God are not different from the key of David. This is confirmed by the fact that in Mt. 16:19, as in Rev. 3:7, Jesus is the One who controls them. . . . We should also note that in the usage of the Bible and later Judaism handing over the keys does not have the sense of appointing a porter. . . . Hence handing over the keys implies appointment of full authority" (*Theological Dictionary of the New Testament,* ed. Gerhard Kittel, trans. Geoffrey Bromiley [Grand Rapids, Mich.: Eerdmans, 1968], 3:749–50). As Scott Butler writes, "The Lord Jesus Christ ultimately holds the authority of all keys and has delegated a certain authority of these keys to Peter on earth. A king never relinquishes his authority to hold the keys, but he may delegate his authority to whomever he pleases. They then both hold the authority of the keys, one by right, the other by delegation" (Scott Butler, Norman Dahlgren, and David Hess, *Jesus, Peter and the Keys* [Santa Barbara, Calif.: Queenship Pub., 1996], 58).

[18] "We may first note that the key is *the symbol of authority.* Here is the picture of Jesus Christ as the one who has the final authority which no one can question" (William Barclay, *The Revelation of John* [Philadelphia: Westminster Press, 1976], 1:127–28). "Christ is now described as having 'the key of David,' a metaphorical

authority, special access, the power to include and exclude, to open and shut, to bind and to loose. They are used as metaphors for authority and official position: "Symbolically, the key is a sign of authority. In Isa. 22:22, the 'key to the house of David' involves the expression of royal authority.... Jesus gave the 'keys of heaven' to Peter. This act must be interpreted in view of the symbolic significance of keys." [19]

Besides that, the keys, be they singular or plural, show us the actual extent of the power given to Peter as Jesus' deputy. The key of David or the key of the house of David is limited, in that it is related to the "house of David" (precisely why Jesus uses this metaphor in dealing with Jews in Revelation 3:7), whereas the keys given to Peter represent official authority in a wider sphere, a larger kingdom: not the Old Covenant people of God, the Jews, but the New Covenant, the eternal covenant embodied in the new wineskins, the Church. The "key" of David has now become the "keys" of the kingdom, a universal, or *catholic*, kingdom. This fits with the overall picture: the national covenant becomes universal; what was limited to the land of Israel now expands to include the whole world—from a house to a kingdom! Peter as the prime minister is not limited to the rule of one nation under an earthly king, but as the deputy he is now to govern the whole world under a heavenly king. St. John Chrysostom understood this when he praised Peter with the words, "At all events the master of the whole world, Peter, to whose hands He [Jesus] committed the keys of heaven, whom He commanded to do and to bear all." [20] The power to open and close is now interpreted by Jesus, in this universal kingdom, as the power to bind and loose in the then current terminology of rabbinic thought.

In Revelation 3:7 Jesus, the risen Messiah, announces to John in a vision that he possesses the key of David.[21] In other words, he

---

expression indicating complete control over the royal household" (Robert Mounce, *The New International Commentary on the New Testament: The Book of Revelation* [Grand Rapids, Mich.: Eerdmans, 1977], 116).

[19] *The Revell Bible Dictionary*, ed. Lawrence O. Richards (Old Tappan, N.J.: Fleming H. Revell, 1990), 603, 604.

[20] *Homily on St. Ignatius*, NPNF1, 9:138.

[21] "In the New Testament this phrase is regularly attached to Jesus. It is in his hands, and no one else's, that the keys are. In *Revelation* 1:18 the risen Christ says: 'I am the living one; I died, and behold I am alive for evermore, and I have

has complete authority over the kingdom of the Jews by holding the key.

This was written during a time of great persecution. In fact, John was in exile while writing Revelation (Rev 1:9). Because the Church is being persecuted at the time of writing, Jesus assures his Church that he is in charge, even if for a while they are being persecuted by "the synogogue of Satan who say they were Jews and are not, but lie" (Rev 3:9). Jesus possesses the key to the new kingdom.[22] Now, in that *new* kingdom he has hand picked his royal steward and has entrusted him with the authority symbolized by those keys. There is nothing here to restrict the one in possession of the keys from delegating them to a deputy. It is clear that no dichotomy can be forced between Jesus and the key of the house of David, and Peter with the delegated keys of the new Davidic kingdom.

In discussing the investiture of royal stewardship upon Eliakim, Protestant Old Testament scholars C. F. Keil and F. Delitzsch comment, "There is a resemblance [with Eliakim] to the giving of the keys of the kingdom of heaven to Peter under the New Testament."[23] Peter is called to mind as we compare these Scripture

---

the keys of Death and Hades.' Again in *Revelation* 3:7 the Risen Christ is described as, 'The holy one, the true one, who has the key of David, who opens and no one shall shut, who shuts and no one opens.' This phrase must be interpreted as indicating a certain divine right, and whatever the promise made to Peter, it cannot be taken as annulling, or infringing, a right which belongs alone to God and to the Son of God.

"All these New Testament pictures and usages go back to a picture in *Isaiah* (Is 22:22). Isaiah describes Eliakim, who will have the key of the house of David on his shoulder, and who alone will open and shut. Now the duty of Eliakim was to be *the faithful steward of the house*. It is the steward who carries the keys of the house, who in the morning opens the door, and in the evening shuts it, and through whom visitors gain access to the royal presence. So then what Jesus is saying to Peter is that in the days to come, he will be *the steward of the Kingdom*" (Barclay, *Gospel of Matthew*, 2:144–45).

[22] "These verses [Revelation 3:7–8] clearly allude to Isaiah 22:22, which speaks of one who had David's key to open and shut, indicating full authorization to rule the house. To Jewish Christians excluded from the synagogue [cf. Jn 9:22], this was Jesus' encouragement that he who rightly ruled the house of David now acknowledged them as his own people" (Craig Keener, *The IVP Bible Background Commentary: New Testament* [Downers Grove, Ill.: InterVarsity Press, 1993], 773).

[23] *Isaiah*, 402. Concerning the "key to the house of David" in Isaiah 22, the *Jerome Biblical Commentary* comments "The key, symbol of the majordomo's

passages; Peter's appointment resembles the unique and singular authority given to Eliakim, the "steward", or official "over the house" in Judah. Messianic Jew David Stern tells us that Jesus makes Peter both *"shammash* ('steward'), with the keys, and *dayan* ('judge'), who, as the one who can prohibit and permit, establishes new covenant *halakhah* [law, customs]." [24]

Protestant biblical scholar F. F. Bruce writes, "And what about the 'keys of the kingdom'? The keys of a royal or noble establishment were entrusted to the chief steward or major-domo; he carried them on his shoulder in earlier times, and there they served as a badge of the authority entrusted to him. About 700 B.C. an oracle from God [through Isaiah] announced that this authority in the royal palace in Jerusalem was to be conferred on a man called Eliakim: 'I will place on his shoulder the key of the house of David; he shall open, and none shall shut; and he shall shut, and none shall open' (Isa. 22:22). So in the new community which Jesus was about to build, Peter would be, so to speak, chief steward." [25]

The Interpreter's Bible confirms this understanding of Isaiah 22. "The keys of the kingdom would be committed to the chief steward in the royal household and with them goes plenary authority. In Isa. 22:22 the key of the house of David is promised to Eliakim. According to Paul, Jesus is the only foundation (1 Cor. 3:11), and in Rev. 1:18; 3:7, Jesus possesses the key of David and the keys of

---

authority to grant or deny admittance to the royal presence, was worn over the shoulder. The images used here to denote the authority of the steward are very similar to those of Mt 16:19 . . . and Jn 20:23" (*The Jerome Biblical Commentary*, ed. Raymond E. Brown, Joseph A. Fitzmyer, and Roland E. Murphy [Englewood Cliffs, N.J.: Prentice Hall, 1968], 276).

[24] David Stern, *Jewish New Testament Commentary* (Clarksville, Md.: Jewish New Testament Pub., 1992), 54. "A similar passage [to Isaiah 22] in the NT is used of the authority Peter is to have in the emerging Christian community (Matt. 16:19). The 'keys' of the kingdom suggest the image of the steward with the keys to the rooms and storechambers of the house. Not only does the bearer of the 'key' have authority to determine who is admitted, the chief steward also has responsibility for overseeing all that takes place in the master's house" (*Harper's Bible Dictionary*, ed. Paul J. Achtemeier [San Francisco: Harper and Row, 1985], 524–25). Remember my earlier reference to R. T. France, who, speaking of Matthew 16, said, "Isaiah 22 [is] generally regarded as the Old Testament background to the metaphor of the keys."

[25] F. F. Bruce, *The Hard Sayings of Jesus* (Downers Grove, Ill.: InterVarsity Press, 1983), 143–44.

death and Hades. But in this passage Peter is made the foundation and holds the keys. Post-Apostolic Christianity is now beginning to ascribe to the apostles the prerogatives of Jesus (cf. [Mt] 10:40)."[26]

Confirming again that Peter is being placed as a steward within the context of a spiritualized monarchical Judah, we read that "Isa xxii 15 ff. undoubtedly lies behind this saying [of Jesus regarding Peter and the keys]. *The keys* are the symbol of authority, and Roland de Vaux (*Ancient Israel*, trans. by John McHugh [New York: McGraw-Hill, 1961], pp. 129 ff.) rightly sees here the same authority as that vested in the vizier, the master of the house, the chamberlain, of the royal household in ancient Israel. Eliakim is described as having the same authority [as Peter] in Isaiah."[27] Also, "The keys of the kingdom of heaven: the phrase [from Mt 16:19] is almost certainly based on Isaiah 22:22 where Shebna the steward is displaced by Eliakim and his authority transferred to him."[28]

Keys represent exclusive dominion. The keys to a person's house give that person exclusive dominion over that house. Possession of the keys necessarily precludes others from dominion or control. Peter is invested with the keys and thereby is delegated exclusive dominion or authority of the kingdom of heaven. This is an amazing appointment, especially when interpreted in light of the scriptural and historical context. With the words and imagery of Isaiah—with the mental image of kings and kingdoms, keys and authority, officials and real delegation—Jesus appoints Peter as the visible and singular vicar or steward of his new kingdom. Peter is the visible representative (vicar) with a commission from Christ to lead and govern visibly the people of the new and eternal covenant during the absence of the visible Christ the King.[29] As we

---

[26] *The Interpreter's Bible*, ed. George Buttrick et al. (Nashville, Tenn.: Abingdon, 1980), 7:453.

[27] W. F. Albright and C. S. Mann, eds., *The Anchor Bible: Matthew* (Garden City, N.Y.: Doubleday, 1971), 196.

[28] D. Guthrie et al., *The New Bible Commentary* (Grand Rapids, Mich.: Eerdmans, 1953), 837.

[29] It is often argued that the other apostles (and, by extension, perhaps all believers) have received the same authority (see Mt 18:18). However, only Peter is given the keys as the steward of the kingdom and appointed as shepherd over the flock (Jn 21:15–17). As observed by J. Jeremias (*Theological Dictionary*, 6:498), "The shepherds are the leaders of the local church; . . . only in Jn. 21:15–17, which describes the appointment of Peter as a shepherd by the Risen

allow Scripture to interpret Scripture, we begin to see more clearly how Jesus, the son of David, was setting up his kingdom as a unified and visible community with a recognized majordomo. Catholic and Protestant scholars alike agree that Jesus' appointment of Peter and the delegation of the keys should be understood against the backdrop of Isaiah 22:22. There is nothing novel in this approach. On the contrary, it is simply studying the New Testament in light of its Old Testament foundations—it is allowing Scripture to interpret Scripture.

Are there other Old Testament passages that shed light on this momentous pronouncement of Peter's stewardship? Let us look at a passage from Genesis, from a completely different period of time, to see if we can glean from Scripture more information that will shed light on Peter's incredible appointment.

VI. Israel's Monarchy Based on the Egyptian Model

We have already discussed the term "vizier" at some length to prepare for this section of our study. Now we look to Genesis to find another example of a steward or vizier ruling a kingdom as a substitute or deputy for the monarch. We find this in the story of Joseph, who was appointed by the Pharaoh as vizier over all the land of Egypt. We will discover here, too, amazing parallels to the appointment of Peter. But first, a little background before we proceed to compare the appointments of Joseph and Peter.

In contrast to the ancient kingdoms, such as Egypt, Israel was a newly formed nation—an infant nation. Egypt had existed as a nation for over one thousand years before Abraham left Ur and

---

Lord, does the whole Church seem to have been in view as the sphere of activity." Peter is appointed the shepherd of *the* Church, whereas the others are appointed shepherds of the *local* Churches. This is borne out in Matthew's Gospel, where Peter is given authority over the Church in chapter 16, whereas the context of chapter 18 is the local Churches, where the other apostles have "judicial" and "legislative" authority to deal with local situations. There is no conflict here, for as governments have various hierarchical levels yet work together as a whole, so the apostolic college had a head, yet each had authority in his proper right and worked together as a governmental whole, in harmony with one another. There is no indication that the authority of the keys was passed on to all believers, any more than the keys of David in the kingdom of Judah were passed on to every individual Jew.

settled in Canaan.[30] *Israel imitated the nations around her and adopted their forms of government.* In 1 Samuel 8:5 the Israelites pleaded for a king like the ones they saw governing the surrounding nations.[31] "The implications of this move were tremendous; we can see in the pages of the OT the increasing complexity of court life. With the kingship came the bureaucracy and the world of officialdom that royalty entails. Egypt would have been the most imposing model for Israel to follow (e.g. 1 Kgs 3:1). . . . The OT provides concrete evidence of the type of court official that functioned in Jerusalem: The list of officials in Solomon's reign (1 Kgs 4:1–6) mentions priests, scribes or secretaries, heralds, . . . and the major-domo of the palace. . . . What [was] more natural than that the training was at least in part patterned after the courtly ideals expressed in the ancient and imposing literature of Egypt?"[32]

Roland de Vaux, universally recognized scholar of ancient Israel, writes, "[In ancient Israel] it is noteworthy, too, that some of these high officials, or their fathers, have non-Israelite names. . . . In fact it was to be expected that the young Israelite kingdom should recruit some of its officials from the neighboring countries, which had an administrative tradition. Even for its organization it had to copy models abroad. Study of some offices suggests the influence of Egyptian institutions, but it does not enable us to decide whether this influence was direct, or whether it came indirectly to Israel from the Canaanite states which Israel displaced. Direct influence [from Egypt] seems the more likely."[33] Young

---

[30] Ancient Egypt was founded as a state as early as 3100 B.C., with kings of the First Dynasty in the Archaic Period from 3100–2650 B.C. (See Christine Hobson, *Exploring the World of the Pharaohs* [London: Thames and Hudson, 1987], and John Baines and Jaromír Málek, *Atlas of Ancient Egypt* [Cairo: Les Livres de France, 1980]). Conservative estimates place the life of Abraham in the Bronze Age, probably between 2000 and 1900 B.C. (*Eerdmans' Handbook to the Bible,* ed. David Alexander and Pat Alexander [Grand Rapids, Mich.: Eerdmans, 1973], 118).

[31] 1 Sam 8:4–5, 19–20: "Then all the elders of Israel gathered together and came to Samuel at Ramah, and said to him, 'Behold, you are old and your sons do not walk in your ways; now appoint for us a king to govern us like all the nations.' . . . But the people refused to listen to the voice of Samuel; and they said, 'No! but we will have a king over us, that we also may be like all the nations, and that our king may govern us and go out before us and fight our battles.' "

[32] Brown, Fitzmyer, and Murphy, *Jerome Biblical Commentary,* 488.

[33] Vaux, *Ancient Israel,* 129. Another scholar concurs: "A royal administrative system began to be organized on Egyptian lines" (G. W. Anderson, *The History*

Israel chose a form of government, including a hierarchy of officials, patterned from the surrounding nations.

The Jews adopted the governmental structure of the surrounding nations. Nowhere in the Old Testament do we find any instructions for setting up a kingdom or appointing the designated
officials. From "Scripture alone" they had no such blueprint from
God. They built their kingdom on the Egyptian model, although
the basic structure was found in all the Eastern kingdoms. The
royal steward was one of the ministerial positions that continued
until the end of the monarchy. Examples abound: Haman held
this position under King Ahasuerus in Persia and was replaced by
Mordecai after the intercession of Esther. Obadiah was "over the
house", or vizier, during the reign of King Ahab of Israel (1 Kings
18:3–16). Ahishar was "over the house" or majordomo over the
kingdom of Solomon.[34] In the time of Jesus, and actually known by
Jesus and the apostles, was a woman named Joanna, who was
healed by Christ and who assisted in maintaining the Lord's itiner-
ant company. She was the "wife of Chuza, Herod's steward" (Lk
8:3), which shows the prevalence of this important and influential
office.

"[In Egypt] toward the end of the third millennium and into
the early second millennium, more and more governmental
authority became distributed among the nobles, and with the
rise of the Egyptian empire in the eighteenth dynasty an enor-
mous bureaucracy had to be established to handle the affairs of
government. The chief officer in this bureaucracy was the vizier
(Egyptian *tjaty*). The description given in Genesis 41–47 of

---

and Religion of Israel [London: Oxford Univ. Press, 1989], 56). Also, "Solomon
set up the office [master of the palace, royal steward] in imitation of the office of
Pharaoh's vizier. Unlike in Assyria and Babylon, where the master of the palace
was a mere administrator of the king's household affairs, in Egypt as well as in
Judah and Israel the master of the palace was the second in command after the
king" (Jaki, *Keys of the Kingdom*, 27–28).

[34] Other biblical examples can be found in Genesis 24:2; 39:4; 1 Kings 4:6;
16:9; 18:3; 2 Kings 10:5; 15:5; 2 Chronicles 28:7; Esther 3:1–2, 8:1–2. "Outside
the Bible, the title [steward or master of the palace] appears in the inscription of
a tomb in Siloam (the name is incomplete: could it be the tomb of Shebna? cf.
Is 22:16), and on a seal-impression in the name of Godolias, doubtless the man
whom Nabuchodonosor installed as governor of Judah after the capture of
Jerusalem (2 K 25:22; Jr 40:7). He would formerly have been master of the
palace under Sedecias, the last king of Judah" (Vaux, *Ancient Israel*, 129–30).

Joseph's responsibilities under Pharaoh reflects the duties of a vizier."[35]

Egypt was very impressive, and its governmental structure was quite familiar to the Israelite people. Joseph had been grand vizier of Egypt, and the Jews had suffered slavery under the Pharaohs for centuries. Moses had been adopted into the royal family by the Pharaoh's daughter (Ex 2:1–10). All the monarchs of the surrounding nations had viziers, and Israel organized their officials according to the same pattern.

VII. Pharaoh, Joseph, and the Office of Vizier in the Egyptian Dynasties

Let us take a look at the story of Joseph. He was the favorite son of Jacob (Gen 37:3) and was sold into slavery in Egypt by his brothers (Gen 37:28). After being a steward of Potiphar's household, he was unjustly cast into prison, where he stayed more than two years (Gen 41:1). Later, Pharaoh had a dream and asked if there was anyone who could interpret his dream. Joseph was brought before Pharaoh, and with the help of God he correctly interpreted Pharaoh's dream—he received a direct revelation from God as to the meaning of Pharaoh's dream. He answered the king's question with words provided by God himself. As a result, he was appointed vizier of Egypt with absolute authority. His only limitation was the throne itself. Pharaoh said, "Only as regards the throne will I be greater than you" (Gen 41:40). The vizier does not seize the throne; rather, the vizier submits to and serves the throne. In order to understand the profound parallels with the appointment of Peter and Jesus' kingdom, let us take a closer look at the appointment of Joseph as the vizier of Egypt.

> And Pharaoh said to his servants, "Can we find such a man as this, in whom is the Spirit of God?" So Pharaoh said to Joseph, "Since God has shown you all this, there is none so discreet and wise as you are; you shall be over my house, and all my people shall order themselves as you command; only as regards the throne will I be greater than you." And Pharaoh said to Joseph, "Behold, I have set you over all the land of Egypt." Then Pharaoh took his signet ring from his hand and put it on Joseph's hand, and arrayed him in

---

[35] Achtemeier, *Harper's Bible Dictionary*, 781.

garments of fine linen, and put a gold chain about his neck; and he made him to ride in his second chariot; and they cried before him, "Bow the knee!" Thus he set him over all the land of Egypt. Moreover Pharaoh said to Joseph, "I am Pharaoh, and without your consent no man shall lift up hand or foot in all the land of Egypt." And Pharaoh called Joseph's name Zaphenath-paneah; and he gave him in marriage Asenath, the daughter of Potiphera priest of On. So Joseph went out over the land of Egypt (Gen 41:38–46).

Joseph later tells his brothers, "He [God] has made me a father to Pharaoh, and lord of all his house and ruler over all the land of Egypt" (Gen 45:8).

Israel based its governmental structure on the Egyptian model, and Jesus appointed Peter according to the Judean monarchy's model. Are there parallels between Joseph and Peter that can instruct us about Jesus' appointment of Peter as vizier of his heavenly kingdom?[36]

What was the basis for Joseph's royal appointment? It was a divine revelation in response to a question from the king. What about Peter? Was he not appointed steward based upon a divine revelation in response to a question from the King, Jesus? Both of their appointments to official office were based, not on "flesh and blood", but on the Father's revelation from heaven. It is amazing that Pharaoh would have so quickly given such great responsibility to a young foreigner. It is just as amazing that Christ would do the same with an uneducated fisherman. But Pharaoh says it all: "Can we find such a man as this, in whom is the Spirit of God?" (Gen 41:38). Revelation was the basis upon which the respective kings recognized the potential and divine calling of Joseph and Peter.

Joseph was given the sign of official authority, which in Egypt was the signet ring of the king. The Pharaoh took the signet ring off his own finger and placed it on the finger of Joseph. In Israel the "key" was the corresponding sign of royal authority, and

---

[36] Commenting on the position of royal steward under the successors of David, John Watts writes, "By Hezekiah's time the position [of royal steward] had grown in importance in much the same way that Joseph's grew under Pharaoh (Gen 40–44; 45:8). Shebna's position must have been very much like that of a vizier in Egypt, 'all affairs of the land passed through his hands, all important documents received his seal, all the officials were under his orders. He really governed in Pharaoh's name . . .' (R. de Vaux, *Ancient Israel*, 130)", (*Isaiah 1–33*, 290).

it belongs exclusively to Jesus.[37] But we are given the valuable glimpse back in time to the city of Caesarea Philippi, where Jesus takes the keys of the kingdom that he possesses and gives them to Peter, as his delegated vicar.

Pharaoh issued Joseph his second chariot, giving him the status, power, and means to travel throughout the land, governing and ruling the entire population of Egypt. Joseph was given the charism of *infallible interpretation* from God and therefore the final word in legal and judicial matters by the king. In terms that reflect the power to "bind" and "loose" given to Peter, Joseph was given authority to control every movement in Egypt: "Moreover Pharaoh said to Joseph, 'I am Pharaoh, and without your consent no man shall lift up hand or foot in all the land of Egypt' " (Gen 41:44).[38] In addition, wherever Joseph traveled in his royal chariot the forward guard bellowed out, commanding the admiring crowds to "Bow the knee!" Peter's power to "bind" and "loose" in the visible Church on earth was ratified by the King himself in heaven. Peter was appointed shepherd to feed (care for, teach) the sheep and to tend (govern, rule) the lambs (Jn 21:15–17) in a universal or catholic sense. The sheep, recognizing the divine appointment of the shepherd, are wise to respond to that appointment with respect and obedience.

As we have mentioned before, name changes in Scripture are very momentous and meaningful. When childless Abram—

---

[37] In the section of the Israel Museum in Jerusalem devoted to Israel's history during the kings of Judah and Israel there is a display of rings, including several signet rings. A clear plastic plaque engraved above the display has the words "Seal-impression of Nathan the Royal Steward from the 7th–8th century B.C. The Royal Steward was the senior official. . . . The Bible mentions several Royal Stewards who served Kings in Israel and Judah. During the divided Monarchy the highest offices appear to have remained unchangeable and continued to be hereditary. This was current among the neighboring people as well." The royal steward served the king; he was the senior official in an office of succession that remained unchangeable, even hereditary.

[38] Psalm 105:17–22 provides insight into Joseph's authority: "He had sent a man ahead of them, Joseph, who was sold as a slave. His feet were hurt with fetters, his neck was put in a collar of iron; until what he had said came to pass the word of the Lord tested him. The king sent and released him, the ruler of the peoples set him free; he made him lord of his house, and ruler of all his possessions, to instruct his princes at his pleasure, and to teach his elders wisdom."

meaning "father"—was promised a son and given the covenant, God changed his name to Abraham ("father of nations"). The name change signified a change in status, commission, or calling. It was a prophecy. The significance could not be seen at the time, but it became obvious later. Simon's name was changed to Rock [Peter] by King Jesus himself, to signify a change of status—from fisherman to royal steward—a new calling, a commission. What about Joseph? Is there a parallel? As soon as Joseph was appointed vizier of Egypt, the king changed his name. "And Pharaoh called Joseph's name Zaphenath-paneah" (Gen 41:45).[39] Two kings each ask a question; two divine revelations are given; two common men are chosen to be stewards of the king's realm; two men are given unquestioned legislative and judicial authority; two men are given the king's own possession as a sign of their royal office; two men are given new names by their kings to mark their new position and status; two men are provided with brides—two men stand in the place of the king.[40] Coincidence?

Joseph was in a unique position, having received the gift of divine revelation in the interpretation of dreams. "The miraculous power of God is to be seen in the fact, that *God endowed Joseph with the gift of infallible interpretation,* and so ordered the circumstances that this gift opened the way for him to occupy that position in which he became the preserver, not of Egypt alone, but of his own family also."[41] As we compare the situations of Joseph and Peter, we again see similarities. Peter has been promised ratification from heaven on his "binding" and "loosing" and must therefore be given assistance from God, something similar to a "gift of infallible interpretation" such as Keil and Delitzsch attribute to Joseph. They write that Joseph was given this "divine gift of infal-

---

[39] There is general disagreement over the meaning of Joseph's Egyptian name. Some think it means "God lives, God speaks", while others believe it means "savior of the world" or "sustainer of life". Stigers writes, "The renaming of Joseph as *Zaphenath-paneah* was the last step in his exaltation. The meaning of Joseph's new name, 'God has spoken, and he shall live'.... By this name, Pharaoh memorialized the gift of interpretation as being the one thing above all others that qualified Joseph for his weighty task" (Harold Stigers, *A Commentary on Genesis* [Grand Rapids, Mich.: Zondervan, 1976], 291).

[40] It is possible that the bride given to Joseph by the Pharaoh parallels the Church given into the custodial hands of Peter by the King.

[41] C. F. Keil and F. Delitzsch, *The Pentateuch,* vol. 1 of *Commentary on the Old Testament* (Grand Rapids, Mich.: Eerdmans, 1978), 352; emphasis added.

lible interpretation" in order to be the "preserver" of Egypt and his family. In a similar way, the Pope has been granted the gift of infallibility in interpreting the revelation of God in order to preserve and feed the people of God—the Church—in unity, faith, and morals. Joseph is a biblical example of God's willingness to protect a man's teaching, in other words, to use a fallible man to give an infallible interpretation.

VIII. Comparing Joseph and Peter

So, we see in Scripture three cases of stewards or viziers invested with the authority of "second-in-command" of a kingdom as a vicar or steward for the king. The king leaves the administration of his kingdom in the hands of his delegated majordomo. The parallels are too striking to be mere coincidence. To understand Christ's words in light of the biblical history is to see that Jesus is establishing his Church with a majordomo in place to rule and govern in his absence. Scripture interpreting Scripture gives us the background so that we can rightly understand the full intention of our Lord Jesus when he gave Peter the keys to the kingdom of heaven.

Probing the Old Testament for light on New Testament passages is "rightly dividing the word of truth". Cultures build one upon another. Revelation builds upon revelation, Scripture upon Scripture. Biblical concepts and truths depend in large measure upon revelation that has preceded. The Old Testament contains the New Testament concealed; the New Testament contains the Old Testament revealed. Is it not then advisable to go to the "law and the Prophets" to understand Jesus and his kingdom in the New Covenant?

Referring to Matthew 16 and the "keys", Protestant commentator Matthew Henry sees the clear correlation and writes, "The power here delegated is a spiritual power; it is a power pertaining to the kingdom of heaven, that is, to the Church.... It is the power to bind and to loose, that is (following the metaphor of the keys), to shut and open. Joseph, who was lord of Pharaoh's house, and steward of his stores, had power to bind his princes, and to teach his senators wisdom (Psa 105:21, 22)."[42]

---

[42] *Matthew Henry's Commentary* (1721; reprint, McLean, Va.: MacDonald Pub., n. d.), 5:233.

In the context of Joseph as the vizier of Egypt, Roland de Vaux writes, "In Israel the powers of the master of the palace were far more extensive and the similarity between his functions and those of the Egyptian vizier is even more important than the verbal resemblances. This vizier used to report every morning to the Pharaoh and receive his instructions. . . . All the affairs of the land passed through his hands, all important documents received his seal, all the officials were under his orders. He really governed in the Pharaoh's name and acted for him in his absence. This is obviously the dignity which Joseph exercised, according to Genesis. . . . The master of the palace had similar functions at the court of Judah. . . . One is reminded of our Lord's words to Peter, Vizier of the Kingdom of Heaven (Mt 16:19)."[43]

To understand Scripture properly, one has to set aside his preconceived ideas about what it was like in the old days and what "the Bible means to me". The life of ancient cultures was very different from what we know today. We must grasp the Egyptian and Hebrew cultures and governmental structure to comprehend the words of Jesus spoken to Peter. "Once the Hebrew figures of speech have been understood, the text [Mt 16:16–19] has no real difficulties. Far from it. St. Peter is here promised the supreme authority in the church in such clear terms, that it is hard to see how the idea could have been expressed with greater force or precision."[44]

Egypt's Pharaoh and his vizier, Judah's king and his steward, Jesus' kingdom of heaven and his vicar—all portray in clear colors the ancient blueprint for Eastern kingdoms. All together they make crystal clear the intent of Jesus' commission to Peter. But now that we have come to this biblically based conclusion, a ques-

---

[43] Vaux, *Ancient Israel*, 130. Professor of Old Testament studies Harold Stigers writes, "Note well that the era of Joseph is to be placed in the Hyksos Era [as] seen in v. 43 where the royal chariot is mentioned, for the chariot was not used in Egypt before this time. The Hyksos introduced it into Egypt and by its use enforced the power of later Pharaoh's [*sic*] in Palestine and Syria. With the Hyksos Era dated to c. 1750–1550 B.C. Joseph's date would be considerably later than the beginning of this era, thus to allow for consolidation of power in Egypt, represented in the aura of power surrounding the Pharaoh" (Stigers, *A Commentary on Genesis*, 290).

[44] Michael M. Winter, *Saint Peter and the Popes* (Baltimore, Md.: Helicon Press, 1960), 18.

tion still remains: What about succession?[45] Even if one concedes that Peter had the primacy and was the royal steward of Christ's new covenantal kingdom, what about the question of succession? Is it possible that the office of Peter is perpetual? And can anyone today possibly claim to be in that office, as Peter's successor?

IX. The Question of Succession

A. *Based on Old Testament Viziers and Stewards*

The Catholic Church has consistently taught from the first centuries that the office of Peter is an office that continues to exist and exercise the authority of the keys. What can we learn from the ancient kingdoms and their office of vizier and steward "over the house" about succession?

The vizier was an office of supreme importance to the kingdom of Egypt. It should be remembered that it was not a person, but an office. When the vizier died the office did *not*. The office continued to exist, and in the event of death or displacement,

---

[45] In general terms succession means the act or process of following in order or sequence. Applied to our study, it means the sequence in which one person succeeds or follows another in continuance of an office or the exercise of authority. With respect to Peter, it means that he had successors who fulfilled the Christ-established ministry conferred on Peter. The *Catechism of the Catholic Church,* quoting *Lumen gentium* 20, explains how this succession to the office in the Church occurs.

"In order that the mission entrusted to them might be continued after their death, [the apostles] consigned, by will and testament, as it were, to their immediate collaborators the duty of completing and consolidating the work they had begun, urging them to tend to the whole flock, in which the Holy Spirit had appointed them to shepherd the Church of God. They accordingly designated such men and then made the ruling that likewise on their death other proven men should take over their ministry" (CCC 861).

"Just as the office which the Lord confided to Peter alone, as first of the apostles, destined to be transmitted to his successors, is a permanent one, so also endures the office, which the apostles received, of shepherding the Church, a charge destined to be exercised without interruption by the sacred order of bishops. Hence the Church teaches that the bishops have by divine institution taken the place of the apostles as pastors of the Church, in such wise that whoever listens to them is listening to Christ and whoever despises them despises Christ and him who sent Christ" (CCC 862).

another man would be appointed to fill the vacant office. Likewise, the presidency of the United States or secretariat of state is an *office*, not a person. When the president of the United States dies, it is a matter of immediate concern. All parties mobilize to invest a new man with the authority of the office. In this case the vice-president automatically succeeds to the position. The presidential seal remains firmly ensconced above the office of the president of the United States. Over the years men have, through succession, sworn the oath of office—the same seal remains over each of them as the symbol of authority and legal succession.

In some Egyptian dynasties the vizier would outlive or outlast several successive pharaohs. We also know that the vizier system within the Egyptian dynasties was "powerful, almost hereditary".[46] The office of vizier was present throughout the dynasties. It was an office that persisted through the centuries, with viziers succeeding one after another. We can see a glimpse of this in the kingdom of the Medes and the Persians. When the wicked Haman, the vizier in possession of the royal seal, attempted to commit genocide on the Jews, he was hung by the neck. Mordecai the Jew succeeded to his office and, as a sign, was given the royal seal (Esther 8:1–2). The majordomo dies, the office does not. There is always a succession of "personnel".

What about our other example, Shebna the steward and Eliakim his successor? I find it rather intriguing that Protestants, who scoff at papal succession, are willing to admit there is a strong relationship between Isaiah 22 and Jesus' words to Peter and to speak of Eliakim *succeeding* Shebna. Fundamentalist Harry A. Ironside writes, "The successor of Shebna was Eliakim."[47] Matthew Henry writes, "It is here foretold, [*sic*] that Eliakim should be put into Shebna's place of lord-chamberlain of the household. . . . To hear of it would be a great mortification to Shebna, much more to see it. Great men, especially proud men, cannot endure their successors."[48] These two Protestant stalwarts do not hesitate to admit that Eliakim was the successor of Shebna and that the posi-

---

[46] *The World of the Bible*, ed. A. S. Van der Woude (Grand Rapids, Mich.: Eerdmans, 1986), 231.

[47] Harry A. Ironside, *Expository Notes on the Prophet Isaiah* (Neptune, N.J.: Loizeaux Brothers, 1952), 130.

[48] *Matthew Henry's Commentary*, 4:121.

tion of steward was one of succession. I would have to guess they would *not* have used such phraseology had they been thinking of this passage in relationship to Matthew 16. However, their comments confirm that the office of "steward" was one of succession. That the office of royal steward is successive (or dynastic) has great weight when one understands the relationship between the prophecy concerning Eliakim and that of Peter. The Old Testament makes a strong case for apostolic succession. Though Evangelicals have ignored this, it must be honestly faced if we want to understand Peter's commission properly. But that is not all; let us look a little farther.

How long had the office of steward existed as an official office in Israel (and Judah), or, in other words, how many years had the "key of David" and the power to "open and shut" been passed down from one royal steward to the next? During the reign of Solomon, we first discover Ahishar, who is "over the house" in 1 Kings 4:6. Ahishar seems to be the first person recorded in the Bible to be delegated with the keys of David, though he is not necessarily the first royal steward. Next we find Arza as steward "over the house" during the reign of King Elah (1 Kings 16:9). The next recorded steward is Obadiah, who was "over the house" during the reign of King Ahab (1 Kings 18:3). About 150 years later, Isaiah prophesies against Shebna and foretells the appointment of his successor, Eliakim. The Scriptures show us that the office of steward was one of succession—it was always filled. The keys of David were passed from one steward to the next throughout the history of Israel and later also in Judah. Since Jesus restored the throne of David, he also restored the office of royal steward. Jesus succeeded David; Peter succeeded Eliakim. Actually, the Pope is a successor not only of Peter but also, in a sense, of the first royal steward from the Davidic kingdom.

Butler explains the parallel successions of king and steward. "What two roles are in this line of succession? The roles of the king and his prime minister rule in parallel lines of succession, one passed on from generation to generation through offspring and issue, the other through appointment."[49]

---

[49] Scott Butler, Norman Dahlgren, and David Hess, *Jesus, Peter and the Keys* (Santa Barbara, Calif.: Queenship Pub., 1996), 51.

B. *Based on the Teaching Authority of Moses*

Now that we have analyzed the royal aspect of Israel and Judah, is there anything to be discovered from the priestly and scribal side of Jewish society that can shed light on the issue of succession? Let us again look back to the Pentateuch, this time at Moses. "On the morrow Moses *sat* to judge the people, and the people *stood* about Moses from morning till evening.[50] . . . And Moses said to his father-in-law, 'Because the people come to me to inquire of God; when they have a dispute, they come to me and I decide between a man and his neighbor, and I make them know the statutes of God and his decisions" (Ex 18:13, 15–16; emphasis added). Moses was the official teacher of Israel—the lawgiver, interpreter, and judge. Like Peter, Moses also had a direct revelation from God while standing at a huge rock, Mount Sinai.[51] Moses was infallible in his teaching and judgments. He sat from morning until night, judging the people and interpreting the law of God. His teaching authority (symbolized by the "seat of Moses") continued through the centuries, through succession, and was still prominent in the synagogues almost two thousand years later. This is prominently mentioned in the Gospels. Matthew tells us, "Then said Jesus to the crowds and to his disciples, 'The scribes and the Pharisees sit on Moses' seat; so practice and observe whatever they tell you' " (Mt 23:1–3). Moses

---

[50] The New International Version renders this: "The next day Moses *took his seat* to serve as judge for the people, and they stood around him from morning till evening" (emphasis added). We learn from R. Alan Cole that "[The words] *sat . . . stood* are technical terms of Semitic law, denoting "judge" and "litigant" respectively" (*Exodus: An Introduction and Commentary*, Tyndale Old Testament Commentaries [Downers Grove, Ill.: InterVarsity Press, 1973], 140). And earlier Cole tells us, "The administration of justice . . . is therefore not between sacred and secular but between difficult and simple matters, those already covered by tradition and revelation as against those requiring a fresh word from God, mediated through His agent, Moses" (ibid.). This is the backdrop of teaching authority in the synagogue and thus, ultimately, in the Church.

[51] Mount Sinai, a huge mountain of solid rock in the southern section of the Sinai Peninsula, is 2,285 meters high and has 3,750 torturous steps up to the summit. When Jesus changed Simon's name to Peter and entrusted him with the keys, he was in Caesarea Philippi, also near a huge rock, this one a precipice five hundred feet wide and two hundred feet high. Jesus seems to have carefully chosen the site to install Peter and to rename him "Rock", just as God had done with Moses centuries earlier.

sat in his seat, and in Jesus' time the scribes and Pharisees continue to sit in Moses' seat (see above, pp. 46–47, n. 61).

Exegetical scholar of the New Testament Floyd V. Filson, informs us, "The scribes, mostly Pharisees, copied, taught, and applied the Mosaic Law. They were pledged to obey and teach both the written law and the oral tradition, which they claimed was an integral part of the Law, *received through a direct succession of teachers going back to Moses.* . . . Moses' seat [was a] synagogue chair which symbolized the origin and authority of their teaching. Jesus does not challenge their claim; he seems here to approve it."[52]

St. Macarius of Egypt (c. A.D. 300–c. 390) saw the same connection. He wrote, "For of old Moses and Aaron, when this priesthood was theirs, suffered much; and Caiphas, when he had their chair, persecuted and condemned the Lord. . . . Afterwards Moses was succeeded by Peter, who had committed to his hands the new Church of Christ, and the true priesthood."[53]

The continuity between the Jews of the Old Testament and the Christians of the New Testament is quite pronounced, but it is certainly what we should expect if the covenants and revelation of God have one source and purpose. Moses and Peter both had revelations, and God appointed both to "seats" of authority. Both spoke God's inspired words. Moses and Peter each had a "seat" (*kathedra,* in the Greek).[54] Both Old and New Testament communities held to two aspects of one revelation: Scripture and tradition. Neither had the truncated concept of *sola Scriptura.* Both Israel and the Church had a recognized teaching authority; both

---

[52] Floyd V. Filson, *A Commentary on the Gospel according to St. Matthew* (New York: Harper & Row, 1960), 243; emphasis added.

[53] *Homily* 26, in Joseph Berington and John Kirk, comps., *The Faith of Catholics* (New York: Pustet & Co., 1885), 2:22.

[54] From the earliest days of the Church the first believers recognized the chair of Peter and the apostolic chairs of the bishops. I have already presented an example in a quotation from Eusebius (see above, p. 47, n. 61).

Regarding the "chair of Peter" we also read in Cyprian, "With a false bishop appointed for themselves by heretics, they dare even to set sail and carry letters from schismatics and blasphemers to the chair of Peter and to the principal Church, in which sacerdotal unity has its source; nor did they take thought that these are Romans, whose faith was praised by the preaching Apostle, and among whom it is not possible for perfidy to have entrance" (*Letter of Cyprian to [Pope] Cornelius of Rome* in about A.D. 252 in William A. Jurgens, *The Faith of the Early Fathers* [Collegeville, Minn.: Liturgical Press, 1970], 1:232).

believed God's people were governed by a hierarchy. Both had a hierarchy before they had a "book", and both "books" (Old and New Testaments) were recognized and collected into authoritative canons through the hands of the respective hierarchies. Both viewed the authoritative teaching office as being one of succession, in other words, the offices would always be filled, never left vacant. "Moses' seat" continued with successors through two thousand years, acknowledged by the Lord Jesus himself, and now the "chair of Peter" is approaching its two thousandth year, and the office has been filled by 264 Popes.

The Semitic mind is far more sensitive to symbolism, metaphor, and analogies than our Western mind, so bent on logical connections and factual evidence. The Jewish mind during the time of Christ would clearly see the ample parallels. The Jews, Matthew's intended audience, understood not only the successive nature of the royal steward's office but also the successive nature of the teaching authority of Moses. Can it be doubted that they applied this understanding, which was a part of their very cultural and religious fabric of life, to Peter's appointment as the "rock" and the steward with the keys? As an Evangelical, I would have contended that Jesus was the King and had sent his Spirit—the Church needs no vizier.[55] If that were the case, I had to ask myself, why did Jesus appoint one? Did Christ the King need a royal steward only during Peter's lifetime, only until A.D. 67? Did the kingdom end and therefore no longer need the vizier? Did the office of royal steward lie vacant after Peter with the keys put in cold storage? In the Eastern kingdoms, the larger the kingdom became, the more necessary the steward became, not the other way around.

Through Semitic eyes, and Semitic history, we see the succession of judicial and teaching authority pass through the various offices of Jewish life (monarchy and priesthood) right into the Church and through the centuries into our very lives. The Catholic Church stands in unquestioned continuity with the visible covenant people of God, people with a recognizable hierarchy, people with a heritage of judicial and teaching authority.

---

[55] The Jews, even with their written Torah and known as "the People of the Book", still understood the need for an authoritative teaching office—a magisterium. Magisterium is simply Latin for "office of teacher".

X. Conclusion: The Primacy of Peter in the See of Rome

While unity of thought about Peter and the power of the keys was consistent for the first fifteen hundred years of the Church, as we saw in part 2 above, that subject provokes no end of contention, dissent, and protest among the Eastern Churches today, and even more so with the heirs of the Protestant Reformation. The average Evangelical in our egalitarian-minded Western world despises the concept of hierarchy, even though that is the undisputed context of the biblical world and the Bible—and, by extension, the Church. Our experience of modern, free democracies taints our understanding of the biblical text and the structure of the kingdom of God. The common assertion today is that one need only "believe" and have a "personal relationship with Jesus", and nothing else is necessary. The need for a Church as the dispenser of grace and sacraments has largely been ignored, even jettisoned. Protestants claim that everyone can interpret the Bible for himself and that no one has the right to force his interpretation on another. The fact that, as Luther stated later in life, there are as many interpretations as there are heads seems not to matter to modern Protestants.

Jesus wanted visible unity in his visible body. He prayed that the Church would be "perfected in unity", as he and the Father were one.[56] This was to be a visible society, unified so that the world could observe and, as a result, conclude that the Father had sent the Son. Kingdoms do not just run themselves, especially if everyone "does what is right in his own eyes". Kingdoms need authority, officials, and obedience. Kingdoms need hierarchies. The word hierarchy simply means "holy government" or the "rule of holy men".[57] Christ appointed and delegated a hierarchy in his kingdom. The apostles spoke clearly in the New Testament of ruling

---

[56] Jn 17:20–23: "I do not pray for these only, but also for those who believe in me through their word, that they may all be one; even as thou, Father, art in me, and I in thee, that they also may be in us, so that the world may believe that thou hast sent me. The glory which thou hast given me I have given to them, that they may be one even as we are one, I in them and thou in me, that they may become perfectly one, so that the world may know that thou hast sent me and hast loved them even as thou hast loved me."

[57] See *The Oxford Dictionary of English Etymology*, ed. C. T. Onions (New York: Oxford Univ. Press, 1966).

bishops, of moral and theological discipline. Paul tells Titus that "a bishop, as God's steward, must be blameless" (Titus 1:7). An offending brother must "listen to the Church" (Mt 18:15–17), Church in the "singular" (not plural), which has judicial authority that is binding on the souls of men. Paul disciplined churches and individuals with an unimpeachable authority that could not be appealed—Paul could not be "taken to the congregation" and overruled. The Church was to be a visible, organized, unity—the "one, holy, catholic, and apostolic Church". The Church is the "household of God",[58] and Peter has been appointed the steward "over the house" of God. Christ the King left his steward, Peter and the successors to his office, in charge of the Church militant, who along with the other apostles and their successors would govern as deputies while Christ was physically and visibly absent.[59] For two thousand years this position has been understood to reside in the papal office, the oldest and longest-standing institution in the Western world—the See of Peter.

As Joseph and his successors governed Egypt, and as Eliakim and his successors carried the keys in Israel, so Peter and his successors govern and pastor the Church of Christ the King, the Son of David. Joseph's brothers had complained, saying, "Are you indeed to reign over us? Or are you indeed to have dominion over us?" (Gen 37:8). One resists and protests against the royal steward at his own peril, for the King has promised to return—he will most assuredly require an accounting from his subjects.

We will close with the words of St. Cyprian of Carthage, which we have previously quoted. In A.D. 251 he wrote, "The Lord says to Peter: 'I say to you,' He says, 'that you are Peter, and upon this rock I will build my Church, and the gates of hell will not overcome it. And to you I will give the keys of the kingdom of heaven: and whatever things you bind on earth shall be bound also in heaven, and whatever you loose on earth, they shall be loosed also in heaven.' And again He says to him after His resurrection: 'Feed my sheep.' On him He builds the Church, and to him He gives the

---

[58] 1 Tim 3:15: "The household of God, which is the church of the living God, the pillar and bulwark of the truth."

[59] Jn 14:2–4: "In my Father's house are many rooms; if it were not so, would I have told you that I go to prepare a place for you? And when I go and prepare a place for you, I will come again and will take you to myself, that where I am you may be also. And you know the way where I am going." See also John 14:28–30.

command to feed the sheep; and although He assigns a like power to all the Apostles, yet He founded a single chair, and He established by His own authority a source and an intrinsic reason for that unity. Indeed, the others were that also which Peter was; but a primacy is given to Peter, whereby it is made clear that there is but one Church and one chair. So too, all are shepherds, and the flock is shown to be one, fed by all the Apostles in single-minded accord. If someone does not hold fast to this unity of Peter, can he imagine that he still holds the faith? If he desert the chair of Peter upon whom the Church was built, can he still be confident that he is in the Church?"[60]

---

[60] *The Unity of the Catholic Church* 4, written between A.D. 251 and 256, in Jurgens, *Faith of the Early Fathers*, 1:220–21.

BIBLIOGRAPHY

Achtemeier, Paul J., ed. *Harper's Bible Dictionary.* San Francisco: Harper & Row, 1985.

Albright, W. F., and C. S. Mann, eds. *The Anchor Bible: Matthew.* Garden City, N.Y.: Doubleday, 1971.

Alexander, Anthony A. *Upon This Rock.* Cleveland, Ohio: Catholic Book Store, 1950.

Alexander, David, and Pat Alexander, eds. *Eerdmans' Handbook to the Bible.* Grand Rapids, Mich.: Eerdmans, 1973.

Allies, Thomas W. *The Throne of the Fisherman.* London: Burns & Oates, 1887.

————. *St. Peter, His Name and His Office.* London: Catholic Truth Society, 1895.

Allnatt, Charles. *Cathedra Petri: The Titles and Prerogatives of St. Peter.* 2d ed. London: Burns & Oates, 1879.

Anderson, G. W. *The History and Religion of Israel.* London: Oxford Univ. Press, 1989.

Anderson, J. N. D. *A Commentary on the Epistles of Peter and Jude.* Grand Rapids, Mich.: Baker Book House, 1969.

Ankerberg, John, and John Weldon. *Protestants and Catholics: Do They Now Agree?* Eugene, Ore.: Harvest House, 1995.

Aquinas, St. Thomas. *Commentary on Saint Paul's Epistle to the Galatians.* Translated by F. R. Larcher. Albany, N.Y.: Magi Books, 1966.

Aradi, Zsolt. *The Popes.* New York: Collier Books, 1962.

Armstrong, Dave. "Forty-five New Testament Proofs." *Hands On Apologetics.* September/October 1995.

Armstrong, John, ed. *Roman Catholicism: Evangelical Protestants Analyze What Divides and Unites Us.* Chicago: Moody Press, 1995.

Arndt, William F., and F. Wilbur Gingrich. *A Greek–English Lexicon of the New Testament and Other Early Christian Literature.* Chicago: Univ. of Chicago Press, 1957.

Auer, Johann. *The Church: The Universal Sacrament of Salvation.* Translated by M. Waldstein. Washington, D.C.: Catholic Univ. of America Press, 1993.

Augustine, Saint. *The Retractations*. Translated by Sister Mary Inez Bogan. Washington, D.C.: Catholic Univ. of America Press, 1968.

Ayer, Joseph Cullen. *A Source Book for Ancient Church History*. New York: Charles Scribner's Sons, 1948.

Baines, John, and Jaromír Málek. *Atlas of Ancient Egypt*. Cairo, Egypt: Les Livres de France, 1980.

Barclay, William. *The Gospel of Matthew*. 2 vols. Philadelphia: Westminster Press, 1975.

———. *The Revelation of John*. 2 vols. Philadelphia: Westminster Press, 1976.

Barnes, Arthur Stapylton. *St. Peter in Rome and His Tomb on the Vatican Hill*. London: Swan Sonnenschein & Co., 1900.

Basso, Michele. *Guide to the Vatican Necropolis*. Fabbrica di S. Pietro in Vaticano, 1968.

Berington, Joseph, and John Kirk, comps. *The Faith of Catholics*. Edited by T. J. Capel. 3 vols. New York: F. Pustet & Co., 1885.

Boettner, Loraine. *Roman Catholicism*. Philadelphia: Presbyterian and Reformed Pub. Co., 1962.

Bottalla, Paul. *The Pope and the Church*. 2 vols. London: Burns, Oates and Co., 1868.

Brezzi, Paolo. *The Papacy: Its Origins and Historical Evolution*. Translated by Henry J. Yannone. Westminster, Md.: Newman Press, 1958.

Brown, Raymond E., K. P. Donfried, and J. Reumann, eds. *Peter in the New Testament*. Minneapolis: Augsburg Pub., 1973.

Brown, Raymond E., Joseph A. Fitzmyer, and Roland E. Murphy, eds. *Jerome Biblical Commentary*. Englewood Cliffs, N.J.: Prentice Hall, 1968.

Bruce, F. F. *The Epistle of Paul to the Romans*. Tyndale New Testament Commentaries. Edited by R. V. G. Tasker. Grand Rapids, Mich.: Eerdmans, 1975.

———. *The Hard Sayings of Jesus*. Downers Grove, Ill.: InterVarsity Press, 1983.

———. *Paul: Apostle of the Heart Set Free*. Grand Rapids, Mich.: Eerdmans, 1977.

———. *Peter, Stephen, James, and John*. Grand Rapids, Mich.: Eerdmans, 1979.

Butler, Alban. *Butler's Lives of the Saints*. Revised by Herbert Thurston and Donald Attwater. Allen, Tex.: Christian Classics, 1995.

Butler, B. C. *The Church and Infallibility: A Reply to the Abridged "Salmon".* New York: Sheed and Ward, 1954.

Butler, Scott, Norman Dahlgren, and David Hess. *Jesus, Peter and the Keys: A Scriptural Handbook on the Papacy.* Santa Barbara, Calif.: Queenship Pub., 1996.

Buttrick, George, et al., eds. *The Interpreter's Bible.* 12 vols. Nashville, Tenn.: Abingdon, 1980.

Cairns, Earle E. *Christianity through the Centuries.* Grand Rapids, Mich.: Zondervan, 1970.

———. *Christianity through the Centuries.* Rev. ed. Grand Rapids, Mich.: Zondervan, 1981.

Calvin, John. *Calvin's New Testament Commentaries.* Translated by T. H. L. Parker. 12 vols. Grand Rapids, Mich.: Eerdmans, 1965.

Carroll, J. M. *"The Trail of Blood"—Following the Christians down through the Centuries.* Lexington, Ky.: Ashland Ave. Baptist Church, 1931.

Carroll, Warren H. *The Building of Christendom.* A History of Christendom, vol. 2. Front Royal, Va.: Christendom College Press, 1987.

———. *The Founding of Christendom.* A History of Christendom, vol. 1. Front Royal, Va.: Christendom College Press, 1985.

———. *The Triumph of Christendom.* A History of Christendom, vol. 3. Front Royal, Va.: Christendom College Press, 1993.

Carson, D. A. *The Gospel according to John.* Grand Rapids, Mich.: Eerdmans, 1991.

Casciaro, José María, et al., eds. *Navarre Bible: The Acts of the Apostles.* Dublin, Ireland: Four Courts Press, 1992.

Catechism of the Catholic Church. Vatican City: Libreria Editrice Vaticana, 1994.

Catechism of the Council of Trent. 2d rev. ed. Translated by J. A. McHugh and C. J. Cullan. 1923. Reprint, Rockford, Ill.: TAN Books, 1982.

Catholic Encyclopedia. Edited by Charles G. Herbermann et al. 15 vols. New York: Robert Appleton Co., 1909.

Chapman, Dom John. *Bishop Gore and the Catholic Claims.* London: Longmans, Green, and Co., 1905.

———. *The First Eight General Councils and Papal Infallibility.* 3d ed. London: Catholic Truth Society, 1928.

———. *Studies on the Early Papacy.* 1928. Reprint, Port Washington, N.Y.: Kennikat Press, 1971.

Cheetham, Nicolas. *Keepers of the Keys: A History of the Popes from St. Peter to John Paul II.* New York: Charles Scribner's Sons, 1982.

Chesterton, G. K. *The Catholic Church and Conversion* and *The Thing: Why I Am a Catholic.* In *G. K. Chesterton: Collected Works*, vol. 3. San Francisco: Ignatius Press, 1990.

———. *Heretics* and *Orthodoxy.* In *G. K. Chesterton: Collected Works*, vol. 1. San Francisco: Ignatius Press, 1990.

Chevrot, Georges. *Simon Peter.* Manila: Sinag-tala, 1984.

Clement, Saint, and Saint Ignatius. *The Epistles of St. Clement of Rome and St. Ignatius of Antioch.* Translated by James A. Kleist. Ancient Christian Writers. New York: Newman Press, 1946.

Cole, R. Alan. *Exodus: An Introduction and Commentary.* Tyndale Old Testament Commentaries. Downers Grove, Ill.: InterVarsity Press, 1973.

Cross, F. L., and E. A. Livingstone, eds. *Oxford Dictionary of the Christian Church.* 2d rev. ed. New York: Oxford Univ. Press, 1983.

Cullmann, Oscar. *Peter: Disciple, Apostle, Martyr.* Translated by Floyd V. Filson. Philadelphia: Westminster Press, 1953.

Daley, Brian, and M. Wiles. "Current Theology: St. Irenaeus and the Roman Primacy." *The Journal of Theological Studies* 44 (1993).

Daniel-Rops, Henri. *The Church of Apostles and Martyrs.* New York: E. P. Dutton & Co., 1960.

D'Aubigné, J. H. Merle. *History of the Reformation of the Sixteenth Century.* Translated by H. White. 1846. Reprint, Grand Rapids, Mich.: Baker Book House, 1987.

Davids, Peter. *The First Epistle of Peter.* The New International Commentary on the New Testament. Edited by F. F. Bruce. Grand Rapids, Mich.: Eerdmans, 1990.

Davis, Leo Donald. *The First Seven Ecumenical Councils (325-787).* Minneapolis: Liturgical Press, 1990.

Denzinger, Heinrich. *The Sources of Catholic Dogma.* Translated by Roy Deferrari. St. Louis, Mo.: B. Herder, 1957.

De Satge, John. *Peter and the Single Church.* London: SPCK, 1981.

Dolan, Thomas S. *The See of Peter and the Voice of Antiquity.* St. Louis, Mo.: B. Herder, 1908.

D'Ormesson, Wladimir. *The Papacy.* Translated by M. Derrick. The Twentieth Century Encyclopedia of Catholicism, vol. 81. New York: Hawthorn Books, 1959.

Douglas, J. D., ed. *The Illustrated Bible Dictionary.* 3 vols. Wheaton, Ill.: InterVarsity Press and Tyndale House Pub., 1980.

Douglas, J. D., and Philip W. Comfort, eds. *Who's Who in Christian History.* Wheaton, Ill.: Tyndale House, 1992. Logos Systems Library 2.1 CD-ROM. Oak Harbor, Wash.: Logos Research Systems, 1997.

Dowley, Tim, ed. *Eerdmans' Handbook to the History of Christianity.* Grand Rapids, Mich.: Eerdmans, 1977.

Dunn, James. *Romans 1–8.* Word Biblical Commentary. Waco, Tex.: Word Books, 1988.

Eberhardt, Newman C. *A Summary of Catholic History.* 2 vols. St. Louis, Mo.: B. Herder, 1961.

Edersheim, Alfred. *The Life and Times of Jesus the Messiah.* Grand Rapids, Mich.: Eerdmans, 1972.

Ellicott, Charles John. *The Epistles to Galatians, Ephesians, and Philippians.* London: Cassel & Co., no date.

El-Meskin, Matta. *Coptic Monasticism and the Monastery of St. Macarius.* Cairo, Egypt: Monastery of St. Macarius, 1984.

Elwell, Walter A., ed. *Encyclopedia of the Bible.* 2 vols. Grand Rapids, Mich.: Baker Book House, 1988.

Empie, Paul C., and T. Austin Murphy, eds. *Papal Primacy and the Universal Church.* Minneapolis: Augsburg Pub. House, 1974.

Eno, Robert Brian. "Pre-History of Papal Infallibility". In *Teaching Authority and Infallibility in the Church: Lutherans and Catholics in Dialogue VI.* Edited by Paul C. Empie, T. Austin Murphy, and Joseph Burgess. Minneapolis: Augsburg Pub. House, 1980.

———. *The Rise of the Papacy.* Wilmington, Del.: Michael Glazier, 1990.

———. *Teaching Authority in the Early Church.* Message of the Fathers of the Church, vol. 14. Wilmington, Del.: Michael Glazier, 1984.

Eusebius. *The History of the Church.* Translated by G. A. Williamson. Harmondsworth, Middlesex, England: Penguin Books, 1965.

Farmer, William R., and Roch Kereszty. *Peter and Paul in the Church of Rome: The Ecumenical Potential of a Forgotten Perspective.* New York: Paulist Press, 1990.

Farrow, John. *Pageant of the Popes.* St. Paul, Minn.: Catechetical Guild Educational Society, 1955.

Fenton, John C. *The Gospel of Saint Matthew*. Baltimore, Md.: Penguin Books, 1963.

Ferguson, Everett, ed. *Encyclopedia of Early Christianity*. New York: Garland Pub., 1990.

Flannery, Austin, ed. *Vatican Council II: The Conciliar and Post Conciliar Documents*. New rev ed. Vol. 1. Collegeville, Minn.: Liturgical Press, 1992.

Fouard, Abbé Constant. *Simon Peter and the First Years of Christianity*. New York and London: Longmans, Green, and Co., 1893.

Fox, Robin Lane. *Pagans and Christians*. New York: Alfred A. Knopf, 1987.

France, R. T. *Matthew: Evangelist and Teacher*. Grand Rapids, Mich.: Zondervan, 1989.

Fremantle, Anne. *The Papal Encyclicals in Their Historical Context*. New York: G. P. Putnam's Sons, 1956.

Frend, W. H. C. *The Rise of Christianity*. Philadelphia: Fortress Press, 1984.

Gaebelein, Frank, ed. *The Expositor's Bible Commentary*. 12 vols. Grand Rapids, Mich.: Zondervan, 1986.

Geisler, Norman L., and Ralph E. MacKenzie. *Roman Catholics and Evangelicals: Agreements and Differences*. Grand Rapids, Mich.: Baker Books, 1995.

Giles, Edward. *Documents Illustrating Papal Authority:* A.D. *96-454*. Westport, Conn.: Hyperion Press, 1979.

Glimm, Francis X., Gerald G. Walsh, and Joseph M.-F. Marique, trans. *The Apostolic Fathers*. The Fathers of the Church. Washington D.C.: Catholic Univ. of America Press, 1981.

Gonen, Rivka. *Biblical Holy Places*. Herzlia, Israel: Palphot, 1994.

Gontard, Friedrich. *The Chair of Peter: A History of the Papacy*. Translated by A. J. and E. F. Peeler. New York: Holt, Rinehart and Winston, 1964.

Grant, Michael. *Saint Peter*. New York: Scribner's, 1995.

Grimal, Pierre. *The Dictionary of Classical Mythology*. New York: Basil Blackwell, 1985.

Guarducci, Margherita. *The Tomb of St. Peter: The New Discoveries in the Sacred Grottoes of the Vatican*. Translated by Joseph McLellan. New York: Hawthorn Books, 1960.

Guettée, Abbé Vladimir. *The Papacy*. 1866. Reprint, Blanco, Tex.: New Sarov Press, no date.

Gundry, Robert H. *Matthew: A Commentary on His Literary and Theological Art.* Grand Rapids, Mich.: Eerdmans, 1982.

Guthrie, D., et al. *The New Bible Commentary.* Grand Rapids, Mich.: Eerdmans, 1953.

Guthrie, Donald. *The Pastoral Epistles.* Tyndale New Testament Commentaries. Grand Rapids, Mich.: Eerdmans, 1980.

Hagner, Donald A. *Matthew 14–28.* Word Biblical Commentary. Waco, Tex.: Word Books, 1995.

Hamell, Patrick J. *Handbook of Patrology.* Staten Island, N.Y.: Alba House, 1968.

Hardon, John. *The Catholic Catechism.* Garden City, N.Y.: Doubleday, 1975.

Harrington, Daniel J. *The Gospel of Matthew.* Collegeville, Minn.: Liturgical Press, 1991.

Hefele, Charles Joseph. *A History of the Councils of the Church.* Translated by H. N. Nutcombe. 5 vols. Edinburgh: T & T Clark, 1896.

Henry, Matthew. *Matthew Henry's Commentary.* 6 vols. 1721. Reprint, McLean, Va.: MacDonald Pub., no date.

Hergenröther, Joseph. *Anti-Janus: An Historical-Theological Criticism of the Work Entitled "The Pope and the Council," by Janus.* Translated by J. B. Robertson. Dublin: W. B. Kelly, 1870.

Hertling, Ludwig. *Communio: Church and Papacy in Early Christianity.* Translated by Jared Wicks. Chicago: Loyola Univ. Press, 1972.

Hill, David. *The Gospel of Matthew.* New Century Bible Commentary. Grand Rapids, Mich.: Eerdmans, 1972.

Hiscox, Edward T. *Principles and Practices for Baptist Churches.* Grand Rapids, Mich.: Kregel Pub., 1980.

Hislop, Alexander. *The Two Babylons.* 2d ed. Neptune, N.J.: Loizeaux Brothers, 1959.

Hoade, Eugene. *Guide to the Holy Land.* Jerusalem: Franciscan Printing Press, 1976.

Hobson, Christine. *Exploring the World of the Pharaohs.* London: Thames and Hudson, 1987.

Howard, Thomas. *Evangelical Is Not Enough.* San Francisco: Ignatius Press, 1984.

Hughes, John Jay. *Pontiffs: Popes Who Shaped History.* Huntington, Ind.: Our Sunday Visitor, 1994.

Hughes, Philip. *The Church in Crisis: A History of the General Councils, 325–1870.* Garden City, N.Y.: Doubleday, 1961.

————. *A History of the Church.* 3 vols. New York: Sheed & Ward, 1948.

Ironside, Harry A. *Expository Notes on the Prophet Isaiah.* Neptune, N.J.: Loizeaux Bros, 1952.

Ironside, Harry H. *James and Peter.* Neptune, N.J.: Loizeaux Bros, 1947.

Jaki, Stanley L. *And on This Rock.* Front Royal, Va.: Christendom College Press, 1997.

————. *The Keys of the Kingdom.* Chicago: Franciscan Herald Press, 1986.

Jedin, Hubert. *Ecumenical Councils of the Catholic Church.* Translated by Ernest Graf. London: Nelson, 1960.

Joers, Lawrence E. C. *Thou Art Peter.* New York: Vantage Press, 1952.

John Paul II. *Crossing the Threshold of Hope.* New York: Alfred A. Knopf, 1994.

————. *The Splendor of Truth.* Boston: St. Paul Books & Media, 1993.

John, Eric, ed. *The Popes: A Concise Biographical History.* London: Burns & Oates, 1964.

Johnson, Paul. *A History of the Jews.* New York: Harper & Row, 1987.

Josephus, Flavius. *Josephus: Complete Works.* Translated by William Whiston. Grand Rapids, Mich.: Kregel Pub., 1980.

Journet, Charles. *The Primacy of Peter.* Translated by J. S. Chapin. Westminster, Md.: Newman Press, 1954.

Jowett, George F. *The Drama of the Lost Disciples.* London: Covenant Pub., 1970.

Jurgens, William A. *The Faith of the Early Fathers.* 3 vols. Collegeville, Minn.: Liturgical Press, 1970.

Kalberer, Augustine. *Lives of the Saints.* Chicago: Franciscan Herald Press, 1975.

Karrer, Otto. *Peter and the Church: An Examination of Cullmann's Thesis.* Translated by R. Walls. New York: Herder and Herder, 1963.

Keating, Karl. *Catholicism and Fundamentalism: The Attack on "Romanism" by "Bible Christians".* San Francisco: Ignatius Press, 1988.

Keener, Craig. *The IVP Bible Background Commentary: New Testament.* Downers Grove, Ill.: InterVarsity Press, 1993.

Keil, C. F., and F. Delitzsch. *Isaiah.* Vol. 7 of *Commentary on the Old Testament.* Grand Rapids, Mich.: Eerdmans, 1978.

————. *The Pentateuch.* Vol. 1 of *Commentary on the Old Testament.* Grand Rapids, Mich.: Eerdmans, 1978.

Kelly, J. N. D. *Early Christian Doctrines*. Rev. ed. San Francisco: Harper & Row, 1978.

————. *The Oxford Dictionary of the Popes*. New York: Oxford Univ. Press, 1986.

Kenrick, Francis P. *The Primacy of the Apostolic See Vindicated*. Baltimore, Md.: J. Murphy, 1855.

Kirschbaum, Engelbert. *The Tombs of St. Peter and St. Paul*. London: Secker & Warburg, 1959.

Kistemaker, Simon. *Acts*. New Testament Commentary. Grand Rapids, Mich.: Baker Book House, 1990.

Kittel, Gerhard, and Gerhard Friedrich, eds. *Theological Dictionary of the New Testament*. 10 vols. Grand Rapids, Mich.: Eerdmans, 1968.

————. *Theological Dictionary of the New Testament*. Translated by Geoffrey W. Bromiley. Abridged in one volume by Geoffrey W. Bromiley. Grand Rapids, Mich.: Eerdmans, 1985.

Knecht, Frederick Justus. *A Practical Commentary on Holy Scripture*. St. Louis, Mo.: B. Herder Book Co., 1930.

Knox, Ronald, trans. *It Is Paul Who Writes, Based on the Translation of the Epistles of Saint Paul and of the Acts of the Apostles by Ronald Knox*. Rearranged by Ronald Cox. New York: Sheed and Ward, 1944.

Kreeft, Peter. *Fundamentals of the Faith*. San Francisco: Ignatius Press, 1988.

Krüger, Gustav. *The Papacy*. Translated by F. M. S. Batchelor and C. A. Miles. London: T. Fisher Unwin, 1909.

Lackmann, Max. *The Unfinished Reformation*. Edited by Hans Asmussen. Notre Dame, Ind.: Fides Pub., 1961.

Lamsa, George. *Old Testament Light*. San Francisco: Harper & Row, 1964.

Lattey, C., ed. *The Church*. Cambridge: W. Heffer and Sons, 1928.

————. *The Papacy*. London: Burns, Oates & Washbourne, 1923.

Liddell, H. G. *An Intermediate Greek Lexicon*. Abridged from Liddell and Scott's *Greek–English Lexicon*. Electronic ed. Oxford: Oxford Univ. Press., published in electronic form by Logos Research Systems, 1996.

Lightfoot, J. B. *The Apostolic Fathers*. Grand Rapids, Mich.: Baker Book House, 1984.

————. *The Apostolic Fathers*. 2d ed. 5 vols. 1889. Reprint, Peabody, Mass.: Hendrickson, 1989.

———. *St. Paul's Epistle to the Philippians.* Lynn, Mass.: Hendrickson Pub., 1982.

Lightfoot, John. *Commentary on the New Testament from the Talmud and Hebraica.* 4 vols. Peabody, Mass.: Hendrickson, 1995.

Likoudis, James. *Ending the Byzantine Greek Schism.* 2d ed. New Rochelle, N.Y.: Catholics United for the Faith, 1992.

Lindsay, Colin. *The Evidence for the Papacy.* London: Longmans, 1870.

Livius, T. *St. Peter, Bishop of Rome.* London: Burns & Oates, 1888.

Loffreda, Stanislao. *Recovering Capharnaum.* Jerusalem: Franciscan Printing Press, 1993.

Longnecker, Richard N. *Galatians.* Word Biblical Commentary. Waco, Tex.: Word Books, 1990.

Lopes, Antonia. *The Popes.* Translated by Charles Nopar. Rome: Futura Edizioni, 1997.

Lowe, John. *Saint Peter.* New York: Oxford Univ. Press, 1956.

Lowrie, Walter. *SS. Peter and Paul in Rome: An Archaeological Rhapsody.* New York: Oxford Univ. Press, 1940.

Luther, Martin. *The Catholic Epistles.* In *Luther's Works,* edited by Jaroslav Pelikan. St. Louis, Mo.: Concordia Pub., 1967.

———. *Lectures on Galatians.* In *Luther's Works,* edited by Jaroslav Pelikan. St. Louis, Mo.: Concordia Pub., 1963.

MacGregor-Hastie, Roy. *The Throne of Peter.* London: Catholic Book Club, 1966.

Maier, Harry O. *The Social Setting of the Ministry as Reflected in the Writings of Hermas, Clement and Ignatius.* Waterloo, Ontario, Canada: Wilfrid Laurier Univ. Press, 1991.

Manning, Henry E. *The Oecumenical Council and the Infallibility of the Roman Pontiff.* London: Longmans, Green, and Co., 1869.

———. *Petri Privilegium: Three Pastoral Letters to the Clergy of the Diocese.* London: Longmans, Green, and Co., 1871.

———. *The True Story of the Vatican Council.* 1877. Reprint, Fraser, Mich.: American Council on Economics and Society, 1996.

Martin, Daniel W. *The Church of the Scriptures.* St. Louis, Mo.: Confraternity Home Study Service, 1959.

Maxwell-Stuart, P. G. *Chronicle of the Popes.* New York: Thames and Hudson, 1997.

McBirnie, William Steuart. *The Search for the Twelve Apostles.* Wheaton, Ill.: Tyndale House, Living Books, 1973.

McBrien, Richard P. *Lives of the Popes.* San Francisco: Harper SanFrancisco, 1997.

McCarthy, James G. *The Gospel according to Rome.* Eugene, Ore.: Harvest House, 1995.

McCord, Peter J., ed. *A Pope for All Christians?* New York: Paulist Press, 1976.

McCue, James F. *Papal Primacy and the Universal Church: Lutherans and Catholics in Dialogue V.* Minneapolis: Augsburg Pub., 1974.

McGoldrick, James Edward. *Baptist Successionism.* Metuchen, N.J., and London: American Theological Library Assn. and Scarecrow Press, 1994.

McKenzie, John L. *Dictionary of the Bible.* New York: Simon & Schuster, 1995.

Meyendorff, John, ed. *The Primacy of Peter.* Crestwood, N.Y.: St. Vladimir's Seminary Press, 1992.

Miller, J. Michael. *The Shepherd and the Rock: Origins, Development, and Mission of the Papacy.* Huntington, Ind.: Our Sunday Visitor, 1995.

———. *What Are They Saying about Papal Primacy?* New York: Paulist Press, 1983.

Morgan, G. Campbell. *The Acts of the Apostles.* Westwood, N.J.: Fleming H. Revell, 1924.

Most, William G. *Catholic Apologetics Today: Answers to Modern Critics.* Rockford, Ill.: TAN Books, 1986.

———. *Free from an Error.* 2d rev. ed. Libertyville, Ill.: Prow Books, 1985.

Mounce, Robert. *The New International Commentary on the New Testament: The Book of Revelation.* Grand Rapids, Mich.: Eerdmans, 1977.

Mourret, F. *The Papacy.* Translated by Robert Eaton. Catholic Library of Religious Knowledge, vol. 8. St. Louis, Mo.: B. Herder Book Co., 1931.

Murphy, J. "Dr. Salmon's 'Infallibility'". *The Irish Ecclesiastical Record.* Vol. 9 (January–June, 1901) to vol. 11 (January–June, 1902).

Nee, Watchman. *The King and the Kingdom of Heaven.* New York: Christian Fellowship Pub., 1978.

Neuner, J., and J. Dupuis, eds. *The Christian Faith in the Doctrinal Documents of the Catholic Church.* 6th rev. and enlarged ed. New York: Alba House, 1996.

New Encyclopedia Britannica, The. 30 vols. Chicago: Encyclopedia Britannica, 1981.

Newman, John Henry Cardinal. *An Essay on the Development of Christian Doctrine.* In *Conscience, Consensus, and the Development of Doctrine.* New York: Image Books, Doubleday, 1992.

Nichols, Aidan. *Rome and the Eastern Churches.* Edinburgh: T & T Clark, 1992.

Nichols, James H. *Primer for Protestants.* New York: Association Press, 1947.

O'Hare, Patrick F. *The Facts about Luther.* Rockford, Ill.: TAN Books, 1987.

Onions, C. T., ed. *The Oxford Dictionary of English Etymology.* New York: Oxford Univ. Press, 1983.

Ott, Ludwig. *Fundamentals of Catholic Dogma.* 4th ed. Rockford, Ill.: TAN Books, 1974.

Otten, Bernard J. *A Manual of the History of Dogmas.* St. Louis, Mo.: B. Herder, 1917.

Pelikan, Jaroslav. *Christian Doctrine and Modern Culture since 1700.* 5 vols. Chicago: Univ. of Chicago Press, 1989.

—————. *The Emergence of the Catholic Tradition (100–600).* Vol. 1 of *The Christian Tradition: A History of the Development of Doctrine.* Chicago: Univ. of Chicago Press, 1971.

Poulet, Charles. *A History of the Catholic Church.* Translated by Sidney A. Raemers. 2 vols. St Louis, Mo.: B. Herder Book Co., 1941.

Quasten, Johannes. *Patrology.* 4 vols. Westminster, Md.: Christian Classics, 1993.

Ray, Stephen. *Crossing the Tiber.* San Francisco: Ignatius Press, 1997.

Rhodes, M. J. *The Visible Unity of the Catholic Church.* 2 vols. London: Longmans, Green, and Co., 1870.

Ricciotti, Giuseppe. *The Life of Christ.* Translated by Alba Zizzamia. Milwaukee, Wis.: Bruce Pub. Co., 1947.

Richards, Lawrence O., ed. *The Revell Bible Dictionary.* Old Tappan, N.J.: Fleming H. Revell, 1990.

Ripley, Francis J. *The Pope: Vicar of Jesus Christ.* Dublin: Catholic Truth Society, 1965.

Rivington, Luke. *The Primitive Church and the See of Peter.* London: Longmans, Green and Co., 1894.

—————. *The Roman Primacy,* A.D. *430–451.* London: Longmans, Green and Co., 1899.

Roberts, Alexander, and James Donaldson, eds. *The Ante-Nicene*

Fathers. Revised by A. Cleveland Coxe. 10 vols. Grand Rapids, Mich.: Eerdmans, 1985.

Ruffin, C. Bernard. *The Twelve.* Huntington, Ind.: Our Sunday Visitor, 1984.

Rumble, Leslie. *Radio Replies.* Edited with Charles Carty. 3 vols. 1938. Reprint, Rockford, Ill.: TAN Books, 1979.

Ryland, Ray. "Papal Primacy and the Council of Nicaea". *This Rock,* June 1997.

Salmon, George. *The Infallibility of the Church.* London: John Murray, 1914.

Schaff, Philip. *History of the Christian Church.* 8 vols. Grand Rapids, Mich.: Eerdmans, 1980.

———, ed. *Nicene and Post–Nicene Fathers,* 1st series. 14 vols. Grand Rapids, Mich.: Eerdmans, 1983.

———, ed. *Nicene and Post-Nicene Fathers.* 2d series. 14 vols. Grand Rapids, Mich.: Eerdmans, 1983.

Schatz, Klaus. *Papal Primacy.* Collegeville, Minn.: Liturgical Press, 1996.

Schimmelpfennig, Bernhard. *The Papacy.* Translated by James Sievert. New York: Columbia Univ. Press, 1992.

Schmaus, Michael. *The Church: Its Origin and Structure.* Vol. 4 of *Dogma.* London: Sheed and Ward, 1972.

Scott, S. Herbert. *The Eastern Churches and the Papacy.* London: Sheed & Ward, 1928.

Scroggie, W. Graham. *Know Your Bible.* Old Tappan, N.J.: Fleming H. Revell, 1974.

Shelley, Bruce L. *Church History in Plain Language.* Waco, Tex.: Word Books, 1982.

Shotwell, James T., and Louise Ropes Loomis. *The See of Peter.* 1927. Reprint, New York: Columbia Univ. Press, 1991.

Simons, Francis. *Infallibility and the Evidence.* Springfield, Ill.: Templegate Pub., 1968.

Soloviev, Vladimir. *Russia and the Universal Church.* Translated by H. Rees. London: Geoffrey Bles, 1948.

Sproul, R. C. *Essential Truths of the Christian Faith.* Wheaton, Ill.: Tyndale House Pub., 1992.

Staniforth, Maxwell, trans. *Early Christian Writings.* Harmondsworth, Middlesex, England: Penguin Books, 1968.

Stern, David. *Jewish New Testament Commentary.* Clarksville, Md.: Jewish New Testament Pub., 1994.

Stibbs, Alan. *The First Epistle General of Peter.* Tyndale New Testament Commentaries. Grand Rapids, Mich.: Eerdmans, 1981.

Stigers, Harold. *A Commentary on Genesis.* Grand Rapids, Mich.: Zondervan, 1976.

Stott, John. *The Spirit, the Church and the World.* Downers Grove, Ill.: InterVarsity Press, 1990.

Stravinskas, Peter M. J. *Our Sunday Visitor's Catholic Dictionary.* On diskette. Huntington, Ind.: Our Sunday Visitor, 1994.

Sungenis, Robert. *Not by Faith Alone.* Santa Barbara, Calif.: Queenship Pub., 1997.

Swaggart, Jimmy. *Catholicism and Christianity.* Baton Rouge, La.: Jimmy Swaggart Ministries, 1986.

Tasker, E. V. G. *The Gospel according to Matthew.* Tyndale New Testament Commentaries. Grand Rapids, Mich.: Eerdmans, 1978.

Tenney, Merrill, ed. *The Zondervan Pictorial Encyclopedia of the Bible.* 5 vols. Grand Rapids, Mich.: Zondervan, 1978.

Theophylact. *The Explanation by Blessed Theophylact of the Holy Gospel according to St. Mark.* House Springs, Mo.: Chrysostom Press, 1993.

Thorne, J. O., and T. C. Collocott, eds. *Chambers Biographical Dictionary.* Edinburgh: W & R Chambers, 1984.

Thurston, Herbert. *No Popery: Chapters on Anti-Papal Prejudice.* New York: Longmans, Green and Co., 1930.

Tillard, J. M. R. *The Bishop of Rome.* Translated by John de Satgé. Wilmington, Del.: Michael Glazier, 1983.

Tixeront, J. *History of Dogmas.* 2d ed. Translated by H. L. Brianceau. 3 vols. St. Louis, Mo.: B. Herder Book Co., 1921.

Torrey, R. A., et al., eds. *The Fundamentals: The Famous Sourcebook of Foundational Biblical Truths.* Grand Rapids, Mich.: Kregel Pub., 1958.

Underhill, Francis. *Saint Peter.* London: Centenary Press, 1937.

Van der Woude, A. S., ed. *The World of the Bible.* Grand Rapids, Mich.: Eerdmans, 1986.

Vaux, Roland de. *Ancient Israel.* New York: McGraw-Hill, 1961.

Vincent, Marvin R. *Word Studies in the New Testament.* 4 vols. 1887. Reprint, Grand Rapids, Mich.: Eerdmans, 1980.

Von Balthasar, Hans Urs. *The Office of Peter and the Structure of the Church.* San Francisco: Ignatius Press, 1986.

Walsh, John Evangelist. *The Bones of St. Peter.* Garden City, N.Y.: Image Books, 1985.

Walsh, William Thomas. *Saint Peter the Apostle.* New York: Macmillan, 1948.

Ware, Timothy. *The Orthodox Church.* New York: Penguin Books, 1993.

Watts, John D. W. *Isaiah 1–33.* Commentary on the Old Testament. Waco, Tex.: Word Books, 1985.

Webster, William. *The Church of Rome at the Bar of History.* Carlisle, Penn.: Banner of Truth Trust, 1995.

————. *Peter and the Rock.* Battle Ground, Wash.: Christian Resources, 1996.

Westminster Larger Catechism. Atlanta: Committee for Christian Education & Publications, 1990, in Logos Library System Library v.2.1 CD-ROM. Oak Harbor, Wash.: Logos Research Systems.

Whelton, Michael. *Two Paths: Papal Monarchy—Collegial Tradition.* Salisbury, Mass.: Regina Orthodox Press, 1998.

White, James. *Answers to Catholic Claims: A Discussion of Biblical Authority.* Southbridge, Mass.: Crowne Pub., 1990.

————. *The Fatal Flaw.* Minneapolis: Bethany House Pub., 1990.

————. *The Roman Catholic Controversy.* Minneapolis: Bethany House Pub., 1996.

Winter, Michael M. *Saint Peter and the Popes.* Baltimore, Md.: Helicon Press, 1960.

Wiseman, Nicholas Cardinal. *Lectures on the Principal Doctrines and Practices of the Catholic Church.* New York: P. O'Shea, Pub., 1843.

Young, Edward J. *The Book of Isaiah.* Grand Rapids, Mich.: Eerdmans, 1969.

INDEX OF PROPER NAMES AND SUBJECTS

Shamma, 43 n. 54
Shebna the steward, 39 n. 46, 273, 284 n. 36, 290–91
Sheen, Archbishop Fulton, 23 n. 4
Shepherd, The (Hermas), 130 nn. 32, 33
Shotwell, James T., 106 n. 22, 151
signet rings, 284, 285 n. 37
Silvester the bishop, 89
Simon Magus, 94
Simon Peter. *See* Peter
Simon, son of Jonas, 23–24, 286. *See also* Peter
Socrates Scholasticus, 224–25
sola Scriptura doctrine, 60 n. 81, 64, 95, 293
Soter, bishop of Rome, 155–56
Source Book for Ancient Church History, A (Ayer), 234 n. 188
Sozomen, 225–27
Sproul, R. C., 253 n. 18
Stephen, Pope, 181 n. 64, 186, 188 n. 78, 189 n. 81
Step Pyramid, 267
Stern, David, 80 n. 34, 278
stewards, 38–41, 266–67, 285 n. 37, 289–91
Stibbs, Alan, 69 n. 9, 97
stone chair (Jewish synagogues), 46 n. 61
St. Peter's basilica, 89–90, 108–9
Strabo, 98 n. 5
Stromata, The, 80 n. 36
Sungenis, Robert A., 53
Swaggart, Jimmy, 102–3

Tacitus, 75 n. 24
Tasker, R. V. G., 30 n. 26
Tertullian, 58 n. 78, 78–80, 123, 168–75
Testament of Hezekiah, 71
Theodoret, 234–35
Theodosius, Emperor of Rome, 217
Theophorus (Ignatius of Antioch), 72 n. 15
"throne of Jerusalem", 222 n. 165
tomb, 76 n. 25
Tome (Pope Leo I), 238 n. 198, 239 n. 199
Trypho, 154 n. 12

Unity of the Catholic Church, The, 182 n. 68
universal Church, 147–48, 252, 253–54, 295–97
universal primacy doctrine, 252

Valdes, Peter, 97
Valentinian, Emperor of Rome, 217
Valerian, Emperor, 189 n. 82
Vatican Council of 1870, 142, 210 n. 131
Vaux, Roland de, 279, 281, 288
Victor, bishop of Rome, 13, 159–61
Vincent, Marvin, 270
vizier, 267, 282–83, 289–90
von Harnack, Adolf, 187 n. 76
Vulgate, 213 n. 140

Waldensians, 97
Walsh, John Evangelist, 108 n. 26
Ware, Timothy, 142
Wars of the Jews (Josephus), 42 n. 53
Watts, John D. W., 38, 40 n. 49, 267, 284 n. 36
Webster, William: on Cyprian's writings, 187 n. 76; on the Fathers regarding primacy of Peter, 12–13, 158 n. 22; on Jacob of Nisibis, 193 n. 93; on Peter interpreted as the rock, 175 n. 56, 177 n. 59; on Peter as part of foundation, 206 n. 125; on references to other Churches, 164 n. 33; on St. Ephriam, 194 n. 95; selective proof-texting by, 183 n. 70
Whiston, William, 42 n. 54
White, James, 36 n. 37, 46 n. 61, 53 n. 71, 202 n. 113, 231 n. 186, 274–75
Winter, Michael, 28, 141, 166 n. 35, 179 n. 62, 201 n. 110, 217 n. 147
Wiseman, Nicholas Cardinal, 254 n. 19
Wycliffe, John, 95

Zaphenath-paneah, 286
Zebedee, 25, 26
Zephyrinus, bishop of Rome, 75, 88

INDEX OF SCRIPTURE